Social Control for the 1980s

Social Control for the 1980s

A HANDBOOK FOR ORDER IN A DEMOCRATIC SOCIETY

edited by Joseph S. Roucek

Contributions in Sociology, Number 31

GREENWOOD PRESS

WESTPORT, CONNECTICUT • LONDON, ENGLAND

Library of Congress Cataloging in Publication Data
Main entry under title:

Social control for the 1980s.

    (Contributions in sociology ; no. 31 ISSN 0084-9278)
    Bibliography: p.
    Includes index.
    1. United States—Social conditions—1960-   —
Addresses, essays, lectures. 2. Social control—
Addresses, essays, lectures. 3. Social institutions—
Addresses, essays, lectures. I. Roucek, Joseph
Slabey, 1902-
HN65.S568   309.1'73'0924   77-91112
ISBN 0-313-20048-3

Library of Congress Catalog Card Number: 77-91112
ISBN:0-313-20048-3
ISSN:0084-9278

First published in 1978

Greenwood Press, Inc.
51 Riverside Avenue, Westport, Connecticut 06880

Printed in the United States of America

10 9 8 7 6 5 4 3 2 1

Dedicated to
Don—*In affectionate appreciation*

CONTENTS

PREFACE

Some of the dilemmas of social control may be illustrated by a human interest story that appeared in the mass press in the spring of 1977. The chief law enforcement officer of a small town noticed that in his hurry he had inadvertently parked in a no parking zone. He dutifully issued himself a ticket. However, when he appeared in traffic court, the judge dismissed the case, for as defendant the lawman refused to testify against himself.

As is true of all living things, man's most basic problem is to survive. The survival of the individual and of the species, however, are sometimes antithetical. Behaviors arise both in human and nonhuman groups which reflect the alternative interests of the group and the individual. A female grizzly that dies protecting her cubs exemplifies instinctive behavior in which the interests of the individual are sacrificed for the group. In humans, where the extensive erosion of biologically preprogrammed behavior has occurred, both the spheres of group behavior and of individual autonomy must be learned or invented. Concomitantly, the problem of the modification of individual behavior in the interests of group survival appears in a qualitatively new form. It is not unfair to say that with man the problem of social control makes its appearance for the first time.

Man cannot survive outside society, yet he has no instincts for being social in any particular way. He learns to be social based on the model of other humans without whose help he could not, even under favorable circumstances, survive before the age of eight to ten. But the individual is able to modify his personality in the very process of modeling it after those around him. He may use what he learns from his group to oppose the group or to exploit it to suit himself.

So long as men lived in very small isolated groups, as they did for many thousands of years, and at a time when most men died young, the problem of social control was relatively simple. There were few specialized control institutions and those that did apear were relatively primitive. Yet, even in the primitive group the problem of the intransigent individual sometimes had to be faced. Ethnographic evidence again and again reveals punishment for violation of group rules and sometimes death or outcasting for continuing intransigence.

In complex societies with conflicting cultural traditions, alternative patterns of socialization, and opportunities for individuals to escape the surveillance of primary groups (such as the family, neighborhoods, and religious institutions), the problem of social control acquires new contours.

Political groups take shape, police forces are established, law codes are drawn up, and court systems are instituted. The problems of social control are parceled out in an array of formal institutions. Ironically, the very dispersion of social power in a variety of specialized control institutions, in some ways, makes the problem of social control more difficult. To take only a single illustration: in a primitive community without a special police force, every community member tends to be alert to deviant conduct, but in a complex community that could not operate without a formal police system, the dilemma arises that much deviant conduct will never be brought to the attention of the police.

In the United States since the end of World War II it is generally agreed that an ever-deepening crisis of control has been developing. In outline, a few of the major factors in our crises of control are (1) a major war (and World War II was no exception) always creates a crisis of control (both civilian and military) by uprooting millions of people from their primary groups, presenting them with alternative ways of life (as in the popular song of World War I, "How can you get them back on the farm once they have seen Paris"), and transforming the social, economic, and political institutions of the country at large); (2) the United States emerged from World War II as the foremost world power confronting many new international and national institutions that had inevitable consequences for her control institutions; (3) the affluent society of the immediate postwar period created unprecedented problems for leisure-time activities, shaking the traditional cultural and recreational institutions; (4) the Korean and Vietnam engagements created quasiwar conditions in ways that had drastic consequences for social control; (5) the black, Chicano, and American Indian movements transformed the shape of the minorities' problems; (6) the rush to the suburbs, simultaneous with the increasing collapse of the traditional rural environment, was related to the hollowing out of the cities and the isolation of the urban ghettoes, forming them into traps of human waste material; (7) the women's and gay liberation movements were cross-tied with the collapse of traditional domestic roles and traditional sexual morality; (8) the Watergate scandal shook faith in government at the highest level, presenting a sorry example of irresponsible personal conduct at the top of American society; (9) the energy crisis and economic recession of the 1970s, with simultaneous inflation, have eroded the economic security of the middle classes and appear to mark a point of no return in the continuing changes of the American economy; and (10) the welfare system is badly in need of overhaul.

These are a few of the many changes that are having both direct and indirect consequences for social control institutions in America. It is because of the crisis and the need for Americans to reassess their control institutions for the decade of the 1980s that the present symposium of eminent scholars has been assembled.

In organizing this anthology, I have not tried to place thinking in a strait-jacket and to impose my own point of view on the participants. It seemed to be of much greater value to sample thinking in the hope of exploring the range of conceptualizations and the various ways the problem of social control appears from the standpoint of diverse spheres of substantive endeavor. All general indices point to the fact that a unity of collective effort unprecedented in American history may be required in the 1980s. If we do not accomplish this unity democratically, by way of the free exchange of diverse opinion, we will run the risk, as Orwell foresaw, of a dangerous slide toward totalitarianism. If there ever was a time America needed a handbook for social control, it is now.

I wish to express my appreciation for the counsel and help extended by the series editor, Professor Don Martindale, and Dr. James T. Sabin, vice-president of Greenwood Press.

Joseph S. Roucek
June 1977

PART I

Compared to human society, the bee hive, ant hill, and termite colony are models of interspecific order. In any insect species, the social organization is of a single invariant type. In contrast, one can hardly find two tribes of the simplest representatives of the human species whose social orders are in all respects identical. Human social order differs from that of insect societies in two fundamental respects: (1) it is qualitatively distinct—a product not of biological preprogramming, but of learning, invention, and conscious choice; and (2) it is not only disorderly and problematic in its individual manifestations, but it is also almost endlessly variable in its forms.

The order in human society is manifest in any given time and place as a somewhat stable process composed of the solutions to three problems: staying alive in nature; transmitting the cultural patterns of the group; and actively maintaining the social order itself in its current forms or undertaking to modify it in various ways. Since the ways these problems are solved are learned or invented, human social order is problematic in a manner that has no counterpart in any other living species of the planet.

The area of social control took shape among the social sciences when the implications of the tentative and problematic character of human order was faced. However, since no two human communities have a completely identical set of social forms, since human societies have been undergoing unprecedented rates of change in the last two centuries (the time period of the rise of the social sciences), and since social theories vary in the way they account for continuity and order, the concept of social control had been subject

History and Theory of Social Control

to varied and, in some measure, conflicting interpretations.

The three essays by Roucek, Janowitz, and Martindale that constitute Part I have inevitable points of overlap and contrast. Roucek approaches the concept of social control in American sociology lexicographically from the standpoint of its formulation in the works of the classical American sociologists; Janowitz writes the intellectual history of the concept from the point of view of the Chicago school of sociology; and Martindale considers the concept analytically from the standpoint of theoretical implications of holism and elementarisms on its scope and thrust.

J.S.R.

Joseph S. Roucek

THE CONCEPT OF SOCIAL CONTROL IN AMERICAN SOCIOLOGY

The concept of social control has been explored and treated rather prolifically and has been given various interpretations in American sociological literature ever since Edward Alsworth Ross introduced it in 1901.[1] In fact, since then the literature dealing with this concept has been as voluminous as the application of the term has been prolific and variegated.

History of the Concept

Although the concept of social control stems from Comte,[2] its roots can be found in the idea expressed by Plato and Aristotle, and ever since by the modern social scientists of every school, that a degree of social solidarity is necessary for the existence of society.

Plato said that the legislator "did not aim at making any one class in the State happy above the rest"; that "happiness" was to be "in the whole State," that "the citizens are held together by persuasion and necessity making them benefactors of the State," and therefore "benefactors of one another."[3] Aristotle asserted that "it is of more consequence that the citizens should entertain a similarity of sentiment than an equality of circumstances."[4] In our times, we think of such American sociologists as Lester F. Ward with his theory of "synergy," Franklin Henry Giddings with his "consciousness of kind," supplemented by "social pressures," and Albion W. Small with his doctrine of "interests" as the processes by which social solidarity is produced. Emile Durkheim devotes Book I of his *The Division of Labor in Society* to the function of the division of labor in producing social solidarity. In fact, the means of achieving the social integration of human beings with widely differing interests, impulses, and attitudes, and especially of groups in divergent cultures, is one of the chief problems for society. Hence, the system of control by which social unity is achieved out of individual and group diversity has demanded our attention.

Every society is characterized by divergent groups, with subgroups having their own value systems, folkways, mores, ideologies, and patterns of behavior varying from or conflicting, to some degree at least, with the dominant elements of the dominant culture. As long as the different culture pattern is not considered subversive to the established pattern of the dominant group pattern, such subgroups are subject only to milder forms of pressures—such as ridicule, sarcasm, neighborly advice, and "peaceful" methods—to conform to societal norms and to specific role expectations. However, if the dominant group feels that the behavior and beliefs of such subgroups are a danger to the welfare of the established order, stronger measures, even including legal punishment, violence, terror, or extermination, may be invoked.[5] At the same time, societies also provide some commonly accepted ways to reduce the frustrations and tensions which social control inevitably produces (game and leisure activities, humor and joking patterns, and the like).

Hence, the aims of social control are (1) to bring into conformity the actions of variant groups with cherished values in order that they may share in what Durkheim calls the "collective conscience,"[6] or, in Giddings' words, in order that they may "know and enjoy their likeness"; (2) to induce and preserve that degree of social solidarity that will ensure the perpetuation of the group (psychologists call it a process of strengthening the approved "social conditioning" process); and (3) in recent years, to study the various devices and techniques of social control utilized by "elites," the "ruling cliques," or "the power-operations of elites," described variously but which can be defined here as "groups of actors who have power."[7]

Difficulties in Definition

Social control may be defined simply as the methods used to get people to conform to societal norms and to specific role expectations. Or it can be defined more complexly as "any social or cultural means by which systematic and relatively consistent restraints are imposed upon individual behavior and by which people are motivated to adhere to traditions and patterns of behavior that are important to the smooth functioning of a group or society."[8] It must be noted, however, that neither definition satisfies all the students of social control.

The semantic aspects of the concept of social control are complicated further when defined in English and in European languages. In French, German, Russian, and other European tongues, "control" implies a much smaller degree of interference than it does in English. In English, "control" usually means power, might, domination, authority; in contrast, in European languages, it generally means supervision, inspection, surveillance, controllership. Complicating this clear-cut distinction between the English and European interpretation in the United States is the fact that some sociologists here accept the one and some the other. For example, the group headed by E. A. Ross and C. H. Cooley uses the term in a sense distinctly closer to the European meaning while other American sociologists think of social control in terms of power, domination, or constraint.

Several specialists in this field have dealt with this concept by limiting their definition to include only those influences by which society consciously tries to regulate the activities of its members. In recent years, however, a whole body of thought as propounded by anthropologists and social psychologists has arisen, showing that human nature and personality can be analyzed only in the framework of the existing culture patterns of the respective group, many of which operate without the individual's consciousness of them and without the identification of any conscious active agent involved. In fact, the most important factors in the development of the socialized personality and in the regulation of human institutions are rooted in the nonrational, irrational, unconscious, but all-pervasive influences that mold the individual without his knowledge, as part of the general culture and which become incorporated there without any conscious awareness on the part of any particular group, or even of a society.[9]

Identifying the processes of social control is also complicated by the rise of urban-industrial and technological culture, which makes use of not only "irrational" aspects of social control (folkways, mores, ideologies) but also the realm of law, operated by government enforcement agencies. This form of social control is generally ineffective compared to the more persuasive influences used by primary groups. Whereas in preliterate society, the elders and traditions were the dominant factors in social control, in modern technological society, especially that confronted with frequent social and political upheavals, the policeman and the soldier are often called upon to control crisis situations. In modern societies interested in the "hereafter," the priesthood is still the dominant factor. In most societies, however, the wealthy, the learned, and the ruling elites have become the most important influences in social control.

Whatever the situation, the basic problem that remains focuses on the perennial questions, "Who exercises social control?", "Who Gets What, When and How?" The usual answers seldom throw light on the subtle social and cultural as well as individual forces hidden under the surface of social processes. In fact, any single pattern that pervades the social order finds its real origin in the interactions of social groups and in the background of all internal and external expressions of the dominant personality's authority of the social control devices. Thus, the leaders ("the elites") use not only a body of customs and traditions but also impersonal forces to attain authority as well as to make people willing to be ruled by that authority. Several studies show that "moral" authority is more important than rule by force.[10]

Introduction of the Concept into American Sociology

In 1894, A. W. Small and G. E. Vincent, discussing the effect of authority upon social behavior, observed that leaders are greatly influenced and limited by the will of their followers. They concluded that "the reaction of public opinion upon authority makes social control a most delicate and difficult task."[11] (Small and Vincent had been influenced by Ward's philosophy.)[12]

Systematic study of social control in America, as an important aspect of social psychology, was introduced by E. A. Ross (1866-1951) in several articles which he published in the *American Journal of Sociology* between 1896 and 1898, and which he then summarized in his book *Social Control: A Survey of the Foundations of Order* (New York: American Book Co., 1901), a study which at times seems almost a free translation of Tarde's *Laws of Imitation*. Ross is more extensively analyzed in Don Martindale's chapter in this volume. Suffice it to note here that Ross, under the influence of the then dominant instinct theories, stressed that biological factors alone could not account for regulation in human society. He recognized that other restraints of predatory persons appeared in the form of public opinion, law, religion, and "other like manifestations of the general will." Thus it was that social and other processes of social control arose by which man superseded and improved the natural order and made it more adequate. Then Ross cited specific forms of control—law, belief, public opinion, suggestion, education, custom, religion, personal ideals, ceremony, art, enlightenment, illusion, social evaluation, and ethical elements—which he called means or "engines of control."

While Ross concentrated on the "social" aspects of social control, during the period before World War I the American social psychologists, headed by William McDougall (1871-1938) and Charles A. Ellwood (1873-1946), featured the question of social values and the problem of social responsibility for social welfare, because, other things being equal, the greater the personal responsibility for social welfare, the less the need for control. If persons were far more socially responsible and socially wiser then than they are now, the problem of social control would be different from what it is now. In answer to the question, "How far do ethical considerations enter into the 'social control' fields," a divided answer was offered. McDougall stressed, "The fundamental problem of social psychology is the moralization of the individual of the society into which he is born as a creature in which the non-moral and purely egoistic tendencies are so much stronger than any altruistic tendencies."[13] Ellwood, like McDougall, emphasized the role of instincts and analyzed their role, as well as the influences of feeling, intellect, imitation, and sympathy as social forces in social life. Ellwood adopted Small and Ross's and Ward's ideas of social forces, Giddings' concept of like-mindedness and sympathy, and Cooley's views of the social mind and popular opinion. In his last work, *Sociology: Principles and Problems* (1943), Ellwood concluded that progress had come by way of organic evolution, as well as cultural evolution; that imitation, sympathy, conflict, and inventiveness all played a part in the process of social development; but that social organization rested basically on conscious social control for improvement (the "meliorism" and "telesis" of Ward and the "order" of Hobhouse), exercised through the various regulative institutions of government, law, religion, morality, and education. Because of the complexity of modern society, he conceded an important place to religion as an agency of social control.

While Ross viewed social control as a *sine qua non* of society, because the selfish nature of the individual made it necessary to restrain his action, another pioneer in this field, Charles H. Cooley (1864-1929), viewed social control as an aspect of the reciprocal relation between the individual and society.[14] He demonstrated how the individual becomes a member of society through association, is controlled by it, and in turn becomes an agent in the process. Cooley concluded that the person's behavior is largely controlled by the development of conscience (the "voice" of the group) as a consequence of association, although the process is withal unconscious and unplanned. Thus, control is implicit in society and as such is transmitted to the individual by association. He discussed such topics as suggestion and choice, sympathy, the social self, hostility, emulation, leadership, and the social aspects of conscience. His famous concept, "the looking glass self" (first used by David Hume), is frequently cited even today. For Cooley, it had three principal elements: "the imagination of our appearance to the other persons; the imagination of his judgment of that appearance, and some sort of self-feeling, such as pride or mortification."[15]

For some reason or other, William Graham Sumner (1840-1910) is seldom given enough credit for his classic contribution to the field of social control.[16] A contemporary of Ward's, Sumner differed considerably from him; he considered sociology to be the scientific study of the "superorganics." While Ward believed in the essential superiority of human society over the rest of the organic world because of intelligence, Sumner, like Spencer, had the mechanistic idea of many organic theories. Because his sociology courses were so popular at Yale, Sumner had an extraordinarily large impact on American intellectual life. Under the influence of Malthus, Spencer, Lippert, Gumplowicz, and Ratzenhofer, he wrote his *Folkways* (1906), interpreting culture "as it is," not in terms of current value judgments, by objectively describing social customs and institutions as the facts and laws of society. Various concepts he used have passed into current sociological usage: folkways, mores, societal forces, syncretism, we-group, in-group, and out-group. He held that mores justify what is considered right at any given time; that civilization developed by means of folkways and mores; and that social forces, "natural" or mechanical in operation, were subject to a strain of improvement toward better adaptation of means to end, and also to a strain of consistency with each other, for the better results obtainable through cooperation. Usages, folkways, and mores were unformulated and undefined, and were enforced largley by means of taboos; through the development of ritual, laws and institutions have assumed a positive character.

Sumner invented the term *syncretism* to mean an automatic selection that determines which of the mores will survive and which will perish. He assumed that the strongest component group in society usually sets the standards and that the inferior groups imitate the dominant one. Very important in group life, Sumner thought, was the distinction human beings set up between the "we-group," that is, the "intragroup" or "in-group," and everybody else, that is, the "other groups," resulting in intergroup relations between the two. He held that society is divided into five divisions, based on talent and earning power: (1) a very small group of geniuses at the top; (2) a larger but still small group of talented people of great social usefulness because of their practical and enterprising character; (3) the bulk of society, the masses, the bearers of the mores; (4) a small group composed of dependents and defectives; and (5) a small antisocial and harmful group, the delinquent and criminal classes. He illustrated this social stratification by means of his famed "onion charts," with its greatest bulk nearer the bottom than the top (see *Folkways*, p. 40).

Sumner considered social reform to be a futile interference with the inexorable working of the mores. He believed that ideals are escape mechanisms that sanctify existing mores but do not change them. Religion for Sumner was merely an irrational set of mores called forth by the aleatory (luck or wish) element of life.[17]

Field Studies: Implicit Social Control Aspects

While even today Ross and Sumner enjoy limited acceptance among American sociologists, during and immediately after World War I, the theories of W. I. Thomas (1863-1947) (and Florian Znaniecki, 1882-1958) were more prominent. Influenced by Small and Ratzenhofer's concepts of interests, Thomas developed his theories of "attitudes." His work marked the transition in American sociology from system-making to the empirical studies of group behavior. Thomas' collaboration with Znaniecki culminated in the classic work *The Polish Peasant in Europe and America* (5 vols., 1918-1921). He contributed largely to *The Old World Traits Transplanted* (published in 1921 under the names R. E. Park and H. A. Miller because of personal difficulties); his famous *The Unadjusted Girl* appeared in 1923; and with his wife, Dorothy Swaine Thomas, he co-authored *The Child in America* in 1928.

Thomas's basic theory is that a person is everywhere and at all times at the mercy of the socially defined environment; every act must have a definition; every definition means the affirmation of an existing social value or the creation of a new social value. The child is born into a situation in which there are ready-made definitions for all the ordinary affairs of every life. These definitions are in the folkways and mores of all groups that have a history and a tradition, and they are inculcated in the thinking and behavior habits of the group members. New circumstances and changed conditions call for new definitions. Social control signifies the social definition of the wishes of the individual and their incorporation in the common attitudes and objectives of the group. The group customs are sanctioned by the attitudes of the group and by the social disapproval which follows infractions of them; group interests overrule individual interests in their development and application. Thomas also developed his well-known theory of the "four wishes" (the wish for new experience, for security, for recognition, and for response) and later linked them to social control through the concept of "the definition of the situation."

Thomas and Znaniecki introduced the cross-cultural approach to the study of social control in *The Polish Peasant*.[18] The work was a study of culture patterns of Polish peasant life in its original setting and of the processes of acculturation in the United States. This grand work remains a valuable mine of illuminating information, as well as a milestone in the development of modern sociological theory and general methodology. Particularly noteworthy are the introductions to the use of personal documents, the classification of human wishes into four groups, the theory of attitudes and values, and the theory of social disorganization (the breakdown of social control).

Influences from Abroad

Several parallel influences from abroad were important in shaping the American sociologists' theories of social control. Herbert Spencer had (and still has) an enormous impact on American sociology, so much so that he is sometimes considered a more important founding father of sociology than Comte was.[19] Spencer was the first to stress the importance of ceremonials as mechanisms of social control. He claimed that "the earliest kind of government, and the government which is ever spontaneously recommencing is the government of ceremonial observances."[20] Ceremonial observances are the most fundamental kind of government or control. According to Spencer, perhaps the most fundamental kind of government is the dance, the mimetic, and gymnastic dances of primitive tribesmen.[21] The idea that folkways and mores include social ritual, ethical judgment, and convention, and that certain acts be done in specified ways, as in etiquette, perfunctory duties, and approach to the divinity, was analyzed by C. H. Wolbert.)[22] The field of taboos of preliterate society interested such anthropologists as Howitt and Smith.[23]

In addition to the influence of McDougall (born in England), we must note that of Gabriel Tarde and Gustave LeBon. Tarde's (1843-1904) impact is especially apparent in Ross. Considered the founder of social psychology and a strong advocate of the statistical approach, Tarde disagreed with Comte's emphasis on environment and Durkheim's stress on social constraint as the basic concepts of social reality. His own theory was built around the process of imitation; all social interaction, he said, is a process of invention and imitation, whereby some social activity or belief originates and is then imitated or copied according to definite rules. Imitation works most effectively among crowds in cities where there is a greater possibility for the people to congregate. He distinguished between logical and nonlogical imitation. He considered customs to be the imitation of ancestors and fashion the imitation of contemporaries. In *Les Lois Sociales* (1898) Tarde proposed that scientists need to study the resemblances to be found in human conduct in order to enumerate and measure them. He described three psychosocial processes leading to human progress: imitative repetition due to mutual sympathy, opposition, and adaptation. He considered imitation to be the most important factor in human development, seeing in it the essential socializing act, and he went so far as to claim that "society is imitation" (*The Laws of Imitation*, 1903 ed., p. 74). Tarde stated that invention contributes to the imitative process because the desire to invent and discover is imitative, while the invention itself is often only a change in something previously done; the spread of civilization simply means that people become more imitative but less aware of the fact. Imitation is either logical (if an invention is adopted because of its usefulness) or extralogical (if it is adopted merely because others have done so).

While Tarde was interested in the psychology of individuals as influenced by society, Gustave Le Bon (1841-1931) was more concerned with the psychology of groups and the influence of society upon the group. He expanded Tarde's sociology of imitation and Durkheim's sociology of the "collective mind." He accepted Gobineau's theory of the inequality of human races and was convinced of the superiority of the white race. Every race, he said, possesses certain definite psychic traits ("the soul of a race"), a national character, and the sum total of all such characteristics are expressed in the totality of civilization. From the standpoint of social control (*The Crowd: A Study of the Popular Mind*, 1903; *The Psychology of Peoples*, 1899; *The Psychology of Revolution*, 1913), he propounded the theory that the crowd forms a collective mind with a psychic unity which is instinctive and mediocre in character—since the crowd is highly susceptible to suggestion of an emotional nature. In his analysis of revolution, he concluded that governments are unsuccessful in stemming such social upheavals. Leaders can sway crowds by suggestion, reckless affirmation devoid of reason and proof, repetition, and emotional contagion. (Pareto further developed the idea of the illogicality of human beings.)

The present epoch is one of those critical moments in history in which the thought of man is undergoing transformation. Two basic factors are involved in this transformation: the destruction of the religious, political, and social beliefs in which all the elements of our civilization are rooted, and the creation of entirely new conditions of existence as a product of modern scientific and industrial discoveries. According to Pareto, we have entered upon an era of crowds; their rule is always tantamount to a barbarian phase of civilization. In crowds, conscious personality vanishes as discernment is lost. The successful leaders of crowds are rhetoricians, agitators, or fanatics obsessed with an idea and dogmatic in method. The procedure of influence is reiteration rather than analysis. An idea once accepted spreads with great rapidity by contagion and imitation. Leaders of crowds maintain their control by prestige (which may have a variety of derivations); they operate by oratory, verbal extravagance, and vagueness.

Prestige

Although the phenomenon of prestige is very definitely in the field of implicit social control, American sociologists have, until very recently, left this area to Englishmen and Frenchmen.[24]

Categories of Social Control

If we accept the definition of social control as all those processes by which society and its component groups influence the behavior of individual members toward conformity with group norms, we must also accept the idea that social control does not imply total determination of the individual's behavior by the group, but only the confining of behavior within an approved range of variation.

Social control may be either informal or formal. Informal social control is exemplified in the functions of folkways and mores. Formal social control is exemplified by the explicit establishment of procedures and the delegation of specific bodies to enforce them (laws, decrees, regulations, codes). The ultimate authority here is the state which exercises coercive power (or, in turn, on behalf of the various groups controlling the state). Although there is no clear dividing line, formal controls are usually characteristic of more complex societies with greater division of labor, heterogeneity of population, and subgroups with different sets of mores and ideologies.

Another division of control types has to do with primary group and secondary group control. Where primary groups are not strong, or where the society is relatively complex, such controls may not be sufficient, and many control functions are turned over to less intimate secondary groups. There controls are more frequently exercised through rules and regulations, law, and other types of formal control, although the influences of mores, ceremonials, etiquette, praise, and blame also are often operative.

A useful division of control processes is that of regulative and suggestive control. In regulative social control, the accent is upon rules, laws, and possible recrimination and punishment. In suggestive social control, the emphasis is upon voluntary conformity through emulation, cooperation, and suggestion.

Social control is not, however, only a question of external influence on behavior. Indeed, external influences are perhaps not as effective in the long run as the internal, voluntary motivation of the individual to conform to group norms. Thus, an important distinction can be made between external and internal controls. External controls are those imposed from without, and internal control are those by which the individual himself is motivated to conform in his behavior (conscience, conditioning processes, attitudes, indoctrination, socialization). Internal control is especially effective in a homogeneous society characterized by consensus as to norms of conduct. Where conflicting groups indoctrinate the young with conflicting conceptions of acceptable and desirable behavior—and even thinking—external controls become more and more necessary.

Here social institutions enter the picture; they are organized for securing conformity to established modes of behavior and thinking and consist of established procedures for satisfying human needs. These procedures carry a certain degree of compulsion. They express themselves in attitudes of loyalty to established values and the desire both to abide by them and to defend them against nonconformists (dissidents). On the negative side, they involve patterns of imposing conformity even among those whose loyalty to them they do not procure. (Thus, attitudes of veneration for the law and obedience are part of the early conditioning of American children; they are taught obedience to properly constituted authorities and an attitude of veneration for institutions such as democracy, religion, free enterprise, and the Constitution). Behind the appeal of such attitudes lies parental authority and the authority of the teacher; in turn, they are backed by the laws supporting and enforcing many aspects of institutional patterns. In a mass society like ours, much control is exercised by individuals and organizations for the specific purposes of advancing their own special interests, without much regard for the interests of those controlled or with the effect of the control upon the well-being of the community or society as a whole. Such exploitative and predatory controls often constitute a violation of the legal conditions of the state and are usually characterized as "corruption."[25]

Social Control Instrumentalities and Techniques

All types of control techniques and instrumentalities are used for such ends as the control exercised in certain instances by various organizations (such as professional associations and unions over members); publicity; the "gang law;" the activities of political machines and bosses; monopolistic activities; censorship and thought-control devices (including propaganda and publicity). In some instances, such control involves violence, intimidation, fear, torture, graft, corruption, fraud, and many unscrupulous forms of psychic persuasion.

Formal regulatory and maintenance control involves the use of techniques and instrumentalities in the interest of society as a whole (usually the state).[26] Such control resolves itself into such forms as the restraints of social parasites, exploiters (usually defined by law), criminals, and all other imperfectly socialized and antisocial persons whose behavior threatens the well-being of society as a whole; and the establishment and preservation of that degree of social adjustment, equilibrium, and social solidarity—"law and order"—among the various parts that will make possible effective joint action on common needs and objectives and ensure the efficient operation, stability, and continuity of the society (such as war efforts).

There is a marked difference between the social control devices used in the "primitive" and the contemporary mass society.[27] In primitive societies, emphasis was chiefly upon magical, supernatural, traditional, and customary sanctions, and less upon the methods made possible by such cultural equipment as the school, press, radio, and television, and still less upon police, courts, correctional institutions, and the available scientific knowledge concerning the manipulation of behavior.

Nevertheless, many of the methods characteristic of preliterate societies persisted into literate societies, although their relative importance was lessened. For example, the pressure of outdated customs and traditions still obtain; gossip and rumors still play a part, together with salty epigrams, proverbs, myths, ostracism, example, and unauthorized force.[28] In fact, whenever most members of a community consider some part of the social heritage sacred (such as the practice of monogamy) or even highly desirable (such as owning one's own home or automobile), the traditions and socially inherited values may be said to be generally in charge of the processes of control. No generation is capable of starting anew to solve all of the problems it is confronted with, and in most cases it accepts the control from the past, leaving, however, its imprint upon them as it transmits them to a succeeding generation.[29]

Specialization

Many European and American sociologists have discussed social control. Although each approaches the problem in a different way, all agree that social control is exercised through social pressures varying from indirect suggestion, socialization, indoctrination, ridicule, praise, blame, urging respect for traditions and folkways and mores to the more direct pressures of ostracism, denial of privileges, imprisonment, persecution, and death.[30] Among the more important pressures (although such a classification is on shaky ground) are control through belief and ideologies; social suggestion; religion; art; leadership; propaganda; formal and informal education; law and administration; and force, violence, and terror.

Notes

1. A. A. Ross, *Social Control: A Survey of the Foundations of Order* (New York: Macmillan, 1901); nineteen titles listed in *Subject Guide to Books in Print 1975*, Vol. 2 (New York: R. W. Bowker, 1975); Don Martindale, *American Society* (Princeton, N.J.: D. Van Nostrand, 1960), Ch. 15; Richard T. LaPiere, *Theory of Social Control* (New York: McGraw-Hill, 1954); L. L. Bernard, *Social Control in Its Sociological Aspects* (New York: Macmillan, 1939); H. D. Lasswell and Abraham Kaplan, *Power and Society* (New Haven, Conn.: Yale University Press, 1950); Joseph S. Roucek, ed., *Social Control* (Princeton, N.J.: D. Van Nostrand, 1956); Ira S. Wile, *Personality Development and Social Control* (New York: Oxford University Press, 1939); C. Ken Watkins, *Social Control* (New York: Longmans, 1975); Herman Bianchi, Mario Simondi, and Ian Taylor, eds., *Deviance and Control in Europe: Papers from the European Group for the Study of Deviance and Social Control* (New York: John Wiley and Sons, 1976); Arnold Birenbaum and Edward Sagarin, *Norms and Human Behavior* (New York: Praeger Publishers, 1976); Julius Fast, *Body Language* (New York: J. B. Lippincott, 1970); Gustave Le Bon, *The Crowd: A Study of the Popular Mind* (Dunwoody, Ga.: N. S. Berg, 1968); Herman Johnston, Leonard Savitz, and Marvin E. Wolfgang, eds., *The Sociology of Punishment and Correction* (New York: John Wiley and Sons, 1962); Albert Mehrabian, *Tactics of Social Influence* (Englewood Cliffs, N.J.: Prentice-Hall, 1970); L. J. Fein, *Schools and Community Control* (New York: Pegasus, 1971); A. C. Heintz, *Persuasion* (Chicago: Loyola University Press, 1970); Eliot Freidson, *Doctoring Together: A Study of Professional Social Control* (New York: Elsevier, 1976); Harry Silverstein, *Social Control of Mental Illness* (New York: Thomas Y. Crowell, 1969); Morris Janowitz, *Social Control of the Welfare State* (New York: Elsevier, 1976); Philip Bean, *The Social Control of Drugs* (New York: Halsted Press, 1974); Paul Lerman, *Community Treatment and Social Control: A Critical Analysis of Juvenile Correctional Policy* (Chicago: University of Chicago Press, 1975); Jesse R. Pitts, "Social Control," in *The International Encyclopaedia of the Social Sciences*, Vol. XIV (New York: Macmillan, 1968), pp. 381-396; Amy Auerbacher Wilson and others, *Deviance and Social Control in Chinese Society* (New York: Praeger Publishers, 1977); Schuyler Jones, *Men of Influence in Nuristan: A Study of Social Control and Dispute Settlement in Waigal Valley, Afghanistan* (New York: Seminar Press, 1974); Denny F. Pace and Jimmie C. Styles, *Organized Crime: Concepts and Control* (Englewood Cliffs, N.J.: Prentice-Hall, 1975); Rachel Sharp and Anthony Green, *Education and Social Control: A Study in Progressive Primary Education* (Boston: Routledge and Kegan Paul, 1975); Eduard A. Ziegenhagen, *Victims, Crime, and Social Control* (New York: Praeger Publishers, 1977); Philip Mason, *Patterns of Dominance* (New York: Oxford

University Press, 1970); Joseph S. Roucek, *The Concept of "Social Control" in American Sociology* (Madrid: Instituto "Balmes" de Sociologia, 1962).

2. Auguste Comte, *Cours de Philosophie Positive* (Paris: 1830-1842), Vol. 2; *Systeme de Politique Positive* (Paris, 1851-1854); David Cohen, "Comte's Changing Sociology," *American Journal of Sociology* 71 (1965): 168-177; Kenneth Thompson, *Auguste Comte: The Foundation of Sociology* (New York: John Wiley and Sons, 1975); Gertrude Lenzer, ed., *Auguste Comte and Positivism: The Essential Writings* (New York: Harper and Row, 1975); Stanislav Andreski, ed., *The Essential Comte* (New York: Barnes and Noble, 1974).

3. Plato, *The Republic*, Jowett's translation, Book VII.

4. *The Politics of Aristotle*, translated by Ellis, Everyman's Library (New York: E. P. Dutton, 1931), p. 44.

5. Joseph S. Roucek, "American Japanese, Pearl Harbor and World War II," *Journal of Negro Education* 12 (1943): 633-649; Donald O. Schultz and S. K. Scott, *The Subversive* (Springfield, Ill.: C. C. Thomas, 1973); Richard Y. Burnett, *Intervention and Revolution: The U.S. in the Third World* (New York: World, 1968); Rose L. Martin, *The Selling of America* (Santa Monica, Calif., 1973); Geoffrey S. Smith, *To Save a Nation: American Countersubversives, The New Deal, and the Coming of World War II* (New York: Basic Books, 1973); James W. Bryan, *The Development of the English Law of Conspiracy* (Baltimore: Johns Hopkins University Press, 1973); *U.S. News and World Report*, ed., *Famous Soviet Spies: The Kremlin's Secret Weapon* (New York: Simon and Schuster, 1976); Louis De Jong, *The German Fifth Column in the Second World War* (Chicago: University of Chicago Press, 1956); Harold Lavine, *Fifth-Column in America* (Garden City, N.Y., 1940); Hugo A. Bedow and Chester M. Pierce, *Capital Punishment in the United States* (New York: AMS Press, 1976).

6. The Durkheim theory is that the division of labor in the social field makes a place for these divergent individuals and groups in the social order and thus produces social solidarity instead of destroying it; see *On the Division of Labor in Society* (New York: Macmillan, 1933), pp. 226-335. See also Talcott Parsons, *The Structure of Social Action* (New York: McGraw-Hill, 1937), Ch. 10.

7. For the various concepts of elites, see Amitai Etzioni, *A Comparative Analysis of Complex Organizations, On Power, Involvement, and Their Correlates* (New York: Free Press, 1971), especially Ch. 5. The government by the few has been noted, analyzed, and criticized since Plato's idea that the most important element in the well-being of society was that it have a class of rulers possessing a profound knowledge of reality and that the rulers govern by the light of philosophic knowledge which only a long period of careful education could develop in them. "Unless philosophers become kings, or those called kings become philosophers, there will be no end of evils for mankind." The idea of "who" should be the governing class was transformed in later history into the concepts of the "divine right of the Kings," "the super-race," "the proletariat," "the majority rule," and so forth. For further analyses, see Francis G. Wilson, "The Elite in Recent Political Thought," Ch. 12, in Joseph S. Roucek, ed., *Twentieth Century Political Thought* (New York: Philosophical Library, 1946); Roberto Michels, *Political Parties* (London: Jarrold and Sons, 1915); Gaetano Mosca, *The Ruling Class* (New York: McGraw-Hill, 1939); Vilfredo Pareto, *The Mind and*

Society (New York: Harcourt, Brace, 1935); Georges Sorel, *Reflections on Violence* (New York: N. N. Huebsch, 1912). In recent years, there has been a lot of literature on the concepts of "leadership" and "charismatic leadership," and the methods of locating the leaders; consult Warren Bennis, *The Unconscious Conspiracy: Why Leaders Can't Lead* (Saranac Lake, N.Y.: Amacon, 1975); M. G. Hermann and T. W. Milburn, *A Psychological Examination of Political Leaders* (New York: Free Press, 1976); Sheldon D. Glass, *Life-Control: How to Assert Leadership in Any Situation* (Philadelphia: J. B. Lippincott, 1976); James G. Hunt and Lars L. Larson, eds., *Leadership Frontiers* (Kent, Ohio: Kent State University Press, 1976); H. D. Lasswell and A. Kaplan, *Power and Society* (New Haven, Conn.: Yale University Press, 1950); Ernest Manheim, "Recent Types of Charismatic Leadership." Chapter 30, in Joseph S. Roucek, ed., *Social Control* (Westport, Conn.: Greenwood Press, 1970).

8. George A. Theodorson and Achilles G. Theodorson, *Modern Dictionary of Sociology* (New York: Thomas Y. Crowell, 1969), pp. 386-387.

9. Bruce R. Joyce, *New Strategies for Social Education* (Chicago: Science Research Associates, 1972); M. Kent Jennings and Richard G. Niemi, *The Political Character of Adolescence: The Influence of Families and Schools* (Princeton, N.J.: Princeton University Press, 1974); S. K. Gupta, *Citizen in the Making: Socialization for the Citizenship Role in a Democratic Society* (Columbia, Mo.: South Asia Books, 1975); Claus Mueller, *The Politics of Communication: A Study in the Political Sociology of Language, Socialization, and Legitimation* (New York: Oxford University Press, 1973); Joseph S. Roucek, "Some Sociological Aspects of Civic Education," *Journal of Human Relations* 11 (1962): 51-67; Alan R. Brown and Connie Thompson, eds., *Modifying Children's Behavior: A Book of Readings* (Springfield, Ill.: C. C. Thomas 1974); O. G. Brim, *Socialization After Childhood: Two Essays* (Huntington, N.Y.: R. E. Krieger, 1976); F. Gerald Kline and Peter Clarke, eds., *Mass Communications and Youth: Some Current Perspectives* (New York: Russell Sage, 1971); David C. Schwartz and Sandra K. Schwartz, eds., *New Directions in Political Socialization* (New York: Free Press, 1974).

10. See especially W. I. Thomas and Florian Znaniecki, *The Polish Peasant in Europe and America* (Chicago: University of Chicago Press, 1918-1920).

11. A. B. Hollingshead, "The Concept of Social Control," *American Sociological Review* 6 (1941): 217-224.

12. Lester F. Ward, *Dynamic Sociology* (New York, 1883); *Psychic Factors of Civilization* (Boston, 1893).

13. William McDougall, *An Introduction to Social Psychology* (Boston: Luce, 1914).

14. Charles H. Cooley, *Human Nature and the Social Order* (New York: Scribner's, 1902).

15. Ibid., p. 152. This concept led to George Herbert Mead's idea of the "generalized others," in his *Mind, Self and Society* (Chicago: University of Chicago Press, 1934), pp. 150-154—the generalized integrated pattern of self essential for the mental health of the individual, with his differentiated roles.

16. For instance, Paul H. Landis, *Social Control* (Philadelphia: J.B. Lippincott, 1956), pp. 10-13, stresses that Ross was the first American promoting "systematic study of social controls," and then jumps from Ross to Frederick E. Lumley, *Means of*

Social Control (New York: Century Co., 1925), and claims that "no other general text on social control appeared until 1925." It is true that Sumner's *Folkways* (Boston: Ginn, 1906) was intended to be a textbook but, at the same time, folkways and mores are probably, next to ideologies, the outstanding methods of social control.

17. Pareto's ideas concerning the nonlogical character of human conduct may have been influenced by Sumner.

18. Thomas and Znaniecki, *The Polish Peasant.*

19. E. Kilzer and E. J. Ross, *Western Social Thought* (Milwaukee, Wis.: Bruce, 1954), p. 332.

20. Herbert Spencer, *Principles of Sociology* (London: Williams and Norgate, 1906), Vol. 2.

21. Ernst Grosse, *The Beginnings of Art* (New York: Appleton, 1897). Frederick E. Lumley, *The Means of Social Control* (New York: Century Co., 1925), dealt interestingly with rewards, praise, flattery, persuasion, advertising, slogans, propaganda, gossip, satire, laughter, name-calling, commands, threats, and punishment. Unfortunately, his treatment depends on only two references. For the more recent studies of this field, see David Hapgood, *The Screwing of the Average Man* (New York: Bantam, 1974); Elihu Katz and Paul F. Lazarsfeld, *Personal Influence: The Part Played by People in the Flow of Mass Communication* (Glencoe, Ill.: Free Press, 1955); Elton Abernathy, *The Advocate: A Manual of Persuasion* (New York: David McKay, 1964); Dan Nimmo, *The Political Persuaders: The Techniques of Modern Election Campaign* (Englewood Cliffs, N.J.: Prentice-Hall, 1970); George Gordon, *Persuasion: The Theory and Practice of Manipulative Communication* (New York: Hastings House, 1971); Gerald R. Miller, *New Techniques of Persuasion* (New York: Harper and Row, 1973); E. P. Bettinghaus, *Persuasive Communication* (New York: Holt, Rinehart and Winston, 1973); Ralph L. Rosnow and Edward J. Robinson, eds., *Experiments in Persuasion* (New York: Academic Press, 1967); Arthur E. Meyerhoff, *The Strategy of Persuasion: The Use of Advertising Skills in Fighting the Cold War* (New York: Coward, 1965); Oren Root, *Persons and Persuasions* (New York: W.W. Norton, 1974); Thomas D. Beisecker and Donn W. Parson, eds., *The Process of Social Influence: Readings in Persuasion* (Englewood Cliffs, N.J.: Prentice-Hall, 1972); J. M. Nuttin, Jr., *The Illusion of Attitude Change: Toward a Response Contagion Theory of Persuasion* (New York: Academic Press, 1976); Winson Brembeck & Will Howell, *Persuasion: A Means of Social Influence* (Englewood Cliffs, N.J.: Prentice-Hall, 1976); Charles Laird, *The Miracle of Language* (Greenwich, Conn.: Fawcett, 1960); Eric Hoffer, *The True Believer* (New York: New American Library, 1951); Julius Fast, *Body Language* (New York: Pocket Books, 1975); Daniel E. Schneider, *The Psycho-Analyst and the Artist* (New York: New American Library, 1950).

22. J. M. Champlin, *The Sacraments in a World of Change* (Notre Dame, Ind.: Notre Dame University Press, 1973); E. O. James, *Christian Myth and Ritual: A Historical Study* (Gloucester, Mass.: Peter Smith, 1973); James D. Shaughnessy, ed., *The Roots of Rituals* (Grand Rapids, Mich.: Eerdmans, 1973); N. K. Whyte, *Small Groups and Political Rituals in China* (Berkeley: University of California Press, 1974); H. L. Nieburg, *Culture Storm: Politics and the Ritual Order* (New York: St. Martin's Press, 1973); Theodore Reik, *Ritual: Psycho-analytic Studies* (Westport,

Conn.: Greenwood Press, 1975); John Abbott, *The Keys of Power: A Study of Indian Ritual and Belief* (Secaucus, N.J.: University Books, 1974); Erik H. Erikson, *Toys and Reasons: Stage in the Ritualization of Reality* (New York: W. W. Norton, 1977).

23. A. W. Howitt, *Native Tribes of South-East Australia* (New York: Macmillan, 1904); W. W. Smith, *The Religion of the Semites* (New York: Macmillan 1907); Hardin Garrett, *Stalking the Wild Taboo* (Los Altos, Calif.: Kaufman, 1973); Harris Marvin, *Culture, Man and Nature* (New York: Thomas Y. Crowell, 1971); Godfrey Lienhardt, *Social Anthropology* (New York: Oxford University Press, 1964); Hutton Webster, *Taboo: A Sociological Study* (New York: Octagon, 1973).

24. Norval D. Glenn, "The Contributions of While Collars to Occupational Prestige," *Sociological Quarterly* 16 (Spring 1975): 184-189; Mariam K. Slater, "My Son the Doctor: Aspects of Mobility Among American Jews," *American Sociological Review* 34 (June 1969): 359-373; L. G. Churchward, *The Soviet Intelligentsia: An Essay on the Social Structure and Roles of Soviet Intellectuals During the 1960s* (London: Routledge and Kegan Paul, 1973); Dean Lan, *Prestige with Limitations: Realities of the Chinese-American Elite* (San Francisco: R. and E. Research Associates, 1976); Peter Cohen, *The Gospel According to the Harvard Business School* (Garden City, N.Y.: Doubleday, 1973); John A. Armstrong, *The European Administrative Elite* (Princeton, N.J.: Princeton University Press, 1973); Robert Presthus, *Elites in the Policy Process* (New York: Cambridge University Press, 1974); Walter Struve, *Elites Against Democracy: Leadership Ideals in Bourgeois Political Thought in Germany, 1890-1933* (Princeton, N.J.: Princeton University Press, 1973); Kenneth Prewitt and Alan Stone, *The Ruling Elites: Elite Theory, Power and American Democracy* (New York: Harper and Row, 1973); Martin Marger, *The Force of Ethnicity: A Study of Urban Elites* (Detroit: New University Thought, 1974); Robert Laporte, *Power and Privilege: Influence and Decision-Making in Pakistan* (Berkeley: University of California Press, 1975); Juan Carlos Agulla, *Eclipse of an Aristocracy: An Investigation of the Ruling Elites in the City of Córdoba* (University: University of Alabama, 1976).

25. Here we are confronted with the whole field of political ideologies, justifying the ends and means of political or state action. For the Marxists, for instance, economic conditions are the basis of life, political and ideological systems being merely the "superstructure" and undergoing changes along with them. Pierre Joseph Proudhon (1809-1865) wrote *What Is Property? An Inquiry into the Principles of Right and of Government* (1938) and answered the question by "Property is theft!"

26. We cannot discuss here the overargued definitions of such concepts as "general welfare," "the public interest," "law and order," "national interests," "the majority rule," and "the minority rights." See, for instance, Gordon Schuber, *The Public Interest: A Critique of the Theory of a Political Concept* (Glencoe, Ill.: Free Press, 1961). Schuber examines the statements about public interest that have been made in recent years, relating fundamental questions about the complex relationships in political theory, political behavior, and scientific inquiry. For the problem of "The Harmony of Interests," see E. H. Carr, *The Twenty-Years Crisis 1919-1939* (New York: Macmillan, 1940), Ch. 4.

27. The process of social change has received considerable attention in recent years. Consult such studies as Francis R. Allen, *Socio-Cultural Dynamics: An Introduction to Social Change* (New York: Macmillan, 1971); D. W. Calhoun, *Social Science in an*

Age of Change (New York: Harper and Row, 1971); Armand L. Mauss, *Social Problems as Social Movements* (Philadelphia: J. B. Lippincott, 1975); Robert Ash Garner, *Social Change* (Chicago: Rand McNally, 1977); Roland L. Warren, *Social Change and Human Purpose: Toward Understanding and Action* (Chicago: Rand McNally, 1977); A. H. Galt and L. J. Smith, *Models and the Study of Social Change* (New York: Halsted, 1976); Henry Kamen, *The Iron Century: Social Change in Europe* (New York: Praeger Publishers, 1971); Louis Schneider, *Classical Theories of Social Change* (Morristown, N.J.: General Learning Press, 1976); Manning Nash, ed., *Essays on Economic Development and Cultural Change in Honor of Bert F. Hoselitz* (Chicago: University of Chicago Press, 1977); Arnold W. Green, *Social Problems: Arena of Conflict* (New York: McGraw-Hill, 1975); George K. Zollschan and Walter Hirsch, eds., *Social Change: Explorations, Diagnoses, and Conjectures* (Cambridge, Mass.: Schenkman, 1976); Iram Adelam, *Theories of Economic Growth and Development* (Stanford, Calif.: Stanford University Press, 1961); Alban G. Widgery, *Interpretations of History: Confucius to Toynbee* (London: Allen and Unwin, 1961); Kenneth B. Benne and Robert Chin, eds., *The Planning of Social Change: Readings in the Applied Behavioral Sciences* (New York: Holt, Rinehart and Winston, 1961); Wm. Bruce Cameron, *Modern Social Movements* (New York: Random House, 1966).

28. W. I. Thomas, *Primitive Behavior* (New York: McGraw-Hill, 1937); E. B. Tyler, *Primitive Culture: Researches into the Development of Mythology, Philosophy, Religion, Art and Customs* (1871); David E. Hunter, "Behavior Control: Formal and Informal Sanctions." Chapter 12 in David E. Hunter and Philip Whitten, eds., *The Study of Anthropology* (New York: Harper and Row, 1976); Philip K. Bock, *Modern Cultural Anthropology* (New York: Alfred A. Knopf, 1969), especially Part Three.

29. Philip K. Bock, *Modern Cultural Anthropology*, Part Two. David Riesman, *The Lonely Crowd: A Study of the Changing American Character* (Garden City, N.Y.: Doubleday, 1953), compares three types of society which enforce conformity and mold social character in definably different ways. The first society is called "tradition-directed" because conformity is ensured by the tendency of its members to follow tradition. The second type is dependent on "inner-direction" and is characterized by increased personal mobility, by a rapid accumulation of capital (teamed with devastating technological shifts), and by an almost constant expansion. Problems arise that are new, and choices are so numerous that people must learn to live socially without strict and self-evident traditional direction; "the source of direction for the individual is 'inner' in the sense that it is implanted early in life by the elders and directed toward generalized but nonetheless inescapably destined goals" (pp. 29-30). The third type of society is "other-directed," best typified by the upper middle class of New York and Boston, which is "in the process of striving itself and the process of paying close attention to the signals of others that remain unaltered throughout life" (p. 37).

30. The more important and systematized means of social control are handled in separate chapters in Joseph S. Roucek, ed., *Social Control* (Westport, Conn.: Greenwood Press, 1970); F. E. Lumley, *Means of Social Control*.

Morris Janowitz

THE INTELLECTUAL HISTORY OF "SOCIAL CONTROL"

In the emergence of sociology as an intellectual discipline, the idea of social control was a central concept for analyzing social organization and the development of industrial society. Originally, the term *social control* dealt with a generic aspect of society and served as a comprehensive basis for a sociological examination of the social order. In fact, it was one intellectual device for linking sociological analysis to the human values and philosophical orientation employed by some pioneer sociologists interested in "social progress" and the reduction of irrationality in social behavior. In the most fundamental terms, "social control" referred to the capacity of a society to regulate itself according to desired principles and values. Sociological analysis has the task of exploring the conditions and variables likely to make this goal attainable.

In this essay,[1] I seek first to set forth the intellectual parameters in the concept of social control as it was originally formulated in order to serve as the basis for a broad sociological frame of reference. Then I examine the early usage and diffusion of the concept. Third, I discuss the efforts, starting in the 1930s, to transform its meaning into the narrower notion of the processes of developing conformity; in this connection, it is interesting to probe the reasons for this attempt to transform the meaning of social control. Finally, I examine the persistence of the classic usage of the concept by selected sociologists during the period since 1945 and thereby assess its relevance for contemporary sociology and for analyzing the crisis of political legitimacy in advanced industrial societies with parliamentary institutions.

Because some sociologists have come to define social control as the social psychology of conformity, sociological theory and analysis have suffered. This type of thinking contributes to the difficulty of relating the sociological enterprise to other social science disciplines as well as to social philosophy and to issues of professional practice and social policy. Either a new term had to be invented or the earlier meaning had to be reconstituted. I have chosen to retrace the intellectual history and usage of social control, since I believe that the concept in its original meaning can help to integrate bodies of empirical data with sociological theory, to codify research findings, and to handle questions of social values in sociological analysis. Moreover, one of my central arguments is that a close examination of the intellectual history of the idea of social control reveals that, despite the constriction of its original meaning in some quarters, its broad and generic meaning has had a strikingly persistent vitality for the study of the social order.

In 1925, George Herbert Mead wrote in the *International Journal of Ethics* that "social control depends, then, upon the degree to which individuals in society are able to assume attitudes of others who are involved with them in common endeavors."[2] He was merely articulating, in his own conceptual terms, a widespread orientation in American sociology that had already been reflected in the first volume of the *American Journal of Sociology* in 1896. There George Vincent, a sociologist who still felt at ease with the language of social philosophy, offered the formulation: "Social control is the art of combining social forces so as to give society at least a trend toward an ideal."[3] Social control has served and continues to serve as a shorthand notation for a complex set of views and viewpoints. It has been a "sensitizing concept," in the terminology of Herbert Blumer, or a "theoretical orientation," in that of Robert K. Merton. Moreover, social control has been directly linked to the study of total societies. It has stood for a comprehensive focus on the nation-state and a concern which has come to be called "macrosociology."

Intellectual Parameters

The intellectual investment in the idea of social control derives from a rejection of economic self-interest theories. Social control has been an expression of the outlook that held that the individualistic pursuit of economic self-interest can account for neither collective social behavior nor the existence of a social order and does not supply an adequate basis for the achievement of ethical goals. Much of the writing about control must be understood as sociologists' efforts to accept the relevance but at the same time to identify the limitations of marginal-utility analysis.

In formal terms, one can think of social organization, the subject matter of sociology, as the patterns of influence in a population of social groups. Social control, therefore, is not to be conceived as being the same as social organization; rather, it is a perspective which focuses on the capacity of a social organization to regulate itself, and this capacity generally implies a set of goals rather than a single goal. Social control is a perspective which, while committed to rigorous hypothesis testing, requires the explication of a value position.

Social control was not originally, and subsequently has not been, necessarily the expression of a conservative political outlook. Many early American sociologists who used the term were religious socialists; others

were adherents of a "progressive" view. It is more to the point to emphasize
that these early formulations parallel sociologists' contemporary interests in
"value maximization." While social control involves the capacity of
constituent groups in a society to behave in terms of their acknowledged
moral and collective goals, it does not imply cultural relativism. The term has
continuity because social control can be conceived as resting on a value
commitment to at least two elements: (1) the reduction of coercion, although
it recognizes the irreducible elements of coercion in a legitimate system of
authority, and (2) the elimination of human misery, although it recognizes
the persistence of some degree of inequality. One should also mention a third
element: a commitment to procedures of redefining societal goals in order to
enhance the role of rationality, although this may be considered inherent in
the first two.

The opposite of social control can be thought of as coercive control, that is,
the social organization of a society which rests predominantly and essentially
on force—the threat and the use of force. Of course, even in the most
repressive totalitarian nation-state the agents of repression are limited in
scope by some primitive, if unstable, set of norms. However, and more
pertinent to the issue at hand, any social order, including a society with a
relatively effective system of social control, will require an element of
coercion, but presumably a limited one circumscribed by a system of
legitimate norms.[4]

Early sociologists in the United States were vague about their social goals
and their notions of the "ideal." Frequently, the ideal they offered was no
better defined than as the spontaneously emergent and spontaneously
accepted consensus. At times, they were no more specific than to assert that
the ideal referred to norms that were rationally accepted and internation-
alized in contrast to the conditions of coercive controls. Sociologists have
become much more specific about the goals they wish to see maximized and
therefore far more precise about the analysis of different patterns and
mechanisms of social control.

Obviously, there are a variety of types and mechanisms of social control.
Each is the result of particular antecedent variables and, in turn, each form
has a different impact on social behavior. The task of empirical social
research is to investigate the forms and consequences of social control. In
essence, this means answering the hypothetical question, which forms of
social control are most effective, that is, which enable a social group to
regulate itself in terms of a set of legitimate moral principles and result in the
reduction of coercive control?[5]

This perspective explicitly negates the assertion that social organization
per se represses personality, social creativity, and collective problem-
solving. In the simplest terms, social control is not the achievement of

collective stability. The vital residue of the classical standpoint is that social control organizes the cleavages, strains, and tensions of any society—peasant, industrial, or advanced industrial. The problem is whether the processes of social control are able to maintain the social order while transformation and social change take place. There is no question that, from this point of view, there is a parallel between social control and stability or repression. The argument that is relevant here is just the opposite: social control, to the extent that it is effective, "motivates" social groups. All this seems painfully obvious; but one purpose of a theoretical orientation is to make the obvious inescapable.

Exploration of the idea of social control requires a recognition that its emergence was part of a continuing critique of and response to the Gemeinschaft-Gesellschaft model. Under the influence of philosophical pragmatism and the impact of empirical research, the dichotomous categories of Gemeinshaft-Gesellschaft were found to be both oversimplified and inadequate.[6] I speak not only of Ferdinand Tönnies' exposition on Gemeinschaft-Gesellschaft but also of the stream of parallel or related writers. These include Henry Maine (status and contract),[7] Emile Durkheim (mechanical and organic solidarity),[8] Charles Horton Cooley (primary and secondary groups),[9] Robert Redfield (folk culture and urban culture),[10] Louis Wirth (urbanism as a way of life),[11] Ralph Linton (ascription and achievement),[12] and Talcott Parsons (pattern variables).[13]

The converging elements of these formulations have had a powerful impact on sociological theory and analysis. At the same time, there is a tradition of criticism of the writings of Tönnies and those who have followed his formulations that is almost as longstanding and enduring as the Gemeinschaft-Gesellschaft model itself. Among the European sociologists who have dissented from Tönnies' orientation are Georg Simmel,[14] Herman Schmalenbach,[15] Theodore Geiger,[16] and René Koenig.[17] The accumulated empirical evidence from anthropological and sociological sources with a historical perspective indicates that peasant societies are not wholly Gemeinschaft entities, as Tönnies used the term. The inability of the model to account for the variety of solitary collectivities that emerge in advanced industrial societies is equally noteworthy.

Much of the criticism of the Gemeinschaft-Gesellschaft approach is not an effort to reject its central concern with societal transformation.[18] Instead, it is an attempt to recast the approach to make it effectively applicable to the analysis of the alternative historical paths by which societies have become urbanized and industrialized. It is difficult, if not impossible, to think of the emergence of modern society in terms of an "evolutionary" transformation from "community" into "society" that is the result of a limited number of basic variables and linear models of social change and societal transformation. Thus, as a consequence of this criticism, the model has been freed from its historical mythography and its conceptual dimensions and variables have been refashioned into testable hypotheses.

As a result, the notion of social control has been formulated and elaborated to provide a more adequate approach to the problems of social change and social order. Sociological theories of the social order thereby have come to reject the assertion that the Gemeinschaft aspects of societal structure are only residues of some previous stage of social organization, while the Gesellschaft dimensions constitute the reality of industrial and urban society. Instead, social organization encompasses, at any given historical moment, essential and elaborated elements of both Gemeinschaft and Gesellschaft in varying scope, intensity, and consequence. The analysis of social control is an analysis of the interplay of those variables that can be related to both Gemeinschaft and Gesellschaft attributes. Moreover, the concept of social control is directly linked to the notion of voluntaristic action, to articulated human purpose and actions—that is, to various schemes of means and ends. Therefore, it is designed to avoid the overdeterministic sociology which has come to be inherent in the Gemeinschaft-Gesellschaft model. Social control presents a format of influence based on the notion of interaction and mutual (two-way) relations among social groups. To speak of mutual influence is hardly to deny the elements of inequality and imbalance in social relations.

Sociologists who have used the concept of social control have in effect been following the intellectual lead of Auguste Comte, for whom the central problem of sociological analysis was the impact of industrialization on the social order and the consequences of the resulting individualism on the moral order. Obviously, the classic writers, including Karl Marx, Emile Durkheim, and Max Weber, addressed themselves to the issues Comte raised. One can translate much of the corpus of sociological writing on macrosociology into the language of the social control framework, but to do so would obscure rather than clarify the issues involved. It is preferable to focus directly on that distinct sociological stream which in varying degree makes explicit use of the idea of social control. Though mainly an American stream, it is influenced by and in turn has influenced European thought and research. It presents both a unity and a continuing elaboration.

First, the original writers and, in time, the subsequent ones as well have manifested a philosophical outlook concerned with the limits of rationality in pursuing social and moral aims. Their outlook has reflected pragmatism in the majority of the writers, but for some it also has included aspects of phenomenology. An essential element of this orientation has been the rejection or, rather, the avoidance of either idealism or materialism.

Second, the adherents of social control have been concerned with informal, face-to-face relations as aspects of social structure. In contemporary language, they have been preoccupied with the interface between micro- and macroanalysis.

Third, the style of these sociologists has been one of persistent concern with empirical exploration of their ideas. They have been self-critical about appropriate empirical techniques, continually in search of various types of documentation and data, and fully aware of the complexities and elusive character of proof in sociology.

Therefore, there is a direct line of intellectual continuity from the earliest efforts to formulate the component elements of social control to its usage by contemporary research sociologists aware of its intellectual background and theoretical purpose. The concept hardly implies that the subject matter of sociology is the "adjustment" of men to existing social reality. On the contrary, since its early use, the thrust of this stream of sociological discourse has been to focus on efforts of men to realize their collective goals. The continuity between the early writers on social control and particular efforts in contemporary research is manifested in such works as the penetrating research on juvenile delinquency by Albert J. Reiss, Jr.[19] Conceptualizing his operational measures in terms of social control, he refers to it as "the ability of social groups or institutions to make norms or rules effective."

Likewise, there is a continuity between the early analysis of social control that included the study of social and political movements—the processes of revolution, protest, and institution-building—as described in the seminal study by Lyford Edwards (1927) and contemporary interest in collective behavior.[20] Thus, the theoretical and empirical tasks of sociologists who use the social control orientation have been and continue to be to identify and, wherever possible, to quantify the magnitude of the variables that facilitate or hinder the group pursuit of collective moral goals.

The pioneer sociologists who thought in terms of social control worked on specific empirical topics and in time applied their efforts to a very broad range of topics in the register of social research. Initially, they did tend to focus on macrosociological issues, such as law and the formation of legal codes, the emergence of public opinion and collective behavior, and informal and mass media of communication, as well as "traditional" elements, such as customs, "mores," and religion. Louis Wirth, an articulate spokesman for this intellectual tradition, asserted the centrality of the processes of "persuasion, discussion, debate, education, negotiation, parliamentary procedure, diplomacy, bargaining, adjudication, contractual relations, and compromise." For him, these processes had to serve as the means for arriving at a sufficient degree of agreement to make the ongoing life of a society possible, despite differences in interests (1948, pp. 31-32).

At this point, an important caveat must be entered. Much of the empirical and substantive writings about social control deals with norms and normative behavior. Norms are often used as the indicators of social control—the dependent variables, so to speak. But social control does not rest on an exclusively normative conception of elements of social organization and society. As will be demonstrated, it did not do so originally and cannot now if it is to serve as a guide to empirical research and to the codification of research findings. On the contrary, the continuing relevance of social control theory reflects the fact that its assumptions and variables incorporate the ecological, technological, economic, and institutional dimensions of social organization.

Early Usage of Social Control

The term *social control* first figures prominently in the writings of E. A. Ross,[21] who was strongly influenced by Gabriel Tarde, a sociologist with powerful insights into French society and deeply involved in empirical social research.[22] Tarde himself did not emphasize the term, but he did present a wide-ranging analysis of the complex processes required to produce social agreement through mass persuasion. He was concerned with the mechanisms required to generate effective leadership and legislation that would regulate social change.

While working at Stanford University in 1894, Ross decided that the idea of social control was a "key that unlocks many doors"; that is, it served as a notion to bridge the various institutions that concerned him.[23] Again and again, he used the concept to explain how men "live closely together and associate their efforts with that degree of harmony we see about us." Basically, Ross was concerned with the social conditions that created harmony. Much of his writing consisted of detailed descriptions of the mechanisms of social control. While he was fully aware of the coercive elements in industrial society, he focused on the devices of persuasion, both interpersonal and institutional. He was impressed with the extent to which persuasion as well as minipulation was operative. His analysis encompassed the processes of face-to-face interaction and sociability and those of public opinion and legal control. However, he was interested not merely in devices of persuasion but also in a generic conception of society that would explain those devices which operate to "find a means of guiding the will or conscience of the individual members of society."[24] His usage of social control brought this term into the center of sociological inquiry, but it remained for other sociologists to use the idea more rigorously and to enrich its intellectual relevance.

During the founding period of sociology in the United States, two major figures—Charles Horton Cooley and W. I. Thomas—gave centrality to social control and its relation to rational control in their writings. There were strong elements of convergence in their interests, but the differences were important.[25] Cooley was a more systematic and coherent thinker than Ross, and his approach to social control was based on a thoughtful, normative orientation. He drove directly to his main preoccupation, which reflected the pervasive influence of pragmatism among the sociologists of that period.[26]

Cooley's approach, of course, rests on an interactional social philosophy he helped to develop. Social control was essential for the growth of the self through the process of interaction. Likewise, it rested to an important degree on self-control. Cooley used the notion of the primary group—face-to-face relations—but he had few constructions for dealing with the internalization norms, although he asserted that "individuality" was a crucial element for effective and meaningful social control.

Cooley was a powerful thinker because he struggled to relate his interactional approach to the larger society. His link with the classic question of social order and his outlook on social control under conditions of industrialization are summarized in his chapter, "Social Control in International Relations." In his words, "A ripe nationality is favorable to international order for the same reasons that a ripe individuality is favorable to order in a small group. It means that we have coherent, self-conscious and more or less self-controlled elements out of which to build our system (of nations)."[27]

Thomas approached social control from a different but related principle of pragmatic philosophy. In his view, the essential issue for both sociologists and persons in public and social affairs was to increase the importance and effectiveness of "rational control in social life." Open mindedly—and in a sense paradoxically—like many European sociologists, Thomas raised the question of the impact of rational thought in weakening the social fabric of society. "We are less and less ready to let any social process go on without our active interference and we feel more and more dissatisfied with any active interference based upon a mere whim of an individual or a social body, or upon preconceived philosophical, religious, or moral generalization."[28]

Unlike Cooley, Thomas was trained in classical literature and history, and he developed an interest in the comparative sociological study of specific cultures and societies. He was fully aware of the writings of Tönnies, whose formulation he rejected because of its simple evolutionary bias, its failure to describe adequately either peasant society or modern social organization, and particularly its implied hostility to individual freedom and creativity. Thomas offered no single set of determinant causes of social change, although he was clearly the most systematic of the founding sociologists concerned with social control. Thomas had a comprehensive outlook toward the dimensions of social organization and social control. He offered a highly differentiated orientation which sought to incorporate variables reflecting ecology, economy, and technology into his analysis of social control. His orientation, of necessity, suffered because of eclecticism. He saw society in institutional terms as consisting of a set of irreducible social groups, from primary groups to complex bureaucratic structures. Social control depended on effective linkages or articulation among these elements; social disorganization resulted from their disarticulation.

While Ross was stimulated by Tarde to propose the term *social control*, the writings of Georg Simmel were important ingredients in fashioning the outlooks of W. I. Thomas and, later, Robert E. Park, both of whom pressed to develop an empirical base for analysis of social control in the urban metropolis. In his classic article, "The Mental Life of the Metropolis," Simmel demonstrated his resistance to the categories derived from the Gemeinschaft-Gesellschaft model.[29] He was, rather, concerned with the changing and alternative basis of group life. He did not conceptualize individuality as inherently self-destructive or destructive of social control. The analysis of individuality had to include the possibilities of forms of autonomy and personal freedom.[30]

Simmel's writings did not express any existing philosophy of history. In fact, they articulated the orientation of American sociologists of the pragmatic persuasion. In particular, Simmel did not conclude that the complexity of modern society and its range of group affiliations automatically implied the loss of individuality or that it was necessarily disintegrative. His "Die Kreuzung sozialer Kreise," translated by Reinhard Bendix as "The Web of Group Affiliation," argues the opposite. In effect, each new group to which a person becomes affiliated "circumscribes" him more exactly and more unambiguously.[31] In other words, as a person becomes affiliated with a social group, he surrenders himself to it. However, the larger the number of groups to which the individual belongs, the more unlikely or improbable it will be that other persons will exhibit the same combination of group affiliations. Therefore, "the person also regains his individuality because his pattern of participation is unique." In essence, Simmel rejected the assertion that participation engendered only social constraint and conformity or, alternatively, individuality resulted only from withdrawal. He held that individuality was the result of a pattern of social participation and the outcome of specific types of social control.

The central themes of Durkheim's writings converge with the early formulation of social control and are thus a related aspect of the intellectual history of the conception. He did not use the term or an equivalent formulation. But his persistent search for the "determination of moral facts" is his version of the problematic issue involved in social control; this is perhaps most clearly seen in *Sociologie et philosophie*.[32] Moreover, his empirical study, *Le Suicide* (1897)[33] has come to supply the link between his work and the subsequent generations of writers concerned with social control.

Obviously, one cannot overlook the existence of a body of literature criticizing Durkheim for his failure to offer an effective analysis of the internalization of the norms on which he rests his analysis. Likewise, Durkheim's framework has not served as a contribution to critical evaluation of the Gemeinschaft-Gesellschaft themes in sociology but has, in effect, been incorporated into this dominant perspective. While his work has been an important stimulus to empirical research, in contrast to the main body of writing on social control as it has subsequently emerged, his orientation has presented a relatively overdeterministic frame of reference with only limited exploration of the voluntaristic elements in the "moral order."

Diffusion of the Concept

By 1920, the term *social control* had emerged in the United States as representing a central theoretical thrust by which sociologists sought to integrate their substantive and empirical interests. For the next twenty years, while sociology was becoming institutionalized as an academic discipline, the writings of both Robert E. Park[34] and Robert M. MacIver[35]—although they were extremely different thinkers—served to maintain the notion that social control was a device for integrating diverse elements of sociological analysis.

Social control was used as the organizing theme of the national convention of the American Sociological Association in 1917. There a wide range of empirical topics were explored, such as child welfare, immigration, labor relations, and economic organization. The papers presented made striking efforts to explicitly evaluate the effectiveness of elements in the process of social control.[36] In 1921, Robert E. Park and Ernest W. Burgess assessed the state of sociology in *Introduction to the Science of Sociology* by asserting: "All social problems turn out to be problems of social control."[37] In contemporary language, social control is the outcome, in various forms and content, of social organization. It is the construct which helps to relate and interrelate the dependent variables of empirical research. Moreover, since they linked social control to social problems, sociologists of that period saw it as a vehicle for joining sociological analysis to issues of social policy and for dealing with issues of deviance.

To understand the full connotations of social control in that intellectual setting, one has only to turn to its references and cross-references. Social control pointedly encompassed law and leadership, key elements for understanding how society regulates itself. In the Park and Burgess volume, the list of cross-references even included the word "participation"; the explication of this cross-reference was based on an analysis of the "immigrant problem" viewed as a problem in lack of participation.[38]

Sociologists of this period did not perceive social control as a mechanism of conformity. Society did not and could not exist on the basis of conformity but required active elements of collective problem-solving. Nor did the explicit philosophical preferences of these sociologists permit them to equate social control with conformity. Social control raised the question of how society regulated itself and changed. In reply, Park and Burgess postulated a sequence of "natural history" of collective behavior that was rooted in conflict and from which few forms of social control could emerge. "Social control and the mutual subordination of individual members to the community have their origin in conflict, assume definite organized forms in the process of accommodation, and are consolidated and fixed in assimilation."[39]

As Ralph Turner has asserted, Park's explication of social control drew on analogies from the competitive processes of ecology, to which he added those forms of social communication that constrained the ecological processes.[40] He posed a formulation of the underlying processes of social control that fused ecological, institutional, normative variables. "Competition and communication, although they perform divergent and uncoordinated social functions, nevertheless in the actual life of society supplement and complete each other. Competition seems to be the principle of individuation in the life of the person and of society—communication, on the other hand, operates primarily as an integrating and socializing principle."[41] He went on to argue that the initial consequence of new forms of communication is to intensify competition. However, "in the long run," improved communication can contribute "to humanize social relations and to substitute a moral order for one that is fundamentally symbiotic rather than social."

In contrast, Robert M. MacIver's interest in political theory and the role of the state led to his concern with coercion, especially legitimate force, as an aspect of social control, a concern that paralleled Max Weber's orientation. For MacIver, an element of coercion was involved in social control; the problematic issues were the amount and the minimization of coercion.[42]

MacIver accepted the idea that social control was the modern equivalent of the classic issue of social order. Social control meant both elements—the institutional mechanisms by which society regulated individual behavior, and the "way in which patterned and standardized behavior in turn serves to maintain the social organization."[43] One striking avenue he investigated was social control in nineteenth-century utopian communities in the United States. MacIver, searching for hypothetical equivalents of existing patterns of social control, was particularly interested in the capacity of purposefully constructed utopian communities to adapt to social change and to engage in collective problem-solving. He concluded that, because the social organization of these communities permitted very limited, or insufficient, individualization, they were incomplete societies and therefore suffered a very high rate of "mortality."[44]

During the 1920s and early 1930s, the term *social control* supplied an essential bridge to the influential work of institutional economists. In the United States, such economists included Thorstein Veblen, John Maurice

Clark, Wesley C. Mitchell, and Walton H. Hamilton.[45] They believed that the mechanisms of the marketplace and competition supplied an essential but only partial basis for understanding economic behavior. Clark, in *Social Control of Business*, presented the core of the institutional economists' effort to make use of the sociological notion of social control.[46] While he was firmly committed to the centrality of effective utilization of market mechanisms for allocating resources, he realized that the basic structure of modern society did not rest in the competitive economic process. Society requires a set of informal and formal norms which highlight "cooperative" arrangements. In effect, he rejected the notion of countervailing power—of society-wide organization as derived from the competition of large-scale or different types of economic organizations. Instead, he asserted that the governmental system, both legislative and legal, supplied the framework of the cooperative elements of the modern economic system.

Comparable to works linking social control with economics was the work of "realist" scholars in law, politics, and psychology. The most outstanding writer in the sociology of law was Roscoe Pound, whose 1942 study, *Social Control Through Law*, anticipated contemporary approaches.[47] In political science, Charles E. Merriam made use of the social control concept in empirical research into political and governmental institutions.[48] During this period, another vigorous intellectual current that fed the concern with social control derived from the writings of Mary Parker Follett, the psychologist of administration. She was groping, with profound insight, toward a sociological formulation of administrative control that would encompass the essential elements of the social process, and she broke with the view of administration as a system of constraints. "We get control through effective integration. Authority should arise within the unifying process. As every living process is subject to its own authority, that is, the authority evolved by or involved in the process itself, so social control is generated by the process itself. Or rather, the activity of self-creating coherence is the controlling activity."[49]

By the 1930s, the American sociologists' theoretical and empirical concerns with social control had begun to have a discernible impact on European thought. Karl Mannheim followed the American literature closely and served as a focal point of interpretation. In his elaborate treatise *Man and Society in an Age of Reconstruction*,[50] Mannheim made social control a central point of departure for his analysis. Interested in political sociology, he introduced and focused attention on the role of parliamentary institutions in the processes of social control in an advanced industrial society. For him, freedom was a particular type and quality of social control; it was required under advanced industrialism if social planning were not to degenerate into authoritarian rule. He believed that, to be effective, the processes of social control had, in turn, to rest on vigorous parliamentary institutions. Under the influence of

Max Weber, he sought to analyze, in the broadest terms, the transformation of social structure and authority relations, and he highlighted the shift that he saw toward indirect authority with the concomitant profound strains on social control. His work was remarkable in its ability to incorporate the detailed findings of empirical sociological research on American social structure. In essence, Mannheim prepared the intellectual groundwork for incorporating political sociology and the analysis of mass society into the study of social control.

Conceptual Continuity

Although *social control* persisted as a coordinating term of reference in American sociology through 1940, the narrow meaning of the term was already coming into force. Sociologists calling themselves social psychologists were postulating the alternate formulation of social control as a process of socialization leading to conformity. This trend becomes evident when one examines, not the theoretical treatises of the period, but the titles of doctoral dissertations and journal articles concerned with socialization and the process of persuasion, interpersonal and mass.

How does one account for this apparent shift?

First, the fact that there is a natural history of sociological ideas may afford a partial explanation. Under the impact of empirical research, broad conceptions that have served as sources of stimulation in time become converted into more specific and delimited topics of research. However convincing in itself, this is hardly an adequate explanation. Review of the literature and interviews with figures active during this period do not permit the conclusion that the diffuseness and shortcomings of the idea of social control—and there are many—account for the apparent transformation. It is necessary to consider additional factors.

Second, the power analysis and modified versions of economic determinism derived from the writings of Karl Marx had the unanticipated consequence of weakening a concern with the voluntaristic and purposeful process of modifying the social order. This occurred during the Great Depression and the New Deal, which created ideological and political currents that impinged on sociology (much as, later, the events of the 1960s did) and made the idea of social control or any equivalent unpopular. The result was an oversimplified focus on power and power relations and on uncritical acceptance of the notion of mass society. To speak of social control was perceived as impeding those social and economic changes that members of the sociological profession considered essential.

As a result, after the interruption in academic life during World War II, the subject matter of social control increasingly came to reflect the specialized interests of sociologists concerned with research on institutions dealing with socialization and resocialization such as the mental hospital or school.[51] The research topics covered under "social control," both at the national and regional meetings and in journal and monograph publications, show that the processes of social control in these terms were investigated in an ever-widening range of institutional settings. Paradoxically, the relevance of these empirical researches rested on their findings, which might well have been anticipated, concerning the limitations of dominant leaders and organization administrators in enforcing norms and the capacity of informal groups to modify norms or participate in redirecting goals. Even in the narrow investigation of the enforcement of norms, such sociologists and social psychologists were forced to recognize the requirements of institutional life and the societal order. They sought to deal with basic issues, relabeling "social control" as "social regulation."[52]

The narrow delimitation of social control as the process of social conformity, although widely used in sociological research, did not and could not displace the classical usage of the concept. Since 1945, the latter, with its broad and fundamental import, has continued to appear and reappear with persistence and vitality in the writings of certain sociologists. Clearly, the new reliance on biological and electronic analogies has not completely displaced or rendered obsolete this traditional line of sociological thinking.[53]

Any review of the continuity and vitality of the idea of social control must accord an important place to the writings and research of Everett Hughes and his students. As the post-World War II expansion of academic sociology was starting, Hughes published his influential essay "Institutions" (1946). For him, one central issue of social control was the socialization and organization of occupational, especially professional, groups. Hughes' theoretical and empirical writings stimulated a crucial body of literature which analyzed and assessed processes of regulation and self-regulation of skilled groups in modern society.[54]

Hughes drew on currents in social anthropology. In particular, the research of certain British and American social anthropologists served to reinforce the interest of students of social control in intensive fieldwork during a period when the emerging trend in sociology was toward survey research methodology. Anthropologists seeking to use the concept of social control to integrate their ethnographic materials and maintain linkages with the intellectual traditions of sociology by this approach included Raymond Firth (1951), S. F. Nadel (1953, 1957), J. S. Slotkin (1950), and Jack Goody (1957).

The post-World War II functionalist maintained a concern with and orientation toward social control. Throughout the body of Talcott Parsons' writing, there is a central focus on the essential elements of a social order. His explicit interest in the social control concept derived from his explication of Emile Durkheim. In Structure of Social Action (1937), Parsons asserted that Durkheim "not only gained great insight into the nature of social control, but also into the role and importance of moral conformity."[55] In *The Social System* (1951), the analysis of social control figures more prominently as a core element in his explanation of the patterning of deviant behavior. Parsons' writings have had a strong influence on the studies of deviance made by a variety of empirical research sociologists.[56]

In the work of a number of Parsons' students, the issue of social control continues to be explicated. In *Human Society*, Kingsley Davis joined his conception of functionalism to the idea of social control. "It is through them (social controls) that human society regulates the behavior of its members in such ways that they perform activities fulfilling societal needs—even, sometimes, at the expense of organic needs."[57] He focused on institutional arrangements for regulation and control by pointedly comparing the mechanisms of social control in totalitarian societies with those in the multiparty states of the West. Likewise, the social control of science has been used to focus attention both on the conditions under which science develops and on the social and political consequences of scientific knowledge. Bernard Barber, in *Science and the Social Order* (1952)[58] has probed the direct involvement of scientists in wartime research and the new orientations toward their social responsibility that have emerged.

The continuing impact of the issues of social order was to be found, after 1945, among a group of sociologists concerned with macrosociology. It was to be expected that Reinhard Bendix and Bennett Berger would display a strong concern with these issues and the conditions under which social order is maintained. Following directly on Simmel's formulations, they postulate alternative consequences of group participation in a fashion that converges with traditional notions of social control. They emphasize that social participation in its generic form produces more than "socializing" effects, the central concern of empirical sociologists.[59] They also stress the potentiality of an alternative set of outcomes, namely, "individualizing" effects, that requires a careful and richer language of analysis. The individualizing effects are not at all equated with personal anomie but are at the root of autonomy, creativity, and problem-solving—elements consistent with and to some degree essential for a social order and effective social control.

In an alternative way, Edward Shils has sought to explicate the dimension of social order and social control of a mass society (1962).[60] The essential transformation of modern society rests not only in its industrial and technological base but also in the effort to incorporate the "mass of the population" into the society's central institutional and value systems as a result of the social and political process of fundamental democratization, to use Mannheim's terminology.[61] Shils has tried to give a normative dimension to the ecological structure of the nation-state with his emphasis on the "center" and the "periphery."[62] The particular relevance of Shils' writings lies in his use of the word "civility" to characterize the patterns of interaction and social relations required for the reduction of coercion and manipulation in the social order of mass society.

It is interesting that George Homans, before his acceptance of "behavioral" assumption of conditioning psychology, made use of "social control" in its traditional meaning. In this, he was stimulated by Mary Parker Follett's writings. "Social control is not a separate department of group life—instead control, to a greater or lesser degree, is inherent in everyday relationships between members of the group."[63] For him, interaction supplies the basis for empirical investigation of social control in "at least two somewhat different languages."[64] Social control can be described in terms of "distribution of goods, such as money, and intangible goods, such as the enjoyment of high social rank."

Barrington Moore, Jr., in a markedly different style, concerned with the historical transformation of societies, poses the question traditionally associated with social control in his essay "Reflections on Conformity in Industrial Society."[65] He considers himself not a student of the abstract principles of the human group but a sociologist of comparative sociopolitical systems. For him, social control involves an element of repression—conscious or unconscious. He feels that "in the mature man, we simply call it self-control. Moore has thus approached social control from the reverse side, namely, how much conformity does an advance industrial society require? First, he is attracted to the idea that, in such a society, more of "this ancient virtue" is required, not less. The societal context for self-control derives from the fact that the practical problem is compounded by a paradox. "There may be less of the self-control now imposed by scarcity," while "a wider range of material opportunities and temptations may require a stronger exercise of this capacity."[66]

Second, Moore, strangely enough, finds the primary need for conformity in the arena of culture, whether broadly defined (as by anthropologists) or narrowly defined to include only certain appreciated cultural, artistic, and intellectual attainments. It is not the arena of technology that generates the need for conformity but "the simple fact that the achievements of human culture require effort and discipline, not only to create them but merely to appreciate them."[67] This line of reasoning is not an expression of sociological perversity; rather, it represents Moore's thoughtful search for the requirements of an advanced industrial society able to regulate and control itself.

Continuing Explication

In summary, the idea of social control has been a central formulation in the origin and development of sociology as an intellectual discipline. Moreover, particular sociologists have not abandoned the intellectual heritage and problematic issues associated with the idea, for there can be no sociology without a concern for the elements of a social order. An inventory of contemporary usage indicates that the efforts to substitute the language of social systems or of biological and cybernetic models do not suffice to supplant older conceptualizations. In fact, Wilbert E. Moore has concluded, in his assessment of "social structure and behavior," that the "old fashioned sociological term, social control, seems appropriate to revive," to handle the combination of external controls and individual internalization of the moral order.[68] The particular term is not the issue, of course. The issue is the analytic formulation that highlights the preconditions and variables that maximize the self-regulation of society and take into consideration the realities of social constraints, whether they have their origins in ecological, economic, or normative factors.

Therefore, I would argue that the idea of social control—in its traditional meaning and contemporary explication—should serve as a powerful antidote to the "crisis in sociology" outlook as exemplified by the writings of Alvin W. Gouldner,[69] among others. No doubt some sociologists have become disappointed with the capacity of their sociological endeavors to alter the sociopolitical process. Others have become personally fatigued and discontented with the life-style of the teacher in the university setting, and as a result they have less zeal for their intellectual tasks. A sociologist who has entered his calling with a belief in the philosopher-king assumption is certain to face a crisis at some point.

The phrase "crisis in sociology" must mean that sociology is progressively more and more unable to explain and clarify social change in contemporary society. There is no need to exaggerate the maturity of sociology and the cumulative character of its research efforts. Nor is there any need to overlook the vast amount of marginal research. But the present state of sociology is to be assessed not in terms of the wide range of its undertakings but, rather, by the vitality of relevant streams—even if they are minority efforts. Therefore, while particular sociologists may experience a crisis, there is no basis for asserting that there is a crisis in the intellectual discipline. Any "crisis" resides in the real world. The advanced industrial nations with parliamentary institutions are experiencing crises in their ability to regulate themselves, particularly in their political institutions. The intellectual *Fragestellung* (posing of the question) linked to the idea of social control constitutes a relevant standpoint for assessing this crisis in political legitimacy.

The reemergence of a focus on social control in its traditional sense (or relabled variously, for example, "social regulation," in contemporary language) has the advantage of being able to draw on increased intellectual self-consciousness among sociologists. The following points are essential, although an adequate explication of them remains beyond the scope of this paper and will be presented in my larger study, "Social Control and Macrosociology."

First, the social control perspective, as it has developed, supplies an appropriate level of abstraction for the study of social organization and social change. In fact, the social control perspective stands in contrast to the post-World War II trend, in which much theorizing used a high level of generality. Originally, social control theory was formulated at a more concrete level of abstraction. It required a set of taxonomic and analytically differentiated categories as the basic elements of analysis. Specifically, social control scholars postulated that social stratification and social class categories were insufficient for the analysis of social organization and social change. There was an explicit concern with institutions and institutional analysis. Under the rubric "institutions," sociologists investigated an endless range of subjects that reflected their personal tastes more than a set of analytic units and objects of analysis. But from the very beginning of their empirical research, sociologists concerned with social control have been aware of the necessity of grouping their subject matters in a broader analytical category system—but one that would not lose sight of the substantive reality.

Thus, slowly, the variety of research of delinquent gangs, work teams, play groups. and the like become more and more explicity fused into the study of primary groups, reflecting the writings of Charles H. Cooley and W. I. Thomas. Under Robert F. Park's stimulus, the host of analyses of territorial units and residential patterns merged into common interest, in community structures. Another core of these subject-matter concerns was the transformation of the study of specific corporate institutions into the analysis of bureaucratic organizations, under the influence of Max Weber and Chester Barnard. From study of a myriad of interesting institutions, there emerged the perspective that such categories as primary groups, community structures, and bureaucratic organizations were essential elements for converting the description of social stratification and socioeconomic class patterns into effective analysis of the "social system" or the nation-state. The random investigation of particular institutions that had fascinated the earlier sociologists has given way to a more pointed focus on the interrelations between basic structural "entities." In the effort to avoid excessive reification or a flight into empiricism, the style of theorizing about social control developed in the 1920s—and explicated thereafter—appears to be markedly viable and appropriate for the continuing tasks of sociologists.

Second, the analysis of social control can be pressed with more pointed concern for causal sequences in social change in particular, with a more explicit and adequate overview of the articulation of "social structure" and political institutions. Sociological analysis is only slowly coming to grips with the crisis of political legitimacy that constitutes the key problematic issue in advanced industrial society, particularly in those nations with multiparty parliamentary institutions.

The noteworthy defect of the early formulations of social control was a viewpoint that saw political institutions as derivative from the social stratification system, almost as if political institutions were thought to be epiphenomenal. The contribution of political sociology since the 1920s has only partially overcome this defect. As sociologists have progressively sought to articulate the relations between social structure and political institutions, they have emphasized the causal priority of the elements of social stratification. They have perceived politics and "political conflict" as manifestations of the underlying social stratification rather than augmenting their approach to politics with an institutional framework associated with the idea of social control.[70] Sociologists have been interested in describing community stratification, in the mode of Robert and Helen Lynd's *Middletown*,[71] or national stratification patterns, by means of the national survey sample, in order to trace the consequences of these hierarchies for political participation, especially electoral behavior. The causal pattern has been from underlying ecological, economic, and occupational structures to social strata to a set of group interests that fashion mass political participation.

Sociologists have yet to explore adequately the implications of an institutional approach to the political process. No doubt the sociological tradition contains examples of an institutional perspective on politics, that is, the viewpoint that political institutions constitute an independent source of societal change and an element for fashioning social structure. But sociologists, including those attached to the social control perspective, have been slow to implement the comprehensive implications of such an assertion. However, the rise and sociopolitical consequences of the welfare state have moved this intellectual agenda into prominence.

The modern political party and modern political institutions penetrate all sectors of society. It is necessary to speak of their decisive consequences for social structure and to recognize that the supremacy of modern political institutions does not ensure either their effectiveness or their legitimacy. As a result, trends in political behavior, especially measures of electoral behavior, become key indicators of the effectiveness of social control in advanced industrial societies with multiparty systems. The crisis in political legitimacy emerges thereby not as a sudden manifestation but rather as the outcome of continuing social change. The cumulative impact of the technological and organizational developments associated with World War II can be taken as the threshold to the new historical era. World War II not only created the institutional base for the welfare state but also contributed to the demand for more extensive political participation.[72]

After a short period of limited adaptation following World War II, Western parliamentary institutions have demonstrated their increased inability to produce effective majorities and to create the conditions for authoritative decision-making. Therefore, the task of students of social control is not only to explain patterns of personal deviant behavior, such as suicide, criminality, and personal unhappiness, important though these may be. The core issue is to help account for the decline of parliamentary opposition and the rise of unstable executive leadership.

The grave difficulties of parliamentary control can be seen in the patterns of mass political participation common to Western nations. In the briefest terms, there have been a long-term increase in the proportion of the population who declare themselves unaffiliated with the major parties, an increase in shifting of the electoral choice from one national election to the next, and a decline in belief in the effectiveness of the legislative process.

The changes in social stratification resulting from technology, occupational structure, patterns of urbanization, and economic resource allocation do not appear to have increased or produced a highly alienated or anomic electorate. On the contrary, the social stratification patterns result in a highly fragmented electorate with a powerful degree of solidarity within the component social elements. These groupings increase their demands for economic benefits, especially governmental benefits. Thereby persons find themselves, under an advanced industrial society, with their own built-in competing self-interests that are not easily resolved or aggregated into integrated and stable political preferences.

In the three decades since the end of World War II, the structure of political parties in the advanced nations, including the United States, has remained relatively unchanged. The descriptive literature on party organization has not been effectively integrated into macrosociology and the analysis of social control. No doubt the parties require vastly greater resources to perform their political tasks, and the mobilization of these resources paradoxically appears to make them less responsive. Nor has the influx of a new cadre of personnel acting for underrepresented groups altered the internal functioning of the major parties. The issue that the social control perspective must face is deep. The opportunity to express political demands and to balance them by periodic national elections becomes less and less effective as a crucial element in social control.

During the second half of the 1960s, the strain of social change and political constriction produced a marked escalation of parapolitical movements outside the institutionalized parties that frequently used violent symbolism and elements of violence. There has also been a striking increase in efforts to extend civic participation into the management of administrative agencies of government and of voluntary associations. These later efforts, in part a response to the impact of the parapolitical movements, have reflected an implicit recognition of the limitations of periodic national elections as mechanisms of social and political control.

There can be no doubt that sociological literature failed to anticipate the scope and intensity of these social movements, although one can find penetrating analyses of the high level of societal strain and the constriction of the processes of social control that an advanced industrial society was

producing. The sociological writings about these agitations often followed
the classic model of the natural history of social movements. Such writings
were perceptive in focusing on the impending transformation of these social
movements into "interest groups" and highlighted their built-in limitations
for influencing patterns of social control.

It was no profound sociological discovery that the protest movements of
this period would lead to increased diffuse political violence but hardly to a
revolution or a "revolution situation." Nevertheless, their explosive
character requires students of social control to reexamine the issue of violence
and coercion in social change. In the sharpest terms, what is the relationship
between reliance on violence and coercion and the search for effective social
control in an advanced industrial society? The question manifests itself at
every point in sociological analysis where existing patterns of social control
are ineffective.

Historians have made it clear that, regardless of the vast and immeasurable
amount of human misery which coercion and violence have produced, the
threat and use of force in the past have been essential for achieving, on
specific and important occasions, more effective social control. But to
explicate the "principles of force" is another matter—that is, to formulate
propositions of the conditions under which force produces positive
contributions to social control. Sociologists have speculated repeatedly on
this issue; but how much further has the analysis been pressed beyond the
hopeful aspirations of Georges Sorel in *Reflections on Violence*?[73]

The perspective of social control is grounded in assumptions about
interaction and mutual influences. Therefore, it raises the persistent and
vexatious issue of the consequences of force and coercion for those who
initiate or manage their use—whether the goal be the maintenance of a social
structure or its change. Perhaps the central proposition that can be explored
is that the use of force and coercion in the search for social control operates
within progressively narrower limits in relations both within and between
industrial societies.[74] This assertion obviously does not deny the extensive
and diffuse patterns of violence under advanced industrialism; nor does it
deny the decisive importance of violence in particular circumstances. But it
does emphasize the emergence of a calculus which points to the expanded
self-defeating implications for those who must rely extensively on force and
coercion in their efforts to achieve social control in its traditional meaning.
Such a calculus of force and coercion reflects at least two trends. There has
been an increase in the professed moral sensibilities of the citizenry (which is
compatible with political indifference under conditions of ineffective
political institutions). Furthermore, the sheer complexity of societal
organization has made anticipating the consequences of force—especially
given the expanded power of force—much more difficult.

In a period of weakened and ineffective social control in advanced
industrial societies, continued conflict and disintegration are alternative or

even simultaneous outcomes. Social disintegration implies a reduction in the ability of a group to control the behavior of its members and a decline in interaction and influence; social conflict implies an increase in interaction between social groups on the basis of antagonistic means and goals. In evaluating the consequences of persuasion and coercion with respect to direct social change, we must confront the problem of whether the existing categories of political ideology—the language of political discourse which dominates sociological analysis—are adequate for analyzing social control.

The alternative outcomes of the search for effective social control cannot be analyzed adequately in terms of conventional ideological categories— radicalism, conservatism or incremental liberalism. There exists a mass of empirical data which highlight the conclusion that these categories are limited in describing mass opinion as well as the realities of institutional practice. Moreover, these categories of political analysis imply a final result, a resolution, and an end state, when in effect we are dealing with a continuous and continuing social process. But the macrosociology and, as a result, the analysis of social control are too often dominated by a narrow format fashioned by political discourse. Thereby the "resolution" or "outcome" of ineffective social control does not necessarily conform to the categories of political ideology. It is necessary at least to assume that, for an advanced industrial society, the alternatives could include such results as chronic and persistent tension and a variety of patterns of stagnation.

In conclusion, it is necessary to return to the point of departure. The core element in social control is the idea of self-regulation of the group—whether the group be a face-to-face primary group or the nation-state. In essence, social control is a perspective toward social organization—one that focuses on the outcome of regulative mechanisms. The use the language of empirical social research, it thereby identifies a set of dependent variables applicable to the fullest range of institutional settings. The empirical content of social control depends on the sociologists' ability to clarify and explicate the content and criteria of self-regulation.

Although some sociologists have transformed the content of the term *social control* into that of social conformity and even social repression, the classical usage has persisted. The major advance in the intellectual history of social control has been its linkages to the political process and to the crisis of "political legitimacy." These linkages can be accomplished, not by means of a sociological reductionism, but by a recognition of the boundaries of political institutions and the "supremacy" of politics in an advanced industrial society.

Notes

1. This article is a section of a larger study, "Social Control and Macrosociology." I am indebted to the Russell Sage Foundation, New York City, for a generous grant in support of this work.

2. George Herbert Mead, "The Genesis of Self and Social Control," *International Journal of Ethics* 35, no. 3 (1925): 251-289.

3. George Vincent, "The Province of Sociology," *American Journal of Sociology* 1, no. 4 (January 1896): 490.

4. Personal control is the psychological and personality counterpart of social control. Personal control focuses on a person's capacity to channel his energies and to satisfy his needs while minimizing disruption and damage to himself and others. It implies mastery over one's psychological environment and encompasses those psychological conditions that enhance rationality. Bruno Bettelheim and Morris Janowitz, *Social Change and Prejudice* (New York: Free Press, 1964).

5. In the contemporary period, Amitai Etzioni defines control in a fashion similar to the classic orientation found in social control. "Control—the process of specifying preferred states of affairs and revision ongoing processes to reduce the distance from these preferred states." His theoretical model is derived from cybernetics. Amitai Etzioni, *The Active Society* (New York: Free Press, 1968).

6. Ferdinand Tönnies, *Gemeinschaft und Gesellschaft* (Leipzig: Reisland, 1887).

7. Henry Maine, *Ancient Law* (London: Murray, 1861).

8. Emile Durkheim, *De la division du travail social* (Paris: Alcan, 1893).

9. Charles Horton Cooley, *Social Organization: A Study of the Larger Mind* (New York: Charles Scribner's Sons, 1909).

10. Robert Redfield, "The Folk Society," *American Journal of Sociology* 52, no. 4 (January 1947): 298-308.

11. Louis Wirth, "Urbanism as a Way of Life," *American Journal of Sociology* 44 (July 1938): 3-24.

12. Ralph Linton, *The Study of Man* (New York: Appleton-Century, 1936).

13. Talcott Parsons, *The Structure of Social Action* (New York: McGraw-Hill, 1937); *The Social System* (Glencoe, Ill.: Free Press, 1951).

14. Georg Simmel, "Die Grosstadt und das Geistesleben," *Die Grosstadt. Jahrbuch der Gette-Stiftung*, Vol. 9. (Dresden: v. Zahn und Jaensch, 1903); "Die Kreuzung sozialer Kreise."Pp. 305-344 in *Soziologie* (Munich: Duncker und Humboldt, 1922).

15. Herman Schmalenbach, "The Sociological Category of Communion." Pp. 331-347 in *Theories of Society*, edited by Talcott Parsons and Edward Shils (Glencoe, Ill.: Free Press, 1961).

16. Theodor Geiger, *Die Masse und ihre Aktion: Ein Beitrag zur Soziologie der Revolutionen* (Stuttgart: Enke, 1926); *Demokratie ohne Dogma. Die Gesellschaft Zwischen Pathos und Nachternheit*. Vol. 5 (Munich: Szczesny Verlag, 1963).

17. René Koenig, "Die Begriffe Gemeinschaft und Gesellschaft bei Ferdinand Tönnies," *Kölner Zeitschrift für Soziologie und Sozialpsychologie* 7 (1955): 348-420.

18. Robert A. Nisbet is representative of those sociological theorists who are aware of the centrality of the concepts of Gemeinschaft-Gesellschaft in contemporary research and emphasize the necessity of departing from the original mechanistic and linear model of change. He writes, "A relationship that begins as a Gesellschaft type may in time become increasingly characterized by Gemeinschaft relationships among members." Robert A. Nisbet, *An Introduction to the Study of Society* (New York: Alfred A. Knopf, 1970), p. 107.

19. Albert J. Reiss, Jr., "Delinquency as a Failure of Personal and Social Control," *American Sociological Review* 16, no. 2 (April 1951): 196-206.

20. Lyford Edwards, *The Natural History of Revolution* (Chicago: University of Chicago Press, 1927).

21. E. A. Ross, *Social Control: A Survey of the Foundations of Order* (New York: Macmillan, 1901).

22. Gabriel Tarde, *The Laws of Imitation* (1890, trans. 1903).

23. E. A. Ross, *Seventy Years of It—an Autobiography* (New York: Appleton-Century, 1936), p. 56, noted that Herbert Spencer had employed the word "control" in 1892 in his *Principles of Sociology*, vol. 2, pt. 4. Although Spencer did not give it central importance in his analysis, his usage undoubtedly influenced Ross. In addition, see Edgar F. Borgatta and Henry J. Meyer, *Social Change and Prejudice* (New York: Free Press, 1959).

24. Ross, *Social Control*, p. 59.

25. William G. Sumner never made explicit use of the term "social control." Yet because of the issues raised in his *Folkways* (Boston: Ginn, 1906), his name is linked to this concept. Sumner defined "folkways" as habits and customs that serve as the basis for the "regulation and imperative" for succeeding generations.

26. Charles Horton Cooley, *Social Organization: A Study of the Larger Mind* (New York: Charles Scribner's Sons, 1909); *Social Process* (New York: Charles Scribner's Sons, 1920).

27. Cooley, *Social Process*.

28. W. I. Thomas and Florian Znaniecki, *The Polish Peasant in Europe and America* (Boston: Badger, 1918-20), vol. I, p. 1.

29. Simmel, *Die Grosstadt*.

30. Donald Levine, *Georg Simmel: On Individuality and Social Forms* (Chicago: University of Chicago Press, 1971).

31. Georg Simmel, *Conflict and the Web of Group Affiliation* (Glencoe, Ill.: Free Press, 1955), pp. 140-141.

32. Emile Durkheim, *Sociologie et philosophie* (Paris: Alcan, 1924).

33. Emile Durkheim, *Le suicide* (Paris: Alcan, 1897).

34. Robert E. Park, *Race and Culture* (Glencoe, Ill.: Free Press, 1950); *Human Communications* (Glencoe, Ill.: Free Press, 1952).

35. Robert M. MacIver and Charles Page, *Society* (New York: Macmillan, 1949).

36. Scott E. W. Bedford, *Social Control*. Publication of the American Sociological Society, vol. 12 (Chicago: University of Chicago Press, 1918).

37. Robert E. Park and Ernest W. Burgess, *Introduction to the Science of Sociology* (Chicago: University of Chicago Press, 1921), p. 785.

38. Ibid., p. 766.

39. Ibid., p. 785.

40. Ralph H. Turner, *On Social Control and Collective Behavior* (Chicago: University of Chicago Press, 1975).

41. Park, *Race and Culture*, p. 43; *Human Communication*, pp. 240-262.

42. MacIver and Page, *Society*.

43. Ibid., p. 137.

44. Other sociologists who pursued the analytic aspects of social control before 1940 include Kimball Young, *Introductory Sociology* (New York: American Book Co., 1934); Paul H. Landis, *Social Control: Social Organization in Process* (New York: Lippincott, 1939); and L. L. Bernard, *Social Control* (New York: Century, 1972).

45. These institutional economists constituted a body of scholars with sociological interest who, for more than two decades, produced important research on industrial and economic organization. With the decline of the institutionalist school of economists, sociologists unfortunately have failed to incorporate fully the topics of social control of economic and industrial life in their domain.

46. John Maurice Clark, *Social Control of Business* (Chicago: University of Chicago Press, 1926).

47. Roscoe Pound, *Social Control Through Law* (New Haven, Conn.: Yale University Press, 1942).

48. Charles E. Merriam, *The Role of Politics in Social Change* (New York: New York University Press, 1936).

49. Mary Parker Follett in *Dynamic Administration*, edited by Henry C. Metcal and L. Urwick (London: Management Publication Trust, 1941), p. 204; see also Paul Pigors, *Leadership or Domination* (Boston: Houghton Mifflin, 1935).

50. Karl Mannheim, *Man and Society in an Age of Reconstruction* (London: Kegan Paul, 1940).

51. Of course, it would be an error to conclude that the narrow sociopsychological definition of social control as conformity was accepted by all social psychologists of either the psychological or the sociological persuasion. A variety of social psychologists concerned with social values resisted. Without effective reference to the previous literature, they came in time almost to reinvent the older concept of social control. A thoughtful example of the counter-trends is found in Paul Scott and Sarah F. Scott, *Social Control and Social Change* (Chicago: University of Chicago Press, 1971), who boldly introduce their work with the assertion: "Even a purely objective attitude toward the phenomenon of social control provides some safeguard against the concept of control by a superman, for either good or evil purposes. This is the fact that control is always a mutual affair" (p. 1). See also the penetrating formulation by Eugene Litwak, "Three Ways in Which Law Acts as a means of Social Control: Punishment, Therapy and Education," *Social Forces* 34, no. 1 (1956): 217-233.

52. Elain Cummings, *Systems of Social Regulation* (New York: Atherton, 1968).

53. For an interesting treatise on continuities in the use of the social control concept, see Richard T. LaPiere, *A Theory of Social Control* (New York: McGraw-Hill, 1954).

54. Everett C. Hughes, "Institutions." Pp. 225-267 in *New Outline of the Principles of Sociology*, edited by Alfred McClung Lee (New York: Barnes & Noble, 1946). Hughes' interest in social control is to be found implicitly in the works of Erving Goffman, Anselm Strauss, and Howard Becker.

55. Parsons' analysis seeks to assess the contributions—plus their degree of convergence—of a variety of classical sociologists to the extension and reformulation of basic questions about the social order. Thus this volume is a key resource in the intellectual history of sociology and the issues involved in social control. In a very compact fashion, Percy Cohen, *Modern Social Theory* (London: Heinemann, 1968), especially chapter 2, has reviewed these linkages, and his effort makes possible the conclusion that "modern sociology" has, in effect, abandoned the older question of how society emerged and concentrates on that of how the social order persists.

56. While a great deal of the writing and research on deviance came to reflect the narrower and more constricted view of social control, the following expositions deal with broad societal issues and thereby reflect earlier formulations: Alexander Clark

and Jack P. Gibbs, "Social Control: A Reformulation." *Social Problems* 12, no. 4 (1965): 398-414; Jack Gibbs, "Conceptions of Social Control." In *Social Control*, edited by Peter K. Manning (New York: Free Press, forthcoming); Richard M. Stephenson, "Involvement in Deviance: An Example and Some Theoretical Implications." *Social Problems* 21, no. 2 (Fall 1973): 173-189.

57. Kingsley Davis, *Human Society* (New York: Macmillan, 1948), p. 52.

58. Bernard Barber, *Science and the Social Order* (Glencoe, Ill.: Free Press, 1952).

59. Reinhard Bendix and Bennett Berger, "Images of Society and Problems of Conception Formation in Sociology." Pp. 92-118 in *Symposium on Sociological Theory*, edited by L. Gross (Evanston, Ill.: Row Peterson, 1959).

60. Edward Shils, "The Theory of Mass Society," *Diogenes*, no. 39 (1962): 45-46.

61. Mannheim, *Man and Society in an Age of Reconstruction*.

62. Edward Shils, "Centre and Periphery." Pp. 305-344 in *Soziologie* (Munich: Duncker and Humboldt, 1922).

63. George Homans, *The Human Group* (London: Routledge and Kegan Paul, 1951).

64. Ibid., p. 94.

65. Barrington Moore, Jr., "Reflections on Conformity in Industrial Society." In *Political Power and Social Theory* (Cambridge, Mass.: Harvard University Press, 1958).

66. Ibid., p. 193.

67. Ibid., p. 186.

68. Moore, "Reflections on Conformity in Industrial Society," pp. 171-219.

69. Alvin Gouldner, *The Coming Crisis of Western Sociology* (New York: Basic Books, 1970).

70. Morris Janowitz, "The Logic of Political Sociology." In *Political Conflicts: Essays in Political Sociology* (Chicago: Quadrangle Books, 1970).

71. Helen Lynd and Robert Lynd, *Middletown* (New York: Harcourt, Brace, 1929).

72. For an analysis of the tranformation of Great Britain into a welfare state under the impact of World War I and World War II, see especially Arthur Marvick, *Britain in the Century of Total War: War, Peace and Social Change, 1900-1967* (Boston: Little, Brown, 1968).

73. Georges Sorel, *Reflections on Violence* (New York: Huebsch, 1914).

74. For this process in international relations, see Morris Janowitz, "Toward a Redefinition of Military Strategy in International Relations," in *Military Conflict* (Beverly Hills, California: Sage Publications, 1975).

Don Martindale

THE THEORY OF SOCIAL CONTROL

The origin of the field of social control in the United States is usually traced to the pioneering work of E. A. Ross in 1901. Once isolated, social control was recognized as a problem as old as human society with an intellectual history as old as social thought. Social control was immediately welcomed as a subdiscipline of sociology. However, Ross did more than establish a new field of inquiry; he bestowed upon it a legacy of ambiguities.

The Pioneering Formulations of Ross

Ross subtitled his *Social Control* "A Study of the Foundations of Order." He traced his own interest in the matter to a series of articles that appeared in the *American Journal of Sociology* between 1896 and 1898. He described the study of social control as a special subdivision of social psychology which he had divided into individual ascendancy, domination of the individual over society, social ascendancy, and domination of society over the individual. Social ascendancy was further subdivided "into Social Influence—mob mind, fashion, convention, custom, public opinion, and the like—and Social Control."[1] In his preface Ward observed:

I seek to determine how far the order we see all about us is due to influences that reach men and women from without, that is, *social* influences. I began the work six years ago with the idea that nearly all the goodness and conscientiousness by which a social group is enabled to hold together can be traced to such influences. It seemed to me then that the individual contributed very little to social order, while society contributed almost everything. Further investigation, however, appears to show that the personality freely unfolding under conditions of healthy fellowship may arrive at a goodness all its own, and that order is explained partly by this streak in human nature and partly by the influence of social surroundings.[2]

Ross argued that much of the order in interpersonal behavior is a product of four properties of human nature—sympathy, sociability, a sense of justice, and a sense of self-interest—which by themselves create a natural, spontaneous order without the need for coercion from the outside.

Sympathy, sociability, the sense of justice and *resentment* are competent, under favorable circumstances, to work out by themselves a true, *natural order*, that is to say, an order without design or art. While such an order is far from perfect, it may permit a considerable unfolding of personal enterprise and mutual aid.[3]

While Ross assumed that the original order of society was spontaneous, traditional communities such as Tönnies' *Gemeinschaft* are not the best examples of natural orders. Particularly when formed out of status equals, new communities may for a time be felicitous examples of natural orders.

When ... men come together from the same economic stratum, as in the Puritan colonies and in the settlements of homesteaders on the public domain, or when people of different conditions are leveled by the powerful equalizing influences of a new environment, as were the gold-seekers of California, natural order is seen at its best.[4]

However, in the course of time, Ross urges, a society must inevitably institute a measure of control over the individual. The resultant system of control is partly natural, partly a matter of deliberate human artifice.

Even in a mining camp, the issues are not always between man and man. In the keeping of arms or whiskey from the Indians, or in the limiting of gambling, there comes to light a collective interest which only collective action can protect.... Among the earliest signs of collective pressure is the endeavor to make kickers, cowards, and shirkers take part in joint undertakings which benefit all.[5]

The system of social control that arises under such circumstances represents the intersection of three groups of interests: the interests of "those who wish to follow a certain line of conduct, that of those who are injured by such conduct, and that of the rest of the community. The second and third *impose* control, the first *limits* it."[6]

Ross concluded his examination of the grounds of social control with a number of generalizations or "laws." These are interesting because they illustrate the fact that Ross visualized social control as defining the relationship between leaders and followers.

1. Social power is concentrated or diffused in proportion as men do or do not feel themselves in need of guidance or protection.[7]
2. The volume of social requirement will be greater when social power is concentrated than when it is diffused.[8]
3. The greater the ascendancy of the few, the more possible is it for social control to affect the course of the social movement.[9]
4. The character of social requirement changes with every shifting of social power.[10]
5. The more distinct, knit together, and self-conscious the influential minority, the more likely is social control to be colored with class selfishness.[11]

While the first part of his study on the grounds of social control showed some inclination to limit the concept to two basic meanings—social ascendancy arising unconsciously or semiconsciously from milieu pressures and social ascendancy arising as a product of deliberate intention and social planning—in the second part of his study where he directed attention to the means of control, Ross appeared to conceptualize control as coextensive with social order without regard to its origins. The means of control, he said, included public opinion, law, belief, social suggestion, education, custom, social religion, personal ideals, ceremony, art, personality, enlightenment, illusions, social evaluations, and ethics. Ross thereby erased the lines between social control and socialization and apparently set aside his distinction between social ascendancy and individual ascendancy. Many of the items he listed as means of control have been the basis for individual resistance to social controls. To take only a single example, the personal ideals of the conscientious objector have often led to heroic resistance to efforts to press him into military service.

In the third part of his study, which was directed to systems of control, Ross outlined his views on two contrasting organizations of social power: class control, the organization of social power in the interests of special groups, and democratic control, the organization and employment of social power in the interests of the average man. He disapproved of class control and approved of democratic control in the interests of a populist politics. Democratic control, he argued, should be limited by the fact that it brings more benefits than inconveniences. It should not be so deployed as to destroy the passion for liberty; it should respect the sentiments of the people which are in support of the natural order; it should not be so paternal as to check the self-extinction of the morally ill constituted; it should not limit the struggle for existence so as to nullify the selective process. The distinguishing criteria of social control, he urged, should be economy, inwardness, simplicity, and spontaneity. It is evident that in these contexts Ross was giving the concept of social control the meaning of social planning in the interest of the average man. However, he shrank from extending his populist vision of social order to the point where it would terminate in a fully constituted socialism and welfare state.

In his last chapter, Ross returned to his concept of natural order, identifying it with Tönnies' concept of Gemeinschaft. He also accepted Tönnies' judgment that over time Gemeinschaft (community) everywhere tended to give way to Gesellschaft (society). As society grows at the expense of community, the sphere of social control can only broaden.

It is likely that certain of the more searching and pervasive means of control will grow in favor. Suggestion, education, and publicity, the choice instruments of the new *folk-craft* that is taking the place of the old state-craft, will be used, perhaps, even more freely and consciously than they now are. The ground for this surmise is the fact that powerful forces are more and more transforming *community* into *society*, that is, replacing living tissue with structures held together by rivets and screws.[12] . . . We are relying on artificial rather than natural supports to bear the increasing weight of our social order, and that a return to the natural basis of social partnership is about as likely as a return to raw food or skin garments.[13]

Thus, in his last chapter, Ross not only returned to the concept of social control as artificially established and enforced order, but also embraced the notion that the expansion of the sphere of social control marked a major drift in social change. Ross writes as if the notion had occurred to him that if the sphere of coercive order grew without limit, the time would come when there would no longer be space for individual freedom. He took comfort from the myth (Ross thought it was a scientific fact) that the psychology of some races inclined them to resist the more coercive systems of control. "There is reason," he argued, "to believe that even today differences in race psychology lead peoples of the same development to adopt different measures of control."[14] At least among Aryan and Anglo-Saxon peoples, Ross thought, controls would not be permitted to become suffocatingly coercive but would adapt to vigorous individualism.

Ross dismissed the possibility that had been suggested by Nietzsche that the controls typical of Christianity[15] and of the modern state were turning into a tyranny of the weak over the strong.

The Strong Man who has come to regard social control as the scheme of the many weak to bind down the few strong may be brought to see it in its true light as the safe-guarding of a venerable corporation, protector not alone of the labors of living men for themselves but also of the labors of bygone men for coming generations, guardian not merely of the dearest possessions of innumerable persons, but likewise of the spiritual property of the human race—of the inventions and discoveries, the arts and the sciences, the secrets of healing, and the works of delight, which he himself is free to enter into and enjoy.[16]

Ross had given the concept of social control a variety of meanings: (1) as activities and instruments for securing social compliance of artificial origin, (2) as all forms of social order, (3) as social planning with a subdistinction between (a) malign types, when of class origin and class interest and (b) benign types, when in the interest of the average man. Along the way, Ross has also used the concept of social control in the relatively restricted sense of (4) management of deviance, especially of crime and delinquency.

Contemporary Status of the Concept

At the time Ross made his pioneering formulations, he was in the process of changing his theoretical position from a holistic (the belief that society is an entity with laws of its own) to an elementaristic type (the belief that only

individuals exist and society is only a name for interpersonal strategies).
From the turn of the century to World War II, American sociology was
dominated by elementaristic points of view, among them Ross's theories.
Various treatises on social control continued to display the same range of
meanings and ambiguities as appear in Ross's account. In structure
functionalism which arose in the post-World War II period, America's first
endemic form of sociological holism was developed.

When the *International Encyclopedia of the Social Sciences* was published
in the late 1960s, two functionalists, Jesse R. Pitts and Amitai Etzioni, wrote
the articles on the concept of social control and organizational aspects of
social control, respectively. According to Pitts:

Much of the impetus for the development and use of the concept of social control
comes from the sociological adaptation of the Darwinian tradition. But there,
however, the major dichotomy was between organism and nature; for the various
theories of social control, it has been that between individual and society. It is
assumed in these theories that society has to control the animal nature of man: if order
is to be established and maintained, man's tendency to pursue his self-interest to the
point of a war of all against all must be limited through learning or selection, or both.
Emergence of the concept of social control, thus, indicated a waning of the utilitarian
concept of the natural harmony of self-interests.[17]

This is a startling formulation. How could Pitts possibly suggest with any
seriousness that sociological adaptation of the Darwinian tradition was
required in order to discover the problem of social control? Surely there has
never been a primitive group anywhere in the last 20,000 years or so that has
not sooner or later discovered it essential to place restrictions on the
individual in the name of group necessity. In any case, in the early hydraulic
civilizations and in ancient China, India, Israel, and Greece, in Rome, in the
Islamic cultural sphere, and in the Western Middle Ages, political, legal, and
police systems among other things were employed to manage deviant
individualism, and there was no lack of thoughtful persons to reflect on the
problems of social control. Moreover, the Social Darwinists who proposed
to adapt Darwinian biology to the study of society were generally opponents
rather than proponents of an expansion in the sphere of social control: any
action by the state beyond minimal peace-keeping was seen as interfering
with the process that facilitated the survival of the fittest and hence the
biological improvement of the race. In fact, soon after the appearance of the
Origin of Species the Russian zoologist Karl Kessler advanced the counter-
hypothesis that cooperation between individuals of the same species was a
major factor in the evolutionary process. The Russian anarchist Peter
Kropotkin proposed the thesis that custom and cooperation, rather than
competition, were the primary factors in the course of human social history.
Moreover, it was Hobbes, in a tradition extending back through Machiavelli

to Polybius in antiquity, who viewed the natural condition of man as a conflict of each against all, hence requiring some arrangement to establish a condition of interpersonal order. Finally, it boggles the imagination to determine in what manner the waning of utilitarianism gave rise to the concept of social control.

Pitts' astonishing derivation of the concept of social control is such a mare's nest of confusions that it is surely more indicative of his theoretical suppositions than of the social history of social control. One may speculate that as a structure-functionalist Pitts subscribed to an entity theory of society. In the long run, proponents of this point of view are inclined to view the individual as presocial, treating all interpersonal order as a social product. Hence, it is quite possible that they are inclined to see any position which appears to dramatize the potential autonomy of the individual as raising the problem of control of the intransigent individual. However, it should be kept in mind that this is speculative.

Following his confusing derivation of the concept, Pitts turned his attention to what he conceived to be the primary problem of the field: what to do about the diverse meanings of the concept which vary from the sources of all order, the sources of coercive order, the management of deviance to social planning. He called attention to various of these usages in the works of Durkheim, Ross, W. I. Thomas, Florian Znaniecki, and Karl Mannheim. His personal choice was to restrict the concept to the management of deviance, an approach he felt only the works of Talcott Parsons had successfully achieved.

It is with Parsons (1951)[18] and LaPiere (1954)[19] that we see the concept of social control become systematically limited to the control of deviance. This approach to the concept eliminates from it the ordinary normative component consisting of social structure, and, more specifically, the aspects of social structure that are concerned with socialization.[20]

This characterization of the virtues of the Parsonian approach to social control (as eliminating from it normative considerations and sharply distinguishing it from socialization) is contradicted in Pitts' description of the Parsonian theory of control.

Pitts regards deviance as any action or behavior which upsets the institutional equilibrium; in turn, he views the institutional equilibrium as the maintenance of normative patterns defined by society's central values. This definition of equilibrium not only presupposes the existence of a single official value system in every society but also treats any behavior that falls short of official requirements as deviant. Thus, an individual who gets sick or breaks a leg is deviating, and the ultimate betrayal of society by the individual would appear to be his death, his final failure to fulfill his social obligations.

Pitts explains that deviance, the inclination to kick over the traces and upset the social equilibrium, is motivated by past learning, personality factors, and pressures and opportunities in present situations. From any or all of these sources, the individual may be made ambivalent, torn between the tendency to conform and not to conform. As a result, he may become socially indifferent, a compulsive conformist, a compulsive nonconformist or each, by turns, depending on the situation.

Illness, according to both Parsons and Pitts, is the prototype of passive alienated behavior. Radical groups may conceal their social antagonisms by claiming to express the real legitimate interests of society. Secondary institutions arise which express alienated feelings, but they ultimately serve the social equilibrium by isolating the deviant behavior and operating as bridges back to conformity. These illustrate some of the derivations from the Parsons-Pitts theory of social control.[21]

The object of social control, according to Parsons and Pitts, is to alter the individual's deviant motivation, leading him back toward unambivalent support of the social system. This object is best accomplished by practices that head off and prevent deviance by preventing the buildup of tensions which incline to deviance, reinforce the desire to conform, clarify what is socially appropriate, and discourage deviance (by punishment) and reward conformity; and by modifying social patterns to accommodate deviant behavior.

Far from sharpening the distinction between socialization and social control, the Parsons-Pitts theory largely erases it.

Following Jesse Pitts' examination of the concept of social control, Amitai Etzioni addressed himself to organizational aspects of social control. Etzioni argued that all social units control their members, but since they are social units which serve specific purposes, organizations are of special interest, for they make informal controls inadequate and require formally institutional-ized allocations of rewards and penalties to ensure compliance with their norms, regulations, and orders.

Etzioni posits the existence of three types of organizational controls: coercive, utilitarian, and normative.[22] Coercive controls are characteristic of concentration camps, prisons, correctional institutions, custodial mental hospitals, and prisoner-of-war camps. Utilitarian controls are characteristic of factories, businesses, financial institutions, and civil service and military bureaucracies. Normative controls are characteristic of religions, ideo-logical-political organizations, colleges and universities, and therapeutic hospitals.

While Pitts had claimed for structure-functionalism the narrowing of social control to manageable limits, in fact he, along with his mentor Talcott Parsons, tended to broaden it to include much of socialization. For his part, as a structure-functionalist, Etzioni extended the concept of social control to its widest possible meaning, visualizing every form of order in interaction as a product of societal management. Groups, he had indicated, do this informally and organizations formally through institutionalized allocations of rewards and penalties.

Toward Clarification

If we take the pioneering sociological formulations of E. A. Ross at the turn of the century and the contemporary formulations by Pitts and Etzioni (who after all are spokesmen for a powerful contemporary school of sociology) as a baseline for establishing the scope and variations in the concept of social control, it would appear that little progress has been made in the last seventy years in standardizing usage as to its meaning. For this purpose, it would be of little value to us to examine the usage by hundreds of other social scientists. Such ethnographic industry would do little to settle the basic question as to why usage varies in the first place. Only an analytical consideration of the rival theories of social life in which social control appears as one aspect of the accounts of interpersonal life can account for the persistent ambiguous usage. A major cleavage from the outset appears between holistic and elementaristic conceptions of social control.

Holism is the idea that society is a superorganic entity with laws of its own that are not reducible to generalizations about interaction; elementarism is the idea that "society" is only a name for a complex dynamic process, consisting of strategies of people individually and in concert, and the only legitimate laws are laws of interaction. Holism visualizes institutions as the organs of society, carrying out the diverse functions that realize its needs; elementarism visualizes institutions as the solutions to interpersonal problems. Holism perpetuates the dichotomy of society versus the individual; elementarism rejects it, treating the reality to be social interaction in which tendencies toward individualism and collectivism are complementary moments. Holism seems inevitably to incline toward a totalistic conception of social control, visualizing all order in interaction as brought about by society; even when holists such as Parsons and Pitts attempt to restrict social control to the management of deviance, the ideas of deviance and its management are conceived in such a manner that they include socialization within the framework of social control. Elementarism is inclined to place the primary meaning of social control in the management of social power.

It is now possible to determine one source of the ambiguities in Ross's account. Ross stated that when he first undertook his inquiries, he had assumed that order arose almost completely from influences outside the individual, but the more he inquired into the subject, the more he was inclined to the view that a "natural" order arises spontaneously within interaction. Ross was in the process of redefining his sociological perspective, substituting an elementaristic point of view for the traditional holistic conception of society. In the first part of his study, he outlined a concept of control that fitted his elementarism; in the second part he reverted back to a holistic conception of control; and in the third part he partially returned to an elementaristic conception of control. The ambiguities in Ross's account were anchored in theoretical confusion.

Moreover, in his concept of a natural order arising spontaneously from common human nature, Ross had subscribed to one of the major rationalist-Enlightenment theories of the individual. A number of seventeenth- and eighteenth-century thinkers had taken it for granted that all individuals are similarly endowed with such basic faculties as sympathy, sociability, a sense of justice and of self-interest. Having made this assumption, they also assumed that left to their own devices, without outside interference, men would spontaneously create an orderly, noncoercive social condition. However, other philosophers at the time had quite different notions of original human nature from which they made contrasting deductions about the original social condition. Hobbes maintained:

Whatsoever . . . is consequent to a time of war, where every man is enemy to every man; the same is consequent to the time, wherein men live without other security, than what their own strength, and their own invention shall furnish them withal. In such condition, there is no place for industry . . . no knowledge of the face of the earth; no account of time; no arts; no letters; no society; and which is worst of all, continual fear, and danger of violent death; and the life of man, solitary, poor, nasty, brutish, and short.[23]

Spinoza, who was familiar with Hobbes' views on human nature and, like Hobbes, viewed the will to live as its essence, urged that enlightened self-interest would lead men to create a state (community) as an essential instrument of self-realization. Self-interest required revolution against the state when it became coercive and failed to promote self-realization. Freedom of speech was essential to keep a state viable.

However plausible it was to argue that the order appearing in human interaction derived from regularities in human nature on the one hand and in the environment on the other, this question clearly could not be settled by speculation, but required empirical investigation. The very different theories of society that seventeenth- and eighteenth-century thinkers derived from *a priori* theories of human nature proved this. Hence, when Ross dusted off one of the Enlightenment theories of human nature, he was treating as axiomatic something that should have been advanced as a hypothesis.

At the very time Ross's *Social Control* appeared, students of comparative social-psychology were beginning to report that what was taken as "human nature" varied between societies and within any given society over time. At the same time, the notion that human conduct rested on a set of fixed faculties or instincts was becoming suspect. Researchers in a number of fields were converging toward the contemporary view that as man expanded his powers of speech and tool-making and a transgenerational stock of learning became available and began to accumulate, the last great surge in his biological evolution occurred, producing the virtually instinct-free creature we know. Whatever remained of man's biologically preprogrammed (instinctive) behavior rapidly deteriorated, leaving him dependent for survival on his capacity to learn and invent.

When one is dealing with the behavior of most nonhuman animals, one is able to take the biology of the animal and properties of the environment as more or less fixed and to visualize behavior as more or less successful resolutions of these forces. In dealing with the human animal, however, one must confront an enormously expanded behavioral potential and an environment that varies continually with the state of accumulating culture. Interaction in terms of the possibilities of the accumulating culture presides over the processes by which any given collection of individuals creates patterns of selfhood and social order.

Ironically, the disappearance of biological preprogramming in the human species increased the individual's dependence on human association for survival. At the same time, basic life problems had to be solved. A particularly significant part of man's accumulating culture consists of his solutions to basic problems, or institutions, which in human behavior perform a comparable role to the animal's instincts. The major categories of problems that must be solved in human associations are the transmission of culture (socialization), survival (mastery of nature), and the management of interspecific relations (the formation and distribution of social power). Solutions to these problems are implemented in a wide spectrum of groups, organizations, and associations. Furthermore, since economies of effort are realized when successful solutions of problems are stabilized and made routine, since the way one resolves one problem inevitably has bearing upon the ways others are resolved, and since problems cycle through the day, the seasons of the year, and the lifetime, the solutions to problems in any given human plurality move over time toward the overall synthesis that leads us to describe the resulting processes as communities.

In terms of these reflections, the contemporary elementarist must abandon both the concept of human nature and of natural order as they appear in Ross's writings, though he does see the counterpart of both as variable printouts of the interpersonal process. Every continuing association over time tends to develop a range of selfhood (social character) peculiar to it and a related form of social order. They are mutually sustaining. One category of the institutions composing the social order is oriented to maintenance of the social order itself. Max Weber analyzed the role of this category of institutions in his concept of legitimate order. He observed that social action may be based on the belief by the actors in the existence of a legitimate order which they uphold out of disinterested motives or rational self-interest. He described such an order as *convention* so far as it was upheld by diffuse sanctions and *law* when conformity was sustained by physical sanctions administered by special groups or persons. Weber observed that legitimacy may be ascribed to an order by subjects acting in the following ways.

(a) By tradition; a belief in the legitimacy of what has always existed; (b) by virtue of affectual attitudes, especially emotional, legitimizing the validity of what is newly revealed or a model to imitate; (c) by virtue of a rational belief in its absolute value, thus lending it the validity of an absolute and final commitment; (d) because it has been established in a manner which is recognized to be *legal*.[24]

Weber's forms (convention and law) and bases (traditionalism affectivity, evaluative rationality, and expedient rationality) of legitimate order are pure types. In any given community, they appear in varying degrees of mixture.

It is now possible to reformulate, in a contemporary elementaristic perspective, the concept of social control. Social control includes all processes that implement the legitimate order of a given community. The institutions which carry out social control (that is, the organization and maintaining the decision processes of a community or its social power) include political, legal, and military and police institutions. The scope of social control ranges from the management of deviance to social planning, which can be viewed as the negative and positive management of power, respectively.

Concluding Note

While the primary purpose of this essay was to provide an analytical perspective for appraising the various concepts of social control that appear throughout this volume, attention has inadvertently been called to some of the major changes in the form of social control over time. There has been a general drift from informal to formal, traditional to rational, conventional to legal types of controls.

Another major phenomenon that has been incidentally touched on in this analytical review is that the various institutional spheres (mastery of nature, socialization, and social control) that constitute any given social order do not necessarily remain fixed over time. From time to time, a strategy by ruling groups has been to employ institutions that had their primary significance in socialization (such as religion or education) as instruments of social control. Moreover, disruptions in any one institutional sphere may have repercussions in others.

One of the most frequent characterizations of American society from the mid-1960s to the present is that it is suffering severe law and order problems. The man on the street as well as the social scientist has repeatedly been led to observe that everywhere one looks the controls appear to be breaking down and that America and much of the Western world are experiencing a crisis of control. However, the millions unemployed and the erosions of inflation are economic problems. The crisis in domestic, educational, religious, and health and welfare institutions signal major troubles in the sphere of socialization. To some extent we seem to be demanding that our control institutions take up the slack and resolve problems that arise elsewhere and for which they are ill adapted to cope.

Notes

1. Edward Alsworth Ross, *Social Control* (New York: Macmillan Co., 1926), p. viii.
2. Ibid., p. viii. Italics in original.
3. Ibid., p. 41. Italics in original.
4. Ibid., p. 42.
5. Ibid., p. 49.
6. Ibid., p. 62. Italics in original.
7. Ibid., p. 78.
8. Ibid., p. 84.
9. Ibid., p. 85.
10. Ibid.
11. Ibid., p. 86.
12. Ibid., p. 432. Italics in original. In a footnote, Ross called attention to the parallels between his conception of natural and artificial order and Tönnies' conception of Gemeinschaft and Gesellschaft. Ferdinand Tönnies, *Community and Society*, translated by Charles P. Loomis (East Lansing, Mich.: Michigan State University Press, 1957). Tönnies' study was first published in German in 1887. Ross insisted that he had arrived at his own distinction long before he read Tönnies.
13. Ibid., pp. 435-436.
14. Ibid., p. 439.
15. The Socratic and Judeo-Christian morality which Nietzsche identified and saw as valid in Europe he describes as a slave morality resting on resentment, as the instinct of the herd opposed to the strong and independent, of the sorrowful and poorly endowed opposed to the fortunate, of the mediocre opposed to the exceptional. See *The Genealogy of Morals* and *Beyond Good and Evil* (New York: Modern Library, 1954).
16. Ross, *Social Control*, p. 442.
17. Jesse R. Pitts, "Social Control: The Concept," in David L. Sills, ed., *International Encyclopedia of the Social Sciences* (New York: Free Press, 1968), Vol. 14, pp. 381-82.
18. Talcott Parsons, *The Social System* (Glencoe, Ill.: Free Press, 1951).

19. Richard LaPiere, *A Theory of Social Control* (New York: McGraw-Hill, 1954).

20. Pitts, "The Concept," p. 383.

21. Although the reference here is primarily to Pitts, he was discussing Parsons' theory. For lack of space, I did not go back to Parsons' original statement.

22. Amitai Etzioni, "Social Control: Organizational Aspects," in Sills, ed., *International Encyclopedia of the Social Sciences*, Vol. 14, p. 396.

23. Thomas Hobbes, *Leviathan* (New York: Macmillan Co., 1947), p. 82.

24. Max Weber, *The Theory of Social and Economic Organization*, translated by A. M. Henderson and Talcott Parsons (New York: Oxford University Press, 1957), p. 130.

PART II

Since it is conventional to describe some institutions as control institutions, it is essential to clarify the scope of the concepts of social control and institutions. This task is complicated by the varied usage of both concepts.

Social control is a generic problem of human social life, arising from the fact that it is potentially subject to challenges by anyone at any time. Like the other two generic problems (socialization—the transformation of men into social beings of a special type—and the mastery of nature), it touches all phases of social life. Institutions are the interpersonal solutions to these collective problems consisting, as Sumner long ago indicated, of an idea (a plan, purpose, or proposal) and a structure (by which Sumner meant the behavioral arrangements that implement the idea).

As long as human societies remained relatively small and simple, the same association carried out all three generic functions. One approach to carrying out the social division of labor was through the formation of special groups for the solution of single problems; this quickly became the standardized way of solving special problems. Hence, in time, institutions became differentiated in terms of their primary function. We can thus speak of institutions for the mastery of nature (the whole complex array of economic institutions—banks, mines, manufacturing establishments, wholesale and retail businesses, professions, and the like), institutions of socialization (families, educational institutions, religious institutions), and institutions of social control (government, legal, police and military institutions).

Institutions for the mastery of nature have incidental control and socialization

Institutions As Elements of Social Control

aspects; those for socialization have economic and control aspects; and those of
social control have economic and socialization dimensions. None of the three, however, can be viewed in isolation, for all
impinge one on the other. When the solutions to the problems of socialization and
mastery of nature grow inadequate in a
given society, its control problems, in turn,
become more difficult.

Gandhi's article in this section emphasizes the impact of the processes of socialization and the formation of the personality
on social control. Gandhi also suggests
that as a result of the present atomization,
fragmentation, and alienation of the self,
socialization and social control are undergoing dramatic changes. A law is a
prescribed pattern of conduct that has the
authority of, and is enforced by, the
governments; Friedlander's essay argues
that these methods of social control are
undergoing major transformation as a
consequence of the modern demands for
nationalistic self-determination. Schoppmeyer's survey of the institutions of marriage (and thus also of the family) describes
significant changes in its means of control
and forms. According to Van Patten,
religion remains firmly established, and
specific forms of religious control depend
on the degree of openness in a society or
culture. Lottich believes that the older
apparatus of educational control, relying
primarily on moral sanctions, the Horatio
Alger idea, and "the American Dream,"
has been gradually, but persistently, giving way to the changing world and social
leveling. Finally, Wolf's treatment of social class and status rests on the assumption that most, if not all, societies are
stratified and thus unequal by nature. This
assumption implies division and inequal-

ity in the acquisition of power and prestige. As part of that structure, social
control ensures the maintenance of the
system.

J.S.R.

Raj S. Gandhi

SOCIALIZATION AND PERSONALITY

Within the social control perspective, E. A. Ross[1] was perhaps one of the pioneers in conceiving the possible interrelationship between social control and such social psychological processes as socialization and personality formation. He did not, however, engage in any detailed discussion of it. Martindale[2] has correctly criticized Ross for sometimes making social control coextensive with sociology, especially when Ross isolated so-called means of social control. Ross did not have a clear perception of the intricate interrelationship between social control, socialization, and individual personalities, for he thought of the last two as "the means of social control." In 1947, Roucek and his associates clearly indicated the role of social control in the process of socialization and the formation of individual personalities when they used the term *social control* to mean "those processes, planned or unplanned, by which individuals are taught, persuaded, or compelled to conform to the usages and life-values of the groups."[3]

The Relationship Between Socialization, Personality, and Social Control

Since man is not born a social being but rather is made so by the society in which he is reared[4], unlike nonhuman creatures, he must socialize himself: "man is one of the most social of all the creatures, but unique in the nature of sociality. He is social by learning and not by instinct."[5] In the process of development man has lost his instincts, and hence, the instinct theory[6] in the context of human socialization has no relevance. Whatever aspects of it we intend to look at, however, socialization involves interaction with one or more persons in a social context.[7] Further, if we consider the configurations of behavior to be personality, then we can conceive of social control as ultimately "the action of one personality upon another, and an understanding of social control necessitates knowledge of the process and elements which enter into personality formation."[8]

Five Major Approaches to Socialization and Personality

If we set aside the instinct theory and adopt an "interactionist" view for assessing the position of social control vis-à-vis socialization and personality formation, we can identify at least five major approaches to socialization and personality: the psychoanalytical, with the Freudian and its neo-Freudian branches; the learning and its more recent variant, Skinner's "operant conditioning"; the role theory; the symbolic interactionist; and the social behavioristic. After a review of the theory of socialization and social person, we will point out the relevant social control perspective within each approach.

The Psychoanalytical Approach

One of the most fundamental problems of socialization is concerned with how individual emotional life is made to conform to social requirements. Freud's analysis of human personality and socialization directly addresses itself to this problem. Although Freud's psychoanalysis dealt with some basic (or innate) driving forces of human behavior, he believed that most of them were manifested only in interactive situations and hence could be comprehended only within its interactive *social* context.[9]

When we look at Freud's analysis[10] of the ontogenesis of socialization,[11] we find that it involves at least two major phenomena: identification and the Oedipus complex. It is through identification that "the earliest form of an emotional bond with another person"[12] is formed. Though early in his development, a boy tends to identify with his father and seeks to model himself on him, he begins to develop an incestuous desire for his mother: "the Oedipal crisis results from the conflict between a boy's incestuous longings for his mother and his desire to please his father."[13] This conflict is resolved through the boy's repression of his sexual desires for his mother and the internalization of parental image, resulting in what Freud calls the superego. The superego formation of a girl is also subject to familial influences and follows the same course of early parental socialization. But her final object of identity is her father and not her mother.[14] This Freud labels the Electra Complex, but according to Freud, it is ambiguous, and as a result women's superego is not clearly formulated.[15]

In Freud's analysis, repression is not the whole story: the interiorization of parental authority and the establishment of superego are equally important. Moreover, the socialization of agression means that it is turned inward and is taken over by the superego, which the superego can direct against the ego. The tension between the harsh superego and the ego that is subjected to it produces the sense of guilt, and it expresses itself as a need for punishment. "Thus, for Freud socialization consists of placing one's sexual and aggressive impulses under the control of a superego, that will then punish one for socially incorrect expressions of either instinct. Socialization thus consists of turning libido outward and aggression inward."[16]

In Freud's view, human personality (in its fully developed form) consists of three main elements: the ego, superego, and id. The id is the innate component of personality, the nonsocial component of self; the ego usually has cognitive capacities, engaging in such strategies as learning, thinking, reasoning, perceiving, deciding, and memorizing.[17] It is through the id that we are able to cope with outer reality. The superego is the social component of self; with the development of the superego one acquires norms, values, morals, and attitudes that are reasonably compatible with society. Thus, the chief components of social control are first acquired via the process of socialization, and in its developed form it represents "an internalized version of society's norms and standards of behavior."[18]

In sum, Freud's main contribution to an understanding of social control lies in bringing society and personality together via the process of socialization and in discovering the process of internalization through which the social control (in the form of the superego) becomes rooted in personality.[19]

Freud's analysis is a landmark in studying the relationship between the process of socialization (and its accompanying process of internalization), personality, and social control. Thus, the writings of such persons as Carl Jung,[20] H. S. Sullivan,[21] and Erik H. Erikson,[22] all of whom have been heavily influenced by the Freudian view, could not be adequately understood without a knowledge of Freudian analysis.

Erikson has recently emerged as an innovator in Freudian analysis. Although he accepts Freud's model of personality as consisting of the id, the ego, and the superego, he considers the ego to be more autonomous than the id. Freud maintained that since basic personality responses are conditioned by early experiences, the early familial influences could be of utmost importance in shaping the social person. Erikson, however, believes that the psychohistorical setting in which the child's ego is molded is of paramount importance and hence one ought to rely on "case studies of people living in different cultures to show how the ego's development is inextricably bound up with the changing nature of social institutions and value systems."[23] Further, unlike Freud who relies exclusively on childhood experiences. Erikson outlines a series of eight universal stages through which the psychosocial development of ego occurs, viz., infancy, early childhood, play age, school age, adolescence, young adulthood, middle adulthood, and maturity. The more recent outcome of the application of his theory is Gandhi's Truth,[24] which is regarded as a sound psychoanalytical monograph.

The Learning Approach

Like the Freudian approach, the learning approach has a long history. It starts with Watson's[25] report that, apart from a few innate reflexes, social behavior is more or less the result of conditioning experiences. The learning approach did not gain the attention of social psychologists until the experimental works of Russian physiologist Pavlov[26] who demonstrated that the simple biological reflexes, which are spontaneous responses to stimuli, could become *conditioned reflexes*. In his classic experiment, Pavlov proved that when presented with food, the hungry dog would respond with salivation, the unconditioned response to an unconditioned stimulus. After being conditioned to a bell which was sounded each time the food was presented, the dog would salivate simply upon hearing the bell. The bell had thus become the *conditioned stimulus*, replacing the original reflex.

Undoubtedly, some learned social behavior may be explained with the help of conditioned reflex theory, but to argue that all learned behavior is the result of conditioned reflexes would be to commit the same fallacy as Marxian determinism. At most, Pavlov's theory provides a number of hypotheses regarding human learning which could be pursued in further studies. This is precisely what B. F. Skinner does in his recent studies.

Although Skinner[27] takes over the Pavlovian argument of conditioning, he rejects the notion that the major portion of human behavior simply consists of conditioned reflexes. Skinner believes that the human organism actively "operates" upon its environment, controlling the environment and being controlled by it. "Operant behavior, (produced by operant conditioning) is determined by the events that follow the response. That is, a behavior is followed by a consequence and the nature of consequence modifies the organism's tendency to repeat the behavior in future."[28] As Skinner puts it, "we make a consequence contingent upon certain physical properties of behavior . . . and the behavior is then observed to increase in frequency."[29]

Skinner applies the same theory to the learning of language.[30] Language, of course, is verbal behavior, but it is acquired through differential reinforcement. Here again the question is: "what reinforcement does the listener give the speaker for speaking and what is accorded the listener for listening and reinforcing the speaker?"[31] Thus, the child's verbal behavior is molded by the child's speech, the sounds he emits during his vocalizations, and the reinforcement provided by his verbal community, his immediate social environment.[32]

In his more recent work, *Beyond Freedom and Dignity*,[33] Skinner addresses himself directly to the problem of social control. Typically, for the solution of problems such as ghettoes, pollution, overpopulation, and disease, he places his ultimate faith in the technology of behavior:

Those who manipulate human behavior are said to be evil men, necessarily bent on exploitation. Control is clearly the opposite of freedom, and if freedom is good, control must be bad. What is overlooked is control which does not have aversive consequences at any time. Many social practices essential to the welfare of the species involve the control of one person by another, and no one can suppress them who has any concern for human achievements.[34]

In short, Skinner's position is that there cannot be a complete freedom so far as social environmental control is concerned; the most one can achieve is some freedom from certain kinds of aversive control. From Pavlov to Skinner, this is a common conclusion, reflecting an anti-intellectual attitude in the area of social control. Thus, the learning approach to socialization, personality, and social control comes to a full circle.[35]

Other social psychologists who have made notable contributions to the social psychology of learning, especially through the "reinforcement" framework, are Miller and Dollard,[36] Bandura and Walters,[37] and Thibaut and Kelley.[38] According to Miller and Dollard, four factors are crucial in learning: drive, cue, response, and reinforcement. While they regard language as important, they see it as a cue-producing response in mediating responses to remote rewards or punishments. They also consider social imitation important in maintaining social conformity and learning, but they assert that imitation occurs because it is tied with reward or reinforcement; the lack of reward may deter an individual from imitating. Bandura and Walters accept the role of imitation in learning, but they modify and add to the reinforcement argument by demonstrating that the different forms of disciplinary interventions in the development of self-control may require the use of negative reinforcers and the withholding of positive reinforcement. Similarly, Thibaut and Kelley subscribe to a sort of "reinforcement" argument when they assume that social behavior is unlikely to be repeated unless its rewards exceed its costs. They believe, however, that the value of an outcome is not determined by its absolute magnitude but by comparison with some standards.[39]

The Role Theory Approach

The role theory approach does not in fact represent any specialized or specific approach; it seems to be an odd mixture of Freudian, learning, symbolic interactionist, and so-called funtionalist theories. Two typical representatives of this approach are Frederick Elkins and Talcott Parsons.

Elkins[40] considers socialization to be the process involving both learning and internalization of values and feelings. He maintains that it is through this process that an individual learns the ways of a given society in order to be able to function in it. There are three preconditions for the socialization of the child: the possession of an adequate biological inheritance, the possession of "human nature," and the ability to establish emotional relationships with others. Similarly, there are expected patterns of behavior—various roles in any given society as well as various status situations—positions in the social structure, and the socialization process involves accommodation of behavior to the requirement of roles.[41] Thus, Elkins prefers to approach the problem of socialization through role theory via the structural-functional framework.

Although the structural-functional framework is basic to Parsonian analysis, Parsons also prefers to connect it with his brand of role theory, while dealing with the process of socialization of individuals. However, when concerned with the "personality system," he tends to borrow some psychoanalytic and learning theory concepts to fit into his framework. Thus, Parsons sees "five cathectic-evaluative mechanisms of learning": reinforcement-extinction, inhibition, substitution, imitation, and identification. The first three do not necessarily involve orientation to social objects, while the last two do.[42] While from the social control point of view all five mechanisms may be important for learning and socialization, Parsons would attach special significance to imitation and identification—imitation indicating the process by which specific items of culture are taken over from a social object, and identification indicating the internalization of the values of a model.[43] Parsons considers the combination of internalized patterns to be "in a very important degree ... a function of the fundamental role structure and dominant values of the social system."[44] Similarly, each society is also believed to possess a basic personality[45] "which is a function of socialization in a particular type of system of relationships with particular values."[46] Thus, imperfect mesh though it may be, the personality system, social system, and the system of culture are intermeshed. Yet, this imperfect mesh represents a certain degree of functional integration. Herein lies the importance of the process of socialization (the acquisition of the requisite orientations for satisfactory functioning in a role) and the mechanisms of socialization (in terms of their functional significance to the interaction system).

The Symbolic Interactionist Approach

Although the symbolic interactionists agree with the Freudians on the importance of childhood socialization,[47] identification, and internalization, they do not consider socialization as more or less based on childhood experiences only. Rather, they view it as a process which continues throughout the life of an individual. Moreover, they do not deny the significance of learning mechanisms such as conditioning, conditioned reflexes, reinforcement-extinction, suggestion, and imitation; but they do not think that these are adequate to explain human socialization and personality development. In extending the process of socialization beyond the Freudian view, the symbolic interactionists also present a far more dynamic view of personality as social self; hence, they also bring social control within the proper interactionist perspective. Just as no artificial distinction between self and society exists for them, in the same way social control and self-control are found to be two sides of the same coin.

Although symbolic interactionism could be traced as far back as the works of William James,[48] W. I. Thomas and Florian Znaniecki,[49] Ernst Cassirer[50] and Jean Piaget,[51] in America, it became prominent especially through the works of C. H. Cooley and G. H. Mead.[52]

For Cooley, the study of personality becomes essentially the study of the development of self-conception within the primary group. The primary group is "fundamental in forming social nature and ideal of the individual."[53] It is characterized by spatial proximity, a small number of persons involved, and the longer duration or relative permanence of interaction and hence face-to-face association and the relative intimacy of participants. Although the role of the primary group in the socialization and the development of self-conception is of utmost importance, it is further reaffirmed in day-to-day interaction with other individuals. Cooley further described man's sense of personal identity as a "looking glass self," by which he meant that "each person's orientation toward himself is a reflection of the manner in which he is treated. He imagines how he appears to someone else, imputes a judgement to the observer, and reacts with pride or mortification to the imputed judgement."[54] Thus, since self-control is impossible without self-images, it has led Shibutani to suggest that social control rests largely upon self-control, which he defines as "behavior that is redirected in the light of the manner in which it is imagined to appear from the standpoint of other people who are involved in a cooperative task."[55]

Similarly, for G. H. Mead, the essence of socialization lies in the emergence and gradual development of the self. Unlike Skinner with his "operant conditioning," Mead considers that an essential characteristic of self is its reflexive character. Much like Cooley, he believes that the self can be both subject and object to itself; it can reflect upon itself. But the self having this "double-edged sword" could arise only in social experience. It is then through the child's communicative contact with others that self develops. "In order to communicate with others he must himself be able to respond to what he communicates. ... Once he has acquired the attitudes of others as part of himself, he can judge how another person will respond by how he himself responds to the words he utters."[56] Mead puts emphasis not only on the reflexive property of self, but also on the use of language (a system of significant symbols) in his account of the genesis of self. Reflexiveness, the essential condition within the social process, not only makes possible the development of mind, but accounts for the internalization of all the others, "the generalized other." Note that the notion of internalization—a significant articulatory process between self and social control—is found in Freud but without Mead's emphasis on reflexiveness.

In short, the imaginative insight of Ross that there is a connection between socialization, personality, and social control is brought to a fruitful conclusion by the symbolic interactionists in observing the fundamental fusion of mind, self, and society, and hence in finding self-control and social control as two aspects of the same phenomenon.

The tradition of symbolic interactionism with its unique perspective on human personality (or self) and the process of socialization is continued in the writings of contemporary social psychologists such as Kuhn,[57] Blumer,[58] Manis and Meltzer,[59] Shibutani,[60] and Kando.[61]

The Social Behavioristic Approach

In its sociological and social psychological conceptualization of socialization and self, social behaviorism is very similar to symbolic interactionism as discussed above. Social behaviorism, however, also turns to the legacies of such prominent social scientists as John Dewey, Gabriel Tarde, Gustave Le Bon, James Baldwin, F. H. Giddings, E. A. Ross, Max Weber, and David Riesman. In particular, Weber and Riesman have made lasting contributions in social historical studies of social control, emergence of and change in the self and character, and socialization. In his study of the relationship between religious orientations and economic attitudes, Weber[62] demonstarted how the ethic of Protestantism as internalized by Protestants regulated their behavior and served as a means of both self-control and rational economic behavior. Riesman[63] studied the changing American social character, from tradition-directed (shaped by the uncritical acceptance of traditions of simple society) to inner- (similar to Weber's typical Protestant, motivated by internal confirmity) to other-directed (regulated by the demands of others and external agencies such as the mass media and audience).

Recently, Martindale[64] has been one of the chief exponents of the social behavioristic perspective on changing character, socialization, and social control. Much like Riesman, in developing the sociology of national character, he has engaged in studies of comparative European national character and German national character and social structure.[65] In examining individuality as a social principle and the social behavioristic theory of social control, he rejects the holistic perspective (e.g., Parsonian functionalism) which reifies society, group, or community:

When an individual observes a custom or convention in his behavior, he does so either because the custom is part of his habitual actions or because he fears various reactions on the part of others. . . . Customary behavior is not imposed from without; it is just as much self-control as social control.[66]

In a penetrating analysis of socialization and community in historical perspective (unlike the conventional approaches to socialization which limit its scope to such agencies as family, school, and peer group), Martindale extends it to encompass the health, welfare, and religious institutions of the contemporary national community. Thus, he finds some basic similarities between such large-scale structures of socialization as the University of

Minnesota and the Mayo Clinic of Minnesota.[67] In his confrontation with impersonal organizations, contemporary man finds his individuality in crisis and his self-conception profoundly shaken. No wonder then that the changing personality of Western man finds a common expression through the common theme of "alienation."

Trends

The five major approaches to socialization and personality as identified in this essay already indicate the typical trends in each and set the tone for the tendencies for the 1980s. The psychoanalytical approach, with its typical perspective of relationship between socialization, personality, and social control as perceived earlier by Freud and continued by neo-Freudians such as Jung and Sullivan, and more recently by Erikson, typically betrays its tendencies for emphasizing unconscious motivation and internalization of social control. Recently, however, it is also likely to be linked with the dilemma of freedom versus control as dramatized by existentialists. This theme will also continue to dominate the scene among psychoanalysts in the 1980s. Among the tendencies that continue to influence the neo-Freudians is the further refinement in psychoanalytical concepts for the analysis of human personality. Although the trend is to continue with the assumption of the basic rationality of human nature, neo-Freudians have generally deemphasized biological determinism. They continue to produce interesting case studies despite their commitment to holism.[68] However, Freud's recognition of the individual's illusion of freedom, and simultaneously his awareness of man's dilemma in choosing an alternative course of action, is likely to be dramatized at the hands of neo-Freudians with more emphasis on freedom than determinism in the 1980s.

Although social psychologists earlier dismissed the Pavlovian argument as physiological determinism, the Skinnerian emphasis on "operant conditioning" and "reinforcement" reflects neo-Pavlovianism. Yet, it is appealing to those learning theorists who regard people to be ultimately scientifically knowable and hence scientifically controllable. Since this kind of approach requires a handful of concepts that could be more easily operationalized, believers in the natural science of human behavior, with their enthusiastic application of scientific methodology to the "conditioned reinforcers," will continue to produce experimental studies.

The 1980s are also likely to witness a decline in functionalism. Functionalism, however, never had its own theory of socialization and personality except the assumption that if socialization and personality were properly controlled by means of social control, they would contribute to the integration of the social system. This is holism *par excellence*. No wonder it goes to Freudian theory and to the role theory approach for certain concepts.

This unhappy blending is bound to lose its popularity, and since it is committed to holism—unless the role theory approach disentangles itself from functionalism—it is not likely to make innovative empirical advances.

Both symbolic interactionist and social behavioristic trends rest on the assumption of elementalism.[69] The latter emphasizes that detailed understanding of the self, and hence self-control, socialization, social control, personality, and changing social character can only be obtained through detailed analysis of constituent parts and precise elementalistic concepts that could be put to empirical test. With the further atomization, fragmentation, and alienation of the self in the 1980s, socialization and social control are bound to undergo far-reaching changes. The symbolic interactionist and social behavioristic perspectives are unusually well equipped to deal with these contemporary changing trends. Moreover, with their unique foresight and social philosophy, they provide a penetrating critique of the "brave new world" if anywhere it is in sight.

Notes

1. E. A. Ross, *Social Control* (New York and London: Macmillan, 1929). See especially Chapter 3, "The Role of Sociability," and Chapter 21, "Personality."

2. Don Martindale, *Institutions, Organizations, and Mass Society* (Boston: Houghton Mifflin, 1966), pp. 284, 299. Elsewhere, commenting on Paul Landis' *Social Control* (New York: J. B. Lippincott, 1939), Martindale credits him with making the problem of social control largely coextensive with socialization. See Don Martindale, *American Society* (Princeton, N.J.: D. Van Nostrand, 1960), p. 359.

3. Joseph S. Roucek, *Social Control* (New York: D. Van Nostrand, 1947), p. 3. This early edition contains two relevant and interesting chapters: Chapter 2, "Socio-Psychic Processes in Social Control," and Chapter 3, "Social Control and the Conditioning of Personality."

4. See Don Martindale, *Community, Character and Civilization* (New York: Free Press, 1963), p. 3.

5. Don Martindale, *Social Life and Cultural Change* (Princeton, N.J.: D. Van Nostrand, 1962), p. 34.

6. William McDougall, in his early publication *An Introduction to Social Psychology*, 30th ed. (London: Methuen, [1908] 1950), gave a long list of instincts.

7. Although this view is expressed by Roger W. Burton in considering the psychological aspects of socialization, Whiting's discussion of anthropological aspects, Greenstein's survey of political socialization, and Brim, Jr.'s account of adult socialization reveal that this "interactionist" aspect is always present in the background. See Burton, Whiting, Greenstein, and Brim, Jr., "Socialization," in David Sills, ed., *International Encyclopedia of the Social Sciences* (New York: Macmillan and Free Press, 1968), Vol. 14, pp. 534-562. For a comprehensive review of recent and some current theory and research on socialization, see John A. Clausen, ed., *Socialization and Society* (Boston: Little Brown and Co., 1968); William H. Sewell, "Some Recent Developments in Socialization Theory and Research," *Annals*

of the American Academy of Political and Social Science 349(1963):163-181; and David A. Goslin, ed., Handbook of Socialization Theory and Research (Chicago: Rand McNally, 1969).

8. Roucek et al., Social Control pp. 43-44.

9. Although there is some outward similarity here between Durkheim's notion of conscience collective as constraining men and Freud's notion of social influences determining personality characteristics, these similarities cannot be carried very far. Durkheim, unlike Freud, resorts to the "over-socialized conception of man." See Dennis H. Wrong, "The Over-Socialized Conception of Man in Modern Sociology," American Sociological Review 26 (1961):183-193. See also Raj S. Gandhi, "Sati as Altruistic Suicide: Beyond Durkheim's Interpretation," Contributions to Asian Studies 9 (1977):141-157. Pope recently maintained that Durkheim in all his works places low valuation on things individual, individuality, and individual personality. See Whitney Pope, "Classic on Classic: Parsons' Interpretation of Durkheim," American Sociological Review 38 (1973):399-415.

10. See S. Freud, Group Psychology and the Analysis of the Ego (New York: Bantam, 1960) and The Ego and the Id (New York: W. W. Norton, 1960). According to Sewell (see note 7 above), "Freud's theories on the importance of the early life experiences for subsequent personality structure was and continues to be a major force in socialization theory and research" (p. 163). Stone and Farberman have recently criticized Sewell's statement that "early childhood experience may have some consequences for later self-formulations" (italics original). They consider "the concept personality . . . too gross and crude to be implemented in socialization studies"; see Stone and Farberman, eds., Social Psychology Through Symbolic Interaction (Waltham, Mass.: Xerox Publishing Co., 1970), pp. 511-512.

11. Freud's account of the phylogenetic origin of the superego is found in his Totem and Taboo (New York: W. W. Norton, [1920] 1950).

12. Robert Hogan, Personality Theory: The Personological Tradition (Englewood Cliffs, N.J.: Prentice-Hall, 1976), p. 43.

13. Ibid., p. 44.

14. Ibid., p. 45.

15. Obviously, in their movement for liberation from male control, women in the 1970s find Freud to be their savior.

16. L. A. Hjelle and D. J. Ziegler, Personality Theories: Basic Assumptions, Research, and Applications (New York: McGraw-Hill, 1976), p. 26.

17. Ibid., p. 26.

18. Ibid., p. 27.

19. Borrowing heavily from Freud, Parsons has also claimed this to be the point of "integration" between what he labels "personality system" and "social system." Cf. Talcott Parsons, Social Structure and Personality (New York: Free Press, 1964), especially Chapter 1, "The Superego and the Theory of Social Systems," and Chapter 4, "Social Structure and the Development of Personality: Freud's Contribution to the Integration of Psychology and Sociology." Note, however, that in Parsonian analysis, there is first the artificial separation between "the personality system" and the "social system" and then, like two trains, they are shunting for a common destination! As per Pope's interpretation (see note 9 above), "Durkheim conceives of the personality as composed wholly of the internalized social factor in

altruistic setting" (p. 406). The important point is to consider *internalization as a social process* in which, in the process of self-interaction, the person is capable of indicating to himself how he should act and organize his action through the interpretation of a situation. See H. Blumer, "Reply to Parsons' Comments," *Sociological Inquiry* 45 (1975):68.

20. C. G. Jung, *Two Essays on Analytical Psychology* (New York: Meridian Books, 1956).

21. H. S. Sullivan, *The Interpersonal Theory of Psychiatry* (New York: W. W. Norton, 1953).

22. See especially E. Erikson, *Childhood and Society*, 2d ed. (New York: W. W. Norton, 1963); *Gandhi's Truth* (New York: W. W. Norton, 1969); "Autobiographical Notes on Identity Crisis," *Daedalus* 99 (1970):730-759; and *Dimensions of a New Identity: The 1973 Jefferson Lectures in the Humanities* (New York: W. W. Norton, 1974).

23. Hjelle and Ziegler, *Personality Theories*, p. 62.

24. Erikson, *Childhood and Society*, 1969. This monograph won both a Pulitzer Prize and the National Book Award.

25. J. B. Watson, *Psychology from the Standpoint of a Behaviorist*, 3d ed., rev. ed. (Philadelphia and London: J. B. Lippincott, [1919] 1929).

26. I. P. Pavlov, *Conditioned Reflexes: An Investigation of the Physiological Activity of the Cerebral Cortex* (New York: Dover, [1927] 1960).

27. B. F. Skinner, *Science and Human Behavior* (New York: Macmillan, 1953).

28. Hjelle and Ziegler, *Personality Theories*, p. 135.

29. Skinner, *Science and Human Behavior*, p. 64.

30. B. F. Skinner, *Verbal Behavior* (New York: Appleton-Century-Crofts, 1957).

31. M. Deutsch and R. M. Krauss, *Theories in Social Psychology* (New York: Basic Books, 1965), p. 104.

32. Ibid.

33. B. F. Skinner, *Beyond Freedom and Dignity* (New York: Alfred A. Knopf, 1971).

34. Ibid., p. 41.

35. Among the sociologists influenced by the Skinnerian analysis of operant conditioning, see G. C. Homans, *Social Behavior: Its Elementary Forms* (New York: Harcourt Brace Jovanovich, 1961); P. Blau, *Exchange and Power in Social Life* (New York: John Wiley and Sons, 1964); and J. F. Scott, *Internalization of Norms* (Englewood Cliffs, N.J.: Prentice-Hall, 1971).

36. N. E. Miller and J. Dollard, *Social Learning and Imitation* (New Haven, Conn.: Yale University Press, 1941).

37. A. Bandura and R. H. Walters, *Social Learning and Personality Development* (New York: Holt, Rinehart and Winston, 1963).

38. J. W. Thibaut and H. H. Kelley, *The Social Psychology of Groups* (New York: John Wiley and Sons, 1959).

39. Deutsch and Krauss, *Theories in Social Psychology*, pp. 116-117.

40. F. Elkins, *The Child and Society* (New York: Random House, 1960), p. 4.

41. Ibid., p. 7.

42. T. Parsons, *The Social System* (Glencoe, Ill.: Free Press, 1951), pp. 209-211.

43. Ibid.

44. Ibid., p. 228.

45. For the notion of "basic personality," see also Abram Kardiner, *The Individual and His Society* (New York: Columbia University Press, 1939), and A. Kardiner, R. Linton, C. DuBois, and J. West, *The Psychological Frontiers of Society* (New York: Columbia Unviersity Press, 1945). For the notion of "modal personality," see J. J. Honigmann, *Culture and Personality* (New York: Harper and Brothers, 1954).

46. Parsons, *The Social System*, p. 228.

47. For an interesting comparison between Freud and Mead, see Guy E. Swanson, "Mead and Freud: Their Relevance for Social Psychology," *Sociometry* 24 (1961): 319-339.

48. W. James, *Principles of Psychology*, 2 vols. (New York: Henry Holt, 1890).

49. W. I. Thomas and F. Znaniecki, *The Polish Peasant in Europe and America*, 5 vols. (Chicago: University of Chicago Press, 1918-1920).

50. See especially E. Cassirer, *An Essay on Man: An Introduction to a Philosophy of Human Culture* (New Haven, Conn.: Yale University Press, 1944).

51. J. Piaget, *The Moral Judgement of the Child* (New York: Harcourt, Brace, 1932).

52. An excellent account of the main representatives of symbolic interactionism can be found in Don Martindale, *The Nature and Types of Sociological Theory* (Boston: Houghton Mifflin, 1960), pp. 339-375. Also see G. H. Mead, *Mind, Self and Society*, C. W. Morris, ed. (Chicago: University of Chicago Press, 1934), and A. Strauss, ed., *George Herbert Mead on Social Psychology* (Chicago: University of Chicago Press, 1964).

53. C. H. Cooley, *Social Organization: A Study of the Larger Mind* (New York: Charles Scribners' Sons, 1920), p. 23.

54. See C. H. Cooley, *Human Nature and the Social Order* (Charles Scribner's Sons, 1922), pp. 183-185; and T. Shibutani, *Society and Personality: An Interactionist Approach to Social Psychology* (Englewood Cliffs, N.J.: Prentice-Hall, 1961), p. 505.

55. Shibutani, *Society and Personality*, p. 92; especially, Chapter 9, "Personal Autonomy and Social Control"; Chapter 13, "Self-Esteem and Social Control"; Chapter 15, "The Development of Social Control"; and Chapter 18, "Social Psychology and Social Control."

56. See Mead, *Mind, Self and Society*, pp. 140-141; and K. Davis, *Human Society*, 21st ed. (New York: Macmillan, 1966).

57. M. H. Kuhn, "Major Trends in Symbolic Interaction Theory in the Past Twenty-Five Years," *Sociological Quarterly* 5 (1964):61-84.

58. H. Blumer, *Symbolic Interactionism: Perspective and Method* (Englewood Cliffs, N.J.: Prentice-Hall, 1969).

59. J. G. Manis and B. N. Meltzer, eds., *Symbolic Interaction: A Reader in Social Psychology*, 2d ed. (Boston: Allyn and Bacon, 1972).

60. Shibutani (see note 54 above).

61. T. M. Kando, *Social Interaction* (St. Louis: C. V. Mosby Co., 1977).

62. Max Weber, *The Protestant Ethic and the Spirit of Capitalism*, translated by Talcott Parsons (New York: Charles Scribner's Sons, 1930).

63. D. Riesman, R. Denney, and N. Glazer, *The Lonely Crowd* (New Haven, Conn.: Yale University Press, 1950).

64. See D. Martindale, "The Sociology of National Character," *Annals of the American Academy of Political and Social Science* 370 (1967):30-35.

65. Martindale, *Community, Character and Civilization,* pp. 183-294.

66. Martindale, *Institutions, Organizations, and Mass Society,* p. 290.

67. Ibid., pp. 478-510.

68. According to holistic assumption, human behavior can be explained only by studying persons as totalities.

69. As opposed to holism, elementalism assumes that persons could be better understood by examining each of their characteristics separately.

Robert A. Friedlander

LAW, GOVERNMENT, NATIONALISM, AND THE STATE

Law and the Legal Process in Historical Perspective

"Where there is society there is law."[1] This Roman legal maxim well illustrates the function of law and the legal process in providing the framework of organized society. Legal systems and legal doctrines have evolved throughout the centuries from conditions and situations that required some sort of formal regulation over the actions of individuals in their relationships to one another. According to Plato, "[t]he laws themselves will explain the duties we owe to children, relatives, friends and fellow-citizens," as well as to the state.[2] As Aristotle later pointed out, the law also has an educative function. First, the citizen, or the sovereign, must be educated as to what law should be, before they themselves can apply the law.[3] In other words, law is essentially a social phenomenon.

During the Middle Ages, law came to be considered an eternal set of principles taken from nature and expressed by conduct. The leading Scholastic philosopher, Thomas Aquinas, was the first influential proponent of the doctrine of natural law since the Roman Stoics. He argued that human law "is derived from the law of nature," but at the same time he acknowledged the importance of divine wisdom as manifested by eternal law. On the one hand, law is the product of man acting as a rational creature; on the other, human law is based upon moral principles derived from a Higher Law.[4] Henceforth, the sometimes contradictory roles of reason and morality were to be fundamental issues in every meaningful inquiry into the significance of law and the nature of legal systems.

Even by the mideighteenth century, the great figure of English jurisprudence, William Blackstone, held law to be "a rule of action dictated by some superior being." Simultaneously, however, he likewise invoked the law of nature and the "exertion of right reason." In reality, Blackstone was a product of the Age of Reason and the European Enlightenment, and therefore in his *Commentaries* on the English Common Law, rationalism predominated. Behind every general Common Law rule, there was almost always an explicit rationale,[5] which led him to declare in a much-quoted phrase: "[f]or when this reason ceases, the law itself ought likewise to cease with it."[6] Yet, with the passage of time, custom and tradition came to rigidify Common

Law precepts so that they were not always applicable to the social, economic, or political problems of societies in change.

Questions on the relationship between law and morality, between ethics and the law, and between a law of nature and a Higher Law, did not abate with the triumph of eighteenth-century rationalism. Nor are they issues devoid of contemporary interest. One of the lessons of the sordid Watergate affair of the early 1970s, in which more than fifty government-connected lawyers were found guilty of criminal activity, was that modern legal theory is still infused with moral principles.[7] Viewed from this perspective, one function of the law is that of goal-setter or of establishing norms towards which both individuals and society should strive. In this way, law reflects the values, the morals, and the basic ethical principles of the community. There are others, however, who reject the idea that law and morals coincide. The seventeenth-century philosopher of state power, Thomas Hobbes, considered injustice merely to be the failure to obey the civil law.[8] There are also those who insist that human law and moral law are separate systems and that morality is an individual matter. Nonetheless, if society makes law, then law becomes part of society and in consequence overlaps with a society's moral structure. In this way, it can be said that moral principles may become part of the legal system.

It was the eighteenth-century English philosopher Jeremy Bentham who tried to reconcile these contradictory theories. According to Bentham, good laws and bad laws can be found in society, but the law itself has to be distinguished from the reason for the law. Law essentially is a command. One should be concerned with the law as it is and not as it ought to be, although pleasure and pain serve as guideposts as to what society should do.[9] Bentham's legal Utilitarianism was later taken up by John Austin and the Positivists in the latter part of the nineteenth century. Austin's credo, simply put, was that "the existence of law is one thing; its merit or demerit is another." Law represents a command of the sovereign authority which imposed on society a habit of obedience or an obligation and duty upon the individual to act or not to act.[10] To this the Basic Norm theory of Hans Kelsen was added in the twentieth century. In this analysis, the legal order is a normative order that regulates human behavior. "The validity of a norm may begin at one moment and end at another." Norms are valid for a specific time and space, for certain individuals, and for a certain territory. They may legitimize the past but they also prescribe the present.[11] Oliver Wendell Holmes, Jr., stated it more effectively in his famous passage: "a legal duty so called is nothing but a prediction that if a man does or omits certain things he will be made to suffer in this or that way by judgment of the court."[12]

The most recent school of legal philosophy in Anglo-American jurisprudence is that of the Realists who view the legal system as an objective manifestation of social behavior. Rules, or laws, serve as instruments of social behavior and reflect community values. The young Karl Llewellyn argued that law was merely the settling of disputes. What officials "do about disputes is ... the law itself."[13] The Realists treated law as descriptive sociology. Case law is judge-made law or reasoning by example. It represents the common ideas of society through the decisions of experts.[14] Thus, law becomes, in effect, social engineering.

In its origins, the Anglo-American Common Law was custom restated and tradition institutionalized, but as the circumstances of society changed, so did the scope of the law. A changing society brought forth innovation and developing standards. Law in England and America became by necessity an instrument of social and economic policy. In the words of Morris R. Cohen, "[t]he law draws its sap from feelings of justice and social need."[15] It was the great technological revolution of the nineteenth century that ushered in new Anglo-American legal principles and new Anglo-American legal theories more amenable to the spirit of the age.

Courts, however, were not intended to be the primary forum for the shaping of public policy, since that is the legislative function. Both Bentham and Austin took note of judge-made law, but whereas Bentham was highly critical of the process, Austin approved of judicial legislation if it was directed to the right ends.[16] The great American jurist of the twentieth century Benjamin Cardozo perceived the judiciary as "the interpreter for the community of its sense of law and order,"[17] commending it for exercising power "with insight into social values, and with suppleness of adaptation to changing social needs."[18] Nonetheless, if a case in controversy did not rest on its merits, the judicial system would merely become enforcement machinery for legislative design.

The American constitutional system, however, has evolved in such a manner that an overlapping of constitutional functions has developed, whatever the original intentions of the Framers. The judicial function runs into that of the legislative process and likewise conflicts with executive authority.[19] As a result, the courts have permanently taken on a nonjudicial role, occasionally stepping into a vacuum created by legislative and executive inaction.[20] The end result has been that courts increasingly have taken upon themselves the role of supreme arbiter of the governmental process.[21] Thus, it was no accident that the judicial branch resolved the dangerous constitutional confrontation between executive and legislature in the quarrel over the Nixon tapes.[22] It also is no accident that constitutional theorists may now speak of judicial supremacy without being seriously challenged. The object of law in the Common Law system, according to Mr. Justice Holmes, is "the prediction of the public force through the instrumentality of the courts."[23] The notion that the law has an individual as well as a collective responsibility has indeed been maintained.

A unique feature of the American constitutional legal system is that it is oriented toward the protection of individual rights. This was the original purpose behind the creation of the Bill of Rights of the U.S. Constitution,[24] and with some deviation the rights of the individual have continued to be accorded legal recognition by the courts. Nowhere is this more apparent than in the administration of criminal justice. Procedural due process as applied by the judicial branch is predicated upon standards of fundamental fairness. Conduct which offends a sense of justice and which is shocking to the conscience of the court will not be tolerated.[25] Arbitrary, capricious, or unreasonable procedures are likewise offensive. These standards, based upon commonly accepted notions of decency and fair play, must also be ascertainable[26] in order to guarantee equal opportunity between the parties (but not parity), so that neither the rights nor the interests of one side are jeopardized vis-à-vis the other.[27]

Other protections are given the accused, not from the language of the Bill of Rights but from decisions of the courts themselves. The so-called Miranda warnings are a doctrine designed to reinforce the constitutional privilege against self-incrimination.[28] The right to counsel granted by the Sixth and Fourteenth Amendments give the accused the right to an attorney, "whether by way of formal charge, preliminary hearing, indictment, information, or arraignment."[29] The exclusionary rule and "the fruit of the poisonous tree" are judicial remedies designed to protect the citizen from arbitrary and unreasonable search and seizures under the Fourth Amendment.[30] On the other hand, the trend of recent Supreme Court decisions in the 1970s indicates that the Burger Court has sought to extend the interests of the community in criminal cases as represented by a greater crime control, while at the same time it has restricted the rights of the accused in limiting due process protections. Often applying a balancing test, the current Supreme Court more often than not has preferred a public policy rationale in deciding cases rather than relying upon narrow constitutional grounds. The late Mr. Justice Black, generally considered to be the most vigorous post-World War II defender of civil liberties, strenuously objected to this new direction. His declaration of faith in the Bill of Rights raises the most controversial jurisprudential issue of the 1970s—is the Supreme Court the supreme arbiter of the Constitution, or does the Constitution speak for itself as the Supreme Law of the land?[31]

In the Common Law system, law itself is relative. Statutes can be repealed and replaced by other statutes; judges can overrule statutes by declaring them unconstitutional, and through judicial precedent judges can make law themselves, until or unless the decision rendered is repealed by statute. As one perceptive scholar has noted, no society "can successfully enforce every rule that governs the behavior of its members."[32] Selective enforcement, therefore, forms an essential part of the government process. The real question is whether "[l]aw is the principal institution through which a society can assert its values."[33] The answer depends not upon the society but upon the nature of the values themselves and upon the will to implement those values, or, to use another term, upon governance.

The Nature of Government: Theories of Sovereignty

Lincoln's Gettysburg Address spoke eloquently of "government of the people, by the people, and for the people," but to the Greek philosophers there was a careful distinction between rulers and ruled, between the select few and the general multitude.[34] Plato maintained that there were two "mother-constitutions"—monarchy and democracy. Yet, he also insisted that the rulers, whomever they might be, must be the "servants of the laws" in that "law is the master of government and government is its slave."[35] Aristotle classified government into five different typologies: kingship, tyranny, aristocracy, oligarchy, and democracy.[36] These classifications have stood the test of time, although the twentieth century has added the nomenclature of authoritarianism and totalitarianism. Aristotle's fundamental emphasis was upon a habit of obedience to law by both the governors and the governed: "it is preferable that law should rule than any single one of the citizens."[37]

The debate over the nature of government and whether it should be the servant or the master of the people has continued inexorably down through the centuries. The Common Law tradition, beginning with *Magna Carta* in 1215 and reinforced during the reign of Edward III (1327-1377), emphasized the due process of law. Its meaning for government was made clear at the beginning of the seventeenth century by Sir Edward Coke, attorney general under James I (1603-1625) and later chief justice of the King's Bench. Opposing James' claim that the king represented the law of the land, Coke replied that kings "ought not to be under men but under God and the law."[38] A short time later in *Dr. Bonham's Case* (1610), Coke held that the Common Law is superior to acts of Parliament and may on occasion render those acts null and void.[39]

The seventeenth century produced the great debate over the nature of government by Thomas Hobbes, advocate of state authority, and John Locke, proponent of limited power and the contract theory of government. To Hobbes the sovereign was all powerful. The sovereign power in the Hobbesian state cannot be challenged and it cannot be changed. What the prince says has the force of law.[40] For Locke, sovereign authority was derived from the consent of the governed and was created by a social contract. Through the social contract, the individual is bound to the sovereign and the sovereign is bound to the individual. The purpose of government is to protect the natural rights of the citizenry.[41]

It was Jean Jacques Rousseau in the eighteenth century with his essay on the *Social Contract* who laid the theoretical basis for the coming age of democratic revolution in America and France. According to Rousseau, sovereignty is formed from a social compact which represents the general will of society. Every citizen places himself under the supreme direction of the general will, and in this way the social contract forms a government based upon the consent, direct or implied, of the governed. There is also, however, an element of compulsion, for if an individual refuses to obey the general will, he will be compelled to do so by the whole state, thus laying a foundation for the totalitarian theories of the twentieth century.[42]

The authors of the American Declaration of Independence, particularly Thomas Jefferson, influenced primarily by Locke but also by Rousseau,[43] proclaimed the doctrine of popular sovereignty based upon the philosophy of natural rights. The language of the Declaration is illustrative: "Governments are instituted among Men, deriving their powers from the just consent of the Governed. . . . ."[44] The principle of representative self-government was given practical implementation by the Constitutional Convention of 1787. The Framers relied heavily on the theories of the "celebrated Montesquieu" and the "judicious Locke,"[45] but the tripartite system of checks and balances they created was aimed not so much at preventing executive dominance as inhibiting legislative encroachment. Hamilton presented his most influential argument in *Federalist No. 78*, which advocated specific functions to be granted the judicial branch in order to provide a bulwark against unbridled legislative power.[46] The impact of the American Constitution was quickly felt in the French, Spanish, and Latin American constitutional experiments in representative government. Although these subsequent experiments were notably less than successful, the final judgment of John Adams cannot be gainsaid:

Our people are undoubtedly sovereign; . . . . the legislative, executive, and judicial powers are carefully separated from each other; the powers of the one, the few and the many are nicely balanced in the legislatures; trials by jury are preserved in all their glory; and there is no standing army; the *habeas corpus* is in full force; the press is the most free in the world. Where all these circumstances take place, it is unnecessary to add that the laws alone can govern.[47]

Alexis de Tocqueville, the most perceptive commentator on American democracy, ascribed the success of constitutional government in the United States to social conditions. Political equality, he maintained, is the inevitable consequence of social equality. Democratic institutions are therefore the product of a democratic society.[48]

The nineteenth-century revolutionary era spawned two alternative theories. Anarchism was diametrically opposed to all notions of government. Leading anarchist theorists, such as Pierre-Joseph Proudhon, Mikhail Bakunin, and Peter Kropotkin, urged the abolition of all governmental authority, and the first two called for popular insurrection as the instrument of governmental destruction.[49] Communism, as developed by Karl Marx, Friedrich Engels, and Vladimir Lenin, ostensibly stood for the withering away of the state, but only after the establishment of a dictatorship of the proletariat. Although the dictatorship of the proletariat was only to last for a transitional period, the regimes of Lenin, Stalin, and their successors have made the party dictatorship a permanent feature of Soviet authoritarianism.[50] In one of the great ironies of history, the supposed classless society engendered a "new class" of technocrats and bureaucrats which not only controls the entire life of communist society but also perpetuates itself by means of a privileged caste system.[51]

The twentieth century provided the world with its most despotic form of government— the totalitarian state. In Nazi Germany, Stalinist Russia, and Maoist China, ideology and terror became inextricably intertwined. The exercise of absolute power became its own justification, and terror was institutionalized as an end in itself. The concentration camp or corrective labor camp associated with totalitarian regimes was literally a vision of hell, and along with the purge it provided the mechanism of totalitarian power. In the words of Hannah Arendt, "[w]hat totalitarian ideologies therefore aim at is not the transformation of the outside world or the revolutionizing transmutation of society, but the transformation of human nature itself."[52]

Democracy survived the Holocaust and World War II, but in the decade of the 1970s it has once again been subjected to attack just as in the decade preceding the outbreak of World War II. Democracy is once again on trial in France, Italy, the Iberian Peninsula, Israel, Japan, Latin America, and even in Great Britain and North America. Watergate tested the American democratic process as it had not been tested since the Civil War era, and the aftermath of that unfortunate episode has partially transformed the nature of the American presidency. International terrorism is on the increase throughout the world, and its primary target appears to be democratic government. In fact, above all else, contemporary terrorism is a technique "for demolishing a State."[53]

The State in History and Law

To the Greeks of the Golden Age, the *polis* or city-state was a limited concept of sociopolitical community.[54] Plato's *Republic* attributes the origin of the city-state to a desire arising "out of the needs of mankind."[55] Aristotle defines the *polis* as "an association of citizens in a constitution."[56] To the Romans, the *cosmopolis* or city of the world was a universal concept of authority and tradition.[57] During the Middle Ages, the competing claims of sovereign authority were divided between monarchy and the universal Church, but with the rise of the nation-state and the theory of absolute sovereignty, centralization of political structures became a hallmark of the sovereign prerogative. Unleashed by the forces of centralized government, the new economic and political dynamism had its greatest effect upon religious orthodoxy and the social order.[58] The result was the birth of the modern state wherein the monarch no longer could proclaim in the manner of

Louis XIV: "I am the state." The means by which this state-building was accomplished was the rule of the law. Succinctly put, "[t]he modern State is a legal system."[59]

Thomas Hobbes' *Leviathan* (1651) is the classic representation of state authority and state power. For Hobbes, the *civitas* or political commonwealth elevates man from a brutish state of nature and provides him with nourishment, protection, and tranquillity.[60] The sovereign power of the state, drawn from an unbreakable covenant between the ruler and the ruled, is absolute. Sovereign power cannot be faulted and cannot be forfeited. What the citizen receives in exchange is the guarantee of peace and security for members of the commonwealth.[61] It was but one short step from this to the twentieth-century philosophies of authoritarian statism—Nazism and fascism. In the words of Giovanni Gentile, the leading philosopher of Italian fascism, "it is not nationality that creates the State, but the State which creates nationality. . . . [t]he State is the universal aspect of the will."[62]

Modern legal theory and international legal practice require four essential characteristics for state recognition: (1) an organized government; (2) a defined territory; (3) a permanent population; and (4) the capacity of entering into independent relations with other states. Before the end of World War II, the general rule was that states were the subject of international law and that individuals were only the objects.[63] Since 1945, the individual also has come to be deemed a subject of international law through the establishment of international human rights principles as propounded by the world community of nations.[64]

Territoriality forms the foundation of modern statehood. The state, by exercising its authority over an identifiable delimited territory, is granted color of sovereignty. In effect, sovereign authority deals with the nature of rights over a given territory.[65] Complications arise, however, over what constitutes a people in the juridical sense and how to determine an identifiable link between people and territory. At least one noted legal philosopher stresses the importance of popular goals. "If there are no goals generally accepted among the given group of people," he argues, "then there is only a group of people in a given territory, but there is no society."[66]

Nationalism and Self-Determination

The concept of nationhood and the development of modern nationalism date from the era of the French Revolution and the Napoleonic Empire. "War, conquest, oppression by one nation meant the rise of national consciousness and loyalty among the conquered and oppressed peoples."[67] Throughout modern history nationalism has been both a unifying and disintegrating force, and the two cataclysmic global wars of the twentieth century had their origins in nationalistic conflicts.[68] Nationalism in the modern sense inevitably and inexorably led to pan-nationalism and to imperialism, providing a dubious legacy for the twentieth century. For many patriots and superpatriots, it became almost a religion in itself. Even the United States succumbed for a time to the lure of the manifest destiny.[69]

Nationalism's legal-political manifestation in the present era is that of self-determination, a dynamic twentieth-century force, providing the juridical justification of new states and a legal rationale for revolution within the confines of established polities. A distinguished international legal scholar has called it "an idea that revolutionized the world."[70] The principle itself can be defined as the "right" of a "people" to shape its own political, social, economic, and cultural destiny. The major issue still facing the world, particularly in Africa and the Middle East, is what constitutes a principle and what is meant by a nation.

A "people" consists of a community of individuals bound together by mutual loyalties, a perceived tradition, and a common cultural awareness, with historic ties to a given territory. A "nation" is a community of peoples, adhering to a single sovereignty, accepting mutually binding authority structures, and occupying a specific territory within ascertainable geographic boundaries. Twentieth-century European nationalism has frequently emphasized cultural unity as the essential prerequisite to national identity. Contemporary non-European nationalism has primarily stressed the political consciousness of a particular people or peoples as the determining factor in securing the right to national sovereignty.[71]

The problem for the 1970s is that, although historically and politically self-determination has been an ideological weapon which purports to champion popular sovereignty on a global scale, in reality it serves to perpetuate deep political and ideological divisions between the countries of the Third and Fourth Worlds and their former colonial masters. As a justification for terrorist acts or a rationale for so-called political crimes, particularly those committed in support of "national liberation movements," it undermines and erodes the very concept of a world public order.[72] If self-determination is truly to become an international legal right, then it must be exercised within a viable international legal system. As long as self-determination is made to serve the cause of violence, it cannot be called a rule of law.

The United Nations has enshrined the cause of national liberation in a large number of resolutions and conventions. For example, the definition of aggression voted on December 14, 1974, specifically endorses wars of national liberation against "colonial and racist regimes or other forms of alien domination."[73]

Sadly, the rule of law throughout the globe in the current decade does not seem to have fared much better than in earlier decades. If one substitutes Lebanon for Ethiopia, Rhodesia for Spain, and Israel for Czechoslovakia, the ambience of the 1930s seems to be reappearing in the 1970s. With the Third World currently engaging in the same sort of political misfeasance or malfeasance as its European predecessors, the words of Raymond Aron take on an ominous and prophetic ring: "[C]ollectivities with a national vocation have disappeared without a trace. In a few years or decades from now, it may be that the human race will destroy itself; or that one people may exterminate all others and occupy the planet alone."[74] The words of the Biblical Prophets still ring true when applied to the law of nations: those who live by the sword will perish by the sword. As for those who are willing to abide by the rule of law, if they do not inherit the earth, they will at least survive. That is the lesson of the 1970s—and of history as well.

Trends in Social Control

Beginning with the Omnibus Crime Bill of 1968 and the Nixon presidency, the Congress and the courts as well as a number of state legislatures have increasingly emphasized legal issues of crime control and personal security. Concomitantly, there has been an ongoing redefinition and gradual restriction of due process rights in the 1970s and a scaling down of judicial remedies such as the Miranda warnings and the exclusionary rule. The underlying rationale is that of the school of legal Realists—law represents community values. The contemporary community must therefore be protected from undue harm even at the expense of individual rights.

Although politicians and legislators have advocated numerous constitutional amendments dealing with questions of equal rights for women, apportionment, abortion, and bussing, in the American constitutional system the United States Supreme Court remains the supreme arbiter of the governmental process. In United States v Nixon (1974), the Court reaffirmed its claim to judicial supremacy and the Congress reasserted its claims to equal partnership with the executive branch of the government. The 1970s have thus brought about a redistribution of governmental power.

During the 1970s, the democratic process has been tested not only in the United States, but throughout the world. England, Canada, and Australia have also been subjected to serious constitutional and political pressures, while such traditional democracies as India, Israel, and France, and the post-World War II democratic regimes of Italy and Japan have come under severe political stress. As in the 1930s, democracy in the 1970s is on the defensive. Terrorism ended the model Latin American democracy of Uruguay and perpetuates military regimes in Latin America and the Third World.

On the global level, the major issue of the 1970s remains self-determination, especially in Africa and the Middle East. The United Nations, as a result of Third World and Soviet pressures, has not only condoned wars of national liberation but actually has promoted guerrilla activities in Rhodesia, South

Africa, and Israel. The prevailing rule of law seems to be that though all peoples are equal, some are more equal than others, and the idea of statehood has been subject to a rising politicization in the world community.

All countries and all peoples continue to advocate a theoretical minimum world order. The fundamental question, however, continues to be: order maintained for whom and by what means? Direct confrontation between nation-states appears to have diminished in the détente era, but ideological competition, as represented by the contradictory attempts to promote international protection of human rights versus political subversion through guerrilla movements, has not abated.

The best that can be said for international law and order in the 1970s is that so far the world still survives. Hopefully, the experiences of the past will become the building blocks of the future in a truly operative global society.

Notes

1. *Ubi societas, ibi jus est.*
2. Book IV, Sec. 7, Plato, *The Laws*, rev. ed., translated by Trevor J. Saunders (Middlesex, Eng.: Penguin, 1976), p. 178.
3. Book III, Ch. 16, Aristotle, *The Politics*, translated by T. A. Sinclair (Middlesex, Eng.: Penguin, 1976), pp. 143-145.
4. Thomas Aquinas, "Law as an Ordinance of Reason," in Martin Golding, ed., *The Nature of Law*, (New York: Random House, 1966), pp. 9-24. See also the excellent short analysis in Martin Golding, *Philosophy of Law* (Englewood Cliffs, N.J.: Prentice-Hall, 1975), pp. 30-37.
5. William Blackstone, *Commentaries on the Laws of England*, I (Oxford: Clarendon Press, 1765), pp. 39-40.
6. Ibid., p. 61.
7. Cf. *Commonweal*, August 9, 1974; *Nation*, August 17, 1974; *Newsweek*, August 19, 1974; *Time*, August 12, 1974; Leon Jaworski, *The Right and the Power: The Prosecution of Watergate* (New York: Reader's Digest, 1976); William Safire, *Before the Fall* (New York: Tower Publications, 1975), pp. 3-17, 688-693.
8. Thomas Hobbes, *Leviathan: On the Matter, Forme and Power of a Commonwealth Ecclesiastical and Civil*, edited by Michael Oakeshott (London: Collier-Macmillan, 1962), p. 113.
9. Cf. H.L.A. Hart, "Law in the Perspective of Philosophy," *New York University Law Review* 51, no. 4 (October 1976): 538-545; Carl J. Friedrich, *The Philosophy of Law in Perspective*, 2d ed. rev. and enlarged (Chicago: University of Chicago Press, 1973), pp. 95-98.
10. Golding, *Philosophy of Law*, pp. 24-27; Dennis Lloyd, *The Idea of Law*, rev. ed. (Hammondsworth, Eng.: Penguin, 1976), pp. 175-186.
11. Hans Kelsen, *General Theory of Law and the State*, translated by Anders Wedberg (Cambridge, Mass.: Harvard University Press, 1945, pp. 30-49.
12. Oliver Wendell Holmes, Jr., "The Path of the Law," *Harvard Law Review* 10, no. 8 (March 1897): 458.

13. Karl Llewellyn, *The Bramble Bush: On Our Law and Its Study* (Dobbs Ferry, N.Y.: Oceana Press, 1973), p. 12. Llewellyn later repudiated this view. See ibid., pp. 8-9.

14. Edward H. Levi, *An Introduction to Legal Reasoning* (Chicago: University of Chicago Press, 1972), p. 5.

15. Morris R. Cohen, "The Place of Logic in the Law," *Harvard Law Review* 29, no. 6 (April 1916): 638.

16. Lloyd, *The Idea of Law*, pp. 260-262.

17. Benjamin N. Cardozo, *The Nature of the Judicial Process* (New Haven, Conn.: Yale University Press, 1974), p. 16.

18. Ibid., p. 94.

19. Roscoe Pound, *An Introduction to the Philosophy of Law*, 2d ed. rev. (New Haven, Conn.: Yale University Press, 1974), pp. 52-53.

20. See *Baker* v. *Carr*, 309 U.S. 186 (1962); *Brown* v. *Board of Education*, 347 U.S. 483 (1954).

21. Robert A. Friedlander, "Judicial Supremacy: Some Bicentennial Reflections," *Rutgers-Camden Law Journal* 8, no. 1 (Fall 1976): 24-36.

22. *United States* v. *Nixon*, 418 U.S. 683 (1974).

23. Holmes, "The Path of the Law," p. 457.

24. Irving Brant, *The Bill of Rights: Its Origin and Meaning* (New York: Signet, 1967).

25. *Rochin* v. *California*, 342 U.S. 165 (1952).

26. Henry J. Abraham, *Freedom and the Court: Civil Rights and Liberties in the United States*, 2d ed. rev. (New York: Oxford University Press, 1975), pp. 90-91. Cf. Lon Fuller, "Positivism and Fidelity to Law—A Reply to Professor Hart," *Harvard Law Review* 71, no. 4 (February 1958): 651-652.

27. Golding, *Philosophy of Law*, p. 121.

28. *Miranda* v. *Arizona*, 384 U.S. 436 (1966).

29. *Kirby* v. *Illinois*, 406 U.S. 682 (1972).

30. Jerold Israel and Wayne R. La Fave, *Criminal Procedure: Constitutional Limitations*, 2d ed. (St. Paul, Minn.: West Publishing Co., 1975), pp. 263-281.

31. Hugo L. Black, *A Constitutional Faith* (New York: Alfred A. Knopf, 1968), p. 42.

32. Burton M. Leiser, *Liberty, Justice, and Morals: Contemporary Value Conflicts* (New York: Macmillan, 1973), p. 31.

33. Alexander M. Bickel, *The Morality of Consent* (New Haven, Conn.: Yale University Press, 1975), p. 5.

34. Raymond Aron, *Progress and Disillusion: The Dialectics of Modern Society* (New York: Praeger Publishers, 1968), p. 25.

35. Book III, Ch. 5, and Book IV, Ch. 6, Plato, *The Laws*, pp. 143 and 174.

36. Book IV, Ch. 1, Aristotle, *The Politics*, pp. 151-152.

37. Book III, Ch. 16, ibid., p. 143.

38. Erwin M. Griswold, *The 5th Amendment Today* (Cambridge, Mass.: Harvard University Press, 1955), p. 33.

39. Edward S. Corwin, *The "Higher Law" Background of American Constitutional Law* (Ithaca, N.Y.: Cornell University Press, 1971), p. 44. This view did not come to be accepted in English constitutional tradition, but it formed a precedent for American judicial review.

40. Hobbes, *Leviathan*, pp. 134-150.

41. Peter Laslett, ed., *John Locke's Two Treatises of Government*, rev. ed. (New York: New American Library, 1965); see especially, Gordon J. Schochet, ed., *Life, Liberty, and Property: Essays on Locke's Political Ideas* (Belmont, Calif.: Wadsworth, 1971).

42. Jean Jacques Rousseau, *Social Contract* (Chicago: University of Chicago Press, n.d.).

43. Harold Lord Acton, *Essays on Church and State* (New York: Crowell, 1968), p. 304.

44. Carl L. Becker, *The Declaration of Independence: A Study in the History of Ideas* (New York: Vintage Press, 1970).

45. Clinton Rossiter, *1787: The Grand Convention* (New York: Signet, 1968), p. 61.

46. Clinton Rossiter, ed., *The Federalist Papers* (New York: New American Library, 1961), pp. 464-472.

47. George A. Peek, Jr., ed., *The Political Writings of John Adams* (New York: Liberal Arts Press, 1954), p. 129.

48. Alexis de Tocqueville, *Democracy in America*, translated by Henry Reeve, abridged ed. (Chicago: Regnery, 1951), pp. 9-16.

49. Roderick Kedward, *The Anarchists: The Men Who Shocked an Era* (New York: American Heritage, 1971), pp. 5-33.

50. Henry B. Mayo, *Introduction to Marxist Theory* (New York: Oxford University Press, 1960), p. 178.

51. Milovan Djilas, *The New Class: An Analysis of the Communist System* (New York: Praeger, 1962), pp. 37-69.

52. Hannah Arendt, *The Origins of Totalitarianism*, new ed. (New York: Harcourt Brace Jovanovich, 1973), p. 458. See also Carl J. Friedrich and Zbigniew K. Brzezinski, *Totalitarian Dictatorship and Autocracy*, 2d ed., rev. (New York: Praeger Publishers, 1965), pp. 161-171, 183, 202.

53. Brian Crozier, *A Theory of Conflict* (New York: Charles Scribner's Sons, 1974), p. 119.

54. Hannah Arendt, *The Human Condition* (Chicago: University of Chicago Press, 1969), pp. 22-28.

55. J.D. Kaplan, ed., *Dialogues of Plato*, translated by B. Jowett (New York: Pocket Books, 1950), p. 241.

56. Aristotle, *The Politics*, p. 106.

57. Hannah Arendt, *Between Past and Future*, new ed. (New York: Viking, 1968), pp. 120-28.

58. Alexander Passerin d'Entreves, *The Notion of the State: An Introduction to Political Philosophy* (Clarendon: Oxford University Press, 1967), pp. 89-103.

59. Ibid., p. 96.

60. Hobbes, *Leviathan*, pp. 132-33.

61. Ibid., 134-141.

62. Giovanni Gentile, *Genesis and Structure of Society*, translated by H. S. Harris (Urbana: University of Illinois Press, 1960), p. 121.

63. Wolfgang Friedman, *The Changing Structure of International Law* (New York: Columbia University Press, 1966), p. 213.

64. Hersch Lauterpacht, *International Law and Human Rights* (New York: Praeger Publishers, 1950), pp. 3-72. See also "Declaration on Principles of International Law

Concerning Friendly Relations and Co-operation among States in Accordance with the Charter of the United Nations," U.N. General Assembly Resolution 2625 (XXV) (1970).

65. James L. Brierly, *The Law of Nations*, edited by Humphrey Waldock, 6th ed. (Oxford University Press, 1963), pp. 126-127, 162-163.

66. Samuel I. Shuman, *Legal Positivism: Its Scope and Limitations* (Detroit: Wayne State University Press, 1963), p. 152.

67. Boyd C. Shafer, *Nationalism: Myth and Reality* (New York: Harcourt, Brace and World, 1955), p. 135.

68. Raymond Aron, *Peace and War: A Theory of International Relations*, translated by Richard Howard and Annette Baker Fox (New York: Praeger Publishers, 1967), pp. 296-299.

69. Cf. Arendt, *Origins of Totalitarianism*, pp. 227-243; Henry Steele Commager, "American Nationalism," in John A. Garraty, ed., *Interpreting American History: Conversations with American Historians*, I, (New York: Macmillan Co., 1970), pp. 95-115.

70. Louis Sohn, "Comment: Radical Perceptions of International Law and Practice," *American Journal of International Law: Proceedings* (1972): 173.

71. The above discussion is based upon Robert A. Friedlander, "Self-Determination: A Legal-Political Inquiry," *Detroit College of Law Review* 1, no. 1 (1975): 71-91.

72. On wars of national liberation in the juridical context, see Natalino Ronzetta, "Resort to Force in Wars of National Liberation," in Antonio Cassese, ed., *Current Problems of International Law: Essays on U.N. Law and on the Law of Armed Conflict* (Milan: Giuffre, 1975), pp. 319-353.

73. U.N. General Assembly Resolution 3314 (XXIX) (1974).

74. Aron, *Peace and War*, p. 787.

Martin W. Schoppmeyer

MARRIAGE AND FAMILY

Belok, citing Murdock, defines marriage as "a complex of customs centering upon the relationship between a sexually associating pair of adults within the family."[1] The medieval Christian philosophers and their modern descendants pointed out that man's natural sociability was activated by a conjugal relationship.[2] Dewey agreed, claiming that sex was a socializing agency fundamental to the family.[3] Marriage, according to Dewey, had to be a long-term arrangement rather than a short mating period as with many animal species because of the prolonged infancy of human young and their need for continued care.[4] In another work, however, he concluded that the permanency of the arrangement was due to the property interest of the husband.[5]

The scholastic philosophers regarded the basis for marital permanence to be the "onerous" duties of parents[6]—a viewpoint which some might construe to be a reflection of their celibate bias. They did stress, however, that marriage had a dual purpose: child raising and the mutual benefits to the married couple.[7] This dualism is quite important, for much of the attitudes toward marriage over the centuries, and even at present, seem to differ depending on which of the two purposes is considered to be the more important. It is on this distinction, too, that much of social control rests. For since most societies have responded to their felt need of self-preservation and continuance, the bulk of social controls have grown to foster the child-raising goal rather than the mutual satisfaction of the spouses. Moreover, it is on this cornerstone of societal interest that a whole collection of contradictory, decorative, nonutilitarian, and involved social practices and controls have arisen. As a result, a natural human relationship has probably been made the basis for more extensive social control than any other single human activity.

Social controls are usually expressed as customs or mores by the group. Dewey and Tufts suggested four means by which they are enforced: public opinion, taboos, ritual, and physical force.[8] An examination of each of these may well provide some clues to current controls.

Public Opinion

Probably because modern America is the most public opinion conscious nation in history, the function of public opinion in other times and places tends to be discounted. Yet, the difference seems to be one of scale rather than of effect. McLuhan stresses that the electronic media have created mass involvement[9]; thus, massive sampling of opinion is needed to determine modern standards. In simpler times, a far smaller number of opinions sufficed. The opinions, whether expressed or implied, of one's immediate neighbors and peers, being the whole world in a space-restricted society, had a definite control on the actions of an individual. A person either complied or risked losing his status in the community, tribe, or clan. Today he risks loss of status in his social group, work group, or even employing organization. In a society where status and its symbols are said to be the basis of a new class structure[10] the gain or loss of status would seem to be an effective social control.

Taboos

Taboos are negative controls; they ban certain contacts which in primitive societies promised reprisals from unseen beings.[11] Modern Americans seem to feel that the only taboos are those described by Margaret Mead in some book about the South Seas, yet they do live with taboos.

Probably the best known and most common taboos have been those against menstrual blood and against incest both as an act and a marital arrangement. Moses condemned almost all forms of incest in Deuteronomy. Hence, the taboo is part of the Judeo-Christian ethic as a modern sin, and is not simply some backward tribal construct. The negative attitude toward incest is quite cross-cultural. The thinking at one time was that the almost universal taboo against incest reflected the recognition of even the least sophisticated society that it led to biological degeneration.[12] Certain royal lines such as the Ptolemys of Egypt practiced incest openly, however, and more recent reigning groups have done so, though with a bit more decorum. The theory of biological degeneration now tends to be disregarded in favor of an explanation based on the unworkability of incestuous marriage.[13]

An almost equally widely recognized taboo is infidelity. Yet, its pattern of rejection is broader and far more democratic than by royal dynasties alone. Charles II may be famous for his infidelities, but far less regal personages have practiced it. It is said to be currently on the rise in the United States.[14] The fiction of marital partnership has never been demonstrated as aptly as by the punishment for infidelity: the unfaithful husband faces but a slight penalty, if any, and in many societies the wife faces death.[15] Infidelity by either partner is decried equally by Christian doctrine.[16] Many societies, however, permit postmarital intercourse with persons other than the spouse.[17] As a taboo, therefore, infidelity has its limits. It, more than any other aspect of the conjugal relationship, seems the best example of Sartre's opinion that "the moral agent . . . is the being by whom values exist."[18] Even though infidelity and premarital sex are not widely considered by polls, they manage to persist. In fact, the main reason given for the fact that infidelity has not grown more rapidly in modern America is that the American adultress makes a poor mistress by foreign standards.[19]

Ritual

Ritual is a positive reinforcement of behavior.[20] Rites supply the basis for courtship, the ceremony itself, and postceremony living patterns. In other words, they are the way a given society does things. Ambrose Bierce's definition of a rite is most germane in this context: "A religious or semi-religious ceremony fixed by law, precept or custom, with the essential oil of sincerity carefully squeezed out of it."[21] The ritual is so ingrained, however, that to do something different, even though reasonable or sincere, would provoke group discipline or criticism. A fatherless bride must still have someone "give" her away to properly commemorate the transfer of male control. Other cultures require ceremonial bathing[22] or children dressed up in wedding costumes to chase or confuse evil spirits.[23] Thus, rice or cans tied to the groom's car can be categorized as part of a ritual to provide good omens and defy evil influences.

The marriage rite itself can range from a short pro forma reading by a justice of the peace, either in an office, in a field, underwater, or a Las Vegas "Wedding Chapel," to a full-fledged Episcopalian or Catholic nuptial Mass. The essence of the ritual is identifiable in all the versions. Promises are made and witnessed, and a third party pronounces the task completed. Although the major American sects place different interpretations on different facets, the ritual has irreducible elements. Not having them is not being married, for it underlines the fact that "a certain degree of social control over sex activity is to be found in nearly every form of human organization."[24]

Physical Force

Physical force, the ultimate control mechanism in even civilized societies, has had many accepted uses relating to marriage. Most such uses have favored the male partner, which is logical since he is physically the stronger. Strength has led to a double standard.

Dewey pointed out that the modern Western family has three roots: Roman, Teutonic, and Christian.[25] In the Roman family the father was supreme, but over the centuries the wife came to be seen as most subservient to her husband rather than to her own father. The Germans were as definite as the Romans in attributing the greater power to the husband. The wife was considered a ward, and like his Roman counterpart before him, the husband could, under certain circumstances, put her to death. The medieval Church, although urged by St. Paul toward the ideal of celibacy, acted to equalize the marriage relationship somewhat. Marriage was not regarded as a perfect partnership, however, as current church doctrine still calls for the primacy of the husband on the basis of the need for the physical coercion of children.[26]

Imposition of physical force on the enamoured couple by external forces has also long been common—for example, the mutilation of Abelard by Heloise's uncle.[27] Another long-standing form of violence has been that stemming from the necessity to defend a marital relationship, as when Andrew Jackson defended the honor of his beloved Rachel against Governor Sevier.[28]

Physical force as a control mechanism is far from dead, as witness the many cases of wife beatings and child abuse currently publicized. As suggested by Skinner, the persistence of this primitive measure could be the result of the failure of other forms of control which have resisted weaker processes.[29]

Modern America

The social controls surrounding matrimony in American society seem to have a basis other than public opinion, taboos, ritual, or physical force. Simply stated it is economics. The economic basis for marriage is well established in other cultures, though not as pervasively as in the American. Marriage is both a status need and a status symbol. To illustrate this thesis, various aspects of matrimony will be discussed in the following sections.

Courtship

"All courtship systems are market or exchange systems."[30] The differences lie in who sells and who buys, what is valued, and how explicit the system is. The tradition whereby parents or an individual paid a fee for a marriage partner is well established. For example, Jacob worked for fourteen years to gain Rachel.[31] Even in the twentieth century in the Middle East it has been stated that:

Courtship and marriage among these Arabs is scarcely more than a purchase and a sale. When the prospective husband finds a would-be bride within his means, he makes his proposal to her father. Then the father inquires if any of her relatives desire her, for they have the first right to her hand; if not, the groom pays the price, from five to twenty liras or its equivalent in camels.[32]

Henry M. Stanley reported the going price for brides in late nineteenth-century Central Africa as one to five head of cattle.[33] In India, on the other hand, the price was paid for the groom.[34] The dowry system was far from unknown in the United States in the nineteenth century. Dowry right in the

Common Law refers to the portion of a husband's estate which the widow can claim without making a specific will.[35] The custom, like the law itself, was brought from England, but its current use is neither nineteenth century nor British. The orthodox Jews of modern New York reportedly still make the marriage contract an essential part of courtship and marriage.[36]

Generally, this commercial aspect seems archaic inasmuch as the modern system of courtship is based on the ideal of romantic love.[37] It might therefore be assumed that the elders in the family of each lover have little or nothing to say regarding the courtship since their economic contributions are no longer necessary to attract the second party. The fact is, however, that family involvement in the choice of a marital partner is neither a thing of the past nor simply a characteristic of less sophisticated societies. Control is still exercised through less direct economic means. The family can control a child's associates[38]; it can and does determine the choice of schools or neighborhoods; and through many modern subdivisions which are built to attract only a certain income level,[39] at least the backgrounds of potential sons- or daughters-in-law can be limited.

Just as family control has become indirect, so has the bargaining process. Bargaining, according to McCall, "implies a certain purposeful awareness of the exchange of rewards."[40] As a result of the reduction of direct family control, courtship has become a period of training in bargaining,[41] with emphasis placed on a unique exchange of rewards in successive relationships. It is built on a permanent availability model,[42] which means that courtship and even marriage are part of a series of relationships that are temporary and can be terminated when a better bargain is in sight. This pattern is in reality a parody of the purchase of successive homes, automobiles, and major appliances: something or someone is retained only as long as it confers status and provides pleasure. The mutual exploitation pattern is a process rather than an event.

Therefore, the modern courtship system has had but a limited effect on mate selection. Persons tend to choose a partner from the same social class; this tendency seems stable and where social upgrading is done, it is done more often by women.[43] Race is another constraint.[44] Hence, the choice of a mate is not without its socially controlled aspects.

The Ceremony

If courtship reinforces class lines, the modern ceremony can often become its public demonstration. The modern economic base of marriage is aptly and often vulgarly displayed in its celebration. The rite becomes subordinate to attempts to demonstrate economic position which in turn maintains a marriage industry. In 1970, $750 million was spent for wedding and engagement rings. If the cost of china and crystal presents are added, weddings represent a billion dollar industry for jewelers.[45] Brides especially are considered a great economic opportunity. Newlyweds spend an average of $3,500 to furnish and equip their home, which means $3.5 billion per year to furniture and appliance firms.[46] Ethnicity is no barrier to display, for the black middle class is quite as prone as the white to make much ado about marriage.[47]

Excesses seem commonplace: $60,000 weddings in San Francisco;[48] a $62,000 wedding for Lynda Bird Johnson;[49] flower bills of $28,000[50] and gifts worth $30,000 in Texas.[51] In less excessive places such as New York, caterers provide wedding lunches for $2,990.[52] The church decorations for Nancy Sinatra cost $25,000. When the Nixons spent "only" $700 for flowers for Tricia, they were called cheap, but an incumbent president has no need to prove his status.[53] So, the ceremony has become something of a potlatch celebration in which families vie in conspicuous consumption. Thus is marriage blessed with an economic kiss.

The Honeymoon

Americans have concocted the idea that the first few days of wedded bliss should be spent in a special location. Even though feminist writers have referred to this practice as ceremonial rape,[54] it seems too popular to be discontinued easily. It is also quite profitable, for it keeps resorts and travel agencies in the black. It is almost treasonable not to follow the trend. Since the social order is said to determine masculine and feminine behavior,[55] there is no reason to assume that it does not determine cooperative behavior as well. The honeymoon does suggest that, regardless of the advertised expansion of premarital sex, the average couple is frightened and seems to appreciate being surrounded by others in the same condition.[56] There seems to be a limit as to the general degree of sophistication regarding premarital experiences.

Family Size

Couples who have a high standard of living or who wish to achieve one generally have smaller families.[57] Having a small family works to the mutual benefit of parents and offspring. Children are taught work values at home[58] and are assigned tasks, somewhat as a matter of heritage. Nineteenth-century America was a frontier nation where childhood did not last long,[59] because children had to perform their share of chores to help maintain their families. Children were, therefore, an economic asset; their very numbers widened the market and provided for economic growth.[60] As industrialization replaced the agrarian system, children became an economic burden; hence, the prudent couple began to limit family size. In analyzing the propertyless "working class" early in the nineteenth century, David Ricardo regarded the workers' own blindness as the basis for population growth.[61] American workers seemed to see more clearly: the average family size in the United States dropped from 6 in 1860[62] to 4.9 in 1890[63] to 4.5 in 1910[64] to 3.3 in 1953.[65] Couples were exercising the self-control which Ricardo had favored but not trusted.[66] To other economists like Adam Smith, female weakness due to prosperity was considered the reason for fewer children.[67] This too seems to provide an economic basis. In truth, the modern small conjugal family emerged because this structure best fits the modern industrial system.[68] Thus, it is the preferred system as it best permits human adjustment to reality and allows maximum benefit from the industrial state.

Child Raising

As the industrial system confers blessings on the conjugal family, the family confers status on itself through its children. They are raised in accordance with the values of their parents' class.[69] Schools reflect the prevalent middle-class values,[70] and school boards reflect the values of its members—business and professional men.[71] The social class of the parents tends to determine the students' choices of curriculum, decisions regarding going to college and which college to attend, and selection of college courses.[72] Thus, the cycle is complete. Marriage joins mates of the same class who train their children in its values who in turn become adults who do the same.

Monogamy

At various times in human history, societies have approved of other than monagamous states. Will Durant, citing Letourneau, noted that every possible experiment has been or is being tried.[73] These include groups in which the marital relationship was free and terminable at will[74] and group marriages of several men and several women in a communal relationship. Caesar reported the existence of such group marriages in ancient Britain. Its vestige is considered the basis for the early Jewish rule that a man must marry his brother's widow. Polyandry, or one wife with several husbands, has existed in several places, notably Tibet, where males outnumber females.[75]

The most common nonmonagamous state, polygamy, was approved by the ancient Hebrews and Mohammed as well as the Mormons. Its root cause was probably the higher death rate for males in primitive societies; the scorn of these groups for childless women may also have been a factor in its origin. The women themselves are said to have favored it as it reduced their frequency of pregnancy.[76] It is argued that it had a eugenic value over monogamy as the ablest men produced more children, which is not the case today. While polygamy still exists, it is dying out, even in the Middle East.

The cause of its decline seems to be an economic one, although a religious reason is also involved. That is, the admonition of the Prophet that all wives were to be treated equally (Sura 4, Verse 3) is now interpreted as meaning that multiple marriage is forbidden.[77] Several Moslem nations, for example, Tunisia, have outlawed it, and it has been severely limited in Syria.

Monogamy became the preferred form of marriage as a result of various economic pressures such as added property,[78] wealth,[79] and less burdensome household work,[80] which lessened the need for cheap labor from several wives working simultaneously and confused estate divisions. It would seem, however, that since divorce permits sequential polygamy without confusing the economic considerations, it has become widespread throughout the world.

Divorce

Will Durant asserted that monogamy is artificial.[81] Whether or not this is the case, it is true that monogamy has become temporary. At present the average American monogamous relationship has only a fifty-fifty chance of lasting.[82] The growing divorce rate is apparently the product of the shifting economic relationships of husband and wife rather than of mere theoretical factors.

The Changing Status of the Wife

Almost a century and a half ago, De Tocqueville was quite impressed with the status of women in America:

nowhere are young women surrendered so early or so completely to their own guidance.

Long before an American girl arrives at the marriageable age, her emancipation from maternal control begins: she has scarcely ceased to be a child, when she already thinks for herself, speaks with freedom, and acts on her own impulse.[83]

[But] in America, the independence of woman is irrevocably lost in the bonds of matrimony. If an unmarried woman is less constrained than elsewhere, a wife is subjected to stricter obligations.[84]

The family was the basis of production, and production was increased through the division of labor.[85] "In no country has such constant care been taken as in America to trace two clearly distinct lines of action for the two sexes . . . American women never manage the outward concerns of the family, or conduct a business or take a part in political life."[86] When production moved to the factory, the father had less contact with his children[87] and the mother assumed their complete care. As family size decreased and the need for labor increased, the mother, too, found a job. By 1949, four families in ten had two or more members in the labor force.[88]

As of 1970, over 40 percent of American wives were working—the second highest proportion in the Western world.[89] The apparent result is more economic independence for the wife, who thereby no longer needs to depend on her husband or to accept an intolerable marriage. It also creates a certain degree of competition. While most women tend to be overeducated for the jobs they hold,[90] in cases where they hold higher status positions than their husbands, some marital role disruption seems likely.

The Changing Status of the Husband

With the female partner in marriage establishing more equality, the male partner has lost his primacy. As husband, he no longer has the legal authority he once enjoyed; more and more, he fits Bierce's definition of the husband as "one, who having dined, is charged with care of the plate."[91] Since the wife now provides a larger share of the family's economic base, the sanctions available to the husband to enforce his desires and decisions have decreased. While he is still expected to be a provider, the kind of job he holds has assumed greater importance. For example, the worker with high morale is usually one who has a job that meets the approval of family and friends and that is sufficient to satisfy family obligations.[92] Approval does not seem to be as important to women workers as to men.[93] Yet the very existence of a wife's income can be a threat to the perceived achievement of some husbands. If men cannot satisfy their need for achievement (which Maslow classifies at the fifth level of his hierarchy)[94] in their family relationships, they will find other sources of satisfaction—whether it be through a hobby, alcohol, the lodge, or other female companionship. Evidently, before American husbands will accept equalization to the extent that their Swedish counterparts reportedly do,[95] a number of beliefs will have to be changed. The social controls over expectations placed upon husbands are evidently out of step with each other's beliefs.

Class and Marital Dissolution

The degree of pressure which the changing status of the husband exerts on both the wife and husband and their willingness to accept these changes seem to be class related because, the divorce rate decreases as the educational level of the couple increases.[96] In most cases of better educated couples, the husband holds a professional or managerial position of recognized status and is threatened neither by his wife's lack of approval nor by her high-status position.

Modern Individualism

In recent years, social scientists have increasingly tended to analyze marriage from an individualistic and behavioral viewpoint. The satisfaction of the individual within the relationship is looked upon as its *summum bonum*; individual behavior is seen as the proper yardstick by which to measure the success or failure of the arrangement. In an era of woman's liberation, "living together," and zero population growth, an emphasis upon personal gratification rather than the procreational aspects of matrimony is quite logical.

The new attitude can reasonably be explained by a sort of reverse economic determinism in which the family is no longer a basic economic unit. Material possessions and children, always somewhat self-exclusive terms, are now quite contradictory. The income which supports the modern post-industrial household is derived from sources external to the family group. Child labor is not only not needed, but the cost of raising and educating a child for entry into a "diploma elite" occupation means the sacrifice of other material possessions.

Today, with the numerous birth control techniques available, children are easily avoided. Birth control is accepted even by persons who are members of religious sects which officially oppose it. Moreover, childless couples no longer bear any stigma in society. Without children to provide a common interest, however, couples may easily drift apart.

The individualistic value further discourages long-range associations and fosters short-term associations for sexual enjoyment alone. Real commitments are postponed or avoided altogether.

While John Dewey's four means of social control still affect the marital relationship, they are but processes. The behavior which is controlled has drastically shifted from the nineteenth-century concept of an income-producing male cohabiting with a female whose role consisted of *kinder, kirche, kuchen*. In a very real sense, the self-serving individualistic attitude represents an extension of childhood in which immediate gratification is a proper goal. In effect, children are being replaced by older persons using childish standards. Modern society, however, is prepared to accept their standards and to utilize its control mechanisms.

Notes

1. Michael Belok, "Marriage and the Family," in James Van Patten, Joseph S. Roucek, Michael Belok, and Martin Schoppmeyer, *Conflict, Permanency, Change and Education* (Moti Katra, Agra 3, India: Satish Book Enterprise, 1976); p. 87. See also Joseph S. Roucek, ed., *Social Control* (Westport, Conn.: Greenwood Press, 1970).

2. Ignatius Cox, *Liberty, Its Use and Abuse*, 3d ed. (New York: Fordham University Press, 1946), p. 296.

3. John Dewey and James H. Tufts, *Ethics* (New York: Henry Holt and Co., 1926), p. 82.

4. John Dewey, *Democracy and Education* (New York: Free Press, 1966), p. 45.

5. Dewey and Tufts, *Ethics*, p. 47.

6. Cox, *Liberty*, p. 297.

7. Ibid., p. 299.

8. Dewey and Tufts, *Ethics*, p. 54.

9. Marshall McLuhan and Quentin Fiore, *The Medium Is the Massage* (New York: Bantam Books, 1967), p. 61.

10. Vance Packard, *The Status Seekers* (New York: Pocket Books, 1961), p. 3.

11. Dewey and Tufts, *Ethics*, p. 55.

12. Bernard Farber, *Family Organization and Interaction* (San Francisco: Chandler Publishing Co., 1964), p. 73.

13. Ibid., p. 84.

14. Vance Packard, *The Sexual Wilderness* (New York: Pocket Books, 1970), p. 271.

15. Dewey and Tufts, *Ethics*, p. 574.

16. Cox, *Liberty*, p. 305.

17. Farber, *Family Organization*, p. 84.

18. Jean-Paul Sartre, *Existentialism and Human Emotions* (New York: Philosophical Library, 1957).

19. Packard, *Sexual Wilderness*, p. 266.

20. Dewey and Tufts, *Ethics*, p. 55.

21. Ambrose Bierce, *The Devil's Dictionary* (Garden City, N.Y.: Doubleday and Co., undated).

22. Edgar J. Banks, *Bismya* (New York: G. P. Putnam's Sons, 1912), p. 49.

23. Ibid., p. 82.

24. Hanna M. Stone and Abraham Stone, *A Marriage Manual*, rev. ed. (New York: Simon and Schuster, 1935), p. 227.

25. Dewey and Tufts, *Ethics*, p. 574.

26. Cox, *Liberty*, p. 326.

27. Carl Stephenson, *Mediaeval History*, rev. ed. (New York: Harper and Bros., 1943), p. 333.

28. Don C. Seitz, *Famous American Duels* (New York: Thomas Y. Crowell Co., 1929), p. 125.

29. B. F. Skinner, *Beyond Freedom and Dignity* (New York: Alfred A. Knopf, 1972), p. 41.

30. William J. Goode, *World Revolution and Family Patterns* (New York: Free Press, 1963), p. 8.

31. Genesis 29:15-28.

32. Banks, *Bismya*, p. 416.

33. Henry M. Stanley, *In Darkest Africa* (New York: Charles Scribner's Sons, 1891), Vol. 2, p. 394.

34. Goode, *World Revolution*, p. 212.

35. William Morris, ed., *American Heritage Dictionary of the English Language* (New York: American Heritage Publishing Co., 1970).

36. Marcia Seligson, *The Eternal Bliss Machine, America's Way of Wedding* (New York: William Morrow and Co., 1973), p. 58.

37. Vance Packard, *Sexual Wilderness*, p. 25.

38. Goode, *World Revolution*, p. 8.

39. Packard, *Status Seekers*, p. 78.

40. Michael M. McCall, "Courtship as Social Exchange: Some Historical Comparisons," in Bernard Farber, ed., *Kinship and Family Organization* (New York: John Wiley and Sons, 1966), p. 191.

41. Ibid., p. 197.

42. Ibid., p. 192.

43. Farber, *Family Organization*, pp. 142-143.

44. Ibid., p. 144.

45. Seligson, *Eternal Bliss Machine*, p. 34.

46. Ibid., p. 43.

47. Ibid., p. 69.

48. Ibid., p. 111.

49. Ibid., p. 108.

50. Ibid., p. 107.

51. Ibid., p. 118.

52. Ibid., p. 150.

53. Ibid., p. 173.

54. Jesse Bernard, "The Paradox of the Happy Marriage," in Vivian Gornick and Barbara K. Moran, eds., *Woman in Sexist Society* (New York: Basic Books, 1971), p. 153.

55. Packard, *Sexual Wilderness*, p. 317.

56. Seligson, *Eternal Bliss Machine*, p. 252.

57. Ernest L. Bogart and Donald L. Kemmerer, *Economic History of the American People* (New York: Longman's Green and Co., 1947), p. 507.

58. William M. Form and Delbert C. Miller, *Industry, Labor and Community* (New York: Harper and Bros., 1960), pp. 407-408.

59. Ibid., p. 407.

60. Barbara Ward, *The Rich Nations and the Poor Nations* (New York: W. W. Norton, 1962), p. 53.

61. Robert L. Heilbroner, *The Worldly Philosophers*, rev. ed. (New York: Simon and Schuster, 1961), p. 79.

62. Bogart and Kemmerer, *Economic History*, p. 507.

63. Form and Miller, *Industry*, p. 388.

64. Bogart and Kemmerer, *Economic History*, p. 507.

65. Form and Miller, *Industry*, p. 388.

66. Heilbroner, *Worldly Philosophers*, p. 76.

67. Smith, *Wealth of Nations*, p. 83.

68. Goode, *World Revolution*, pp. 10-26.

69. Packard, *Status Seekers*, pp. 196-197.

70. Form and Miller, *Industry*, p. 252.

71. Ibid., p. 249.

72. Ibid., p. 253.

73. Will Durant, *Our Oriental Heritage* (New York: Simon and Schuster, 1954), p. 38.

74. Ibid., p. 38.

75. Ibid., p. 39.

76. Ibid., p. 40.

77. Goode, *World Revolution*, p. 101.

78. Ibid., p. 39.

79. Goode, *World Revolution*, p. 188.

80. Ibid., p. 102.

81. Will Durant, Oriental Heritage, p. 41.

82. Packard, *Sexual Wilderness*, p. 256.

83. Alexis De Tocqueville, *Democracy in America*, edited by Richard D. Heffman (New York: Mentor Books, 1956), p. 234.

84. Ibid., p. 235.

85. Adam Smith, *An Inquiry into the Nature and Causes of the Wealth of Nations*, edited by C. J. Bullock (New York: P. F. Collier and Sons, 1909), p. 11.

86. De Tocqueville, *Democracy*, p. 244.

87. Dewey and Tufts, *Ethics*, p. 591.

88. Form and Miller, *Industry*, p. 388.

89. Judith Blake, "The Changing Status of Women in Developed Countries," *Scientific American* 231, no. 3 (September 1974): 136-147, 142.

90. Ibid., p. 143.

91. Bierce, *Devil's Dictionary*, p. 91.

92. Form and Miller, *Industry*, p. 393.

93. Ibid., p. 393.

94. Henry C. Lindgren, *Psychology of Personal and Social Adjustment*, 2d. ed. (New York: American Book Co., 1959), p. 31.

95. "Report to the United Nations, 1968: The Status of Women in Sweden," in Mary Lou Thompson, ed., *Voices of the New Feminism* (Boston: Beacon Press, 1970), pp. 155-177.

96. Packard, *Sexual Wilderness*, p. 257.

James Van Patten

RELIGION

Religion may be defined in a variety of ways.[1] One common definition is that it involves man's relationship with supernatural powers and entails interwoven forms of worship, awe, and prayer or belief systems adhered to with faith and ardor. Regardless of the difficulties of defining religion, throughout history it has exerted a powerful and continuing influence on the lives of individuals. While modern civilizations have seen external changes in religious rituals as a result of expanded scientific inquiry, many old functions continue to survive, for the most part unchanged. Religion continues to serve as an explanation of an unknown future through supernatural powers which individuals honor, worship, and praise. Religion provides creative expression for communicating with a god or gods, and it also provides control through voluntary and involuntary restraints on those behaviors seen as antiestablishment, antireligious, or antisocial.

This essay will attempt neither to trace nor to describe all religions or theological doctrines. The primary focus is on the methods, avenues, and resources of religious institutions for social control. The relationship between religion and both individual and social behavior will be explored through forms of social control. Brief glimpses of historical religious thought as well as the roles of individual belief systems will be given to clarify these relationships.

Overview

Religion has served to explain occurrences in nature and in society. From the beginning of recorded history, the destructive forces of nature and even irrational acts of man were viewed as the wrath of supernatural powers termed deities. Violence among men was seen as evil personified. As civilizations developed, supernatural power played a changing role, with scientific inquiry explaining formerly unexplained events. For Homer, causation was found in capricious deities whose undependability led to acceptance of a blind faith called will. Later, Hesiod gave more structure to supernatural forces; and during the classical era of Socrates, Plato, and Aristotle, the role and function of deities were explained through a comprehensive intellectual system. The system based on reason blended into the Christian era of St. Augustine and St. Thomas with a focus on faith and revelation to interpret the role of supernatural powers. The people of Israel combined reason and faith to define themselves as a nation of destiny. From Abraham forward, there were some who carried the message of faith from generation to generation.[2] Thus, the Judeo-Classical-Christian period brought together forces of reason and faith. Through reason, man could interpret and understand his role in the universe and through faith, he could develop a personal and deep relation to God.

With the age of empirical inquiry from Francis Bacon onward, scientific inquiry expanded the horizons of knowledge of both man and the universe. The role and function of religion were modified to deal with fewer unknowns and to focus more on the human condition, its promise and fulfillment. To this day, armies pray to their God before engaging enemies in combat; sports arenas witness team prayers before and after athletic events; and individual contestants in life's battles stand in awe and reverence before the diverse belief systems to which they adhere. Righteousness and victory are viewed as inevitable companions. Governmental leaders invoke the blessings of deity on taking office; and currency often contains reference to supernatural powers. Prayers are given to bless food and its partakers. Civic events, community endeavors, activities of social and political clubs, betting events, marriages, and deaths call on infinite wisdom and seek the blessings of a powerful, benevolent, loving, and caring God.

These are but a few of the many social uses of religion that serve as a unifying influence on humankind.

Methods of Social Control Through Religion

Historically, social consensus provided a base for rewarding and punishing behavior patterns. How this consensus was achieved seemed less important than the unity of belief and action it provided. In primitive societies, unity and survival were partners permitting no dissent in religious activities. Eventually, leadership figures accepted their positions as representing divine right under the fabric of belief systems from Judaism, Buddhism, Islam, Christianity to Manichaeism. Every religion begins with a unique event carried into historical legend by those who witnessed it.[3] Individual pronouncements had the effect of law and became the basis for both action and belief. Private testimony, transcendentalism, dogmatism, absolutism, traditionalism, and authoritarianism typified their method and mode of operation. Yet, these mutifaceted forms of dogmatic authority served the basic social and security needs of people very well. Security, for example, provided a feeling of belonging to a culture with a set of values and perimeters within which acceptable behavior was defined. Thus, a unifying, coherent, comprehensive, and consistent set of values was developed to provide a social fabric. Answers to fearful questions gave hope, faith, and even expectation of a better future. Thus, religions formed a central place in the hearts and minds of people.

Even though religions differ depending on the amount of scientific inquiry, understanding, and information in a given culture,[4] in general they have three basic dimensions: (1) the theoretical dimension which encompasses beliefs and doctrines regarding deity and the nature and destiny of man and the world; (2) the practical dimension which involves rites of worship, sacramental acts, and forms of meditation; and (3) the sociological dimension which includes groupings of leadership and relationships between religious groups and society.[5]

The theoretical dimension weaves a comprehensive interrelated system of ideas within which most, if not all, of man's questions may be answered. A theory is developed which ties together systematically existing knowledge of individuals and their universe. Interpreting unknown factors is achieved through speculation from what is known to the unknown. Faith and revelation explain the world that is through the world that ideally ought to be. The function of theory is to promulgate a structure for broad questions about reality, truth, appearance, existence, death, and the meaning of those terms. Theory may be simple or complex. Primitive peoples developed myths to exist more comfortably with their doubts, whereas more advanced peoples wove a more intricate web of complex theories such as those of St. Thomas, St. Augustine, or Guatama Buddha. In modern times, theories have been adapted, modified, and integrated to meet the demands of peoples with advanced knowledge and fewer unknowns to fear.

There have been various forms of rites and ritual throughout history; these provide organizational strength and unity. The concept of myth in primitive religions illustrates both theory and ritual. In imitating the mythical accounts of supernatural beings, archaic and primitive men repeated and participated in the primordial act of creating cosmos out of chaos, and this implied establishing and maintaining norms and forms as well as order.[6] While myth plays a lesser role in modern religion, it is still prevalent.

Ritual in religion helps control human behavior through developing role expectations for members. It also provides for mass participation in worship, which encourages institutional conformity as well as industrial subservience to instructional mores.

The sociological dimension provides for the sense of belonging, which is vital for religious institutional health. It calls into service both the theory and ritual dimensions of religion, for both open up routes for social unity and purpose under a common belief bond. Both theory and ritual justify adherence to a wide range of values whether they are transcendental, moral, or sacred, or combinations of these. Historically, methods of control have been physical, material, and symbolic. Normative power or use of symbols to control behavior is generally used by religious institutions in the twentieth century. Methods of control in normative organizations are generally more dependent on personal qualities or influence. Individuals with these qualities combine positional normative power as in the status of priest with personal power such as a persuasive personality.[7] These charismatic leaders are often founders of bureaucratic organizations.

Each of these dimensions offers methods of social control and organizational structure with a hierarchy of authority. While methods, ritual, theory, or leadership may differ depending on the stage of social advance, religion is found universally among all human beings. Primitive religion often used fear of the unknown as a source of control and power, but despite vast increases in scientific knowledge the influence of religion today is still very strong. Scientists themselves are often most religious, many of them believing that man and nature are equally unexplainable without God, and concurring with Kant[8] that "Two things fill the mind with ever new and increasing admiration and awe, the oftener and the more steadily we reflect upon them: the starry heavens above and the moral law within."[9] Nevertheless, peoples in modern civilizations tend to consult experts in secular fields in their attempts to control and manage physical and social environments. Accountants, medical specialists, scientists, economists, computer analysts, and management systems experts are frequently consulted to determine ways and means of more effective control of specific areas of environment. The all-encompassing methodologies of the Judeo-Classical-Christian era seen in the work of Aristotle, St. Thomas, Plato, and St. Augustine have been replaced by narrow fields of specialization where experts are highly trained within perimeters of structured fields. The comprehensive systems of master analysts wherein most fields of inquiry were covered have been replaced by teams of specialists, each in one narrowly defined area of investigation. Thus, whereas historically one might consult a religious leader or an oracle for answers to most of men's questions, modern times tend to provide multi-approaches to these questions. A religious leader might refer a parishioner to a psychiatrist, law enforcement agency, marriage counselor, medical clinic, or social welfare agency. Thus, a cooperative team approach provides responses to individual and social needs. Whenever individuals are concerned with value judgments as to the rightness or wrongness of a given act or belief, however, religion is called upon to provide aims and directions. These aims are often directed toward the development of an internalized set of values which enable an individual to control emotions and act in a disciplined manner. Thus, social control is attained through efforts by religious institutions to give individuals the tools by which they may attain emotional and intellectual self-control.[10] Modern religious beliefs often stress open encounters, free from restraints, to explore individual choices and meanings. In a sense, social control in these systems involves participation in dialogue.

Scope of Religious Authority

The scope of religious authority depends on the level of knowledge a culture has attained. Primitive man attributed vast powers to supernatural forces. Religious authorities provided socially accepted structures and a system of rewards and punishments. With few competing sources of information, the word of religious authorities was accepted, honored, and obeyed. Since these authorities were men with strengths and weaknesses, it was only natural that they frequently sought to extend and promulgate their spheres of influence through vast powers accruing to them through dogma, tradition, and unquestioned adherence to and acceptance of their doctrine. Religious institutions evolved which codified and provided a carefully organized system of hierarchy of authority. Justification and reinforcement of this system consisted of transcendental, moral, and sacred values. The religious institution became imbued with properties over and above those of the reality it represented. The institution developed a modern bureaucratic organizaton which, as Max Weber pointed out, contained an authority structure of the rational-legal type whereby rules and prerogatives of authority became separated from the person and personality of the wielder of authority. Thus, charismatic founders of religion were eulogized in perpetuity through bureaucratic organizations. This organizational structure developed, in addition to its maintenance system, an elaborate formal role pattern, clear authority structure, adaptive structures, and explicit formulation of ideology to provide for strengthening of system norms and to support the authority structure.[11] Religious institutions therefore developed a corporate identity which allowed them to exist apart from the personalities functioning within the organization.

Religion and Adaptability

Religious institutions have been maintained amazingly strong and durable through the ages, and organizational structure has been an important force in this permanence. Within the organizational structure, religious institutions solve four basic problems which Talcott Parsons described as adaptation, goal achievement, integration, and latency.[12] Religious institutions have continually accommodated their systems to the demands of the society served and in addition have continually sought to influence society. Fuse[13] states that religion managed to survive as one of man's viable social institutions partly because it has accommodated itself to a secular society and rationalized its demands and claims. In a study of attitudes of orthodox beliefs over a forty-year period, Eckhardt[14] finds a marked tendency to religious submersion and conformity rather than compassion. Religion historically has been a conservative force operating to effect compromise and reconciliation with existing political systems. Thus, religion has been and is a viable force in dictatorships, democracies, monarchies, and oligarchies as well as in Communist governments. Caporale[15] maintains that the process of adaptation to new social environments provides avenues of new church influence. Eckhardt[16] believes that continuing efforts are underway to modify church positions toward nonconformism and nonviolence. In a study of the Jesus People Movement, Balswick[17] finds attitudes and goals of counterculture, subjectivity, informality, and spontaneity with new media and communication forms emerging. He notes that in order to decrease the new group's potential power, established churches might well encompass the movement's ability to adapt to a new social environment. On the other hand, Balswick suggests that a new church could grow out of the movement. The present-day influences modifying institutional functions and aims are to be found in membership pressure, exertions of religious power, social ostracism, use of hallucinogens in subcultures, and antiestablishment movements, in addition to legitimate doctrinal reformations.

Goal achievement is attained in religious institutions through careful elucidation of objectives in broad transcendental or supernatural terms. The Ten Commandments provide objectives for social moral obligations; these objectives are so broad in connotation that they have been interpreted in different ways at different periods in history. Resources may be mobilized to provide enforcement of these rules of conduct. Historically, the death penalty was invoked for infidelity, theft, or murder, but in recent times, in response to changes in social mores and folkways, interpretation of the Ten Commandments has been modified. Perhaps the best example of this change is the evolution of process theology and situational ethics. Joseph Fletcher[18] indicates that decisions should be made in the context of a given situation and not be based on any concept of the preordained rightness or wrongness of an act. This ethical relativism is a form of religious adaptation to social changes and traditional modes of thinking. Ahlstrom[19] observes that this shift toward situational ethics is based in part on a deep change in the presuppositional substructures of the twentieth-century mind. He suggests that as a result of the impact of science, relativism, and technology, there is an increased suspicion of the supernatural and awareness of contradictions in ideal and actual, profession and performance. Bianchi[20] points to a shift in religious doctrine from the classicial-conservative to historical-progressive position. He believes the doctrine of infallibility is being seriously questioned, and in the church's response to this challenge he sees the development of a flexible and situational ethic. Certainly this viewpoint seems to be close to Auguste Comte's central theme regarding historical progress in human thought and action. In a study of dissenting Catholics, Berzano[21] notes that their most evident features are fluidity, experimentation, and anti-institutionalism. Bruce and Sims,[22] in a research study of radical left university students, conclude that apostates are not converts to radical ideology in any significant proportion, but are clearly disenchanted with society and more critical of its basic institutions. Critical disengagement rather than substitute conversion was the response of the students studied. Harrison[23] reports that the new religious movements are distinguished by spontaneity, with a sense of direction by the Holy Spirit, often speaking in tongues and prophecy as well as immerged in Pentecostal friendship networks. The trend in the new movements is to lead intense devotional lives and to display great tolerance for diverse styles and varying degrees of involvement. Such tolerance facilitates broad recruitment and tends to be present in most of the successful social movements. It should be noted that rather than decrease the power and authority of religion, these shifts make religious institutions more viable and permanent in culture.

Through the ages, it has not been uncommon for religious organizations to modify their aims and directions during times of social upheaval and then slowly return to their conservative position as society becomes more passive.

In integrating members into the organization, religious institutions have been able to invoke a high degree of loyalty. Whether such integration is developed through extraorganizational loyalties[24] or through symbiotic relationships, religious organizations have been able to unify memberships to strive for transcendental values and ends. Other means to achieving this integration have been ritual and ceremony. These processes, coupled with awe, honor, and worship involving concepts of altruism, unselfishness, and universal love, create adherence to religion. Use of the same concepts in the face of social change is accomplished through adaptation of meanings and intent of ritual. Rituals vary from elaborate to simple and are important in creating a religious consciousness which unifies emotive and intellectual behavior. The universality of religious role and function throughout the world of men is noted in Braeker's[25] study of Asian religion. He finds that the teachings and dogmatic variations of Buddhism in Southeast Asian countries paved the way for adaptation of goal achievements to past and present political systems in those countries. In China, the general populace has tended to identify Buddhism with national consciousness and with independence movements since the fifteenth century. Mainland China has, he continues, recognized the vital role and function of religious structure in Southeast Asia. Its long-term foreign policy has stimulated the creation of a Chinese Buddhist Academy to push its political ideology. Thus, a two-way adaptation operates in religious institutions: first, they adapt to social changes, and second, they find political and other social institutions adapting to their modes of operation.

Latency, or the maintenance of religious organizations' motivational and cultural patterns, may also be noted through the use of guidelines and regulations for chuch membership. Housekeeping rules set up by religious institutions indicate perimeters of behavior within which a member may operate. An example is the Roman Catholic Church's historical emphasis on increasing childbirth. Interfaith marriage is frequently termed grounds for expulsion from membership. However, social change has required modification and adaptability even within religious institutions. Formerly restrictive rules imposed on individual members are being eliminated for institutional survival. Parsons[26] refers to an ecumenical integration which is coming to the fore based on the activist forces operating in society. He sees evidence that the ecumenical process is beginning to transcend the Judeo-Christian world and is bringing about a new relationship with other great religions of the world and the societies in which these religions exist. Hadden[27] reiterates this new relationship by noting that an increasingly pluralistic world has forced the church to alter its doctrine to remain relevant in a changing environment. He views ecumenicism as the thrust of institutional survival. The fact that religious institutions have been amazingly durable and permanent in all social orders does not result totally from their ability to adapt to social changes but must also be attributed to man's basic need for religion. Henderson[28] observes that religion is as fundamental to man's nature as his need for food.

Aspects of Life Controlled Through Religion

Religion and Education

Historically, education was a responsibility of religious institutions. Moral indoctrination with rote memorization of classical subjects, coupled with rigorous discipline, was the diet of early church schools. Curriculum was taught through the particular religious doctrine espoused. Rippa[29] points to Cotton Mather's dictum that teachers not only pray with scholars daily, but take occasion, from the public sermons and from remarkable occurrences in their neighborhood, frequently to inculcate the lessons of piety in children. Although twentieth-century Western civilization for the most part maintains a doctrine of separation of religious and public education, there remain powerful methods of religious control over public education. Some are vested in local and state boards of education whose membership is largely derived from special interest groups; members frequently instigate investigations of curriculum and textbook materials, and through pressure, textbooks are often changed. Teacher conduct and behavior in public schools are also frequently criticized by religious groups, who sometimes bring pressure to have offending individuals removed from public schools. The degree of success of this pressure depends largely on the social environment and culture where it occurs. Liberal areas are less influenced by these forces than traditionally conservative communities. Hence, religion still plays a universally important role in education in Western civilization.

Religion retains direct power in public education in Central and South America, where religious organizations instituted, maintained, and supported the educational system. Today, although the state maintains many schools, informal ties with the church remain strong and durable. Because of the instability of public education in Latin America, religious schools provide a measure of permanence, order, and stability, particularly in secondary and higher education.

There is a worldwide renewal of concern for moral and ethical education, together with what Harold Fallding[30] refers to in his book, *Sociology of Religion*, as the needed balance between material and spiritual concerns. Fallding writes of the totality of the human experience where persons will have to learn to experience health and well-being; to love learning and cultivation; and to involve themselves in leisure, pleasure, and worship. Smart[31] suggests that a balance will have to be found for the opposition in learning about religion and the living power of religion. The influence of religion in education is either direct or indirect, formal or informal, progressive or retrogressive, depending on the social, political, economic, and cultural environment in which schools are located.

In the broader sense, the curriculum of schools reflects the prevailing attitudes, folkways, and mores of the community. Thus, expressions of traditionalism to antiestablishment counterculture religion may be found within our schools. On a broader scale, indirect influences in schools may be found in the international efforts of the World Council of Churches, National Council of Churches, and Free Church Federal Council, organizations seeking modern church unification through either interdenominational efforts or ecumenical movements. The educational themes of universal brotherhood and internationalism are found in many school curriculums.

Religion and Marriage

Religion continues to play an important role in family life and marriage. The increase in the number of one-parent family heads and in the divorce rate has decreased neither the scope of religion in marriage nor the role of marriage as an institution. Radically changing mores and folkways have not negated the institution of marriage, and religious organizations in general support and receive support from the institution. Since religious organizations operate on the basis of ordered systems and traditional modes of thought, it is advantageous to support the stability of the family. One long-standing method of maintaining religious organizations, intermarriage between members of a given faith, is breaking down as societies become more mobile and provincialism declines. It remains true, however, that marriage, the family, and religious institutions have long been and continue to be mutually supporting agencies. Churches have always recognized the necessity of reaching the young for that purpose and maintain Sunday Schools where they indoctrinate students into accepted rules of conduct and reinforce acceptable behavior patterns. Channels of influence from Sunday School through adult Bible study groups provide activities for all family members and; by encouraging virtuous and moral living, aim to protect the family.

Abdal-Ati[32] provides an alternative to contemporary Western marriages which today are too often ending in divorce and are negatively affecting the children. He suggests that the Moslem family ideal should be explored. Members of Islam are bound together in a web of reciprocal relationships to God. Marriage is a contract and a sacrament, a commitment and fulfillment, and is rooted in a system based on individual conscientiousness of societal care. Many young people in the West who are searching for alternatives to Western marriage are joining Eastern religious groups as well as counter- or subcultural groups.

Many churches are making an effort to adapt to more flexible social mores, For instance, many religious institutions are cooperating with health and welfare agencies in the dissemination of birth control information, even though historically sex outside of wedlock has been discouraged by churches. Birth control is more widely supported by the religious institutions of advanced industrial nations than of underdeveloped countries, where large families are seen as an economic necessity and as an important end result of marital union. Most churches in these countries consider birth control practices a sin. In all societies, however, the church offers families supportive service. The social contacts and informal activities give them a sense of belonging. Many religious leaders are trained in counseling so that they can respond to parishioners' needs in the areas of drug abuse and sexual problems.

Religion and Health

The semireligious rites of the witch doctors who invoke spiritual powers to cure dreaded, unknown diseases have been superseded by modern medical treatment based on advanced research and applied technology. Religious institutions continue to maintain social control in the areas of health and treatment of the diseased by operating and staffing many hospitals, rest homes, and medical schools. Clergymen work in medical centers, and hospital chapels are found in most treatment centers. Medical schools maintained by religious organizations throughout the world are dedicated to the service of mankind and provide excellent channels for spreading church doctrine and influence. A secondary but important purpose of religious institutions involved in medical work is to fulfill theological functions for the dead and dying. The church sees one from the cradle to the grave, and this lifelong connection with its members gives religious institutions unique and powerful control. The sense of security it provides its members often becomes more dear and precious with the passing years.

Religion and science are united in the idea that faith is often as important as medical treatment in the cure of disease. Accordingly, increasing attention is being paid to the emotional health and attitudes of the dying. William James spoke of the will to believe as important in reconciling man to God and to health, and religious institutions have provided the means by which men can develop this will to believe. They further encourage their members to conduct themselves in such a manner as to promote physical and mental well-being. Oliver,[33] in discussing Block's hope principle, notes that eschatology (a religious language about the future which cannot be tested in ordinary ways) is a viable contribution to the individual and society.

Religion and Politics

The church and the state were united for centuries with kinds ordained by the clergy and claiming to serve by divine right. The power of the church in the state is seen clearly in the political history of Latin America.

The political constitutions of most modern nations, however, provide for separation of church and state. Nevertheless, religious institutions are powerful control agents in government and politics. In some countries—and even in the United States until recent years—divorced men have not easily attained public office. Religious doctrines have been so inculcated through teaching and preaching the sanctity of the marriage covenant that divorce frequently is not acceptable for governmental leaders. Codes of behavior are rigorously enforced for political leaders through religious agencies that often function as informal watchdogs. Although there have been many value judgment changes in recent times, great pressures of public opinion can be brought to bear to ensure that public figures live up to ideal religious codes and standards.

Religious institutions also exert social control through their economic wealth, although the amount of pressure they thereby bring on political institutions varies from nation to nation. Because economic wealth has continually tended to place religious institutions squarely in the corner of the vested landed gentry and propertied interests, they have long had a strong conservative influence on politics. Through their formal and informal channels of communication, religious institutions can sometimes dictate acceptable and unacceptable role behavior in political institutions.

Religion and Authority

Loyalty to religious institutions has been developed through fear, physical coercion, or threats of banishment from the group. Crucifixion, excommunication, and social ostracism have been instruments to ensure organizational discipline and loyalty; these punishments have been invoked in the name of deity to punish evil. In earlier times, anti-organizational behavior, i.e., nonconformity, was viewed and dealt with as a sin to be punished. In modern times, such methods of social control have generally been rejected by ever more enlightened societies. Persuasion, symbolic values, and appeal to altruism (the brotherhood of mankind, love of one another) now provide some control of members' behavior. Specific forms of religious control depend on the degree of openness of a society or culture. Closed societies, which are far less permissive than open societies, are found as frequently in advanced as in underdeveloped social orders.

Religion and the Future

Religion appears to be firmly established in the world, although its power to control individual and social behavior varies according to society. Yet, it is universally accepted as a force that must be reckoned with. It may be hypothesized that religion tends to exert more control in times of social disorder and upheaval than in times of calm and peace. Physical coercion, social ostracism, and excommunication are occasionally witnessed even in advanced industrial societies in the twentieth century when such societies are in a period of stress.

The ability of religious institutions to adapt to changing mores and folkways gives them great resiliency. The future of religious institutions will continue to depend on how responsive they are to social forces and to the demands of new challenges. They can contribute a great deal to resolving national and international crises and in the future might well provide the basis for unifying men and nations.

The relation of religion to processes of stability, change, and control is an area for continued study. Communications networks between individuals and groups within society are intertwined with religious beliefs affecting the social systems. In the future, there will be increased application of research techniques of sociology to the study of the role and function of religion within social systems; in such as study, an interdisciplinary approach appears to offer the most promise. Drawing on economic, cultural, environmental, and educational research will enable sociologists to study the multitude of bridges between individuals and society.

Notes

1. See Joseph S. Roucek, *Social Control* (New York: D. Van Nostrand Co., 1947), and James Van Patten, Joseph Roucek, Michael Belok, and Martin Schoppmeyer, *Conflict, Permanency, Change and Education* (Moti Katra: Agra-3, India: Satish Book Enterprise, 1976). These sources provide the structure for this essay.

2. Quirinus Breen, *Christianity and Humanism* (Grand Rapids, Mich.: William B. Erdman's Publishing Co., 1968), p. 246.

3. Hans-Joachim Schoeps, *The Religions of Mankind* (Garden City, N.Y.: Anchor Books, 1968), p. 40.

4. Roucek, *Social Control*, p. 102.

5. For further information see Joachim Wach, *The Comparative Study of Religions*, edited by J. M. Kitagawa (New York: Columbia University Press, 1975). It is also interesting to note Auguste Comte's *System of Positive Polity* (London: Longmans, Green and Co., 1875), Vol. 2.

6. Mircea Eliade, *Myth of the Eternal Return*, translated by W. R. Trask (New York: Pantheon Books, 1954), pp. 10-11.

7. See Amitai Etzioni, *Modern Organizations* (New York: Prentice-Hall, 1964), Ch. 6.

8. Stella Van Petten Henderson, *Introduction to Philosophy of Education* (Chicago: University of Chicago Press, 1947), pp. 87-88.

9. Immanuel Kant, *Critique of Practical Reason*, translated by T. K. Abbott (London: Longmans Green, 1927), p. 260.

10. Roucek, *Social Control*, pp. 102-103.

11. Daniel Katz and Robert L. Karn, *The Social Psychology of Organizations* (New York: John Wiley and Sons, 1966), pp. 47, 54.

12. Talcott Parsons, *Structure and Process in Modern Societies* (Glencoe, Ill.: Free Press, 1960), pp. 16-96.

13. Toyamasas Fuse, "Religion, Society, and Accommodation: Some Remarks on Neo-Orthodoxy in American Protestantism," *Social Change* 12, no. 6 (1965):345-358.

14. William Eckhardt, "Religious Beliefs and Practices in Relation to Peace and Justice," *Social Compass* 21, no. 4 (1974):463-472.

15. Rocco Caporale, "The Dynamics of Hierocracy: Processes of Continuity-in-Change of the Roman Catholic System During Vatican II," *Sociological Analysis* 28, no. 2 (Summer 1967): 59-68.

16. Eckhardt, "Religious Beliefs and Practices," pp. 463-472.

17. Jack U. Balswick, "The Jesus People Movement: A Generational Interpretation," *Journal of Social Issues* 30, no. 3 (1974):23-42.

18. Joseph Fletcher, *Moral Responsibility* (Philadelphia: Westminister Press, 1947), pp. 7-29.

19. Sydney E. Ahlstrom, "The Radical Turn in Theology and Ethics: Why It Occurred in the 1960's," *Annals of the American Academy of Political and Social Science* 387 (January 1970):1-13.

20. Eugene C. Bianchi, "John XXIII, Vatican II, and American Catholicism," *Annals of the American Academy of Political and Social Science* 387 (January 1970):30-40.

21. Luigi Berzano, "Ideology and Utopia in the Diocese of Rome: Analysis of Noninstitutionalized Ecclesiastical Communities and Groups," *La Critica Sociologicia* 32 (Winter 1974-1975):71-84.

22. William Bruce and John H. Sims, "Religious Apostasy and Political Radicalism," *Journal of Youth and Adolescence* 4, no. 3 (September 1975): 207-214.

23. Michael I. Harrison, "The Maintenance of Enthusiasm: Involvement in a New Religious Movement," *Sociological Analysis* 36, no. 2 (Summer 1975): 150-160.

24. Anthony Downs, *Inside Bureaucracy* (Boston: Little, Brown, 1966), p. 157.

25. Hans Braeker, "Communism and Buddhism: On the Religious and Asia Policies of the Soviet Union and China," *Moderne Welt* 8, no. 1 (1967): 50-64.

26. Talcott Parsons, "Religion in a Modern Pluralistic Society," *Review of Religious Research* 7, no. 3 (Spring 1966):125-146.

27. Jeffrey K. Hadden, "A Protestant Paradox—Divided They Merge," *Trans-Action* 4, no. 8 (July-August 1967):63-69.

28. Henderson, *Introduction to Philosophy of Education*, p. 87.

29. Alexander Rippa, *Educational Ideas in America* (New York: David McKay Co., 1969), p. 50.

30. Harold Fallding, *The Sociology of Religion* (New York: McGraw-Hill, 1974).

31. Ninian Smart, *The Science of Religion and the Sociology of Knowledge* (Princeton, N.J.: Princeton University Press, 1973).

32. Hammerdah Abdal-Ati, "Modern Problems, Classical Solutions: An Islamic Perspective on the Family," *Family Journal of Comparative Family Studies* 5, no. 2 (Autumn 1974):37-54.

33. Harold H. Oliver, "Hope and Knowledge: The Epistemic Status of Religious Language," *Cultural Hermeneutics* 2, no. 1 (May 1974):75-88.

Kenneth V. Lottich

EDUCATION

John D. Rockefeller, III, philanthropist and practical humanist, sees man as an integral part of nature. To teach his peculiar values, one must seek a balanced and symbiotic compact with the environment—if for no other reason than that in the long run nature is stronger than man. So pragmatic humanists see man as basically good, primarily needing only to develop his inherent qualities related to love and trust, with respect for each unique individuality. Rockefeller's man-centered and institutional approach invokes a technique termed *management by objectives* and attempts to utilize "reason and collaboration" in opposition to what he views as the conventional coercion and threat.[1]

But here the reader may properly inquire, What is the role and function of teaching, or, for that matter, education itself?

Every people, in addition to their basic drive for sustenance and living space, is custodian of a characteristic culture which they seek to transmit from generation to generation. Indeed, it is solely through this process of cultural transmission that any society is competent to continue its existence. In societies where the culture is relatively simple, the young learn all that is necessary for life in the base group through ordinary daily associations and contacts, an artless form of "education." Brown and Roucek present a somewhat wider definition of this achievement, stating that it may be designated as "the sum total of the experiences which mold the attitudes and determines the conduct of both the child and the adult."[2]

Robert Hogan, professor of psychology at Johns Hopkins, agrees with the thesis that learned responses are the *sine qua non* for societal development. He sees the process as one of developing a philosophy (or ideology) of life, i.e., the shaping of such necessary moral antecedents of the group fellowship as a three-step execution.[3]

The young are educated in three stages: (1) socialization (and here the celebrated remark of H. G. Wells concerning a deprived "human" child reared away from his normal human baby culture and his consequent failure to arrive at any human or manlike plateau applies); (2) empathy, wherein the subject becomes conversant with, and part of, his given fellowship; and (3) autonomy, when as a teen-ager or culture neophyte, he develops a personal identity (although within the well-controlled close precincts of his native world).

Of course, some failures of the young may, and do, occur at any of these stages. Such failures are one of the dilemmas and discouragements of the current age. Nevertheless, some adaptation of human acculturation does appear to hallmark the induction of the juvenile into an ongoing society. It also presents an appropriate way to speak of the process of education as both a formal and informal action, although, as we intend to show, the formal school not infrequently plays a peripheral role.

History demonstrates that, as the social order becomes more complex and reaches out to a "higher" stage of social or economic development, its members tend to become quasi-specialists: warriors, farmers, traders, merchants, teachers, shamans, or priests. Thus, in an extremely complex society (the civilizations so identified by Arnold Toynbee fit this description), the inducting of the juvenile becomes a much greater task for the simple reason that now there is so much more to learn. Moreover, the individual has to adjust continually because of culture change and the multitude of new contacts and personal decisions made. Clearly, the task of instructing the young cannot be left to chance association or hit-and-miss learnings. Neither can the "apprenticeship," which is indispensable for earlier stages or ages, be invoked. Each child must be taught with a definite goal in mind. The objective of society thus becomes the aims of that society. In order to guide the training of young members of a group along lines deemed essential to the continued security of the society, schools are established as basic engines of social control. Education, whether engineered by the fellowship, the family, or the state, signifies the acceptance of the worth of cultural continuity on the part of a given tribe, clan, fellowship, or nation.

Ever since the genesis of that stage in biological development that distinguished man from lower species of creations,[4] formal education, as typified by the evolution of the school, has been considered the province of the state—whether of a priestly, tribal, imperial, or national entity. Formal education, through its agency, the school, is presumed to develop the young into the desired types of citizenry. This procedure is infinitely more rigid in the totalitarian, or even paternally despotic, regimes than in the so-called democratic or republican states.[5]

Yet, despite its form or philosophy, the state generally deems that its vested interest in achieving an effective body of like-minded participants is secured through the efforts of its formal school system. Although not so rigidly structured as in a variety of other countries, formal education in the United States is, by its Constitution, remanded to the political entity identified as the "State." The presumed autonomy of each of its fifty states, however, is becoming more and more fictional, regardless of local machinery or appurtenances to be described in further analysis, as the interpretations and dicta of the U.S. Office of Education—an integral part of the cabinet post designated Health, Education and Welfare—are propounded and implemented through constitutional amendments and, the Supreme Court's interpretations.

Religious institutions, too, when they choose to operate basic schools within the United States, commonly make them quite mutually agreeable to the country's political mores and patriotic judgments. Consequently, it may be observed, without bias, that public or parochial schools in the United States mirror the achieved culture of the American nation as it has arisen historically. To further this end, schools have been designated to provide an education for all classes of society, without prejudice to color or ethnic origin, at a minimum cost to individual members, providing, in many cases, free textbooks, free lunches, and free transportation.

Philosophy of Education

J. Donald Butler identifies four philosophies in the exercise of education: naturalism, idealism, realism, and pragmatism.[6] Of these, naturalism is the easiest defined: within man there is nothing that transcends the natural, no soul, no world of ideas. Idealism, sidestepping its name, deems reality to be made up of minds or ideas. i.e., ideaism. Realism focuses its attention on the human problem "What is real?" and insists that the world as we see it is not subject to mind. *It exists.* Pragmatism places the utility of things higher than the knowledge of things—use is all important, thus favoring problem-solving. (Rockefeller's pragmatic humanism combines a certain experimentation with the thesis that man is essentially good.)

For those who would prefer more simplicity in their apprehension of philosophy of education, two rubrics only need be suggested: (1) traditionalism or essentialism, including the perennialists, even the disciplinists; and (2) progressivism, embracing the reconstructionists or planned program advocates. The naturalists, of course, would share the progressive post on the more liberal left, while moralists and other rightists would side with the traditionalists. In the historical evolution of American education, traditionalists merit the designation "Jeffersonians," while the advocates of popularism in education, "Jacksonian."[7]

Education for Citizenship

Schools operate in anticipation of producing more discerning, if not more intelligent, members through its selection of subject matter, courses of study, and methods employed. Each of these derives from the philosophy of the school and this philosophy, in turn, from philosophy in general. Totalitarian states demand an infinitely more supervised and regulative variety of method. Indeed, their expectation of doctrinal continuity rests on the indoctrination of youth with not only the consistent views appropriate to the particular ideology under which they live, but also veneration for their current leaders or political ideologues. Their philosophy embraces a peculiar type of idealism along with the sheer pragmatism of action.

Charles E. Merriam has said it well: "the political society constantly seeks to develop and maintain its solidarity through the impression of its traditions upon young and old alike," for "the fund of common memories is an important possession of the tribe or nation; its cohesive value is very large, and it is never neglected in any system."[8] Thus, sociologists or any student of social control may well maintain that the difference between education in democratic and totalitarian countries is merely one of degree—although they may see a vanishing parallel as cruelty, force, or some other brutal method of suasion is indicated.

As yet, however, no universally accepted or exact meaning for the expression "citizenship education" has been arrived at although, as indicated above, the problem becomes much simpler when determining its import within Communist or Fascist regimes. In the West (non-Communist Europe, North America, and parts of Latin America), citizenship education has come to be identified with the rights and duties of the "good citizen," including his liabilities within a democratic society. Such an admittedly narrow description emphasizes the political inferences of a participating citizenship. Moreover, in an all-embracing sense, citizenship education is related to all ethical, moral, social, and economic aspects of living as well as the cited party aspect. Thus, the present trend is toward this latter and more inclusive demarcation. The school must become its supreme surrogate.

Contemporary perception of citizenship education demands that it not be a curriculum for social studies classes alone, but that whole school and total community aspects and contacts are necessarily mandated. While, legitimately, basic knowledge must never be ignored, attitudes, behavior, and social skills are further imperatives. The mental health concept of the well-adjusted individual within his society has to be the chief foundation for an effective citizenship. The development of such a position appears likewise to be the proper goal of citizenship education, much as the reduction of rank ethnocentrism and prejudice can lead to individual and group social effectiveness.

Social Control and the Family

Long before the formal school took charge of the subject to be educated within its broad or narrow scope—depending on time, place, or philosophy —the family was the child's most intimate instructor and the agent of the broader culture group, such as the ethnic group, nation, social class, and (frequently) its religious orientation. In this close manner, the child absorbed the particular ways of his family's class, race, nationality, and religion. The many studies of "simpler" societies described by cultural and social anthropologists provide an essential base for the comprehension of socialization processes within the American (or European) fraternity. They are especially important for understanding the possibilities for variation in the socialization of the individual when cultural conditions are altered.

Even more directly related to the educational problem is the expanding knowledge concerning the relationship of formal education to the several cultural subgroups: e.g., one subculture can relate to the product of an integrated school, another to one segregated, yet a third to the graduates of a scholastic academy, collegiate institution, or private school.

Conversely, education of varying degrees can assist one person to achieve membership in a different social group from that in which he was born or raised, to transcend his family limits, or, in extreme cases, to suffer retrogression. There are likewise individuals who have learned, through education, to withdraw from all previous associations—to become rebellious or inconoclastic. Therefore, education, as indicated, can help reduce (or augment) social mobility; or maintain or diminish the distance between social groups. Studies of the relation of schools and colleges to social class, social distance, social mobility, and ethnic relationships generally establish the fact that American public education is geared to middle-class family expectations and values. They show further that lower-class pupils either must learn middle-class mores or suffer discrimination, or even grave social disadvantage, until they apprehend the system and learn to conform.

Classic American novels dealing with status or social class such as *An American Tragedy*, *Washington Square*, and *The Great Gatsby* surely serve to conform this sociological conclusion. On the other hand, Donald Reeves' *Notes of a Processed Brother* details the struggle and success of a brilliant black boy who, according to his own testimony, learned to work against, for, and finally through the American socioeducational value system in his transit of a trio of leading American educational institutions.[9]

Social attitudes directed toward groups other than one's own particular cluster reveal that a realization of the distinctions set up by peers and family are well under way by age five and that by fourteen they have become crystallized in the majority of children. Sometimes such attitudes do remain subject to modification by new social or educational experiences.[10]

Social Effectiveness Through Education

It is commonly agreed that education over an extended period of time and in an immediate fashion, through the specific direction of those activities deemed beneficial to society, can effect desired behavior; and that the greater the degree of education amassed, the more broadened the educand. This follows because education's role is to confront (or modify) behavior patterns, attitudes, understandings, interests, and competencies.

Thus, the major business of schools as engines of social control are (1) to create in youth an understanding of and an appreciation for his native social order; (2) to act as agencies of society to conserve and to transmit, by deliberate inculcation, the cultural values of the established order to succeeding generations; (3) coincidentally, to provide the learner with sufficient training and tools to enable him, hopefully, to exist economically; and (4) to ensure social progress in the group, insofar as any institution can assure its own "progress."

Interpreted either strictly or loosely, education mirrors the Gestalt of its society; yet, conversely, education may (and quite often does) reflect its special influence on society in return. Thus is established what may loosely be called "a moving equilibrium." If this constitutes "progress," then one may rightly assume that education has become doubly significant. In such manner, the sociological approach to education becomes simply another method of interpreting the evidence of learning as "social control."

In its educational phase, social control attempts to mold its subjects according to a diversity of social purposes, e.g., training the subjects' emotions to reflect the subtleties of his individual culture, that is, to exhibit those general tendencies or "peculiarities" falsely considered by chauvinists to be inherent "racial" or group characteristics; to develop a respect for its ideologies, folkways, mores, codes, laws, and institutions; and to ensure personalities that either consciously or unconsciously will contribute to that culture their acquired and, by now, ingrained belief of what they think their proper role of social helpfulness should be.

The social knowledge amassed tends to affect the entire community since the social effectiveness of individuals in many areas of life is profoundly influenced by their education. The new knowledge influences not only demonstrated abilities, but in like manner also voluntary activities, personal mobility, fads, attitudes, misconceptions, superstitions, and even occupational adjustment. So it is that the community as well as the customary cultural requirements must be taken into consideration when educational planning is contemplated.

Community Requisites

The initiation of any school program should be undertaken only when anteceded by a careful analysis to ascertain what the community requires from the school and what, in turn, the school can gain from its community. Although a basic (Jeffersonian) curriculum ought to be offered in all communities, many programs may be modified to become more closely related or geared to the activities and interests of the given locale. Thus, in many communities (so taking a leaf from the totalitarian book) provisions have been made for the leisure-time activities of both children and adults. It should be stated quickly, however, that communities place these activities in democratic perspective rather than invoking the goals of the totalitarians. Obviously, communities differ in their bare physical requirements. Salvation of the ecology, conservation of natural resources, development and preservation or implementation of communication facilities, and culture patterns—all these must be part of the school if it is to serve as a bona fide social development institution.

The American Educational Evolution

Two lines in the historical evolution of the American school system are generally discerned: the New England model and the county system of the American South and Central states. The origin of these sites of local control is important to an understanding of the sociology of the U.S. school, for with a few exceptions related to the private and/or parochial school situations, the mechanics of control shown here represents both the advantage and disadvantage of developing school agencies in a pristine setting.

In New England, the first unit of a public school system was based on the "town," a terminology that may be unclear to many citizens outside that area. The New England town, varying in size up to perhaps as much as forty square miles (and not to be confused with the "township" of the Middle and Far West), was based on the historical course of settlement and political-geographical assimilation. In a process somewhat akin to that of cell division, citizens of an older town might migrate and form a new entity at the periphery of the old, complete with the several appurtenances of the former, i.e., a village, church, school, and perhaps a port or river "city." Selectmen chosen as representatives held authority for the affairs of the new town, although this power, both in practice and in theory, frequently was foreshortened, or even abrogated, by the town's citizens who periodically assembled at their "town hall."

While democratic indeed, such a process did not ensure large financial or even philosophical commitments to education. As the population of the town grew it became expedient to mandate a "moving school" which held sessions for several months in the various segments of the town; and next, to divide the area into "districts," each sharing in responsibility (and, of course, finances, which by now had shrunk to small and frequently inadequate proportions). Yet, the institution persisted and actually attracted a great deal of loyalty, if not respect, for its endeavor.[11]

In the South, the units were larger because of agricultural necessities and the nature of settlement there. Following the old English model, a county was usually the unit of local government and of educational planning, when such planning was not done by individual effort (as frequently was the case, especially in the Tidewater area). Further west, a combination of county and township developed. This township is not to be identified with the New England town; it is merely a conveniently sized geographical or population entity thought suitable for political and, later, educational efforts. Yet, in some regions the township, with its trustees, held a virtual autonomy; in others, the county became the arbiter and the county superintendent wielded real administrative clout.

In about the middle of the nineteenth century, the office of city superintendent became popular and this office, too, for its area, held close command—excepting sometime strictures now imposed by rising state legislatures and by the state superintendency from 1837. Yet, in the city and in the county, parish, or township units, board members (or sometimes trustees) retained genuine authority over the schools, the teachers, and the curriculum. They often had great powers, even extending to prescribing dress, actions, and proper associates for their pedagogical employees.

Fortuitously, well into the twentieth century the federal Office of Education exercised little or no power over the states (being circumscribed by the U.S. Constitution); it was largely, if not exclusively, a normative, fact-finding, or statistical-reporting organization. Foreign visitors stood amazed at a structure that was in such vivid contrast to that generally operated by the governments of Europe and Asia.[12]

But on May 17, 1954, the Supreme Court, in a landmark decision, held that in Brown v. Board of Education (Topeka, Kansas) separate schools for whites and blacks violated the Fourteenth Amendment to the federal Constitution, in spite of the 1896 Plessy v. Ferguson verdict that had held them to be legal. Chief Justice Earl Warren wrote that the segregation of blacks from others of similar age and qualifications "generates a feeling of inferiority as to their status in the community." Less than a year later, the court mandated that "all deliberate speed" be applied to the integration of black and while schools, schools that were more prevalent in the South but de facto in many Northern and Western communities.

The effect of this determination on the antecedent authority of city and local school boards as institution was to sublimate local tradition and/or feeling and to reduce the board's authority, historically derived, to a serious degree. Subsequently, a great deal of friction ensued (and continues), with dangerous confrontations in Little Rock, New Orleans, Mississippi, and Alabama. Eventually, problems also arose in Boston and Louisville, where busing as a means of effecting integration became a thorny and continuing issue.

Such agitation moved north in 1968, when under the authority of Title VI of the newly enacted Civil Rights Act, legislation prohibiting the use of federal funds for any activity involving discrimination made pertinent a suit against the school board of South Holland (a suburb of Chicago). Soon boards in California, New York, and Gary, Indiana, were also involved in such suits. Our purpose here is not to detail the action stemming from *Blocker* v. *Board of Education of Manhasset, New York, Bell* v. *School City of Gary* or *Balabin* v. *Rubin*. Suffice it to say that, for all the conventional fiscal purposes, the fulcrum of authority had now passed from the local boards to Washington, D.C.[13]

Before looking at a monolithic structure in the nation's capital, which is the current mode for social and legal dominion of manners, morals, and social cohesion, let us again consider the historical purpose of schools and education. According to Charles A. Beard, its task is "to guard, cherish, advance, and make available in the life of coming generations the funded and growing wisdom, knowledge, and aspirations of the race."[14] Although on the surface Beard's statement appears merely to be a truism, upon closer inspection it will be found that building the mechanics and providing the personnel for such an essential task is anything but simple. The facts show that a vast, highly indigenous, establishment arose over the approximate four centuries of the American national existence, First developed as a colonial appanage and then as a democratic republic, it was geared to the process of fostering the mental and moral development of its citizens and their offspring in the direction (a la Beard) of as durable and virtuous a mode as made possible by their community and state. Although the debate has widened to encompass the matter of the relative contributions of New England and the South to the process, philosophy, and product, as of 1977 it can truthfully be said that nowhere does one find such a conglomeration of institutions as has developed within the American public school complex for the achievement and furtherance of its aims.

The American School Board Authority

Following Yeager,[15] it is apparent that the U.S. local and state-operated common school has become the principal and highly operative socializing device for general induction of childhood into the American culture.

The organization for education within the state is truly an extraordinary thing. The federal Constitution grants each state authority over its educational apparatus, although the federal Office of Education has now begun to assume more and more control through civil rights legislation passed by Congress and through its custodianship of the funds voted by Congress to sustain court decisions and enhance their enforcement.

The state office is, in turn, both augmented and circumscribed by various other agencies of the state and local government and personnel associations. To catalogue these briefly, one must list (1) professional organizations, including state and commonwealth educational associations and units of the American Federation of Teachers, state vocational education bodies, state library associations, state historical associations, fine arts and scientific societies, and many more; and (2) auxiliary agencies such as the Congress of Parents and Teachers, State Federation of Business Women's Clubs, Inter-scholastic Athletic Associations, Safety Councils, school service organiza-tions, and civic, patriotic, and religious groups—all concerned with the organization and policies (to say nothing of the philosophy) of the schools. Generally, the membership in such auxiliary agencies is elective.

In addition, there are myriad consultation groups whose counsel to the state superintendent of public instruction or highest state school office becomes highly barometric. Among these are the state office staff, frequently made up of influential state and national figures with thorough experience and higher education training; the presidents of state teachers' colleges and some liberal arts colleges; the deans of university schools (or colleges) of education; and tenured professors of the college (or school) of education faculties. Then there are the district, county, and city superintendents of schools; a number of influential secondary and elementary school principals (from whose ranks the superintendent may have come); and other ad hoc groups that make up the state superintendent's consultative quorum. Even further than this, one finds an overlapping with other state departments, including the attorney-general's office as well as the offices of health, highway, agriculture, motor vehicles, welfare, publicity, and ecology. And, of course, the state office must have national contacts with the U.S. Office of Education, the National Education Association, national teachers' union bodies, the American Council on Education, American Library Association, National Council of PTAs, Federal Bureau of Vocational Education, and UNESCO. Tangential to these are the Peace Corps and Work Corps (national).

At the local level, much of the foregoing is duplicated, though on a smaller scale. The local boards on the city, county, or township level are chosen by the people and are generally unsalaried and untrained. The fact that they are the dispensers of public funds, from the locality and state, as well as from the federal government, suggests that both the philosophy and execution of education can, at best, but suffer.

The Illusion of Power

Bendiner[16] reports the Hobson's choice now facing these citizen-staffed local (and sometimes state) agencies which are so beset with the paradox of cultural aspiration and enfeebled dominion. The problems are manifold: philosophy, wherein the devotees of progressivism continue to debate the essentialists or Jeffersonians; the decline of the city and the flight to the suburbs which not only reduces the tax base but also leaves unrepresentative distributions of cultural or ethnic groupings within the central city; continued strife over busing or other related recourses to equalize education;

and the extended expense of rehabilitating school buildings at the core and providing structures appropriate to changed conditions and philosophies at the periphery. Taxpayers' revolts, mothers' marches, and opposition to the school's increasing secularization tend to further reduce the effectiveness of the American board of education. Indeed, the accent on humanistic education, believed by some to be a godless emphasis and a challenge to Christian values, has, along with busing, affirmative action (quota enrollments and teacher percentages), and the new anti-sex discrimination enforcements, become a rallying cry for both pros and cons in the latest educational enbroilments.[17]

With continuing strife in Boston, the birthplace of the school committee, and unalleviated uproar in Louisville and in Indianapolis regarding busing, the board—financially dependent on the community and politically unable to cope with the rising power of federal suasion—finds itself much in the position of the fabled dodo.

In addition to these external obligations, the 1960s and the 1970s experienced the teacher rebellion. Teacher strikes for higher salaries, optimum working conditions, and representation through new affiliations— whether of the National Education Association or the American Federation of Teachers—have now become commonplace. Thus, it may well be that the American school board is fast becoming inadequate or, at the least, unrepresentative of the nation's current goals.

While the school is not solely responsible for the transmission of culture from one generation to the next, as a formal institution it has until now served society well in providing the young with the requisite linguistic, physical, social, and mathematical skills and habits.

Yet the school is not all. Throughout his lifetime the individual continues his education through his family, neighborhood, and community relations, as well as through books and the media.

Auxiliary Agencies

The existence and influence of both government and nongovernment auxiliary agencies, as extensions of the education process described above, should also be considered. Of course, the government-arranged youth groups of the U.S.S.R., China (mainland), and the captive nations of Eastern Europe wield great influence and extract a high degree of loyalty, if for no other reason than that they shrewdly capitalize on the gregarious and emulative drives of youth. The route to personal fame—and even a state stipend—may lie in the athletic or other cultural achievement of the most proficient Marxist-Leninist members of the Young Pioneers, Red Guards, or Organization Ernest Thaelmann. Proficiency may even carry the participant to Olympic fame and international recognition. While the political factor is also present, it is hardly the hurdle that American-oriented elders might judge; even the state "maturity festivals" (substitutes for Christian religious confirmation or Jewish Bar Mitzvah) tend to partake of political indoctrination as an expected goal.[18]

An extension of the educative process as it relates to the United States, though without the political orientation of the totalitarian, may include United Nations materials and the campaigns directed by UNESCO and UNICEF, adult and youth activities sponsored by the National Council of Churches, Roman Catholic and other denominational church activities, Knights of Columbus, Luther and Epworth Leagues, YMCA and YWCA, Young Hebrew Association, Big Brother and Big Sister Federations, Boy and Girl Scouts, Cub Scouts, and Campfire Girls, and activities for males and females organized by high schools, junior and senior colleges, and universities. Even professional athletic groups are not without an effect on youth—both in terms of fostering hero worship and in terms of creating the desire for emulation (with its possibility of an attendant high salary and popular prerogatives).[19]

The Youth Revolt

In the 1960s and 1970s many of the traditionally conventional sanctions of family, school, and social status appeared to be going "by the board." The issues of race relations, the Vietnam War, and other ideological clashes, including the debate on educational philosophy and the condition of the environment, were rife throughout much of the student population—indeed spilled over into adult society. Middle-class parents felt the "college crunch" as they endeavored to enroll sons and daughters. Even state-supported institutions, to say nothing of the private sector, found their going rough as they attempted to provide the usual offerings in the face of inflated costs, curriculum challenges, and a declining birthrate. The most bitter campus confrontations in the 1960s occurred at Berkeley, Columbia, Kent State, and Harvard.[20]

Both church and family influence suffered in these years. The conventional explanation of this decline in the power of family, school, and adult sanctions has been that tracing it to drugs, television, movies, and music. While possibly extreme, an illustration of the negative application of hoped-for value formation is illustrated in David A. Noebel's *Rhythms, Riots, and Revolution*. Noebel seeks to demonstrate that youth are being swayed from conventional values in religion, politics, and even personal behavior through the adoption of strange or compulsive hypnotic rhythms and through "perversion" of the revered lyrics of standard hymns or even patriotic soliloquies.[21] In fact, a near-classic of movie-making art, *The Blackboard Jungle*, took such a musical composition as its theme in delineating a contemporary inner-city American high school.

Professor Wilfrid Mellers of York University (England) reaches similar conclusions. He describes the Beatles' music (for example) as a "reborn tribal primitivism," which answers the needs of a new generation of tribal villagers. Mellers states that the composition "Things We Said Today" "hints of the possibility of a loss, with a weeping chromatic descent into triplet rhythm, with a rapid but dreamy tonal movement flowing from B-flat by way of a rich dominant ninth to E-flat: the subdominant triad of which then serves as a kind of Neapolitan cadence dropping back to the grave pentatonic G-minor."[22] Of course, this new music is not the only source of distraction from the conventional and normative control.

Speaking in Miami at a consultation on the young adult ministry sponsored by the National Council of Churches, anthropologist Margaret Mead, among others, bewailed the decline of the family as a close-knit entity and instructional unit. Mead believes that the increase of single-parent households in lieu of the old, conventional family structure will result in a society that cannot provide for its own continuity—the essence of any definition of education. She says that "We cannot go on with the present situation (leading to) a mass of children from broken homes." With youth lacking the family training opportunity, Mead feels that the future for adolescents can hold little or no reality in terms of formerly accepted values.[23] Howard M. Kahn's study of a New England milltown, "Yarborough," leads to similar conclusions.[24]

Another problem touching on the operation of public schools by boards of education and the existence of formal or informal youth groups is that posed by Title IX of the U.S. Office of Education Rights Enforcement. This regulation mandates that for any student on athletic teams to qualify for federal aid, education and athletic programs must be sexually nondiscriminatory. Housing too seems to fall within this same nondiscriminatory ukase, with the shocking result that boarding schools and colleges are finding it difficult to preserve "standards" long thought to be hallmarks of their special function. Recent reactions to HEW's regulations suggest that the enforcement of its orders may easily result in a shortfall hazard to private business's right to independent action. In the long run, it may lead to an unwarranted interference in a state's right to autonomy in matters that have long been recognized as its prerogative.[25]

New Directions

The U.S. Department of Health, Education and Welfare's recent decree ordering unisex sports leaves partisans of the schools gasping. On the one hand, the principle of equality for women—in this case, females of all ages—certainly is justified and *just*. On the other, Pandora's box has indeed been opened, for equality in all sports would appear to be impossible— women truly excel in some and men undoubtedly in others. Maturation too, poses its problems; this, as everyone knows, is a female advantage, but the stress and strain invoked by HEW's order may well be fraught with psychological—even dim, Freudian—pits. Without becoming hysterical or maudlin, let us merely mention the glee club, the wrestling team, the hockey squad, and the more ridiculous issues of dressing rooms, baths, and toilets.

Sociologist Paul Blumberg of the City University of New York sees abrupt shifts in the precipitous changes now occurring in the American culture pattern. Yet some of these shifts appear to signal, if not a return to the older values, at least some sort of accommodation to the status quo, a lifestyle based on the lure of environmentalism, the reality of living in a noncompetitive economy via-à-vis Japan and West Germany, with unfavorable trade balances and the specter of inflated $50,000 to $75,000 homes.[26]

Concurrent with the financial strain and lack of jobs which young people are facing has been the development of a changed climate among some students and their mentors. "Liberal" thought in the 1960s encouraged some questioning of the traditional positions in American life; as a result, some flew to extreme positions on the right or on the left. At the same time that cries of opposition to the so-called military-industrial complex were being uttered, new fields of endeavor were appearing as counterweights to the old. These included the computer revolution, the ever-widening electronics industry, the quest for new forms of energy, the harnessing of sun power, as well as development of peacetime nuclear strength. Such "progress" offered expanded hope for a return to the work ethic, though with contemporary variations. Some new approaches to education were also offered.

John Pfeiffer sees systems analysis as the practical approach to current problems in education and to a rebirth of individual opportunity. Pfeiffer's organizational approach to educational decision-making rests on four bases: definition of the problem by (1) clarifying objectives; (2) considering measures of effectiveness; (3) viewing constraints and uncontrollable variables; and then (4) establishing the controllable variables. In pursuit of such goals, Pfeiffer would choose a two-pronged attack: define subfunctions and alternates for each subfunction, and synthesize subsystems; and develop a model, collect data, and select the most appropriate road to the problem solution.[27] Indeed, method may ultimately revitalize the common historical approach to educational organization and planning. Yet, the basic problem remains: the schools are far too frequently labeled social liabilities rather than national assets.

A Declining Status System?

Paradoxically, in the 1960s and 1970s, just as the American standard of living neared its zenith, many of the status signs of our society seemed to have lost their former appeal. The upper, middle, and lower echelons, as described by Warner's analysis of American society, appeared to weaken. Such status symbols as enormous automobiles, ostentatious art display, lavish "coming-out parties," and other examples of conspicuous consumption began to be considered crassly vulgar. The new indices of status now included travel (not necessarily the "Grand Tour"), private clubs, bicycles, and enrollment in participatory sports.

College degrees too have lost some of their allure, although Ivy League diplomas still rate high. Richard B. Freeman reports that in the early 1970s, B.A., M.A., and Ph.D. holders faced a virtual shrinkage in the job market. Many have been forced to accept positions that are radically different from and lower-paying than, those for which their college or university specializations prepared them.[28] And, as a further sign of the times, Arizona State University reported in February 1977 that few of their 30,000 students were interested in seeking Rhodes Scholarships, being content with merely entering graduate schools of business or engineering.[29] Traditionally, the prestigious Rhodes Scholarship has been called "the million dollar award."

Obviously, the older apparatus of control, relying primarily on moral sanctions, the Horatio Alger myth, and the American Dream, has gradually, but persistently, given way to the specter of world change and social leveling.[30] At least one persistent, nagging conclusion is that personal or world relationships will eventually supersede the familial and national educational ideal.

Notes

1. John D. Rockefeller, III, *The Second American Revolution* (New York: Perennial Library, Harper and Row, 1974), pp. 44-47.

2. F. J. Brown and J. S. Roucek, eds., *Our Racial and National Minorities* (New York: Prentice-Hall, 1937), pp. xii-xiii.

3. See Patrick Young, "How We Learn Life's Rules; We Begin at Birth" *The National Observer*, January 8, 1977.

4. See Kenneth V. Lottich, "Some Distinctions Between Culture and Civilization," *Social Forces* 28, no. 3 (March 1950): 240-250.

5. See Joseph S. Roucek and Kenneth V. Lottich, *Behind the Iron Curtain* (Caldwell, Idaho: Caxton Printers, Ltd., 1964).

6. J. Donald Butler, *Four Philosophies and Their Practice in Education and Religion*, 3d ed. (New York: Harper and Row, 1968), pp. 38-39.

7. See Elmer H. Wilds and Kenneth V. Lottich, *The Foundations of Modern Education*, 4th ed. (New York: Holt, Rinehart and Winston, 1970), pp. 474-490, 500-515.

8. Charles E. Merriam, *The Making of Citizens* (New York: Charles Scribner's Sons, 1931), p. 23.

9. Donald Reeves, *Notes of a Processed Brother* (New York: Pantheon Books, Random House, 1971).

10. C. B. Stendler, *Children of Brasstown* (Champaign, Ill.: University of Illinois Press, 1949); Albert Blumenthal, *Small Town Stuff* (Chicago: University of Chicago Press, 1932).

11. See Richard B. Gross, ed., *The Heritage of American Education* (Boston; Allyn and Bacon, 1962), pp. 430-433.

12. Wilds and Lottich, *Foundations of Modern Education*, pp. 341, 349, 353, 519.

13. Robert Bendiner, *The Politics of Schools, A Crisis in Self-government* (New York: Harper and Row, 1969).

14. As quoted in William A. Yeager, *School-Community Relations* (New York: Dryden Press; Holt, Rinehart and Winston, 1951), p. 99.

15. Ibid., pp. 123ff, *passim*.

16. Bendiner, *Politics of Schools*, pp. 43-82.

17. Elizabeth L. Simpson, *Humanistic Education: An Interpretation* (Cambridge, Mass.: Ballinger, 1977).

18. See Kenneth V. Lottich, "Extracurricular Indoctrination in East Germany," *Comparative Education Review* 6, no. 3 (February 1963): 209-211; Hans Granqvist, *The Red Guard—A Report on Mao's Revolution* (New York: Praeger Publishers, 1967).

19. See Bessie L. Pierce, *Citizens' Organizations and the Civic Training of Youth* (New York: Charles Scribner's Sons, 1933). Although old, this work is most complete.

20. See E. J. Kahn, Jr., *Harvard Through Change and Through Storm* (New York: W. W. Norton, 1969); John Searle, *The Campus War, A Sympathetic Look at the University in Agony* (New York and Cleveland: World Publishing Co., 1971).

21. David A. Noebel, *Rythm, Riots, and Revolution* (Tulse, Okla.: Christian Crusade Publications, 1966), pp. 21ff.

22. John Rockwell, "Beatle Music—Is It Primitive?," New York Times Service, March 13, 1976.

23. "Anthropologist Condemns Rise of One-parent Home," Miami, Florida, Religious News Service, February 5, 1977; "The American Family, Can it Survive Today's Shocks?" *U.S. News and World Report*, October 27, 1975, pp. 30-31.

24. Howard M. Kahn, *Yarborough, Living in a City That Time Forgot* (Boston: Little, Brown and Co., 1973).

25. See George Roche, III, *The Balancing Act* (LaSalle, Ill.: Open Court Publishing Co., 1974); Cecelia Goodnow, "Private-College Presidents Assail U.S. 'Interference,'" Phoenix, *The Arizona Republic*, December 5, 1976; see also *The Wall Street Journal*, January 25, 1977, p. 20, for two reproductions of the intricate web of authority exercised by the U.S. Department of Health, Education and Welfare, and including its vast proposed restructuring.

26. As quoted in *U.S. News and World Report*, February 14, 1977, pp. 41-42.

27. John Pfeiffer, *A New Look at Education, Systems Analysis in Our Schools and Colleges* (New York: Odyssey Press, 1968), pp. 16-32.

28. Richard B. Freeman, *The Over-Educated American* (New York: Academic Press, 1976).

29. "Few ASU Students Seek Rhodes Scholarship," Phoenix, *The Arizona Republic*, February 22, 1977, p. A-22.

30. See Kahn, *Yarborough*, pp. 203-211; Vance Packard, *The People Shapers* (Boston: Little, Brown, and Company, 1977), pp. 26-39, 93-127.

Charlotte Wolf

SOCIAL CLASS, STATUS, AND PRESTIGE

Most societies are stratified and thus are by nature unequal. By definition, social stratification means that there is a societal system of higher to lower categories or strata into which people are ranked. The top-ranking strata within the hierarchy have or get a disproportionate share of power and privilege; conversely, lower ranking strata are always disprivileged and with lesser power relative to those above them. For a system of structured inequality to remain operative— that is, for people to be kept in line, more or less, believing that they are getting what they deserve, particularly if they aren't getting much—requires adequate social control mechanisms.

Types of Social Stratification Systems

Estate, Caste, and Class

Although the contours of stratification systems vary from time to time and place to place (as do the prevailing modes of social control), historically the major forms of stratification have been those of estate, caste, and class. Estate and caste have represented basically closed situations for their members, involving ritually prescribed behavior and social distance between highly stratified groups. The estate system was rooted in an agricultural economy and feudalistic type of social organization. Subordinates were linked to superordinates by ties of obedience and protection; superordinates depended upon subordinates for most of the work and the production of food and goods. Each stratum had its own differentiated function and honor, and was thus set off from other strata. A hereditary landed aristocracy of lords and warriors constituted the topmost strata, next came merchants and artisans, then peasants, and finally at the bottom were the broad strata of serfs, propertyless but tied to the land. In medieval Europe, a parallel hierarchy of ecclesiastical orders existed at the middle and upper levels, highly related yet separate. A world view of place and function stamped with the seal of God's approval was the connective tissue of this system. As F. Antal, in reviewing St. Thomas Aquinas's organic model of the estate-based society, succinctly states: "The orders of society, and their various kinds of work, are ordained by God; each order has its special *raison d'etre*, each individual must remain in the station to which it has pleased God to call him—he must stay in his own order and his own work."[1] While it was not impossible to move out of one's stratum, given the strong barriers of custom and law, the slow rate of change, and the low level of education, it was infrequent, as were challenges to any part of the established pattern. Although empirical examples of estate-type of stratification systems have differed, those of feudalistic Europe, India, Japan, China, Egypt, and Achaea still resembled one another in broad outline.[2]

The notion of caste involves a hierarchy of groups in which membership is ascribed by birth and is considered permanent, and contacts between caste strata are rigidly defined and formal. Within the delimited boundaries of the caste group, members live, work, marry, and die. Mobility from one caste group to another is in principle impossible. Lower ranking castes, as with lower ranking estate groups, are characterized by subjection and deprivation; members of higher groups, by birth alone, receive deferential treatment and prescribed rights and privileges. The inequities between strata historically have been reinforced by the religious and legal institutions of the society; inflexible enforcement of caste privilege and control has been essential to maintenance of the system. It is as Jesse R. Pitts reminds us: "Every failure of the caste system to enforce its norms decreases the power of these norms."[3] The Indian caste system and the caste relations between blacks and whites in the United States are probably the best known examples of this type.[4] Today the caste boundaries between blacks and whites in the United States have greatly deteriorated; in India, the system has become moderated with increasing industrialization.

The stratification pattern of class as ordinarily defined differs from that of estate and of caste in the critical sense that it is an open system, in which people and groups can move freely up or down the hierarchical ladder, changing position relative to others. The bases of class assignment are by individual achievement, as well as by birth or ascription. Class frequently has been used as the master classification of contemporary stratification systems.

Karl Marx (1818-1883) developed the concept of class into a powerful instrument for the analysis of economic systems, particularly that of capitalism, and of social change. For Marx a class was made up of a group of people who bore the same relationship to the society's mode of production. He maintained that throughout history social classes, as rooted in the economic foundations of a society, had been divided into two main groups, those of the oppressors and of the oppressed. Thus, as conflict was inherent to the class system, history itself was but a long and bitter account of class misery and struggle. This dichotomized conception of class cuts into and lays bare the relationships of groups that are unequally disposed in a stratification system. With pounding impact Marx made the point that social control under capitalism is always problematic since the system is one of exploitation of one class by another. Yet his brush, while powerful and compelling as an ideological weapon, has too broad a sweep for the analysis of a wide range of phenomena. Marx did not apprehend the distinction between class and status dimensions of a stratification system. For this distinction, many sociologists turn to the incisive work of Max Weber.

Social Class, Status, Prestige, and Party

In distinguishing between the economic and social orders of society, Weber (1864-1920) drew from these the stratification elements of classes, status groups, and parties, as "phenomena of the distribution of power within a community."[5] For Weber, class, status, and party represented three analytically separate dimensions of a stratification system—analytically separate only, because empirically there is a high degree of correspondence between them.

Classes, then, are narrowly defined by Weber as being differentiated from one another on the basis of income and wealth only. Aggregates of people who bear a roughly similar relationship to the market, and as derived from this have similar life chances, are considered to share the same class situation. Weber stressed the importance of property ownership as a basis for class; yet, wages and other sources of income in contemporary life have become increasingly significant to class placement. Also included in this category, as Frank Parkin has mentioned, are "security of employment, promotion opportunities, long-term income prospects, and the general array of social and material advantages."[6] Class labels, such as "the poor," "the middle classes," "the working classes," and "the rich," direct attention to these distinctions, the degree of income discrepancy between these groups being the key variable here. Yet, as Weber emphasized, the particulars of sharing a class situation with other people do not seem to automatically encourage either community formation or class organization. For either to occur, members of a class must be able to recognize their *shared* class situation clearly, and as Weber trenchantly puts it, the onset of this perception seems "linked to the *transparency* of the connections between the causes and the consequences of the 'class situation.' "[7]

Status groups are stratified on quite different grounds. The positive or negative estimations of honor and of honor as expressed in a particular style of life are the bases for the ranking of people in a status hierarchy. Status claims and appraisals, more or less dependent on visible characteristics, tend to be made on a local level, although there are national status groups as well. A number of years ago, Thorstein Veblen in his penetrating analysis of stratification pointed out the linkage between claims to status and consumption patterns. He depicted "conspicuous leisure" and "conspicuous consumption" as both potlatch glorification of personal and group worth and as a means of demonstrating status superiority and distance.[8]

Communities of equals and near-equals are a frequent outcome of the ranking process. A status community will develop when a number of people, ranked similarly, recognize and identify with one another, and consequently tend to interact. A small world can evolve, maintained by group solidarity and bolstered by restrictive membership, the encouragement of endogamous marital arrangements, the monopolization of privileges, and the punctilious regard for status qualifications and differences that set the group apart. The style of life that distinguishes a group can involve "proper" or "appropriate" manners, dress, speech, education, possessions, titles, physical appearance, and so on. The group culture by closing out others is often used as a means of monopolizing opportunities and perpetuating group privileges.

T. H. Marshall graphically describes this process in his discussion of English gentlemen, who from the sixteenth century on with great verve and determination defended their charmed circle against the encroachment of *nouveaux riches* by "constructing barriers out of those attributes and symbols of social differences which are most difficult to acquire. Conspicuous expenditure can be copied by those who get rich quick, but correct manners, the right accent, and the 'old school tie' are esoteric mysteries and jealously guarded monopolies."[9] Positively honored communities, if sufficiently strong, can weather many generations, stabilizing their positions and passing on their privileges to their children. With their tightly ingrown emphasis on family, property, life-style, and honor, such groups tend toward closure and in many respects attest to the amazing resiliency and persistence of estate and caste characteristics. For that matter, it is worthy of note that Weber defines caste as a closed status group.

The ascriptive criteria of race, ethnicity, and sex are important variables in the assignment of people to positions in class and status hierarchies. The linkage between negative social honor, disadvantage, and ethnic groups was traced by Weber. It has been more extensively conceptualized in Don Martindale's theory of ethnic communities. Martindale sees the growth of segregated and semisegregated communities as characteristic of immigrant and minority groups faced with a more or less hostile society. The response of the minority or ethnic group to the continuing crises of external cultural impact is that of closure and protective adaptation of their ethnic "community formula." The extent of inequality in power relations between themselves and external groups is determinative of their success in meeting these crises.

These theoretical frameworks, valuable as they are, appear to lend only lateral insight into the peculiar and disvalued social position of women. Many theorists have maintained that women's status in a society is devolved only from that of their fathers or husbands or families.[10] In some of the recent work, however, women have been seen as constituting a separate caste, or a separate class, or simply a lower status group vis-à-vis men.[11] Regardless, the income and power differentials between men and women, as between whites and blacks, are widely disparate.

Prestige

Although not abstracted as an element of stratification by Weber, prestige can be studied as a dependent attribute of class or status or party. It can adhere to such a motley collection of people as movie stars, politicos, scholars, musicians, and thieves. The term can be and often is used interchangeably with that of honor, and similarly there can be negative prestige as well as positive prestige. Both subjective and objective dimensions of prestige have been noted: subjective prestige is dependent upon one's perceptions of one's own renown; objective prestige is that esteem accorded by others. Presumably, there are prestige rating processes, which could be either local or national. Surely, an immense number of prestige values exist in a complex society and provide various bases for esteem and for community.

Hans Speier in an early discussion on social planning treated prestige as a manipulable element of social control. He suggested that it was possible to disrupt the norms pertaining to property by substituting honor or prestige as the stellar reward. As an integral aspect of preliberal or precapitalistic or military societies, he believed that honor might be revived as a basic kind of social control to neutralize the effects of capitalism.[12]

Parties

According to Weber, power can be defined as "the chance of a man or of a number of men to realize their own will in a communal action even against the resistance of others who are participating in the action."[13] Parties are instruments of domination and control. They are groups organized for and directed toward achieving a calculated goal, such as a public cause, personal gain, or perhaps both. Aimed at influence and representing interests that are narrowly defined, they may appear as separate groups, class parties, or status parties. Parties, then, are specialized groups organized as the human thrust of power.

Interrelationships of Stratification Hierarchies

Class, status, prestige, and power are related in numerous, tension-filled, and dynamic ways. Status without wealth will tend to disappear, for certain styles of life are not possible without adequate income. Yet, at the same time, status groups arrogantly oppose the crass pretensions of wealth, although firmly cemented to its foundations. The wealthy seek status eagerly to sanctify and preserve their money through respectability. Status and class are laced together by power, the means to control and perpetuate advantages. Prestige legitimates power, changing its course toward authority and palliating its harsh coerciveness. The parvenu is welcomed nowhere; still, rank in one hierarchy will be utilized to gain corresponding rank in others. And usually this will come. However, if status groups are closed to the wealthy or to the prestigious, such closure can constitute a crisis for individuals or for groups. Gerhard Lenski conceptualized the disjunction between class and status as status incongruency or status inconsistency and found it to be a major source of discontent and of structural danger to the system.

Identity

The social structure provides the context and the constraints for the development of identity. There is little question that status and class leave their rough or gentle marks upon the self-concept. Data are limited on the wealthy, the powerful, the honored, but the poor, the powerless, and the not-so-honored have been accessible to investigation.

Identity as the critical reference point of self is created and achieved out of role experience. Roles of relative social significance are available for higher status persons, but lower status persons have limited role choices. Exclusion from roles of responsibility and initiative, the roles that are valued by society, means both exclusion from access to the social goods inherent in those roles and deprivation of recognition for filling roles of social worth. Thus, those toward the bottom of class and status hierarchies are restricted in how they see themselves and in how others see and respond to them. Subordinate status and class position—limited opportunities, boring jobs, lack of autonomy, negative honor, the struggle of coping with the tightness of everyday living—can have crushing effects upon aspiration, upon hope, upon identity. Melvin Kohn tells us that "men of higher class position are more self-directed in their views of social reality and men of lower class position more conformist."[14] And Parkin points out: "Ambition does not readily flourish in an atmosphere thick with warnings against the danger of getting 'big ideas' . . . the working class view of limited opportunities becomes a self-fulfilling prophecy."[15] Indeed, abundant research demonstrates that lower classes tend to be dissatisfied and unhappy and to think poorly of themselves.[16] Oppression does not *necessarily* result in negative feelings about oneself, but the denial of inadequacy often comes with rationalization or with mystification. The argument might be with one's position or with one's bad luck, not with a stratification system in which the distribution of positive self-concepts, as well as goods and honor, is inevitably unequal.

Social Control

A stratification system, then, implies division and inequality; social control as part of that structure ensures that the system is maintained. Assurance of continuity emerges both from the normal ongoing processes of routine life, such as custom, socialization, and interaction with others, and from the shadowy outlines of institutionalized power exerted to preserve a system more advantageous to some than to others.

Levels of Control

The study of social control mechanisms can be focused on individual and interpersonal behavior, group behavior, and on the institutional and societal levels. From every level, sanctions may be imposed on those whose responses are approved or disapproved. Conformity is usually rewarded and deviance is punished, although the kind and the extent of the sanction are related to the individual's position in the stratification system.

Both internal and external means of control are manifested on a group level. Within class and status aggregates, discipline is brought to bear to keep members in line. With all strata, external constraints are used to control outsiders, as means both of protection and of exploitation. On the one hand, status communities are likely to defend group boundaries against trespass; on the other, these same communities push toward the outside to expand power and privileges and to enforce deference. Those at the lower and less organized end of the status and class scales must attempt to defend themselves from the inroads of upper imperiousness, while at the same time pressing to improve their position. In this adagio of wins and losses, Ralf Dahrendorf argues that there are limits to exploitation of subordinate groups by dominant groups: when pressures from above become too oppressive, he says, the interests of subordinate groups will surface and countercontrol measures will be undertaken. This is often true, yet on the basis of a cursory review of history, it is indeed difficult to discover what those limits and their time-frames might predictably be. Surely, some groups have exploited others with impressive ruthlessness, and countercontrol measures have not arisen within the margins of dignity or life itself. In contemporary sociology, as a matter of fact, several highly provocative studies have been made of white gains from black subordination and of business gains from the perpetuation of male-female stereotypes.[17] Suffice it to say that neither situation is one of recent emergence.

Institutional reinforcement of the stratification system, particularly in the areas of education, religion, and law, are essential aspects of formal control.

Legitimation

Social inequalities are bearable to the extent that people feel them to be legitimate and to reflect societal values. As Parkin cogently suggests: "How could sharp differences in material reward be formally justified if it was widely held that all occupations were of equal social value?"[18] The dominant value system must validate both the unequal distribution of goods and privileges on the basis of moral and cultural principles and the means for encouraging or enforcing conformity to these principles. People tolerate a system of stratification and its attendant means of control either because they accept it as legitimate or because they cannot do anything about it. Obvious discrepancies between value and reality might presage challenge from those who both are aware and have sufficient power resources to do so. Nonetheless, belief in the legitimacy of the stratification system appears to vary, attenuated in lower ranks and celebrated in higher. The more completely class and status groups do identify with and endorse the existing social order, however, the more likely there will be both individual and group compliance.

Differential Access to the Means of Control

It is not necessary to believe in the conspiracy of the powerful or the confluence of evil forces to be cognizant that people in the highest ranks of status and class strata have more power and greater command of the mechanisms of social control in a society than do others not so fortuitously placed. This occurs in two ways. First, the centers of influence in any society are at the top of the major agencies for social control, communication, and socialization; typically, people in top status and class positions are in control of these agencies. Second, the dominant definition of reality in a society is a function of power. As Marx claimed over a century ago, the ideas of the ruling classes are always the ruling ideas. Societal values, such as justice and honor, are tied to the chariot wheels of the upper classes and placed in the service of legitimating the status quo. In other words, the strategies of both definition and direct control are to a great extent in the hands of the rich, the honored, and the powerful.

Types of Social Control

Societies have arsenals of controls that are remarkable in their scope, variety, and nuance. The kinds of control that emanate from a stratification system range from the subtleties of etiquette and laughter, compliment and gossip, moral suasion and earnest advice, to threat and ridicule, deprivation, torture, and chains. Sanctions can be positive or negative, formal or informal, direct or indirect, and can encourage or discourage. They can be classified, as Amitai Etzioni has suggested, on the basis of their normative, material, and coercive aspects.[19]

The most powerful kind of class control is economic sanction. A secondary, but nonetheless effective, kind of control is that of mobility. Upward mobility, real or spurious, has such positive effects for the maintenance of a class system as being a "safety valve" on lower class discontent, providing personal satisfaction for individuals who make it or models for those who do not, diluting lower class solidarity, being antithetical to class consciousness, and discouraging through the process of anticipatory socialization lower class sociality, being antithetical to class consciousness, and discouraging through the process of anticipatory socialization lower class sociality and cohesiveness. Apparently, even downward mobility poses no threat of discontent or revolution for a system since evidence indicates that "skidders" make no trouble. They retain their pretensions to former class membership and rigorously resist lower class identification.

Status symbols are also likely to be a means of both internal and external control. Expectations for the behavior of members who display certain symbols might be very rigorous and precise. Symbols of higher status groups might also serve as a means of control for lower groups. In an affluent society, such status symbols as automobiles, fake fur, and phony diamonds are easily available to many people. These symbols represent spurious mobility, the status usurpation of the transient in an impersonal society. Changing the name of one's occupation, let us say from garbage collector to sanitary engineer, is but one more example of spurious status mobility.

It is occasionally difficult to tell clearly when class controls cease and status controls commence, if indeed one can separate out the strands of difference at all. Yet, on the whole, status systems usually exert different kinds of control, touching on different sensitivities and activating different motivations. The ritualization of everyday life in a status community makes it rich in meaning for its members, but it also exerts a stringently disciplinary effect. The uses of honor and reputation are among the strongest sanctions, and at the far extreme of punishment stands the threat of status degradation. Erving Goffman in his discussion of status rituals argues that deference behavior occurs not only in dominant-subordinate relationships, but also in symmetrical deference which social equals pay to one another. The two broad types of deference behavior, avoidance rituals and presentational rituals, trace out one's rights and privileges, one's areas of sanctity and accessibility vis-à-vis others, based on one's class and status standing. Deference behavior is a way of demonstrating appreciation for others, but beyond its superficial aspects it is a first-rate means of reinforcing status position.

Among the most interesting status control mechanisms to study are those that obtain between upper and lower status groups—for example, between whites and blacks and between men and women. More than forty years ago, Bertram Doyle, in his book *The Etiquette of Race Relations*,[20] noted that etiquette between the races was a form of social control utilized by whites to keep blacks in their places; blacks, by responding in predictable ways, reinforced this system. Daily contacts between the two groups were carefully defined by reference to status boundaries. In this same vein, Dana Densmore has called the chivalry that men show to women "the iron hand in the velvet glove."[21] Nancy Henley and Jo Freeman have discussed the etiquette of social distance and subservience holding between men and women as consisting of such patterns as nonreciprocal first-naming and touching, the subtle reminders of superior physical strength that whisper caution and passivity, and conversational tactics of control, such as initiation, interruption, change of topic, pointing, and so on.[22] Rose Laub Coser has hypothesized that jokes and humor are seldom "just for fun," but, rather, insistently and insidiously function as a means of telling people where they belong.[23] Goffman, perhaps, has best summarized these forms of social control when he says: "The gestures which we sometimes call empty are perhaps, in fact, the fullest things of all."[24]

The Failure of Social Control?

It has been asked, why do people conform? And it has also been asked, why do they not? Both questions make sense in the light of stratification history. There is always a sustained tension between the stratification and control system and its human participants. Routine changes occur. Individuals and groups negotiate, conform, adapt, and escape in millenarianism or deviance or passive alienation; groups reject prevalent value systems and form new status or ethnic communities. Class aggregates become radicalized and insurgent, quixotic as that usually is, for structured inequality and the control to make it stick involve power.

Yet, inseparable from the notions of division and dominance has drifted the simple and elusive hope of equality. In the face of this hope has been built the overwhelming bulwark of promises, rationalizations, regulations, and ameliorations by those who profit by the system as it exists. Ultimately, though, there always has remained the spare and elliptical question: how long will these suffice?

Notes

1. F. Antal, *Florentine Painting and Its Social Background* (London: Kegan Paul, 1947), p. 39.

2. In particular, see Marc Bloch, *Feudal Society*, translated by L. A. Manyon (Chicago: University of Chicago Press, 1961).

3. Jesse Pitts, "Social Control: The Concept," *International Encyclopedia of the Social Sciences* (New York: Free Press, 1968), Vol. 14, p. 388.

4. An excellent discussion of this can be found in Gerald D. Berreman, "Caste in India and the United States," *American Journal of Sociology* 66 (September 1960): 120-127.

5. Max Weber, *From Max Weber: Essays in Sociology*, translated and edited by H. H. Gerth and C. Wright Mills (New York: Oxford University Press, 1938), p. 181.

6. Frank Parkin, *Inequality and Political Order* (New York: Praeger Publishers, 1971), p. 31.

7. Weber, *From Max Weber*, p. 184.

8. Thorstein Veblen, *The Theory of the Leisure Class* (New York: Modern Library, 1934).

9. T. H. Marshall, "The Nature and Determinants of Social Status," *Sociology at the Crossroads* (London: W. Heinemann, 1963), p. 190.

10. For a recent example of this, see Charles H. Andersen, *The Political Economy of Class* (Englewood Cliffs, N.J.: Prentice-Hall, 1974), p. 317. For an excellent discussion of this problem, see Joan Acker, "Women and Social Stratification: A Case of Intellectual Sexism," *American Journal of Sociology* 78 (January 1973): 936-945.

11. Jo Freeman, "The Legal Basis of the Sexual Caste System," *Valparaiso University Law Review* 5 (Symposium Issue 1971): 203-236; Juliet Mitchell, *Woman's Estate* (New York: Pantheon Books, 1972); Constantina Safilios-Rothschild, "Dual Linkages between the Occupational and Family Systems: A Macrosociological Analysis," *Signs* 1 (Spring 1976): 51-60.

12. Hans Speier, "Freedom and Social Planning," *American Journal of Sociology* 42 (January 1937): 463-483.

13. Weber, *From Max Weber*, p. 180.

14. Melvin Kohn, *Class and Conformity. A Study in Values* (Homewood, Ill.: Dorsey Press, 1969), p. 196.

15. Parkin, *Class Inequality and Political Order*, p. 67.

16. For a review of this literature, see Louis Kriesberg, *The Sociology of Social Conflicts* (Englewood Cliffs, N.J.: Prentice-Hall, 1973), pp. 39-42.

17. George W. Dowdall, "White Gains from Black Subordination in 1960 and 1970," *Social Problems* 22 (December 1974): 162-183; Albert Szymanski, "Race, Sex, and the U.S. Working Class," *Social Problems* 21 (June 1974): 706-725; Albert Szymanski, "Racism and Sexism as Functional Substitutes in the Labor Market," *Sociological Quarterly* 17 (Winter 1976): 65-73.

18. Parkin, *Class Inequality and Political Order*, p. 44.

19. Amitai Etzioni, "Social Control: Organizational Aspects," *International Encyclopedia of the Social Sciences* (1968), Vol. 14, pp. 396-402.

20. Bertram Doyle, *The Etiquette of Race Relations in the South. A Study of Social Control* (New York: Schocken Books, 1971).

21. Dana Densmore, "Chivalry—The Iron Hand in the Velvet Glove," *No More Fun and Games: A Journal of Female Liberation* (Cambridge, Mass.: November 1968).

22. Nancy Henley and Jo Freeman, "The Sexual Politics of Interpersonal Behavior," in Jo Freeman, ed., *Women: A Feminist Perspective* (Palo Alto, Calif.: Mayfield, 1975), pp. 391-401. Also see Don H. Zimmerman and Candace West, "Sex Roles, Interruptions and Silences in Conversations," all in Barrie Thorne and Nancy Henley, ed., *Language and Sex: Difference and Dominance* (Rowley, Mass.: Newbury House, 1975), pp. 105-129.

23. Rose Laub Coser, Roundtable Meeting on Sexism and Humor, American Sociological Association Meetings, San Francisco, 1975.

24. Erving Goffman, *Interaction Ritual: Essays on Face-to-Face Behavior* (Garden City, N.Y.: Doubleday, 1967), p. 91.

Paradoxically, concurrent with the rise of dictatorships and totalitarian regimes which tightened up all modern devices of social control, especially the use of propaganda, violence, and terror, the traditional means of social control have been breaking down throughout the world. In American society social control has turned increasingly to manipulation and technological controls. Our behavior is controlled, mostly without our knowledge, or manipulated, by those who control the mass media of communications.

Individuals and groups are led to behave in ways that are predictable through at least two major kinds of processes. The first type, socialization (see Part II), promotes conformity to expected patterns by providing a preconditioning for the interpretation of situations in socially accepted ways.

Social control processes of the second type are those mechanisms that members of a social system utilize to prevent deviants from proceeding beyond tolerable limits. In Martindale's words, "study of social control is the sociology of how social order in maintained" (Don Martindale, *American Society*, Princeton, N.J.: D. Van Nostrand, 1960). Martindale suggests that influence and power are necessary to maintain order and that, in this sense, social control may be thought of as "the maintenance of influence and power" (p. 364). However, he cautions that the control of deviance is only one of the functions of power.

Basically, social control may be thought of in terms of the processes whereby the individual is made to respond to the behavioral expectations of other members of his social system, especially of the group which in the narrower sense "controls" the

PART III

Means and Techniques of Social Control

social system. The means by which social
control is exercised are built into the various status positions within given systems
and into their institutionalized arrangements. The types of mechanisms used vary
for many reasons, including the nature of
the goals involved. It is often difficult to
differentiate between the "legitimate" and
"illegitimate" application of such devices.

Of the important forms of social control
exerted in contemporary mass society,
ideologies stand out as the dynamic devices for molding a "climate of opinion."
As Roucek's opening essay in Part III
shows, ideologies are based on unscientific
premises, but they make use of some
well-established assumptions and techniques that have widespread influence.
Although many institutions aim to maintain law and order in a society, the article
by Unkovic and Brown demonstrates that
it is the police who are charged most
distinctly with preventing and controlling
crime and that, as the same time, police
officers must indeed be jacks of all trades.
Zinam's essay suggests that the role of
economic control is basic and essential,
but it is not the most important aspect of
social control. Martin's survey of violence,
terrorism, and nonviolence as means of
social control indicates that today terror
and violence are employed both by revo-
lutionaries and by the defenders of "law
and order." Hulicka's description of the
phenomenon of charisma explores the
various types of leaders who have emerged
in recent decades. Wilke's essay attempts
to determine what types of art and literature play a role in social control. Roucek's
survey of the function of music supports
his contention that this most intimate of
the arts not only enhances man's enjoyment of leisure but often has ritualistic

significance that may be employed for political and military purposes. This view is at least as ancient as the Spartans of Greek antiquity who believed that only the Dorian musical mode enhanced military efficiency. Owen maintains that significant personality values are acquired and confirmed in man's leisure-time activities and that the institutions which are arising to structure contemporary man's recreation have important control functions.

Secret societies and guerrillas, according to Krase, have increasingly employed terrorist activities so as to confound traditional control agencies. In view of the "primitivism" which in one sense this terrorist activity represents, it is of value to examine its status in the simpler societies from which all complex civilizations have sprung. Finally, Roucek's historical and contemporary survey of capital punishment indicates that its employment as an ultimate control device has become one of the most controversial subjects of our times.

J.S.R.

Joseph S. Roucek

IDEOLOGY

In recent years, we have been hearing the word "ideology" more and more frequently. Our language abounds in references to the "war of ideologies," to Fascist, Communist, New Deal, socialist, conservative, radical, and other ideologies. But while the word is used so frequently, very few people can actually define it. Some newspaper writers have used the term to mean "unmitigated bunkum" as opposed to "the voice of reason;" others seem to believe that the concept means some system of ideas that has come to be the accepted scheme of thinking of a group, e.g., of the Communist party, the Nazi party, or the English Tories, as distinguished from the theories of democracy or the humanitarian aims of the United States.

An ideology has numerous definitions. It may be defined as a system of ideas or a confession of faith characterizing the way in which a particular group of persons views life, in terms of its aspirations, morality, law, religion, and philosophy. It has been defined by some writers as a system of ideas that contemporaneously dominates social behavior, as opposed to the ideas of other groups. For our discussion, ideology is defined as a theory of social life that approaches social realities from the point of view of a political and social ideal and interprets them both consciously and unconsciously to prove the correctness of the analysis and to justify the ideal. In ideologies, we find an explanation of the future state of affairs for the improvement of society, together with a quasi-scientific explanation of contemporary and past social realities. The desired future state of affairs is obviously scheduled to come about logically or morally, or because of "natural" laws.[1]

Historical Roots

The word "ideology" was used for the first time in 1801 by Destutt de Tracy (1755-1836) in his *Elements d'ideologie* (4 vols., Paris, 1801-1815).[2] He employed it to refer to the empirical analysis of the human mind (most consistently formulated in the eighteenth century by Condillac and originally rooted in the "new way of ideas" first formulated by John Locke in his *An Essay Concerning Human Understanding*). This approach, which claimed that sensation is the origin of all ideas, was used by the spokesmen of the French Revolution as an indispensable weapon for attacking authoritarian political and religious dogmas. The recognition granted to this analysis as the philosophy of the Revolutionary government resulted in the use of the word "ideologues," referring to the only recognized philosophy of the day.

Another twist to the term was given by Napoleon Bonaparte who referred to his critics as "ideologues," those believing in any republican or revolutionary ideas. His reference to such mongers of metaphysical trash introduced the popular connotation of the term as visionary moonshine, and the term took on a derogatory meaning which it retains even today.

The pejorative character of the concept was reinforced by the writings of Karl Marx and Friedrich Engels, who, in their joint work, *German Ideology*, identified the term with philosophy, especially any philosophy they believed was inimical to their own philosophy (that is, ideology) of history. According to Marx, particularly in his *Poverty of Philosophy*, ideology is a cloak for class interests, an outwardly rational instrument of propaganda, a veil of argument produced to disguise and defend an established social order. In Marx's words, "The same men who establish social relations conformably with their material productivity, produce also the principles, the ideas, the categories, conformably with their social relations." Thus, Marx attacked the social theories of his own time and of earlier ages as ideologies meant to maintain capitalism, feudalism, and imperialism. The social ideas and ideals that Marx invoked to explain the behavior of men and institutions mask the clash of economic interests; a struggle for acceptance is waged by conflicting social ideals and whichever set triumphs in the end determines the ruling beliefs of an epoch. The prevailing ideology of any particular epoch is both the outward rationalization of that epoch's economic organization and also the tool used by the dominant class to stop history from continuing on its inevitable path. For history is a perpetual progress through time, propelled irresistibly by the class struggle, though at varying rates of advance. (*The Communist Manifesto* proclaimed: "All history is the history of class struggle."). Throughout this unfolding pattern of dialectical change, combining revolution and evolution, ideology serves both to mask and then to unmask "objective reality."

Marx also used the concept of ideology as a comprehensive term for myths. All social philosophies and theories, he said, are either myths or scientifically grounded doctrines. He explained that myths are of two kinds: ideas that are false or refutable by evidence, and ideas that, although capable of rallying and inspiring or discouraging and demoralizing large masses, are too vague to be tested. Both categories of myth function as psychological rationalizations of interests which, if openly proclaimed, would not be accepted. Thus, all social philosophies which teach that interests are common in a class society are myths.

Marx and Engels also distinguished between illusion, the unclear ideas of the majority of people, and knowledge, the result of scientific investigation. "A clear ideology," Engels concurs with Marx, is "the deduction of the reality not from the reality itself, but from imagination." Engels adds: "The real driving force which moves it [ideology] remains unconscious, otherwise it would not be an ideological process."[3]

The Marxian approach is the closest to our modern conception of the ideology that analyzes the social dependence of human thinking in all its aspects on its framework. The tragedy of the Marxist reasoning, however, is that Marxism, just like all the "scientific" theories designed for social action, is an ideology *par excellence*. Marxism's insight into the ideological character of all cultural creations is vitiated by its interpretation of consciousness as merely the reflection and the product of material conditions.

In Marxism, ideology is the term given to any form of thought invaded by the vested interests of a ruling class or the aspiring intentions of subordinate classes. Ideologies are "unmasked" or "evaluated"—that is, behind apparently objective or disinterested or noble attitudes, a covert, perhaps unconscious, class interest is shown to exist. A systematic attempt to eliminate the influence of ideology from the social sciences was made by Emile Durkheim.[4] Although Durkheim used the word "doctrine" rather than "ideology," he has helped our sociological understanding of ideology. He has shown that the "doctrine" concept does not grow from a study of reality but that it is a logical argumentation for preconceived ideas.

In 1848, the year Marx and Engels published their famous *Communist Manifesto*, Vilfredo Pareto was born in Paris; he was to become one of the most skillful sociological students of the great Marxian synthesis.[5] His view of society as a system of equilibrium has been extremely influential. He insisted that sociology should adhere strictly to scientific method, what he called the logico-experimental method. His *Socialist Systems* (1902) presents a theory of elites; his major sociological work, *The Mind and Society* (1935), mainly gives his theory of residues and derivations, which he classified into diverse groups. The expression of sentiments out of which nonlogical actions arise are called residues by Pareto. (The concept is related to what Allport terms "prepotent reflexes" and to what many psychologists refer to as "complexes," and "inferiority complex" or "drives".)[6] Derivations, on the other hand, are speech reactions—deductions that aim to explain, justify, and demonstrate the residues. There are the explanatory, theoretical, justificatory, persuasive, and doctrinal elements in social behavior (ideologies). Residues and derivations are mutually dependent forces which act on society in different degrees at different times and under different conditions; they are complex variables in the determination of social conduct. Pareto finally reached the same conclusions Machiavelli, Frazer, LeBon, and others had—that illusions and ideologies are indispensable to society's processes.

One of the greatest sociologists of all time, Max Weber, made explicit the central issues in sociology—value, freedom, and the development of Western society. In addition, the concrete problems he dealt with—the division of authority into charismatic, traditional, and rational-legal; legitimation of power in the state and society; and bureaucracy, class, and status, to take the most notable ones—are basic features of modern sociology. Weber's inspiration, method, and example are clearly visible in sociology today. Specifically, he pointed out that the politician is forced to treat the world "as it is" and has to make use of ideologies for his own purposes.[7]

Probably the most popular recent interpreter of the concept of ideology has been Karl Mannheim. In his *Ideology and Utopia* (1929, translated 1936), he argues that knowledge functional in man's adaptation to the environment varies with the environment. Knowledge is of two types, he says: true knowledge based on scientific criteria; and knowledge relative to classes, e.g., religion, philosophy, and traditional knowledge. Sets of ideas that promote and defend interests are also of two types: utopias—those promoting the interests of underprivileged groups and placing their social objectives in the future; and ideologies—those defending the interests of privileged groups.[8]

Since the appearance of Pareto's work in translation, and with the persistent intensification of ideological conflicts, American social scientists have demonstrated growing interest in the various aspects of ideological elements. Ideological reasoning has especially influenced Talcott Parsons' works which focus on the theory of action,[9] Pitirim A. Sorokin's impressive works on the history of civilization and sociology,[10] and A. J. Toynbee's massive *A Study of Civilization*.[11]

Programs, Panaceas, and Components of Successful Ideologies

The hopes and claims of solving social problems both of the present and of eternity are especially expressed in political ideologies. The political ideologist promises to relate theory and practice. Rooted in the burning issues of the day, he vocalizes the problems, seeks their solutions, and offers the means whereby these solutions can be realized. To believe and work for this or that ideology is the solution offered. Critics and dissenters are relegated to the categories of "cynics," "Fascists," or "Communists," or "atheists," "non-believers," and so on.

All promises made by every ideologist can be tested only by accomplishments, but accomplishments can be evaluated only in a historical perspective. Hence, the ideologist asks his followers (the "believers," the "faithful" ones) to have faith in the coming of the millennium.

Although some ideologists believe that faith is enough to solve all of men's problems,[12] most ideologists know that faith alone cannot effect social change. Man's faith must be bolstered by reason, although irrational ideas have more immediate effect than rational ones. Most ideologies are, therefore, a rather strange mixture of scientific and rational statements, of philosophies, generalizations, and principles, and of faith, as well as of the most absurd mythical elements. These presentations are transmitted by words and symbols, related to the subjective world of feelings, emotions, and irrationality. All persons associate most words with fears, hates, pleasures, wishes, and aspirations. Thus, we hate or prefer democracy, communism, nazism, fascism, anarchism—and all other ideological terms. Much that passes for language has little value as objective comments on the world, most of it being subjective expressions of ideological conditioning. Vast words like loyalty, treason, ideals, pacifism, justice, individualism, and mankind are mere high-order abstractions meaning different things to different people.

The function of language is to communicate ideas, and the ideologist manipulates words within the context of his ideology. ("You know what I mean!"). He indulges in orgies of verbomania, defining his own words since they are mere symbols.

Slogans usually arise in critical times: "Thumbs up"; "All Aid Short of War"; "A War to End War"; "Make the World Safe for Democracy"; "All Power to the Soviet"; "Peace, Bread and Land." After popular reactions are established by repetition, the hearing of familiar sounds and slogans or the sight of certain characters and symbols (written words, the flag, swastika, red star, elephant, donkey) calls forth intense passions and convictions, leading to thinking and acting. Important are "glow words"; these carry strong and prevalent emotional tones, as for example: "racial tolerance," "racial superiority," "liberty," "justice," "equality," and "fatherland."

Myth is an indispensable component of all ideologies. It is a highly symbolic account or story of a supernatural or extraordinary event within a culture or subculture, and is continually retold and contemplated for its wisdom, philosophy, inspiration, or practicality. As Pareto pointed out, myth is a system of ideas, very often utopian, that is set up to inspire action. Ideologies create fictitious ideals that glorify the charismatic leaders and the exploits of a group or some of its members. They enshroud happenings in sentiments and protective pathos, and offer dreams in order to allow the group an escape from the hard facts of reality in the vision of a glorious future ("the pie in the sky" idea). They give concrete expression to the desire for a better social order, offering both a criticism of the old and a picture of the new. The future, the "better future," is sometimes pictured as an altogether too distant divine event, but more frequently as a "just around the corner" proposition. Successful ideologies must promise a reign of justice in the planned-for world, and must claim that the "good" will be rewarded and the "wicked" punished, and that the "Better World" will ensure lasting security and uninterrupted comfort.

If an ideology is to provide the impetus to social movements, it must be presented as a scientific truth. For instance, "scientific socialism" is built on the principle that it can "scientifically" predict the future. But what is regarded as "science" by one school may be called "ideology" by its critics. What, for instance, is Marxism? To this writer it is mere ideology, but for the Marxists it is science.

There is a basic difference in the methods and aims of ideologists and scientists. The essence of the scientific approach is not so much the content of its specific conclusions as the method whereby it arrives at them. Ideology utilizes, consciously or unconsciously, illusions and even errors. Science questions everything while ideology takes its illusions for granted, declines to question them, and refuses to correct the distorting influences of its selected facts. Hence, ideology often sees what does not exist, and ideological guessing is presented as a scientific conclusion. Science describes and explains "what is" and says nothing about what "ought to be"; it recognizes only facts that are "indifferent." The subjective evaluation, the "value-judgment," is left to the ideologist.

Excessive simplification of all social problems is an important part of every ideology; it makes it easy to comprehend an otherwise very complex phenomenon. Man hungers for the explanation of the what and why of the troubles facing him and his world; if the explanation is "rational" or "logical," the propagator has a powerful weapon. Ideologies, to be effective, must be transplanted through simplification and popularization from the sphere of theoretical thinking into the sphere of political, social, or religious thinking, programs, and slogans.

The human mind seems to need the certitude of acting on "principles." In order to justify a series of "ought to be" social propositions, ideologies have them rooted in a variety of fundamental doctrines: original sin, divine law, natural law, dialectic materialism, absolutism, communism, individualism, liberalism, fascism, and the like.

If an ideology is to find starry-eyed followers, it must express and provide philosophical justifications and arguments for the ideals of social classes and for their personal and collective values, such as social status, power, income, and prestige. However, it is always preferable not to talk directly about the specific material interests involved but to submerge the real motives in a set of lofty doctrines.

Since the ideologist "knows" the coming state of affairs, he divides mankind, in general, into two groups: those who "know" the way to open the door to the "better world" (those who are willing to make the necessary sacrifices to bring about its realization) and those who, in spite of all their chances to join the movement which is ready and eager to transform this "vale of tears" into the promised paradise, only retard the process by their obstinate obstructionism and opposition. The world is thus divided into the "vanguards of progress," "the elite," "the believers," "the Superior Aryan race"; and "the unbelievers," "the heretics," "the pagans," "the deviationists," "the Jews," "the capitalists." Those who follow the "true" ideology become the "moral kind," "the superior sects," "and the like," because they represent that which is "moral" and "superior." Since there is no room for disillusionment in an affective social platform, the creed is sweetened by what is known as "hokum." Human frailties are assigned only to the opponents, the scapegoats, those who are responsible for contemporary and past social predicaments.

In spite of their claims to offer "simple" explanations, all ideologies usually present complex interpretations of fundamental principles. All ideologies, sooner or later, degenerate into verbal or even physical struggles between the orthodox proponents of the ideology and the "liberal" or "progressive" wings. The battle over the "meaning of meaning" is expressed in sectarian misunderstandings, disputes over interpretations of ideological principles, and antagonistic factional movements that claim to adhere to the same theoretical teaching but that quarrel about its interpretations. (Examples are China's Mao Tse-tung versus the Moscow clique; Tito and polycentrism versus Moscow; and the arguments in the U.S. Supreme Court over the Constitution.)

Fanaticism, especially as it relates to the rise of contemporary crime, terror and violence, seems to have become almost the normal instrument of social life, especially of politics in Northern Ireland, Great Britain, Lebanon, and Argentina. In the United States, the Law Enforcement Intelligence Units (LEIU) is also worried about terrorist activities, since kidnapping and violence for ransom or for political blackmail have mushroomed into today's most pernicious "growth industry."[13] Yet, the sociologist has devoted very little attention to the phenomenon of fanaticism.[14]

There are three main categories of terrorists, although the dividing lines are usually blurred: (1) Students invariably bearing the "true believer" stamp[15] who inhabit a fairy-tale ideological world of good guys versus bad guys. The conspirators feel they are living a life of adventure (reminiscent of the high-seas pirates romanticized in books). Their ideological claims are often only a pretext for them to give free rein to criminal tendencies. A growing number of adolescents refuse to grow up and to assume adult responsibilities; many become eternal students, reaching age thirty or forty without ever having held a responsible job. (Soviet terror schools teach their agents to exploit such social and economic dropouts). (2) Rootless rebels, goaded by an outraged sense of injustice, who come from ethnic and national minorities— America's urban black youth, the Quebec French, the Palestinian refugees, Spain's Basques, for example. Deprived of cultural or national identity, they latch onto the revolutionary role-model offered by extremist propaganda. (3) Criminal gangs of extortionists, robbers, and kidnappers who frequently pose as political terrorists, adopting revolutionary slogans and rationales for their convenience. Terrorists often hire criminal types, exploiting their skills and antisocial drives.[16]

From one point of view, heretics can be included in the category of fanatics.[17]

Trends

Today no single system of thought is not influenced by the present war of ideologies. The great ideologies—those of democracy, totalitarianism, and nationalism—have provoked an ever-increasing morass of opinions that are more varied than ever before in the history of the world. The larger size library, the plethora of books, and the impact of the mass media have made possible a greater number of permutations of ideologies than ever before. There is an altogether unparalleled use of the weapons of criticism, and all aspects of each ideology are under attack by numerous antagonists. (An interesting example can be found in the changing orientation of American sociologists, who, no longer content merely to analyze the problematic aspects of our society, are becoming "action"-oriented.)

Although libraries are overloaded with studies on the dominant ideologies, much is yet to be contributed by empirical sociologists. Utilizing the methods of the behavioral sciences, they are inquiring, in depth, into the workings of the various ideologies, the methods of inducing social control in various cultures and subcultures, the causes of deviance, and the complex determinants of social changes within the ideological framework. In other words, our approach in this section is to help us look at ideologies as one of the many modern forces that is shaping our lives, influencing what we are and, more importantly, what we will be.

Notes

1. For the development of the concept of ideology, see Joseph S. Roucek, "A History of the Concept of Ideology," *Journal of the History of Ideas* 5 (October 1944): 479-488; Fernand Dumont, *Les Idéologies* (Paris: Presses Universitaires de France, 1974); K. Bruce Miller, *Ideology and Moral Philosophy, The Relation of Moral Ideology to Dynamic Moral Philosophy* (New York: Humanities Press, 1971), bibliography, pp. 187-192; Thomas Remington, *The Origin of Ideology* (Pittsburgh: University Center for International Studies, 1971); John Plamenatz, *Ideology* (New York: Praeger Publishers, 1970), bibliography, pp. 145-146; Arne Naess, *Democracy, Ideology, and Objectivity* (Oslo: Oslo University Press, 1956); Karl Marx and Friedrich Engels, *The German Ideology* (New York: International Publishers, 1939); H. D. Aiken, *The Age of Ideology* (Boston: Houghton Mifflin, 1957); Edward Shils, "The Concept and Function of Ideology," in *International Encyclopedia of the Social Sciences* (New York: Macmillan and Free Press, 1968), bibliography, pp. 75-76; Harry M. Johnson, "Ideology and Social Systems," in ibid., pp. 76-85; H. C., "Ideology," in *The New Encyclopaedia Britannica* (Chicago, 1974), valuable bibliography, p. 198; Alvin W. Gouldner, *The Dialectic of Ideology and Technology:*

The Origins, Grammar, and Future of Ideology (New York: Seabury Press, 1976); James T. Borhek and Richard F. Curtis, *A Sociology of Belief* (New York: John Wiley and Sons, 1975); L. N. Moskvichov, *The End of Ideology Theory: Illusions and Reality; Critical Notes on a Fashionable Conception* (Moscow: Progress Publishers, 1974); Joseph S. Roucek, "Scientific Claims and Methods Versus Ideological Claims and Methods," *Wisconsin Sociologist* 2 (Fall 1963):1-6; Peter Stadler, *Karl Marx: Ideologie und Politik* (Goettingen: Musterschmidt Verlag, 1966).

2. See the references in the previous note.

3. From a letter to F. Mehring, quoted by Sidney Hook, *Toward an Understanding of Karl Marx* (New York: John Day, 1933), p. 341.

4. Stephen Lukes, *Emile Durkheim: His Life and Works* (New York: Harper and Row, 1973); Ernest Wallwork, *Durkheim: Morality and Milieu* (Cambridge, Mass.: Harvard University Press, 1972); Dominick LaCapra, *Emile Durkheim: Sociologist and Philosopher* (Ithaca, N.Y.: Cornell University Press, 1973); George Simpson, *Emile Durkheim: Selections from His Work, With an Introduction and Commentaries* (New York: Thomas Y. Crowell, 1963); Robert Biersted, *Emile Durkheim* (New York: Dell, 1966); Robert Nisbet, *The Sociology of Emile Durkheim* (New York: Oxford University Press, 1974); Emile Durkheim, *Sociology and Philosophy* (New York: Free Press, 1974).

5. Vilfredo Pareto, *The Mind and Society* (New York: Harcourt, Brace, 1935), 4 vols.). This translation produced bitter controversies: Bernard de Voto, "Primer for Intellectuals," *Saturday Review of Literature* 9 (1933):569-581; Bernard de Voto, "Sentiment and the Social Order," *Harper's* 167 (1933):569-581; G. C. Homans and G. P. Curtio, *Introduction to Pareto* (New York: John Wiley and Sons, 1934); W. McDougall, C. Murchison, J. H. Tufts, and F. N. House, "A Symposium on Pareto's Significance for Social Theory," *Journal of Social Philosophy* 1 (1935):36-89; A. G. Keller, "Pareto," *Yale Review* 24 (1935):824-828; C. Perry, "Pareto's Contribution to Social Science," *International Journal of Ethics* 11 (1935):14-48; L. G. Henderson, *Pareto's General Sociology* (Cambridge, Mass.: Harvard University Press, 1935). The controversy is still going on; see: "A Symposium on Vilfredo Pareto: Reflections on a Rich Legacy," *Social Science Quarterly* 54 (1973):451-533.

6. For their discussion, consult Pitirim A. Sorokin, *Contemporary Sociological Theories* (New York: Harper, 1927), pp. 48-50.

7. *From Max Weber: Essays in Sociology*, translated by H. H. Gerth and C. Wright Mills (New York: Oxford University Press, 1946).

8. Gunther W. Remmling, *The Sociology of Karl Mannheim: With a Bibliographical Guide to the Sociology of Knowledge, Ideological Analysis, and Social Planning* (Atlantic Highlands, N.J.: Humanities Press, 1975); Gunther W. Remmling, ed., *Towards the Sociology of Knowledge* (Atlantic Highlands, N.J.: Humanities Press, 1975). The concept of ideology is integrated with the sociology of knowledge approach; this field is often considered to be a branch or specialty in the broader field of sociological inquiry. The sociological literature contains frequent references to the persons responsible for its development—whether ancestors such as Marx, Durkheim, Scheler, and Mannheim, or contemporaries such as W. Stark and Robert K. Merton. More often than not, however, allusions to the sociology of knowledge are rather vague, indicating some kind of social determination of knowledge or the products of knowledge. Especially because "knowledge" is a central dimension of religiosity, either as ideology or as a partial component of belief. The sociology of

knowledge has been pertinent to the study of religion. The field is concerned with the relationship between knowledge or systems of thought (scientific, religious, philosophical, aesthetic, political, legal, and so forth) and social and cultural factors. Consult Carroll J. Bourg, "Story and the Study of Man," *Sociological Analysis* 3 (1975):267-276; K. Bruce Miller, *Ideology and Moral Philosophy: The Relation of Moral Ideology to Dynamic Moral Philosophy* (Atlantic Highlands, N.J.: Humanities Press, 1971); Alasair MacIntyre, *Against the Self-Images of the Age, Essays on Ideology and Philosophy* (New York: Schocken Books, 1967); Robert Benewick and R. N. Berki, eds., *Knowledge and Belief in Politics; The Problem of Ideology* (New York: St. Martin's Press, 1973); Lucio Colletti, *From Rousseau to Lenin: Studies in Ideology and Society* (New York: Monthly Review Press, 1973); Adam B. Ulam, *Ideologies and Illusions: Revolutionary Thought from Herzen to Solzhenitsyn* (Cambridge, Mass.: Harvard University Press, 1976); Ukandi G. Damachi, *Leadership Ideology in Africa: Attitudes Toward Socioeconomic Development* (New York: Praeger Publishers, 1976); Irving Louis Horowitz, *Philosophy, Science and the Sociology of Knowledge* (Springfield, Ill.: C. C. Thomas, 1961); Don Martindale, "Fact, Truth and the Sociology of Knowledge," *International Journal of Contemporary Sociology* 9 (1972): 117-131.

9. Talcott Parsons, *The Structure of Social Action: A Study in Social Theory with Special Reference to a Group of Recent European Writers* (New York: Free Press, 1949). Parsons' originality has been quite overrated; see, for instance, David G. McKee, "The Metaphysics of Talcott Parsons," *International Journal of Contemporary Sociology* 12 (1975):89-94; Whitney Pope, Jere Cohen, and Lawrence Hazelrigg, "On the Divergence of Weber and Durkheim: A Critique of Parsons' Covergence," *American Sociological Review* 40 (1975):417-427; Alfred L. Baldwin, "The Parsonian Theory of Personality," in Max Black, ed., *The Social Theories of Talcott Parsons: A Critical Examination* (Englewood Cliffs, N.J.: Prentice-Hall, 1961).

10. Pitirim A. Sorokin, *Social and Cultural Dynamics* (New York: American Book Co.; New York, 1937-1941, 4 vols.; one-volume edition, Boston: Porter Sargent, 1957); For the studies analyzing Sorokin's works, see Edward A. Tiryakian, ed., *Sociological Theory, Values and Sociocultural Change: Essays in Honor of Pitirim A. Sorokin* (Glencoe, Ill.: Free Press, 1963); Philip J. Allen, ed., *Pitirim A. Sorokin* (Durham, N.C.: Duke University Press, 1963); Joseph S. Roucek, "Sorokin's Impact on Contemporary Global Sociology," *Indian Journal of Social Research* 8 (1967):197-206; W. Warren Wagar, *The City of Man, Prophecies of a World Civilization in Twentieth-Century Thought* (Baltimore: Penguin, 1963), pp. 93-97, and *passim*.

11. A. J. Toynbee, *A Study of History* (New York: Oxford University Press, 1934-1961, 10 vols., abridgment by D. C. Somervell, 1947-1957). Analyzed in Wagar, *The City of Man*, pp. 84-92, and *passim*; Nicholas S. Timasheff, *Sociological Theory: Its Nature and Growth* (New York: Random House, 1967), pp. 273-276, and *passim*; Joseph S. Roucek, ed., *Contemporary Sociology* (Westport, Conn.: Greenwood Press, 1969), pp. 49ff.

12. Theodor Laurence, *The Miracle Power of Believing* (West Nyack, N.Y.: Parker, 1976); Paul L. Holmer, *C. S. Lewis: The Shape of His Faith and Thought* (New York: Harper and Row, 1976); Maurice Claude Burrell, *Whom Then Can We Believe?* (Chicago: Moody Press, 1976); Norman James Young, *Creator, Creation, and Faith* (Philadelphia: Westminster Press, 1976); Harminus Martinus Kuitert, *The Necessity*

of Faith: Or, Without Faith You're as Good as Dead (Grand Rapids, Mich.: W. B. Eerdmans Publishing Co., 1976); Elizabeth Maclaren, The Nature of Belief (New York: Hawthorn, 1976); James L. Merrell, ed., The Power of One: Men and Women of Faith Who Make a Difference (St. Louis, Mo.: Bethany Press, 1976); Charles E. Cluff, Parapsychology and the Christian Faith (Valley Forge, Pa.: Judson Press, 1976).

13. "Behind the Rise in Crime and Terror," U.S. News and World Report (November 13, 1972), pp. 41-49.

14. Paul Wilkinson, Political Terrorism (London: Macmillan and Co., 1974), bibliography, pp. 152-160; Joseph S. Roucek, "IMRO," in Slavonic Encyclopedia (New York: Philosophical Library, 1943), pp. 531-532; Roucek, "Sociological Elements of a Theory of Terror and Violence," American Journal of Economics and Sociology 21 (1962):165-172; Roucek, "Guerrilla Warfare: Its Theories and Strategies," International Behavioural Scientist 6 (1974):57-80; Hannah Arendt, On Revolution (London: Faber and Faber, 1964); Hannah Arendt, The Origins of Totalitarianism (London: Allen and Unwin, 1967); Paul Avrich, The Russian Anarchists (Princeton, N.J.: Princeton University Press, 1967): Richard Cobb, Terreur et Subsistances, 1793-1795 (Paris: Libraries Clauvreuil, 1964); H. Eckstein, ed., Internal War (New York: Free Press, 1964); Louis Feuer, The Conflict of Generations (London: Heinemann, 1969); Sigmund Freud, Civilization and Its Discontent (London: Hogarth Press, 1963); Feliks Gross, The Seizure of Political Power (New York: Philosophical Library, 1957); Feliks Gross, "Political Violence and Terror in 19th and 20th Century Russia and Eastern Europe," in Assassination and Political Violence, Vol. 8 of A Report to the National Commission on the Causes and Prevention of Violence, edited by J. F. Kirkham, S. G. Levy, and W. J. Crotty (Washington, D.C.: U.S. Government Printing Office, 1969), pp. 421-476; Eric Hobsbawm, Bandits (London: Weidenfeld and Nicholson, 1969); Simma Holt, Terror in the Name of God: The Story of the Sons of Freedom Doukhobors (Toronto/ Montreal: McClelland and Stewart, 1964); Carl Leiden and Karl M. Schmitt, The Politics of Violence (Englewood Cliffs, N.J.: Prentice-Hall, 1968); Albert Londres, Terror in the Balkans (London: Constable, 1935); Jay Mallin, ed., Terror and Urban Guerrillas: A Study of Tactics and Documents (Coral Gables, Fla.: University of Miami Press, 1971); Thomas P. Thornton, "Terror as a Weapon of Political Agitation," in H. Eckstein, ed., Internal War (New York: Free Press, 1964), pp. 71-99; Eugene V. Walter, "Violence and the Process of Terror," American Sociological Review 29 (1964): 248-257; George Woodcock, Anarchism: A History of Libertarian Ideas and Movements (Cleveland: World Publishing Co., 1962).

15. S. M. Lipset, Student Politics: Student Movements—Past and Present (New York: Basic Books, 1967); Joseph S. Roucek, "The Role of Students and Intellectuals in the Arab Middle East," Il Politico 40 (1975): 296-305; Joachim Remak, The Origins of the Second World War (Englewood Cliffs, N.J.: Prentice-Hall, 1976).

16. Robert S. Strother and Eugene H. Methvin, "Terrorism on the Rampage," Reader's Digest 54 (November 1975):73-77.

17. Thomas Szasz, Heresies (Garden City, N.Y.: Anchor Press/Doubleday, 1976); R. I. Moore, The Birth of Popular Heresy (New York: St. Martin's Press, 1976); Max Nomad, Political Heretics: From Plato to Mao Tse-tung (Ann Arbor: University of Michigan Press, 1963).

Charles M. Unkovic
and William R. Brown

POLICE

While many institutions function to maintain law and order in a society, in the final analysis, it is the police who are charged most directly with preventing and controlling crime. It is popular today to tear down our regulatory agencies, as Philip Wylie did in his classic book, *Generation of Vampires*.[1] Some current writers seem to delight in chipping away at the power base of the police, so much so that the effectiveness of this agency is dangerously undermined. The media remind us daily that crime is rampant—that anticrime programs have not lived up to their expectations despite billions spent to better equip more policemen. What are the latent effects of torpedoing the social agency which has evolved to protect its citizens?

In the period when Gemeinschaft patterns of relationships dominated societal life, society did not require a specialized group to control its members. As societies evolved toward Gesellschaft patterns, more complex social systems could no longer resolve differences among their members. There had developed a greater division of labor, wider circles of travel, fewer personal ties, and thus a higher degree of anonymity and impersonality. Gradually, the police concept began to emerge as a means of keeping order.

The concept of police probably has existed as long as man has needed to be protected from his fellow man. Historians cannot agree as to the one source of the word "police." Most of the recognized authorities believe that the term goes back to the Greeks and was probably derived from the word "polis," a word meaning "city." The term is loosely defined as an executive and judicial system that functions to protect life, limb, and property by ensuring that the laws are obeyed. Other authorities believe that the word "police" derives from the French word "policier," which refers to the power of the people. The purists may prefer this term since it is more conceptual than the Greek definition and suggests more directly the process of social control. Both the Greek and French advocates, however, agree that the title of police was officially and unanimously accepted in the 1829 Act of Parliament under the Leadership of Sir Robert Peel. Although Peel is sometimes ignored in our modern textbooks, his insights led to our modern concept of the police.[2]

Before reviewing the role of police agencies in society and the transitional problems that they face today and that affect their image, let us first examine the role that an individual policeman plays in our society. What is an officer up against in trying to ensure "law and order" as he/she interacts with an impersonal and sometimes hostile public under ever-changing conditions?

An Analytical View of the Role of Police

The cultural, social, and psychological process relevant to social control can best be discussed by using a dyadic illustration. In subsequent sections, we will return to the sociological perspective and view police as a collectivity. As a means of understanding the role expectations and limitations of a police officer, it is useful to analyze him/her as a possible source of influence when interacting with a (potential) offender. Neither the officer nor the offender lives and acts in a vacuum. Complex "classes" of variables affect the degree to which the officer can effectively control the offender, including the intensity and kinds of motive states present within both the offender and the officer. We will focus on these interaction processes in some detail, for they are at the heart of problems involving the ability of law enforcement officers, acting collectively, to achieve what we call social control at the societal level.

Figure 1 schematically illustrates the cybernetic processes that *can* occur when an officer confronts a would-be offender. In some situations, whole classes of variables may not even be present, but they must be considered as potential factors in a theoretical model. For ease of reference, these classes of variables are labeled via a letter in the lower right corner of each "cell." Let us call the police officer "Pratt" (cell b) and the potential offender "Owens" as we analyze the interaction processes. Note also in Figure 1 that cells a, b, and c are *external* influences affecting the offender (Owens), while cells d through i are Owens' *internal* factors.[3] Broadly stated, cells a and b represent direct, external pressures as means of social control; cell c depicts a range of incentives that strongly affect behavioral choices; and cells e, f, and g portray internal states that can also affect an individual's behavioral motives.[4]

What can Pratt do as a social control agent to prevent or cope with Owens' deviant behavior? What can't Pratt do? Does criticism of the police system stem in part from the public's unrealistic expectations of its ability to cope with deviant behavior? What other external factors inhibit or strengthen Pratt's ability to prevent Owens from committing socially unacceptable acts? These are some of the questions we hope to answer more clearly via a systematic analysis of the processes related to social control.[5]

Forces External to the Offender

As a police officer, Pratt has authority, that is, legitimate power, to intervene should Owens be in the process of committing an unlawful or

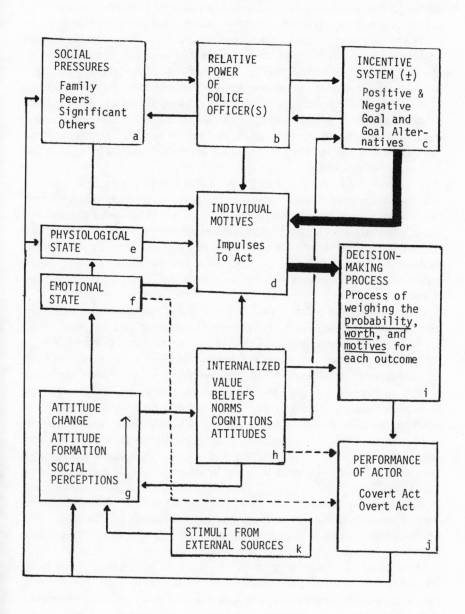

FIGURE 1. *Interaction Model Portraying the Role of Police Officers (b) As Agents of Social Control*

dangerous act. Pratt's authority was assigned to him by the police agency. Although numerous specific rules and regulations condition his authority, regulations cannot cover all situations. Pratt must have some degree of discretion to act or not act in ambiguous situations. Rigorous training is intended to assist law officers in the use of their authority. Even so, charges of abuse of authority are frequently leveled.[6] It should be noted that a "power" source that is "assigned" by others can also be taken away by the assigners; hence, Pratt's use of authority is constantly subject to scrutiny. Although we cannot pursue here why police officers abuse authority, it should be pointed out that police, being mortals, are subject to the same influences as those shown to affect Owens' motives in Figure 1 (note the sources by tracing the arrows back from cell d).

Before viewing forces external to Owens that compete with Pratt's power over him, we will note another source of police authority that is derived from the cultural values, beliefs, and norms of a society. The higher the relative status afforded police within a society, the easier it is for police to prevent and control crime. Over a period of time, flagrant abuses of authority tend to lead to decreased societal support of their status and therefore seriously erode police power. Continuous outcries against police, which are sometimes exaggerated and/or unfounded, have the same detrimental effect on this consensual source of police power. Nonetheless, Pratt does have authority over Owens inasmuch as he can arrest and even shoot him—at least to the degree that Owens perceives this outcome as a real possibility or probability.

In addition to Pratt's direct power threat over Owens, he has another less direct tool in his social control "bag." Collectively, police officers can affect the availability of some, but certainly not all, incentives (cell c) that are prime human motivators. For instance, Pratt, or one of his cohorts, can use his power to help Owens by protecting him or his family, coming to his rescue, overlooking a minor rule infraction, or in some other way doing something for Owens that exceeds Owens' level of expectations for a policeman's behavior. Such behavior eventually results in Owens' building up a reservoir of positive "social credits" (i.e., attitudes) toward Pratt and other policemen (cells g and h). In contrast, Pratt can use his power to violate Owens' level of expectations for fairness (or to block his access to a goal) and thereby cause Owens to accrue a reserve or balance of negative "social credits" regarding Pratt and, by association, other policemen.

These social credits are accrued as a function of the frequency, duration, direction, and degree of discrepancy from Owens' perceptions of Pratt's acts to Owens' current level of expectations. Owens' level of expectations (or comparison level) is based on his previous cognitive experience and is thus subject to change as he has new experiences with Pratt (or other officers). According to the norm of reciprocity, there is a tendency to "pay back," or "get even" with, "one's creditors." Owens may want to cooperate with Pratt because of a positive "bank" of accrued social credits, or he may have an impulse to rebel or even use violence against Pratt (or less powerful others) to vent his frustrations from accrued negative social credits.[7]

In sum, the police can (and often do) use their authority in a positive manner to more effectively accomplish social control within the populace, or they may abuse their authority (and often do) to make social control even more difficult as a result of an erosion of their power differential. Building up an overall surplus of positive social credits facilitates effective social control. The importance of social control via the police achieving goodwill within the community was recognized, although not heeded, when the Englishmen Rowan and Mayne developed the first set of principles for modern law enforcement agencies.[8]

Owens has other external influences that compete with the power Pratt may exert and with the incentives that may attract or repulse him. Owens must often contend with pressures (cell a). These social pressures may be "mixed"; that is, some of one valence (e.g., positive parental influence) and other influences may be negative (e.g., peer pressures). In addition, all of the forces motivating Owens vary in intensity as well as in the degree to which he respects the person(s) exerting the pressures(s).

One last comment regarding external forces is crucial to understanding the plight of police in preventing crime. An offender usually tries to commit a serious crime when there is minimal likelihood that a law enforcement agent will observe him/her. The crime may be carried out in a strictly anonymous setting or in the presence of an accomplice only. Anonymity adds greatly to the probability that the offender will get a highly desirable reward without incurring a great risk of being caught. Police cannot be everywhere at once; incentives of one kind or another are everywhere. The worth of the incentives and the probability (risk) of apprehension and subsequent significant punishment are key factors that are weighed during the decision-making process (cell i) prior to the behavioral act (cell j). Potholm and Morgan report that the "current odds are approximately 50 to 1 that a person committing a burglary will not get caught for that burglary and approximately 100 to 1 that he will ever spend a day in jail."[9]

Pratt's *power* to prevent Owens and countless others from committing criminal acts is simply not enough to assure conformity to societal rules. There are too many incentives out there, too many illegal means of obtaining tempting goals, too many social pressures egging him on, and no practical way to increase the number of police to sufficiently guard all the worldly goals that are desirable. In a nutshell, police power has to compete with the external forces overviewed above, as well as the internal factors discussed in the next section.

Internal Forces as Motivators

Cells e through i in Figure 1 represent classes of variables related to the internal processes that affect Owens' impulses to act (cell d). Even if Pratt were present every time Owens (or others) were tempted to commit criminal acts, the police power factor would have to be viewed as only one of several motives affecting Owens' actions. We shall briefly consider other major, often competing, internal forces.

The most basic human needs (hunger, thirst, warmth, sleep, sex, freedom from pain) must be satisfied before higher level motivation factors become important. To the extent that the body is seriously deprived of any one of these basic needs, the physiological state (cell e) takes precedence over other motives illustrated in Figure 1.[10] A closely related class of motives is the emotional state (cell f) of the person. By definition, irrational behavior occurs when the emotions are in control over cognitions. The cognitive and semicognitive processes (cells g to i) may simply be bypassed, should Owens be in a rage over a recent happening. (Note the dotted arrow in Figure 1 from cell f to cell j.) If Owens were in a severe, negative physiological or emotional state, Pratt's effectiveness in deterring Owens from crime or in coping with him after a crime would be largely impaired. It is to the credit of law enforcement officers that they are able to peacefully resolve as many dangerous episodes as they do. Thanks to the nature of the mass media, however, we are more apt to be aware of their unsuccessful cases.

Our internalized values, beliefs, norms, cognitions, and attitudes (cell h) are the product of ongoing socialization processes involving complex social perceptions, attitude formation, and attitude change (cell g).[11] Since we have already touched on attitudinal motivation tendencies derived from the buildup of social credits, we will restrict most of our remaining comments regarding cell h to the importance of internalized values in achieving social control.

Value systems are learned over long periods of time. Once broad values are well internalized, they are more impervious to change than are the more specific attitudes.[12] Values, together with specific attitudes accrued through the social credit process, have dual functions in the motivation processes, although they are closely related. First, they play an affective role (cell h to cell d) as major influences for what one wants to do or not to do. In our example, Owens would need to have strong socially approved values to resist a criminal act to obtain some enticing outcome, especially if the situation were, or could be planned to be, under anonymous conditions. Most crimes (a frequent exception being irrational acts) are committed by those who have less deeply embedded societal values or values different from those of the dominant society.[13]

Second, values and specific attitudes determine the worth of the incentives in cell c. What is one man's meat is another man's poison. Hence, through socialization processes we learn what goals and goal alternatives are worth pursuing. (Note arrows from cell h to cell c, then to cell d.)

Freudian psychiatrists argue that much of our behavior is unconsciously determined.[14] To the extent that this is true (and it is very difficult to support empirically), the decision-making process is by-passed, as illustrated by the dotted arrow from cell h to cell j. Likewise, we are unaware of habitual types of behavior unless an important or threatening situation arises.

Finally, in the decision-making process (cell i), each of the various motives that are salient in a given situation are weighed along with the worth of each possible outcome. The probability or risk of obtaining each outcome is also weighed. The ability to calculate these probabilities is a function of the cognitions from previous experiences (cell h). Any one of these three major dimensions can negate the other two.[15] For instance, Owens could highly prize a truck load of CB radios and hold weak internalized values about theft, but because of Pratt's presence and power, Owens might well decide that the probability of being caught is too great a risk.

Obviously, Owens is constantly exhibiting some sort of behavior (cell j). His acts can directly affect his perceptions and expectations about himself (self-concept), his physiological state, and also people with whom he interacts. These cybernetic processes are, of course, dynamic and not static as must be depicted in Figure 1.

In summary, we have analyzed social control as a complex series of interrelated but often competing processes. Viewed in this manner, the limitations of a police officer such as Pratt are clear. We have seen how damage to the societal power base of the police can further curtail their effectiveness. As also noted, the police can improve their position in the eyes of the populace by performing in such a way that will lead to a positive reservoir of social credits. Today police human relations departments are charged with this task, but the behavior of individual officers is crucial to community goodwill. The tendency for citizens to want to cooperate with police and obey the regulations with which they are charged to enforce can be enhanced to an appreciable degree, whereas police behavior that culminates in a negative reserve of social credits only adds to the perilous social control status they hold. Let us turn now to the role of police as viewed from other perspectives.

Police in Society

The limitations of police officers as enforcement agents illustrated by means of the dyadic interaction skeletal model become glaring when we view the recent track record of the criminal justice system.[16] In 1974, amid the multibillion dollar anticrime program of the Law Enforcement Assistance Administration (LEAA), reported crime rose by 18 percent, the largest jump since the FBI began compiling records. In LEAA's eight years, $4 billion have been spent, yet violent crime has increased by 60 percent nationally. Police departments have gotten a disproportionately large share of these funds, about 50 percent. Less than 15 percent has gone to the courts and something less than 40 percent can be traced directly to correctional facilities and programs.[17] Relatively little emphasis has been placed on the prevention of crime.[18]

Viewing social control in terms of spending more money for the latest in patrol cars, communication, and the like, or even in passing laws making punishment more or less severe, or in terms of developing new experimental rehabilitation/diversion programs, research techniques, and/or the latest in crime lab technologies, is too narrow a focus to fully understand or effectively cope with the prevalence of crime in a society. The fact that societal institutions (family, economic, political, religious, educational) are all undergoing major transitions greatly compounds the problems of police. Laws and the social organizations that create them and attempt to enforce them must be viewed as dynamic, evolving processes, not as static sets of rules.[19] More sophisticated sociological systems analysis techniques are being developed to analyze these cybernetic forces in order to better identify, trace, explain, and predict major sources of dysfunctions evidenced by high crime rates in a social system.

Should the roots of high crime rates be more convincingly documented as basic societal problems (that is, problems costly to battle such as poverty, inequity, internalization of more functional societal values), will society be willing to take the giant steps necessary to effectively combat crime?[20] The police alone cannot. Boston Police Chief Robert diGrazia emphatically states, "We cannot reduce crime. That's something beyond our capabilities and I wish that politicians would recognize it."[21] Nothing short of establishing crime reduction as a major superordinate goal (i.e., a common goal of all groups) seems to have a chance of effecting significant crime reduction. Are we ready to pay the price, a price that could conceivably lead toward "1984" types of surveillance? The present trend is to give the police less legal discretion in America,[22] although they apparently still exercise a great deal of discretion in the field.[23] Today, there are approximately 450,000 law enforcement officers who serve in over 43,000 separate agencies, many of which overlap. Consolidation of departments, once thought to be a major remedy, has not lived up to expectations. The agencies range in size from an average of 5 in Maine to 31,000 in New York City. (Interestingly, in New York City, there are rarely over 1,000 officers on patrol at any one time.) On the average, there are 1.9 police officers per 1,000 inhabitants in the United States, including the FBI, which in a sense is a "national" police system with 9,000 agents and 10,000 support personnel.[24]

In recent years, the educational levels of police officers has been upgraded. Currently, an average of 37 percent of new police recruits have had at least one year of college. Officers are usually encouraged through tuition support or promotional credits to complete their education while serving on the force.[25] For some writers, education is the key to professionalization;[26] others point out the need to study the type of training the officer should experience.[27]

Female and minority race police officers are being more actively recruited, but they have been only slowly accepted.[28] In the past, policewomen have been assigned protective tasks rather than a full range of duties. Black policemen, especially, have identity problems, often being viewed as representatives of an alien white influence in their black communities.[29]

Despite the failures of the criminal justice system cited above, some positive points can be made on behalf of police. Police officers must indeed be jacks of all trades. More than 60 percent of their time is spent dealing with *non*criminal matters, be it helping a child retrieve a cat, directing traffic, tending the injured, or intervening in family crises. Wilson notes that only 10 percent of incoming calls to police involve law enforcement.[30] When we view the changing roles of police, the fact that social control per se has thus far eluded police agencies can be in part rationalized away, depending on how police roles are to be defined in our evolving society.

Perceptions of Police

If you were to go out on the street and ask ten people, "Who are the police and what do they do?," you would probably get ten different answers. To the businessman, a policeman is the man who protects his business and watches over it while the rest of the world is watching TV or sleeping; to the teenager, the policeman is the guy who breaks up an innocent riot, which is a lot of fun, after a football game; to the ghetto black, the policeman is the guy who is out to get him; to the aged, the policeman is the guy who helps him across the street; to the criminal, the policeman is the guy who will gladly take away his freedom; to the average Joe and Jane, the policeman is the authority figure who makes them more paranoid than usual.

This network of complexity, accompanied by unlimited responsibilities, makes it extremely difficult for the policeman to maintain a clear role identity. Hence, the policeman sometimes changes roles, from social worker to tough cop. To say that this shift confuses the public is a gross understatement.

Role confusion does not just happen. The myth that the major role of the policeman is to prevent crime is inculcated to the bright-eyed children in elementary schools and to the bright-eyed police recruits. Most crimes occur out of sight of the police; this situation can only be significantly altered by radically modifying the mores and folkways of a culture and its incentive system. Still the myth persists, and everyone from the raw rookie to the superior "super cop" pretends it is true. As one day follows another, the myth becomes part of the officer's value system, and he really believes he is in the business of preventing crime. Then suddenly, the middle-class conservative law officer has to battle internal conflict when his looking-glass concept can no longer be avoided. As James Q. Wilson commented regarding the standard police reaction to the public pressure that they can and ought to prevent crime: "Their response was perfectly rational and to be encountered in any organization that is judged by a standard it can't meet—they lied."[31]

The policeman is also told that it is his job to enforce laws. What laws? Arthur Niederhoffer, a former New York policeman, says: "No policeman enforces all the laws of a community. If he did, we would all be in jail before the end of the first day."[32] The policeman becomes judge and jury. How, then, does the policeman decide which laws to enforce, and on whom? Many factors go into these decisions, including the mores of the community in which he works, those of his own past, and those of his own peers.

Margaret Mead, writing about police and community attitudes, says, "It is their job to provide whatever the community will support or tolerate in the way of law and order, including order that is outside the law."[33] Clearly, this places the policeman in the position of policy-maker as well as enforcer. It gives him a degree of discretion which, indeed, he could not operate without, unless the general behavior and mores of the community he patrolled were the same as his. Edwin Lemert calls the policeman's role "a policy forming police administration in miniature." He adds:

The policeman's art consists of applying and enforcing a multitude of laws and ordinances in such a degree or proportion that the greater degree of protection will be secured. The degree of enforcement and the method of application will vary with each neighborhood and community . . . each patrolman must, in a sense, determine the standard to be set in the area for which he is responsible.[34]

The heart of the problem is that the policeman must realize that he plays a multifaceted role and that he should be aware he must be objective and fair in his performance as social control agent and law officer. Based on the analytical discussion presented earlier, we would add that the police should consciously seek additional ways to strengthen their image by individually and collectively generating a surplus of positive "social credits." Such a reservoir can enhance their ability to maintain social control and enforce the laws; moreover, it is an objective that police can accomplish. It is sound advice to "spend" their social credits as conservatively as possible so the reserve will be "there" to draw on when needed.

Notes

1. Philip Wylie, *Generation of Vipers* (New York: Farrar and Rinehart, 1942).

2. See John L. Sullivan, *Introduction to Police Science*, 2d ed. (New York: McGraw-Hill, 1971), pp. 1-2; William J. Bopp and Donald O. Schultz, *Principles of American Law Enforcement and Criminal Justice* (Springfield, Ill.: C. C. Thomas, 1972), p. 24; and Alvin W. Cohn, *Crime and Justice Administration* (Philadelphia: J. B. Lippincott Co., 1976), p. 224.

3. Caution must be taken so as not to reify the constructs used herein to portray internal states. As yet, we have relatively little physiological understanding of mental processes. The sequences depicted in Figure 1 are intended to be insightful, but in reality, processes analogous to these occur at electrochemical speed—their order is unknown.

4. Richard T. LaPiere, *A Theory of Social Control* (New York: McGraw-Hill, 1954).

5. For a more complete model of attitude formation, attitude change, and the decision-making processes, see William R. Brown, "A General Model of Social Interaction and Decision-Making Processes," paper submitted at the 77th annual meeting of the American Sociological Association, August 1977.

6. Arthur Niederhoffer and Abraham S. Blumberg, *The Ambivalent Force*, 2d ed. (Hinsdale, Ill.: Dryden Press, 1976), pp. 149-164.

7. See Alvin W. Gouldner, "The Norm of Reciprocity: A Preliminary Statement," *American Sociological Review* 25, no. 2 (1960):161-178; Peter M. Blau, *Exchange and Power in Social Life* (New York: John Wiley and Sons, 1964); Brown, "A General Model."

8. See Robert C. Trojanowicz and Samuel L. Dixon, *Criminal Justice and the Community* (Englewood Cliffs, N.J.: Prentice-Hall, 1974), pp. 24-28.

9. Christian P. Potholm and Richard E. Morgan, *Focus on Police: Police in American Society* (New York: John Wiley and Sons, 1976), p. 397.

10. A. H. Maslow, *Motivation and Personality* (New York: Harper, 1954).

11. Brown, "A General Model."

12. Ezra Stotland and Lance K. Canon, *Social Psychology: A Cognitive Approach* (Philadelphia: W. B. Saunders, 1972).

13. Numerous studies covering the problems of crime and the administration of justice have appeared in recent years, such as Bopp and Schultz, *Principles of American Law Enforcement*; David J. Bordura, "Police," in *International Encyclopedia of the Social Sciences* (New York: Macmillan, 1968); Cohn, *Crime and Justice Administration*; Larry T. Hoover, *Police Educational Characteristics and Curricula*, U.S. Department of Justice, LEAA, July 1975; C. Ray Jeffery, *Crime Prevention Through Environmental Design* (Beverly Hills, Calif.: Sage Publications, 1971); La Piere, *A Theory of Social Control*; Harry W. More, Jr., *Critical Issues in Law Enforcement* (Cincinnati: W. H. Anderson Co., 1972); Arthur Niederhoffer, *Behind the Shield: The Police in Urban Society* (Garden City, N.Y.: Doubleday, 1967); Niederhoffer and Blumberg, *The Ambivalent Force*; Potholm and Morgan, *Focus on Police*; Sullivan, *Introduction to Police Science*; Robert C. Trojanowicz and Samuel L. Dixon, *Criminal Justice and the Community* (Englewood Cliffs, N.J.: Prentice-

Hall, 1974); Wylie, *Generation of Vipers*; Jerry Wilson, *Police Report* (Boston: Little, Brown, 1975).

14. Mervin E. Shaw, *Theories of Social Psychology* (New York: McGraw-Hill, 1970).

15. J. W. Atkinson and N. J. Feather, *A Theory of Achievement Motivation* (New York: John Wiley and Sons, 1966.

16. Gerald M. Caplan, "Criminology, Criminal Justice, and the War on Crime," *Criminology* 14, no. 1 (May 1976):3-16.

17. Mitchell C. Lynch, "Federal Law Enforcement Aid," *Wall Street Journal*, July 7, 1976.

18. See Jeffery, *Crime Prevention Through Environmental Design*.

19. Joseph S. Roucek, "Law and Sociology," Chapter 12, in James Van Patten, Joseph Roucek, Michael Belok, and Martin Schoppmeyer, eds., *Conflict, Permanency, Change and Education* (Moti Katra: Agra-3, India: Satish Book Enterprise, 1976), p. 217.

20. Potholm and Morgan, *Focus on Police*, pp. 375-412.

21. Caplan, "Criminology", p. 5.

22. Joseph S. Roucek, "The Sociology of the Police Control," *International Journal of Legal Research* 8 (1972):66.

23. Niederhoffer and Blumberg, *The Ambivalent Force*, pp. 169-196.

24. Potholm and Morgan, *Focus on Police*, pp. 398-401.

25. Hoover, *Police Educational Characteristics and Curricula*.

26. Ibid., p. 2.

27. Wilson, *Police Report*, pp. 169-177.

28. Ibid., pp. 186-193.

29. Potholm and Morgan, *Focus on Police*, pp. 181-212.

30. James Q. Wilson, "The Police and Their Problems, a Theory," *Public Policy* (1963).

31. Ibid., p. 134.

32. Arthur Niederhoffer, *Behind the Shield*, p. 12.

33. Margaret Mead, "The Police and the Community, *Redbook*, June 1969, p. 38.

34. Edwin M. Lemert, *Human Deviance, Social Problems and Social Control* (Englewood Cliffs, N.J.: Prentice-Hall, 1967), p. 24.

Oleg Zinam

ECONOMIC CONTROL

Economic control is a basic and essential aspect of social control but not its most important element. Social control encompasses all means, methods, and institutions that provide the incentive and sanctions necessary for the orderly performance of vital social functions. Economic control facilitates the orderly and peaceful performance of economic functions relating to (1) the use of scarce material resources to produce goods and services for the satisfaction of human wants and (2) the distribution of income among those who contributed to their production. At any given point in time, the existence of this economic control is manifested in the rules of the game controlling the economic activities of production, exchange, distribution, and consumption. These rules emanate from two principal sources: (1) ethical standards embodied in the customs, mores, and traditions of society and (2) explicit norms of behavior formulated by lawgivers. The first are the results of a subconscious evolutionary process leading back to the very roots of the origins of social order, and the second are explicitly formulated by legislatures to modify existing laws.

Rules of the game regulating both traditional and legal economic activities are given in the short run. In the long run, however, these rules, as well as rules for making rules themselves, can be altered. Hence, the long-run includes the choice between alternative types of socioeconomic control systems. This result can be attained through either an orderly democratic process or through the violent overthrow of the existing order. In Hayek's words, "If in the long run we are makers of our own fate, in the short run we are captives of ideas we have created."[1] Philosophically, in libertarian societies, the choice among different types and degrees of economic control involves the perennial dilemma of reconciling conflicting requirements of preserving human freedom while maintaining orderly performance of economic functions. "Since freedom and all change conflict more or less with order, the primary essential," according to Knight, is that "a delicate balance must be struck and maintained."[2]

Economic Control and Pure Types of Economic Systems

At any given point in time, the existing rules of the game determine who in a given society has power to decide what is going to be produced, how resources are to be allocated for this production, and for whom economic goods and services are produced. How this central question is answered depends primarily on certain important characteristics of the economy's decision-making structure. Whether the government or individuals in their capacity as producers and consumers possess this ultimate power, and to what extent, depend primarily on society's organizational and power structure emanating from it. Of crucial importance is whether political organization is highly centralized and controls economic organization, or whether it is decentralized by the principle of division of power and separated from economic organization. The role of ideologies and their impact on the formation of preferences is essentially different under these alternative organizational and power structures. Of crucial importance, however, is the effect of organizational and power structures on *whose* preferences become effective.[3]

Understanding economic control is important not only because it is essential for formulating economic policies but also because its characteristics and extent have thoroughgoing implications for economic efficiency, quality of life, freedom, and human dignity. The almost unsurmountable difficulties in defining quality of life, freedom, and human dignity are fully recognized. Yet, any society must reach some implicit or explicit degree of consensus on the content and meaning of these concepts.

To facilitate the analysis of real economic systems as they exist in the outside world in an impure or mixed form, it is necessary to resort to the use of ideal or pure types in the Weberian sense.[4] These pure types will reveal how control is exercised in diverse economic systems with strikingly different organizational and power structures. The ideal or pure types used in this study are denoted as Perfect Market Economy or M-P-D (Market-Private Ownership of Capital-Democratic Political Structure) and Absolute Command Economy or K-C-T (Command-Collective Ownership of Capital-Totalitarian Political Structure).

In terms of crucial variables of organization, power, value-systems, preferences, and effective freedom, these ideal types have the following characteristics:

In a Perfect Market Economy, political and economic organizations are separated and neither dominates the other. Political organization is decentralized and is based on separation of power. Capital is privately owned and is permitted to be used for private profit. This type of organization leads to separation of political and economic power, a political system based on checks and balances, competitive political order, and political democracy.

On the ideological level, the individual is considered supreme over the collective. Society exists primarily to assist individuals to attain their destiny. In both economic and political realms, individuals have the right to make their own choices.

Separation and decentralization of economic and political orders in such a society facilitate the existence of competing ideological systems and protect the individual's right to dissent. Under the M-P-D order, individual preferences become effective, while the government's preferences tend to reflect those of the individual. In the realm of economics, market forces determine the opportunity functions of individuals. All of these characteristics assure freedom of consumer choice, occupational choice, and freedom of business decisions within the framework of government, which limits itself to external defense, upholding law and order, and control of natural monopolies.

At the opposite pole of the spectrum, in an Absolute Command Economy political organization dominates economic order. Governmental central planning fully controls economic activity, while political order is totalitarian. Factors of production are collectively owned; the power structure reflects society's organization; and all political and economic power is concentrated in one center. It is a closed power system in which a self-appointed elite enjoys a monopoly of all political and economic power. In such an ideal socioeconomic order, ideology stresses superiority of the collective over the individual. Only the rulers' ideology is permitted; any ideological dissent is ruthlessly suppressed. Education and systems of information are geared to the conditioning of individuals' beliefs and preferences. Government's preferences are effective, while the preferences of individuals are rendered ineffective by restricting their opportunity functions and by conditioning. Government enjoys most of the effective freedoms in both political and economic realms. Consumer sovereignty is replaced by planners' sovereignty.[5]

All real socioeconomic systems are a mixture of elements contained in extreme pure types. Nevertheless, the implications of organization and power structures in pure types and the impact of these structures on the ideologies, preferences, opportunities, and effective freedom of individuals, groups, organizations, and governments must be thoroughly studied because they have a definite effect on the quality of life of the people,[6] their freedom, and their human dignity.

Economic Controls, Efficiency, Well-Being, and Human Dignity

Economic controls affect total human well-being or quality of life, though the impact on economic well-being seems to be more immediate and more evident. Whether the impact of controls is measured in terms of per capita income or rate of growth of total per capita national income, the problem is always one of efficiency. Yet, efficiency alone is not enough since ill-advised objectives pursued with rigor and efficiency can be even more damaging to an economic system and the well-being of individuals than a sound economic policy implemented inefficiently.

If a society agrees on its economic objectives, what level of controls is just right to attain these objectives? If costs and benefits from economic controls, as well as economic controls themselves, were homogeneous and infinitely divisible, an optimum level of controls could be defined as that point where marginal benefits just equal marginal costs. But this is very rarely the case, and marginal analysis utterly fails in most attempts to calculate the optimum volume of controls needed to attain certain reform or change in the rule of the game in the market.

This situation is aggravated by an almost inevitable divergence in economic and social costs. It has been argued that much of economic efficiency might be associated with the infliction of social costs which are disproportionately large in comparison to the economic benefits secured. Moreover, on the global level and in a broad historical perspective, economic well-being does not guarantee the good life and happiness of a society. Some writers even condemn economic growth as detrimental and destructive to some important human values. Advocates of zero economic growth policy seem to echo the contentions of John Stuart Mill that a stationary state, contrary to Ricardo's views, should be considered a blessing rather than a calamity. Most economists, however, defend the necessity for improvement in material well-being on the grounds that it broadens the human range of choice for good or evil. If people misuse their freedom to reduce their overall well-being by an imprudent life-style, that is their problem and not the concern of economists.

Nevertheless, there are some disquieting signs that "the quest for higher standards of living is becoming an end in itself, with these standards being defined in exclusively economic terms" and that "higher things are esteemed according to their usefulness for the lower things."[7] This raises the question of the primary purpose of aiming at higher and higher material well-being. It should lead to a higher overall well-being which is extremely difficult to define—even in terms of a weighted quality of life index including the most important facets of human existence: political, social, moral, and others along with economic.

As stated before, in the short run controls are given and the concept of quality of life cannot be substantially changed, while in the long run the rules of the game and even the rules for making or changing the rules themselves can be substantially or even drastically altered. This adds an additional dimension to the concept of overall well-being—that of a society's effective freedom to change both the quality of life desired as well as the type and character of controls determining the rules of the game in socioeconomic life.

Effective freedom to participate in decisions molding the destiny of man is closely associated with the concept of human dignity and with the idea that human dignity cannot be maintained unless some minimal levels of overall well-being are provided to every human being within society. The rest of this essay analyzes the crucial question of the impact of alternative methods of socioeconomic organization providing different types and amounts of economic controls on quality of life and human dignity.

Some Recent Historical Examples

Among the objectives set by governments in their efforts to improve the material well-being of their citizens, one usually finds full employment, adequate economic growth, price stability, and equitable distribution of income and wealth. In libertarian countries, governments frequently include, implicitly or explicitly, the goals of maintaining or even expanding economic freedoms such as the freedoms of consumer choice, occupational choice, and business decisions.

In some cases, there is need for a trade-off between economic freedom and efficiency in attaining other important economic objectives. In others, controls are carried too far, and efficiency can be improved only by their diminution, or even removal. Economists disagree at what point economic controls reach the optimum beyond which their increase becomes harmful.[8]

In the United States, proponents of "managed capitalism" like Paul Samuelson, Walter W. Heller, John K. Galbraith, and Alvin H. Hansen, accept more governmental intervention in economic affairs, while "free economy" economists such as Arthur Burns, Milton Friedman, Frank H. Knight, Henry C. Wallich, and George J. Stigler believe that controls are already beyond the point of diminishing returns.[9] In Great Britain, the Labor government went too far in its push to equalize income and reduce inequality of wealth and is paying for violating Wallich's admonition that "we must furnish welfare without destroying initiative and provide security without doing injury to incentives"[10] by high rates of inflation and unemployment.

But even in totalitarian governments, in which "importance attributed to an individual is notably absent" and is valued "only in so far as he serves the state,"[11] economic controls can become too stringent and overcentralized. Such an economy might suffer from diminishing returns to overcentralization as a result of its complexity rapidly outrunning the capabilities of control mechanisms to deal adequately with the consequences of rising complexity.

This was the case in the Soviet Union in the 1960s. Some Soviet economists and academicians proposed an economic reform to liberalize the system and make it more efficient. Yet, when under Khrushchev an attempt at economic reform was undertaken and a considerable amount of decision-making was shifted from the center to individual republics, the fear of political implications of such a drastic change in the economic sphere led to the

Brezhnev-Kosygin counter-reform, which essentially returned power to central ministries and curbed powers delegated to republics.

The counter-reformers felt that "there is no advance assurance that such a process of transformation would not disrupt the whole intricate web of centralized control levers that make up the authoritarian political system of the USSR."[12] This is a case of controls being carried well beyond the optimum at which freedom and efficiency become complementary, and to increase efficiency, controls have to be reduced. The leaders in the Kremlin refused to gain economic efficiency at the cost of granting more decision power to lower authorities and the people themselves.[13]

The opposite can be illustrated by the policies of the British Labor government in the years immediately following World War II. It refused to restrain the political freedom of its citizens, even though it believed that the imposition of some more stringent controls would improve economic efficiency and thus raise the individual's standard of material well-being. The Labor government considered political as well as net economic freedom an essential part of the overall quality of life. Contrary to John Jewkes' view that a centrally planned economy and preservation of freedom of the individual are incompatible,[14] many other critics agree that central planning never did threaten Britain's free society.[15]

In the long run, a socioeconomic system can gradually evolve from a predominantly free market to a different type of system called democratic socialism. In Great Britain, this happened after World War II. The landslide victory of the Labor party in 1945 was at least partially the result of a shift in the preference of the majority of the English people from one concept of freedom to another. In Hayek's terms, allegiance to "freedom from coercion, freedom from arbitrary power of other men," was substituted by the acceptance of a new freedom from "despotism of physical want," from the "restraints of the economic system," and "from the compulsion of circumstances which inevitably limit the range of choice of all of us, although for some very much more than for others."[16]

Competing Concepts of Freedom

In planned command economies, the rulers use this second concept of freedom, together with another much broader and nobler concept of voluntary subjection to highest value, which could be defined as altruistic service to a collective, usually a nation. This type of freedom involves sacrifice which can be very appealing, especially to young idealists desiring to lose themselves in a cause greater than themselves.

Unfortunately for the individualistic type of freedom, it also includes freedom to relinquish freedom and "to be relieved of the necessity of solving [one's] own economic problems."[17] Moreover, a nation's quest for security at any given historical time might become so overwhelming that people would stress that "without economic security, liberty is not worth having."[18] The prevalence of such a concept of freedom, or rather escape from freedom, greatly contributed to the victory of England's Labor party in 1945. In a democratic market economy, a violent revolution is much easier to achieve. It makes it much easier to replace the existing order with an autocratic command economy than to reverse such a change.

In most theoretical treatises, egoistical behavior is usually attributed to individuals, but very seldom to governments. There exists "a common supposition that government's proper function is the maximization of social welfare." Many theorists "fail to apply the self-interest axiom to governments, although it is the foundation of analysis concerning private economic agents."[19] Since governments are not run by altruists, they cannot be adequately treated by any theory which disregards its organizational and power structure. A government in a command economy controls greater coercive power and can disregard preferences of individuals to a much higher degree than in a libertarian market economy.

A totalitarian government has a much greater potential than a democratic one to "force people to act against their own immediate interests in order to promote a supposedly general interest" and "to substitute the values of outsiders for the values of participants" either by telling them what is good for them or by taking from some to benefit others.[20]

For ideological reasons and to attract people's allegiance, they claim to have formulated superior concepts of freedom and human dignity than their adversaries. Indeed, in their purely theoretical form they are deeper and nobler than libertarian definitions based on individualism. They emphasize an altruistic aspect of these terms. Freedom becomes a voluntary subjection to the highest values embodied in the highest aspirations of a collective, be it society or nation, or of universal union of all workers of the world, while human dignity is derived from a degree of selflessness in serving the collective of which the individual is an organic part.

An Astounding Historical Paradox

Despite the apparent ethical superiority of socialist concepts of freedom and human dignity, historical evidence suggests that economies based on these principles have in no way performed better than predominantly market economies. Paradoxically, the capitalist systems based ideologically on a rather egoistical motto, "from each according to his will to contribute, to each according to his marginal product," have fulfilled the yearnings of men for a higher quality of life and human dignity much better than their socialist counterparts founded on the romantic and more humane credo "from each according to his ability, to each according to his needs."

The reasons for this paradox are manifold and complex. The founding fathers of both the laissez-faire type of social order and the American republic had realistic views of human nature and of its relations to power, society, and government. They saw individuals as potentially egoistical and, when endowed with power, corruptible. They believed that absolute power corrupts absolutely and, therefore, did not entrust anyone with complete control of power. One of the principal merits of the social order based on the division of power advocated by Adam Smith and his contemporaries is "that it is a system under which bad men can do least harm" and that it makes it possible "to grant freedom to all instead of restricting it, as their French contemporaries wished, to 'the good and wise.' "[21]

The assumption of altruistic and perfectible individuals, and the superiority of collective ownership, central planning, and governmental control of economic activity underlying socialist doctrines have led to unintended paradoxical consequences. The socialist theorists, fearful of private exploitation, did not envision the possibility of exploitation of individuals by powerful centralized governments ruling in the name of the collective, or of society as a whole. The attractive slogan "all power to the people" in practice turned out to be "no power to the people" but all power to government acting in the name and, presumably, in the interest of the people. The eventual destruction of market forces under such a system leads to severe restrictions of individual economic and political freedoms and to suppression of human rights and aspirations.

The abysmal difference between the utopian promises of the Marxist-Leninist revolution and the grim reality of the regime imposed by it is common knowledge. Marxism-Leninism promised an end to the exploitation of man by man; the greatest freedom to the largest possible number of people; the withering away of the state; an end of colonialism and imperialism; the fostering of brotherly cosmopolitanism; a classless society; the elimination of bureaucratic abuses and an era of abundance for all. What it delivered is very well known: exploitation of the masses on an unprecedented scale; slavery to the largest number of people in history; a totalitarian state; the greatest colonial empire on earth; oppression of weaker nations by stronger ones; a rigidly stratified class society; the most oppressive and inflexible bureaucracy the world has ever seen; and continual denial to citizens under its control of the level of quality of life they would have attained in a free society. With their freedom reduced to serfdom, the citizens who yearn for freedom and are courageous enough to stand for their rights have a choice between the dignity of martyrdom or the dignity of resistance in the face of overwhelming odds.

Because of their realistic assumptions about human nature, society, and government, free enterprise countries have achieved what other systems, based on less realistic premises, promised but utterly failed to attain. The benefits the free market systems have provided their people in terms of quality of life are unprecedented in the history of man. Relying on market forces, peaceful competition, and cooperation of all social groups within a democratic political setting of individualism, popularism, and pluralism, the United States, the most advanced postindustrial market economy, has built the closest approximation possible to the classless society. Two major factors in market economies contributing to respect for human dignity are the relatively high measure of effective freedom in making decisions affecting the individual's own destiny and a relatively high level of quality of life he can attain with the economic means at his disposal.

Capitalism's greatest strength lies in the powerful incentive to compete based on the healthy self-interest of individuals, in the flexibility and adaptability of its institutions, and in the economic and political freedoms made possible by the democratic political system based on division of power. Among its weaknesses are lack of automatic macroeconomic controls, the tendency toward the formation of oligarchies and monopolies, and the possibility that self-interest misunderstood and carried too far might severely damage, and even destroy, the free enterprise system. Paradoxically, the very success of the system in creating a high quality of life and in giving the people a broad range of choices harbors the danger of all successful orders: they are taken for granted and the forces that sustain their existence are not clearly understood. The resulting indifference and lack of willingness to defend such an order is reinforced by the decline of competition, separation of ownership from control, and restrictions imposed on freedom of contracting.[22] In addition, such forces of modernization as the "revolution of rising entitlements," anomie, and the decline of the philosophy of individual responsibility are endangering the very foundation on which the free competitive system rests.

Notes

1. Friedrich A. Hayek, *The Road to Serfdom* (Chicago: University of Chicago Press, 1944), p. 2.

2. Frank Knight, *Intelligence and Democratic Action* (Cambridge, Mass.: Harvard University Press, 1960), p. 34.

3. For a detailed description of the theoretical framework dealing with this problem, consult Oleg Zinam, "The Economics of Command Economies," in Jan S. Prybyla, ed., *Comparative Economic Systems* (New York: Appleton-Century-Crofts, 1969), pp. 19-46; "Cross-Sectional Analysis of Economic Systems: Functional-Structural Approach," *Rivista Internazionale di Scienze Economiche e Commerciali* (April 1974):312-333; and "Method of Specialized Holism: A Model for the Comparative Study of Socio-Economic Change," *International Behavioral Scientist* (September 1974):39-56.

4. Max Weber, *The Theory of Social and Economic Organization*, translated by Henderson Parsons (New York: Oxford University Press, 1957), p. 14.

5. Zinam, "Cross-Sectional Analysis of Economic Systems," pp. 322-325.

6. For a brief treatment of the quality of life in relation to population problems, see Oleg Zinam, "Optimum Population Concept and the Zero Population Growth Thesis," *Economia Internazionale* (May 1974):6; "Optimum Population Growth and Quality of Life," *International Behavioral Scientist* (September 1975):32, 34; and "Zero Population Growth, Optimum Population Growth, Optimum Population and Quality of Life," *Journal of Economics* 1 (1975):69.

7. Werner Levi, "Economic Development and Human Values," in H.C.H. Harlan, ed., *Readings in Economics and Politics*, 2d ed. (New York: Oxford University Press, 1958), p. 727.

8. In technical terms, if use of controls is suboptimal, freedom (in the sense of controls) and efficiency are competitive goods or substitutes, hence the argument of trade-off. Yet, after the optimum point is reached, freedom and efficiency become complementary; consequently, less controls would mean more efficiency.

9. Allan G. Gruchy, *Comparative Economic Systems* (New York: Houghton Mifflin, 1966), pp. 224-228.

10. Henry C. Wallich, *The Cost of Freedom* (New York: Harper and Brothers, 1960), p. 11.

11. Heinz Koehler, *Welfare and Planning: An Analysis of Capitalism Versus Socialism* (New York: John Wiley and Sons, 1966), p. 163.

12. U.S. Congress, Joint Economic Committee, *New Directions in the Soviet Economy* (Washington, D.C., 1966), pp. X-XI.

13. Oleg Zinam, "Soviet Russia at the Crossroads," a paper presented at the meeting of the Ohio Association of Economists and Political Scientists, Worthington, Ohio, March 1967.

14. John Jewkes, *Ordeal by Planning* (London: Macmillan and Co., 1948), p. 9.

15. Ben W. Lewis, *British Planning and Nationalization* (New York: Twentieth Century Fund, 1952), p. 41.

16. Hayek, *The Road to Serfdom*, p. 26.

17. Ibid., p. 92.

18. H. J. Laski, *Liberty in the Modern State* (New York: Pelican Edition, 1937), p. 51.

19. Ibid., p. 293.

20. Milton Friedman, *Capitalism and Freedom* (Chicago: University of Chicago Press, 1962), p. 200.

21. Friedrich A. Hayek, *Individualism and Economic Order* (Chicago: University of Chicago Press, 1948), pp. 11, 12.

22. Joseph A. Schumpeter, *Capitalism, Socialism and Democracy* (New York: Harper and Brothers, 1947), pp. 140-142.

L. John Martin

VIOLENCE, TERRORISM, NON-VIOLENCE: VEHICLES OF SOCIAL CONTROL

On May 17, 1974, six suspected members of the Symbionese Liberation Army died in a gun battle and an ensuing fire that erupted after police surrounded their Los Angeles hideout. Thus, for all intents and purposes, ended the brief but violent saga of a small group of dissidents who referred to themselves as urban guerrillas. Violence and the threat of violence had been their medium of communication. It had been the currency in which they chose to barter. The security forces of the government had accepted the challenge and had paid them in their own coin.

The incident is instructive in that it illustrates that violence is the instrumentality both of those who have alienated themselves from society or been cast out by it and of those who have social and political legitimacy. The former may be terrorists or have criminal intent, and the latter may be guardians of the public integrity and the laws of the land. Violence, therefore, is a neutral term, despite the fact that in common parlance it has negative connotations. It is a means of interaction, an instrumentality of social—or antisocial—control, a linguistic vehicle rather than a medium or a message.

Violence As Behavior

A person can receive bodily injury with or without human intervention. A rock or a tree can fall on him, or he may drop into an open sewer. None of this is referred to as violence unless some human being caused the event to occur. The term *violence* is reserved for those acts of human beings that are inflicted upon other human beings. Nor do we consider an accidental injury caused by one person to another as violence. Violence is an act of human volition, and as such, it is a form of human behavior. Not all behavior is volitional; some behavior is reflexive. The term *violence* is seldom used in connection with involuntary, unmotivated behavior.

Another form of human behavior is verbal. Communication theorists speak of verbal behavior to distinguish it from other types of behavior that do not use words. Nonverbal behavior includes gestures, facial expressions, posture, laughter, voice quality, dress and cosmetics, color, space, time, and numerous other cues to meaning.[1] The key word is *meaning*. All human behavior—at least that of the nonreflexive type—carries meaning. If we think of a symbol, such as a word or a gesture, as being the conveyor of meaning to the mind, and the hand as writing the word or making the gesture, the hand would be the medium.

Now let us turn to violence. The hand or an extension of the hand, such as a gun, can do violence. Violence, therefore, is a vehicle or a language; it is not the medium, since the hand or a gun would be the medium. In a model that describes the interaction between two persons, violence has the same function as words or gestures. In other words, violence is symbolic behavior that conveys meaning between two individuals.

Violence and Power

Joseph Roucek has defined violence as "the willful application of force in such a way that it is physically or psychologically injurious to the person or group against whom it is applied."[2] It is used for purposes of coercion, which Roucek defines as "the use of either physical or intangible force to compel action contrary to the will or reasoned judgment of the individual or group subjected to such force."[3] Key concepts in these definitions are the implication of dominance and compliance by the parties concerned—a clear instance of the exercise of power. Bertrand Russell defined power as "the production of intended effect,"[4] and R. H. Tawney termed it "the capacity of an individual, or group of individuals, to modify the conduct of other individuals or groups in the manner which he desires."[5] Roucek states that "violence is but one aspect of the techniques of politics and all politics is but a struggle for power."[6]

Hannah Arendt distinguishes between power and violence by pointing out that numbers are an important requisite of power, whereas violence depends on implements.[7] "Power," she says, "needs no justification, being inherent in the very existence of political communities."[8] Power, she continues, has legitimacy which violence does not. According to Roucek, however, the legitimacy of violence depends on the user.[9] The state, which presumably has numbers on its side, can claim legitimacy, while a group of outlaws cannot.

While power may be acquired without violence, given the express or tacit consent of those over whom the power is exercised, violence can, at least temporarily, put power into the hands of a few. Throughout history, power has frequently passed into the hands of usurpers who have either used or threatened to use violence. But unless consent follows, power cannot long rest in the hands of those who have nothing but weapons with which to assert their claim. Weapons can change hands, as they did in the Hungarian revolution. "Where commands are no longer obeyed, the means of violence are of no use," Arendt says.[10]

Terrorism and Violence

Terrorism is an aspect of violence that is very much in the news today. It differs from violence in three important ways. (1) Although, like violence, its instrumentality is force, it quite frequently stops at the threat of force; (2) in common with violence, it seeks power, but frequently it has more limited objectives, such as the preservation of the identity of the group it represents, or simply publicity for the cause it espouses; (3) unlike violence, the effectiveness of terrorism rests principally on the element of surprise and fear. Terrorism differs from other crimes that use or threaten to use violence in that terrorists always claim to be acting for a cause other than their personal benefit. A terrorist's first loyalty is not to himself but to his cause, just as a soldier's is to his country. Hence, terrorists generally are willing to take greater risks than criminals, whose concern is their own safety.

Yet, terrorism is classed as no different from crimes of violence by most governments, especially those against which, or against whose citizens, the terrorists are operating. The reason is that terrorism is a challenge to the power of the state, as is any criminal activity. The survival of the state depends on its ability to enforce its laws.

On the other hand, while the term *terrorism* has a pejorative meaning in everyone's vocabulary, there is no consensus as to the referent. "One man's terrorist is another man's freedom fighter," says Jeffrey A. Tannenbaum in a series of articles on terrorism in the *Wall Street Journal*. It explains, he adds, why the United Nations has been unable to define terrorism after years of debate.[11] Nor does terrorism have a legal definition in international law.[12] In fact, the General Counsel of the United Nations, Eric Suy, flatly says that the cause of terrorism is not a legal question, and its cure will not be found in treaties and conventions.[13] Many jurists consider terrorism to be a political problem, and there are no workable definitions for political crimes.

One tends to think of terrorist activities today in terms of small groups. "Terrorist groups, by their very nature," says Alexander, "are too small and too weak to achieve an upper hand in an open struggle for sheer power."[14] As a group becomes larger, it tends to change its name to insurgent, and finally it becomes a revolutionary force that wages civil war. Yet terrorism can also refer to the acts of a government. According to Friedlander, the term originated with the Jacobin "reign of terror" that accompanied the French Revolution,[15] and the tactics of other governments are occasionally referred to as terror tactics. The term is used, of course, only when the government is not a friendly one; otherwise, the government would be said to "squash dissident factions with a firm hand."

In the eight years from 1968 through 1975, 3,688 incidents of terrorism were counted by the U.S. Central Intelligence Agency, one-third of the victims being U.S. citizens.[16] Between January 1973 and October 1976, 737 terrorist acts were committed, resulting in 292 deaths. It has been pointed out that compared with the 20,000 homicide victims in the United States in 1975 alone, or the 100 million violent deaths caused by human beings in the first seventy-five years of this century, this is a drop in the bucket.[17] What makes death at the hands of terrorists a more macabre act, however, is that someone in political power is generally forced to decide between the life of one or more hostages and submission to the demands of the terrorists. In view of this grim choice, it is not surprising that the State Department has calculated that terrorists have an 80 percent chance of escaping death, a 50 percent chance of having all or some of their demands met, and a 100 percent chance of getting all the publicity they want.[18]

Terrorism and Communication

Communication derives meaning from the whole gamut of human behavior so long as at least two individuals are interacting. Terrorism is a form of human behavior that is loaded with significance. Let us examine the symbolism.

Terrorism, as we have said, uses or threatens violence against a victim who normally is not the one for whom the message is intended. In fact, if the victim were the main audience, the effectiveness of the violence or its threat would be reduced, since he cannot both carry out the demands and suffer the consequences of not carrying them out. Thus, the South Moluccans who hijacked a Dutch train in December 1975 to dramatize their revolt against their new rulers in Jakarta and to demand the release of South Moluccan prisoners in Indonesia could not have shot the train's engineer and two passengers one by one when their demands were not met. Obviously, the victims were the objects rather than the subjects of their demands, and communication with their audience had a totally different objective than the victims themselves.

This is one important respect in which terrorism differs from other crime. Most other crime is of a personal nature in which the victim is a central figure and generally the main audience. As Watson indicates, "terrorism must not be defined only in terms of violence, but also in terms of propaganda. The two are both in operation together."[19]

If we think of communication behavior as ranging on a continuum from purely mental to purely physical, the printed word would be at one end of the continuum and violence at the other. As a term in communication behavior, terrorism has the unusual function of operating at both ends of the continuum. Propaganda, diplomacy, advertising, persuasion, education— all operate exclusively at the verbal or mental end. Violence, force, torture, and third degree use physical means to attain their objectives. Terrorism and brainwashing are initiated for communication purposes at the mental end, but are escalated, as the communication progresses, to the physical end of the continuum.

Purpose of Terrorism

When in 1972 eight members of the Black September group—a Palestinian terrorist organization—entered the Israeli quarter at Olympic Village in Munich, where they killed an athlete and the coach and grabbed nine other Israeli athletes, they demanded the release of 200 Arab and other terrorists in Israeli jails. They failed in this particular demand, but the German government acceded to their fallback demand for a helicopter and permission to leave Germany with their nine hostages by plane from Munich airport. In addition, they received much publicity in the world's press. Only a blunder at the airport speeded the terrorist act from limited violence to total violence when a gun battle killed all nine hostages, five terrorists, and a German policeman.

Ironically, all this carnage was perpetrated not in an effort to attain the ultimate goal of the terrorists—the "liberation" of Palestine or the restitution of the land and homes of Palestinian refugees—but for an intermediate goal. The initial demand (and even later demands, had they succeeded) would have given the terrorist group no more than the capability of continuing its terrorist existence.

Terrorists seldom demand the full realization of their cause. This may be because they do not expect to achieve it all at once. It may be, as Watson suggests, because achieving their goals would force them to relinquish the power they have accumulated. "People who lay out a clearly stated proposition—'you do this and we will do that'—are leaving themselves open to someone accepting the terms. The terrorists' game would thus be over," Watson writes.[20] He believes that terrorists want political power above everything else and will not trade it away by negotiating to achieve their ultimate goal.

But terrorism may be resorted to as a change in the vehicle for delivering the messages after the vehicle of words has failed. Just as people may not expect their words to succeed right away, especially if the message or meaning is unpalatable, terrorists do not expect their vehicle of terror to succeed. But they are willing to continue the interaction until they have achieved their goals through perseverance.

Effectiveness of Terrorism

Under certain circumstances, terrorism has been successful. Effectiveness here is not measured in terms of the number of individual battles won or, for that matter, *any* battles won. As we have said, the war terrorists are waging is for a cause; the battles are merely for their survival. The Arab and Jewish terrorists who nibbled away at the British mandatory government in Palestine, often taking turns at harassing the British (although never working in collusion with each other), finally wore the British government down so that it gave up the mandate. Granted, terrorism was not the only reason why the British left Palestine, but it certainly accelerated the final withdrawal. Similarly, the violence that disrupted life in the United States during the 1960s was not the sole factor that changed American values on racial and other inequalities, but it did much to speed up the anti-discrimination process.

All changes that are given an impetus by violence and terrorism are normally those that are ripe for the evolutionary process. There is development in the desired direction because the pressure is for an idea whose time has come. On the other hand, terrorism that pushes in a direction for which there is little popular support lacks power. Thus, many terrorist movements lead nowhere, as was true of the Symbionese Liberation Army or Charles Manson's family. They lacked a power base or a constituency to which they could appeal.

Often, terrorist groups that have a plausible cause dissolve back into the population that spawned them, not because their cause failed to gain popular support, but because their program was overtaken by history and even left behind. Thus, even in recent history, we find that such rousing and antiestablishment causes as those of the Weathermen, the Yippies, and the Black Panthers faded into oblivion, not for lack of sympathy among large elements of the population, but because many of their ideas were more generally accepted than their proponents thought. They were ideas whose time came—and went. The proponents were simply left behind.

This may very well be the fate of some of the most notorious terrorist groups. The Tupamaros in Uruguay had the support of many respectable people and probably most of the countryside. The police had great difficulty keeping up with them in the early 1970s. Similarly, the various Arab terrorist factions not only had the sympathy of the man in the street in most of the Arab world, but they often had the active support of Arab governments. These are causes that probably will be swallowed up by the inexorable march of time, not because their goals are unrealistic, but because they are so obvious. While the terrorists rant and rave and violently press their case, others, operating at the verbal end of the continuum, plod on to a resolution.

Nonviolence

Nonviolence is a misnomer. It looks and sounds like a form of human behavior that belongs at the mental end of the communication continuum, but it does not. It fits right next to violence at the physical end.

Others have pointed out that it is a form of communication. "Non-violent resistance is in effect a sort of language, a means of communicating feelings and ideas," according to Richard B. Gregg.[21] He continues: "Even in situations where words can be used little or not at all, conduct alone may be a rapid, accurate and efficient means of communication." At the same time, it is not to be mistaken for nonphysical behavior. Gene Sharp has emphasized that the class of behavior variously referred to as "nonviolent resistance," "satyagraha," "passive resistance," "positive action," and "nonviolent direct action" may not be violent, but "it *is* action, and not inaction."[22]

Sharp distinguishes between nonviolent protest, nonviolent noncooperation (i.e., the various types of boycotts), and nonviolent intervention. All these activities must be termed violent, although the violence is not normally perpetrated by the protester or resister. Instead, the action *invites* the violence of those in power. Nonviolence clearly attempts to represent the opposition as violent, which is a pejorative characteristic.

Staughton Lynd refutes the popular belief that nonviolence was conceived by Gandhi, or even by Tolstoy and Thoreau, who are known to have influenced the Indian leader.[23] Lynd suggests that the philosophy had its origins in seventeenth-century America with Quakers such as William Penn and John Woolman, abolitionists, and others. Clarence M. Case traces "nonviolent coersion" back still further—to Confusius, Lao-tse and Buddha in China, Jesus and the Essenes in the Middle East.[24]

Whatever its origin, most of its proponents advocate it as an effective form of social action. Gandhi admitted that the progress of nonviolence was terribly slow, and he reminded his followers that "in non-violence, bravery consists in dying not in killing."[25] He suggested that it was better to be violent, if violence was in a person's heart, than nonviolent to cover up impotence. Like many other advocates of passive resistance, however, Gandhi was under the misapprehension that nonviolence "is not a policy for the seizure of power,"[26] and that "those who die unresistingly are likely to still the fury of violence by their wholly innocent sacrifice."[27]

This clearly is a misconception of the purpose of nonviolence and the reason why it often works. Gandhi stated that nonviolence leads to a transformation of relationships to the point where "a peaceful transfer of power [is] effected freely and without compulsion."[28] What is peaceful about an act that invites forceful reprisal? The effectiveness of nonviolence, in fact, depends in most cases on repressive measures. If that is not compulsion, then neither is violence.

Violence and Morality

The United States was conceived in violence and was nurtured by it. Although Americans have been among the leading pacifists, conscientious objectors, and proponents of nonviolence, U.S. history and tradition is replete with aphorisms and legends glorifying violence. "Apart from its role in the formation and preservation of the nation," writes Richard M. Brown, in a historical study of American violence and vigilantism, "violence has been a determinant of both the form and the substance of American life."[29] But this is true of most cultures.

While there is some scientific evidence that man is instinctively aggressive and violent,[30] others refute it, suggesting that the use of violence is a learned response and that it is just as easy to learn to become a nonaggressive person.[31] Innate aggressiveness should manifest itself as an expression of emotion. While one might become violent because of anger or a felt hostility, violence is most often resorted to not in rage, but as an instrument of power. When used instrumentally, one can reasonably assume that it is a learned act rather than an intuitive response to fear or danger.

The question of morality is most relevant when violence manifests itself as an intellectual rather than as a spontaneous act. How do people view violence as an instrument of social change or of social control? Historically, and in some contemporary cultures, violence is unequivocally an accepted instrumentality. It was the hallmark of chivalry, the vindicator of honor, the symbol of masculinity; in some cultures today, it is viewed in the same way.

In most European countries and especially in the United States, violence is seen as an instrument of last resort. One may fight back but should not fight. Some have even agonized about the morality of fighting back; at least in principle, they believe that the most moral thing to do in the face of violence is to turn the other cheek. Violence is "immoral because it seeks to humiliate the opponent rather than win his understanding," the Times of India quoted Martin Luther King as saying.[32] "It creates bitterness in the survivors and brutality in the destroyer."

In a 1969 nationwide study of 1,374 males between the ages of sixteen and sixty-four living in the United States, about 90 percent said that, while some social change was desirable, they believed such changes could be brought about without police action involving property damage or personal injury. Only 10 percent believed that protests involving extensive property damage and possible deaths were necessary, and 20 percent thought some property damage and personal injury would be necessary to bring about change at a sufficiently rapid rate.

On the other hand, 80 to 87 percent of American males thought police arrests could "almost always" or "sometimes" be made during disturbances without the use of weapons, while 76 to 80 percent believed that clubs but not guns should be used.[33]

International law is ambivalent about violence and terror. Although the United Nations Secretariat has interpreted the international consensus to be that "the legitimacy of a cause does not in itself legitimize the use of certain forms of violence, especially against the innocent,"[34] there is less agreement about who is innocent. Tourists, diplomats, and foreign employees are not necessarily uninvolved. The problem appears to be one of divorcing terrorism and other forms of criminal violence from rebellion or revolution, "which are generally recognized remedies in international law."[35] And this requires drawing a fine line between "civil strife which is basically criminal and that which is an expression of the will of the people."[36] This is no mean task. What it often boils down to is legitimizing shooting but not being shot at, rebelling but not being rebelled against.

Countering Terrorism

Dealing with terrorism is easier in theory than in practice. Faced with the impending injury or death of a human being, a decision-maker may find it difficult, if not impossible, to stick to the rules. Yet guidelines need to be written.

Probably the most effective method used to combat terrorism is prevention. Security checks at airports in recent years have reduced skyjackings to negligible numbers. Terrorists still manage to find chinks in the security system in countries that fail to take the threat seriously. But the cost to the terrorists, and the risks, are greater than ever before. In Northern Ireland, where terrorists have used mailboxes for mailing letter bombs, postal authorities have controlled some of the bombings by altering the slots of mailboxes so that only thin letters can be mailed in them.

Terrorism as a form of communication should be analyzed in terms of the communicator rather than in terms of the intended audience. Most communication theorists today believe that people initiate communication to reduce tension or to resolve some discontinuity.

To resolve his discomfort or discontinuity, the terrorist formulates a message, for communication is a tension-reducing mechanism for him. If we accept terrorism as the vehicle or language for communication, then the terrorist will continue to discourse in that language, much as a child cries if it discovers that crying will elicit quick action. By playing up a terrorist act in the press or in negotiation, one tends to lend more importance to this form of communication that it need have. Terrorist groups must be conditioned to feel that they will get more sympathetic and faster action by operating at the verbal end of the communication continuum than at the physical end. Reinforcement must be limited to nonviolent behavior.

If at all possible, the mass media should be encouraged to hold off any mention of a terrorist act until after its resolution. Publicity is necessary to keep a terrorist organization in operation, and success is a great morale booster. With every success, terrorists tend to get bolder. To the extent that anything is reported, emphasis should be focused on the hurt to the families and children, and on the dead and the injured as by-products of terrorism. All mention of the terrorists themselves must be negative and should be limited to the terrorist act. Terrorism should not be mentioned in the context of any legitimate aspirations of the organization or the people the terrorists claim to represent.

Terrorism is a vicious language that is likely to stay with us. Fears have been expressed that future targets may include nuclear installations that may be sabotaged with great loss of life and property losses. "Everything appears in the terrorists' favor," says Michael Flood of the University of London's Department of War Studies.[37] Deeds of terror "are more easily tolerated than prevented," writes J. Bowyer Bell for the Hoover Institution on War, Revolution and Peace.[38]

All this is true. But while we cannot possibly undo the many wrongs that man continues to inflict upon his fellow man, which, in turn, means we will have more terrorist groups, we can work on reducing the currency of the language of terror and violence. This can be done by conditioning would-be terrorists to prefer more peaceful vehicles because they result in faster and better responses.

Notes

1. For a brief overview of various types of nonverbal communication, see Randall P. Harrison, "Nonverbal Communication," in Ithiel de Sola Pool, Wilbur Schramm, et al., eds., *Handbook of Communication* (Chicago: Rand McNally, 1973), pp. 93-115.

2. Joseph S. Roucek, *Social Control* (Westport, Conn.: Greenwood Press, 1970), p. 331.

3. Ibid., p. 330.

4. Bertrand Russell, *Power* (New York: W. W. Norton, 1938), p. 35.

5. R. H. Tawney, *Equality* (New York: Harcourt, Brace, 1931), p. 230.

6. James Van Patten, Joseph Roucek, Michael V. Belok, and Martin Schoppmeyer, *Conflict, Permanency, Change and Education* (Moti Katra: Agra 3, India: Satish Book Enterprise, 1976), p. 209.

7. Hannah Arendt, *On Violence* (New York: Harcourt, Brace and World, 1969), p. 41.

8. Ibid., p. 52.

9. Joseph S. Roucek, "The Sociology of Violence," *Journal of Human Relations* 3 (Spring 1957):12.

10. Ibid., pp. 48-49.

11. *Wall Street Journal*, January 4, 1977, p. 21.

12. See Robert A. Friedlander, "Terrorism and Violence: Some Preliminary Observations," *International Studies Notes* 3, no. 2 (Summer 1976):1-3.

13. Quoted by Robert A. Friedlander, "Terrorism and Political Violence: Do the Ends Justify the Means?" *Chitty's Law Journal* 24, no. 7 (1976):240.

14. Yonah Alexander, ed., *International Terrorism: National, Regional, and Global Perspectives* (New York: Praeger Publishers, 1976), p. xiv.

15. Friedlander, "Terrorism and Violence," p. 1.

16. *Wall Street Journal*, January 4, 1977, pp. 1, 21; see also *Revue Internationale de Droit Pénal* 46, no. 3/4 (1975), book review by Friedlander.

17. See *Wall Street Journal*, January 4, 1977; also Michael Flood, "Nuclear Sabotage," in *The Washington Post*, January 9, 1977, p. C1.

18. *Wall Street Journal*, January 4, 1977.

19. Francis M. Watson, *Political Terrorism: The Threat and the Response* (Washington, D.C.: Robert B. Luce Co., 1976), p. 15.

20. Ibid., p. 34.

21. Richard B. Gregg, *The Power of Non-Violence* (Philadelphia: J. B. Lippincott, 1935), p. 60.

22. Gene Sharp, "The Technique of Nonviolent Action," in Joan V. Bondurant, ed., *Conflict: Violence and Nonviolence* (Chicago: Aldine, Atherton, 1971), p. 153.

23. Staughton Lynd, ed., *Nonviolence in America: A Documentary History* (Indianapolis: Bobbs-Merrill, 1966), p. xv.

24. Clarence Marsh Case, *Non-Violent Coercion: A Study in Methods of Social Pressure* (New York: Garland, 1972).

25. Thomas Merton, ed., *Gandhi on Non-Violence* (New York: New Directions, 1965), p. 26.

26. Ibid., p. 23.

27. Ibid., p. 46.

28. Ibid., p. 23.

29. Richard Maxwell Brown, *Strain of Violence: Historical Studies of American Violence and Vigilantism* (New York: Oxford University Press, 1975), p. 4.

30. See inter alia, Konrad Lorenz, *On Aggression* (New York: Harcourt, Brace and World, 1966).

31. See, for example, Jeffrey H. Goldstein, *Aggression and Crimes of Violence* (New York: Oxford University Press, 1975).

32. Quoted by S. A. Bari, *Gandhi's Doctrine of Civil Resistance* (New Delhi: Kalamkar Prakashan Private Ltd., 1971), p. 109.

33. Monica D. Blumenthal, Robert L. Kahn, Frank M. Andrews, and Kendra B. Head, *Justifying Violence: Attitudes of American Men* (Ann Arbor, Mich.: Institute for Social Research, 1972), pp. 39-40.

34. Robert A. Friedlander, "Terrorism," *Barrister* 2, no. 3 (Summer 1975):13.

35. Robert A. Friedlander, "Sowing the Wind: Rebellion and Violence in Theory and Practice," *Denver Journal of International Law and Policy* 6, no. 1 (Spring 1976):84.

36. John C. Novogrod, "Internal Strife, Self-Determination, and World Order," in M. Cherif Bassiouni, *International Terrorism and Political Crimes* (Springfield, Ill.: C. C. Thomas, 1975), p. 113.

37. Flood, "Nuclear Sabotage," pp. C1, C4.

38. J. Bowyer Bell, *Transnational Terror* (Washington, D.C.: American Enterprise Institute for Public Policy Research, 1975), p. 89.

Karel Hulicka

LEADERSHIP AND CHARISMA

This essay discusses leadership status, charisma, and charismatic leaders as agents of social control and change, as well as the value of the concept of charisma as a tool for social analysis. Leadership may be defined simply as a relationship between a person exerting an influence and those who are influenced,[1] or as a behavioral process in which others are stimulated to act integratively toward the achievement of group goals.[2]

Charisma and Charismatic Leadership

The word "charisma" comes from Charis, one of the Graces, who according to Homer was a divinely endowed being of rare charm and beauty who, through her ability to emanate joy, influenced all who knew her. The concept of charisma has evolved to include the notion that rare individuals are endowed, through supernatural intervention or divine grace, with extra-ordinary gifts of mind and character. This charisma, based on unusual and exemplary attributes, enables the gifted individual to influence large masses of people and to secure their devoted allegiance.

As a result of the writings of Max Weber,[3] the concept of charisma, with its derivatives charismatic leadership and charismatic authority, has been used frequently in analyses of leadership. He incorporated charisma into a theoretical formulation of authority which included the traditional, charismatic, and rational-legal basis of rule. Weber applied the term *charismatic leader* to an individual who acquires and maintains leadership status on the basis of real or perceived extraordinary personal characteristics and who uses his leadership status as a catalyst for social, political, or ideological change.[4] Thus, he stipulated that the leader "preaches, creates or demands *new* obligations" and that charismatic authority exists "only in the process of originating."[5] As such, charismatic authority functions as a "revolutionary force," and its success results in "a radical alteration of the central system of attitudes and directions."[6]

Weber held that the charismatic leader's power to act "springs from ... devotion to the extraordinary and unheard-of, to what is strange to all rule and tradition and which therefore is viewed as divine."[7] This legitimacy is derived neither from custom or law nor from the follower's consent, but rather from a transcendentally based absolute devotion. The charismatic leader would have to subscribe to the proposition "It is written . . . , but I say unto you . . . ."[8] His unique authority must derive from his own extraordinary qualities:

The term "charisma" will be applied to a certain quality of an individual personality by virtue of which he is set apart from ordinary men and treated as endowed with supernatural, superhuman, or at least specifically exceptional qualities or powers. These . . . are regarded as of divine origin or as exemplary and on the basis of them the individual concerned is treated as a leader.[9]

Some of Weber's statements suggest that he intended to limit the term *charisma* to a description of a relationship between followers (or believers) and a leader (or prophet) rather than to denote an attribute of the individual. He stated: "It is recognition on the part of those subject to authority which is decisive for the validity of charisma."[10] However, perhaps because Weber sometimes attributed charisma to the leader rather than to a leader-follower relationship, and perhaps because of reluctance to accept divine grace, many sociologists employ the term as if it referred simply to some extraordinary, above-average, personal competence.[11]

In popular usage, the term *charisma* is applied to almost any person whose company, because of personal qualities and attractiveness, is sought by others. Indeed, it is sometimes assumed that charisma can be manufactured for politicians and entertainers by publicists and "image-makers" through public pronouncements, staged rallies, and coaching with respect to style and content of speeches, mode of dress, and even hair style. Such notions are, of course, far removed from Weber's intended meaning. In the 1960 presidential campaign, according to some observers, Kennedy had an advantage over Nixon because he had more charisma. Although some people may have been more attracted to Kennedy because of real or assumed attributes, he could not, according to Weber's analysis, be described as a charismatic leader because his pronouncements generally relied on legal and historical precedent, his relationship with most of his followers was not based on attributed supernatural or even extraordinary qualities, and he did not aspire to effect radical social changes. On the other hand, scholars who adhere closely to Weber's views have described persons such as Hitler, Mussolini, and Castro as charismatic leaders on the basis of attributed extraordinary powers, the source and use of authority, personal magnetism, and goals for modification of the social order.[12] Others who have been described as charismatic leaders by Weberian scholars include Moses, Jesus, Confucius, St. Francis of Assisi, Mohammed, Buddha, King Alfred the Great, Joan of Arc, John Hus, Brigham Young, Rasputin, Gandhi, Lenin, Nasser, Eva Peron, and Albert Schweitzer.

Some scholars have assumed that institutional as well as personal charisma can exist in that the supernatural mandate of a leader can become associated with his "office" and be "inherited" by his successors.[13] Thus, until the defeat of Japan in 1945, the Japanese emperors were believed by their subjects to have infallible wisdom because of divine origin. Incidentally, the emperor's apparent loss of charisma after the defeat of Japan supports the generalization that continued success is a prerequisite for the survival of a charismatic relationship.[14] Another example of the institutional survival of charismatic rule is the Papacy. The concept of institutional charisma has also been vulgarized in popular usage; thus, the family and associates of the president of the United States and, within a narrower circle, those of the president of a major organization may be described as charismatic and treated as if they possess extraordinary personal attributes.

Leadership Status

Acquisiton

Distinctions must be made between the acquisition and retention of leadership status. "Imposed" leadership refers to the designation of a leader by superior authority; "emergent" leadership refers to acceptance of influence and hence is conditional upon consent of the followers.[15] Within each of these categories, leadership status may be acquired in different ways. A leader could be imposed on the basis of tradition (e.g., a hereditary monarch), by appointment within an organization, or through use of force or power (e.g., revolution, purchase of office, threats, and bribes). Emergent leadership status could be acquired by election or informal consensus.

The dichotomy between imposed and emergent leaders is not complete. A superior authority may consult with and acquire consent from a group prior to the appointment of a leader. Although we prefer to believe that the election of officials reflects the consent of their constituents, in fact, candidates for office may be imposed on the electorate by cliques who have preempted the power of selection, and the citizen may use his franchise only to vote for the least objectionable of several candidates. Conversely, an imposed leader may acquire enthusiastic consent from group members. For example, an heir apparent may undergo training to prepare for the fulfillment of future responsibilities, and at least some appointed leaders are selected on the basis of their potential acceptability to group members. Apart from those who have acquired institutional charisma, most persons who have been described as charismatic leaders fit the emergent rather than the imposed category.

The acquisition of leadership status has been studied by many scholars. Early theorists tended to favor the "great man" theory, which assumes that some individuals, endowed by nature with superior characteristics, are destined by their own actions to rise to positions of leadership.[16] Lincoln and Napoleon, both men of humble origins who influenced the course of history, are offered as examples in support of this theory. It is assumed that their eminence was inevitable, although under different circumstances they might have made their mark in different ways. Consistent with the "great man" theory is the attempt to identify leadership traits. Advocates of the trait theory, though not claiming that certain individuals will inevitably become leaders, assume that factors which permit acquisition of leadership status are primarily qualities of the individual. Identified as general leadership traits are imagination, foresight, flexibility, versatility, and inhibition; personality, manner, use of language, tact, cheerfulness, courtesy, and discipline; force of will, breadth of knowledge, strength of convictions, and self-sufficiency.[17] The concept of charismatic leadership is consistent with the "great man" and trait theories, but not with the "times make the man" or the situational approach, which assumes that stature as a leader is a function of time, place, and circumstances. Leadership does not reside in the person but is a function of the occasion; the situation calls for certain types of actions and the leader is the instrument through which the solution is achieved.[18] Gerald Ford, if deemed a great president, could serve as an example to support the notion that greatness is a function of circumstances. An obvious problem with this theory is that not all crisis situations produce a leader equal to the occasion.

The "great man," trait, and situational theorists attempted to explain leadership as an effect of a single set of forces with a concomitant disregard for the interaction effects of individual and situational factors, and the impact of group dynamics on leadership behavior and effectiveness. Contemporary theoreticians, using variants of a situational-personal approach, have used a variety of labels such as the expectancy-reinforcement, path-goal, motivational, contingency, and social exchange theories of leadership to summarize their positions.[19] Although differing in specific details, most modern theorists agree that effectiveness of leadership requires an adequate fit between the qualifications and behavior of the leader and situational demands, including external factors and the goals, expectations, and behavior of group members.

Leadership Types

For centuries, attempts have been made to categorize leaders according to function and/or style. Plato identified three types of leaders—the philosopher-statesman, the military commander, and the businessman—and specified their major functions. In 1918, Bogardus categorized leaders as autocratic, democratic, executive, and reflective-intellectual, and speculated about differences in functional goals and modes of operation.[20] Weber proposed three tpes of authority, each associated with a different type of leadership: the bureaucratic leader whose authority is based on legal and normative rules; the patrimonial leader whose authority is based on tradition; and the charismatic leader whose authority derives from the devotion of followers to his sanctity and from normative patterns ordained by or revealed to him.[21] Weber suggested that the bureaucratic leader operates with a staff of deputies, the patrimonial leader with a staff of relatives, and the charismatic leader with a staff of disciples. The patriarch tends to defend vigorously the status quo on which his authority is based, the bureaucrat might attempt to facilitate gradual change within the existing structure, and the charismatic leader is the sponsor of causes and revolution designed to effect drastic and precipitous changes.

Subsequently, leadership typology proliferated. Stogdill identified the six most frequently used descriptive labels as the authoritative (dominator), persuasive (crowd arouser), democratic (group developer), intellectual (eminent man), executive (administrator), and representative (spokesman) leaders.[22] However, he pointed out that, recently, the persuasive, intellectual, and representative categories have seldom been used; the authoritative and democratic types have been relabeled the task-oriented and the person-oriented types; and the executive type has been classified as task-oriented or person-oriented, depending on the dominant mode of operation. Thus, very recent studies have tended to focus on identification of conditions under which task-oriented or person-oriented styles of leadership are more successful in terms of designated outcome variables.[23] Although charismatic leadership has apparently not been subjected to appropriate analysis, perhaps because it cannot be studied easily in a laboratory, it seems to correspond more to the task-oriented than to the person-oriented typology. According to Weber, charismatic leaders must have a mission; hence, they must be task-oriented.

Leader Effectiveness

Not everyone who acquires leadership status retains it. Some people voluntarily relinquish leadership positions, and many are removed by superior authority, the formal or informal withdrawal of support from followers, force, the emergence of a competing leader, or a combination of several factors. Although factors extraneous to role performance may be relevant, it is generally true that the retention of leadership status is influenced by how well leadership functions are fulfilled. It is axiomatic that there are "good" and "bad" leaders and that a leader's effectiveness is assessed as a function of his performance in relation to the needs and expectations of group members and/or superior authorities within the context of situational demands. Hollander defined leader effectiveness as "an influence process wherein the leader is able to muster willing group support to achieve certain clearly defined group goals with best advantage to individuals comprising the group."[24] This definition is relevant to the effectiveness, and hence retention, of the leadership status of emergent and imposed, as well as charismatic and noncharismatic, leaders. It therefore requires that leadership be viewed as an interactive process involving the leader as an influence agent who may also be influenced by group members, with both the leader and the group functioning within a particular but changing social structure.

Persons responsible for the selection and training of potential leaders are particularly interested in determinants of leader effectiveness. Stogdill, on the basis of a comprehensive review of leadership studies, identified six major leadership factors: (1) capacity (intelligence, alertness, verbal facility, originality, judgment); (2) achievement; (3) responsibility (dependability, initiative, persistence, aggressiveness, self-confidence, desire to excel); (4) participation (activity, sociability, cooperation, adaptability, humor); (5) status (socioeconomic position, popularity); and (6) situation (mental level, status, skills, needs and interests of followers, group objectives).[25] Effectiveness, though not dependent upon a universal set of personality traits, does appear to be contingent upon several basic prerequisites, including the competency of the leader, his fulfillment of group expectations, his perceived motivation, and his adaptability to changing requirements of a situation.[26] Such factors, relevant to the attainment of group goals, must be assessed within the context of the group's operation at a given time.

Although competence in the performance of specific tasks may facilitate attainment of leadership status, leader competency pertains primarily to characteristics and behaviors that contribute to the productive operation of the group and the materialization of its primary goals. Competency factors may include a broad rather than detailed informational base; awareness of the goals and activities of the entire group and its members; perceptiveness to changes within the group and external conditions which impinge on it; expertise in communication and motivation-manipulation; innovation in modification of group structure and goal definition; and strong advocacy skills. Since behaviors crucial to goal attainment under one set of circumstances may be irrelevant or detrimental under changed internal or external circumstances, perceptiveness to changing demands and flexibility of behavior would appear to be important ingredients of leader effectiveness.

Every leader is expected to fulfill certain functions, with specific expectations varying from group to group and from time to time within groups. Generally, leaders are expected to establish or modify structure; to identify, support, and facilitate materialization of long- and short-term goals; to be instrumental in the distribution of rewards and recognition; to facilitate communication within the group; to make or influence decisions affecting the group; and to serve as an advocate for the group with other groups or superior authorities.[27] A leader who fails to fulfill group expectations may serve as a barrier to the attainment of group goals, in part because his presence as a leader prevents others who are capable of performing certain functions from acting on behalf of the group.

Group members are unlikely to judge a leader to be effective unless he is perceived as being loyal to group goals and acting in terms of the group's interests rather than in terms of his own interest or those of a superior authority. Common sense, supported by some empirical evidence, suggests that the effective leader is able to reconcile conflicting interests of superiors and subordinates, and to satisfy the expectations of both.[28] This ability requires that he be simultaneously a good leader and a good follower. He must identify sufficiently with his superiors that he is able to fulfill their expectations with efficiency and enthusiasm; and he must have sufficient influence with them that he is able to act on behalf of the interests of his group. His advocacy for group members must be sufficiently apparent and effective that they willingly support his leadership.

A number of behavioral processes appear to be prerequisites for leader effectiveness. Among these are communication, restraint and predictability, and advocacy.[29] A leader is expected to provide and implement group structure to ensure a two-way flow of communication. Group support, and hence the potential for the leader to influence the group, generally requires that members participate in, or at the very least have advance information about, decisions that affect them.[30] Although the leader should serve as a source of ideas, he should also be receptive to ideas, suggestions, and problem identification from others. The group should know where the leader "stands" and what "he" stands for.[31] Both vacillation and maladaptive rigidity on the part of the leader impede progress toward group goals and hence weaken leadership status. Restraint, good judgment, and predictability are particularly important with respect to the distribution of rewards. Both respect by group members for the leader and attainment of group goals are supported by the reward of behavior consistent with the interests of the group and the nonreward, or even punishment, of behavior inimical to group interests. The leader must communicate to higher authorities and to other groups the goals, potentials, and positive attributes of his group, and he must have a reasonable degree of success in negotiating or otherwise obtaining from higher authorities or other groups the resources and other essentials for the fulfillment of his group's goals. As Hollander indicates, an understanding of effective leadership cannot disregard how followers fare in the relationship.[32] Leader effectiveness depends on an equity in social exchange, with the leader gaining status and influence as a function of the attainment of group goals and the simultaneous attainment by individual members of social and other rewards such as security, recognition, achievement, and self-actualization.

Most effective leaders rely more on influence and authority than on power for the regulation of group processes. In general, the locus of authority is in the individual, while the locus of power is in a position or in instruments or conditions external to the individual. For example, a Nobel Prize winner may because of his expertise be able to influence others, though he may have no power to enforce compliance; a man with a gun may have no basis for authority but sufficient power to regulate the behavior of others. A person in a leadership position, particularly within an organizational structure, may have considerable authority and power, or he may have much of one and little of the other. Thus, a leader with significant mechanisms for the administration of rewards and punishments, and few controls over their use, may rely almost entirely on power for group regulation. Conversely, an emergent leader of an informal group which is competing with an organized group for influence over some segment of society may, by virtue of his own attributes, have considerable authority over group members but relatively little power in relation to them or to other groups. An organization may allocate responsibilities in such a way that an official with considerable personal authority must also serve as an agent of power as, for example, with the renewal or nonrenewal of employment contracts. On the other hand, individuals in positions with a power base are often perceived by themselves and others as authorities. Stalin, for example, who commanded tremendous power, was perceived by others and apparently by himself as an authority whose expertise ranged from military strategy to genetics.

Effective Versus Charismatic Leadership

It may be concluded that persons who can be described as charismatic leaders function within certain situations, bounded by time, as effective leaders, but that most effective leaders are not simultaneously charismatic leaders. The charismatic leader is, indeed, defined as a person with extraordinary leadership qualities. His effectiveness is attributed to his exceptional qualities and the unique relationship he holds with his followers rather than to authority and/or power derived from traditional or legal norms. Indeed, most people who have been identified as charismatic leaders have functioned, at least initially, as outsiders and often as rebels with respect to tradition and the established power structures. However, some, such as Hitler and Castro, have used their followers as a source of power to wrest control from incumbent leaders within the established order and then have used power as an additional source of control.

Historical personages who have been identified as charismatic leaders have, without exception, been people with a high degree of competence, as exemplified by intelligence, social perceptiveness, ingenuity, innovativeness, foresight, communication skills, and ability to identify the most urgent goals, needs, and discontents of a significant proportion of the populace. They have clearly articulated these goals and have suggested or initiated action designed to facilitate their materialization. Their motivation has been perceived by followers as completely unselfish and directed toward the attainment of group goals. They have served as eloquent and effective advocates for the group, and they have been persistent, stable, and unshakable in their defense of the cause which, under their direction, the group has espoused. They have relied almost exclusively on influence for in-group regulation, though some have used the group and its resources as a source of power to gain control over other groups. A charismatic leader could thus be described as one who with great effectiveness uses his own real or perceived qualities, skills, and attributes to acquire the support of others in the struggle to attain designated goals. Modification of the prevailing order and the eventual materialization of other goals would be perceived as benefiting all members of the group, although the leader might clearly articulate the need for current members to make extreme sacrifices for the benefit of future group members rather than for themselves.

A major reason for distinguishing between effective and charismatic leaders—over and above the fact that extraordinary powers and qualities are not attributed to most effective leaders—is that most effective leaders function within an established organizational or social setting, and the goals which they articulate and attempt to materialize are generally consistent with prevailing social expectations and norms. Charismatic leaders, on the other hand, are disenchanted with the traditional and prevailing institutions, practices, aspirations, and/or ideologies (though obviously not all disenchanted leaders are charismatic). Ordinarily, the changes they desire are perceived as being too radical to be attained through the gradual modification of the existing order. Moreover, for many reasons, there are usually rigid barriers to radical social change. Thus, the advocate of radical change is not an acceptable candidate for leadership within the established order and, if he is to be an instrument of change, he must work against the established order. If he is to acquire an extensive following, then the goals he espouses must correspond to the basic needs or desires of large numbers of people. Usually, his pronouncements reflect an articulation of widely perceived needs, and in addition he proposes new strategies and reinforces hope that the goals can be materialized. His appeal to basic needs, his persuasiveness, and the hope that he offers may be sufficiently great that his followers are willing to accept extreme danger and self-sacrifice and to engage in behaviors that violate established traditions. The charismatic leader is thus an effective leader who strives to change the social order and ordinarily works, at least initially, outside and against the established social and legal structure. As such, he may function as an instrument of social disruption and change, and depending on his goals and success in achieving them, as an instrument of social progress or destruction.

Comment

The concepts of charisma and charismatic leadership are used with various nuances of meaning, conflicting definitions, and even without definition as descriptive labels. Because of an erroneous assumption that if something is named it is explained and understood, these labels tend to serve as impediments to the objective analysis of social relationships. According to Downton,

few concepts in the social sciences have gained as much notoriety as charisma and few have been as indiscriminately applied to describe the emergence of a popular leader. Yet a concept that has been applied so indiscriminately loses its usefulness for analytic purposes, except as a residual category for describing what we cannot fully understand or explain.[33]

How valuable is a concept that can be applied equally well to Jesus and Confucius and to Hitler and Mussolini? The concept does not allow for a necessary distinction between the social and psychological aspects of leader-follower relations.[34] Since there can be no leader without followers, if charisma is to be understood there should be more emphasis on the charismatic relationship rather than almost exclusive attention to charismatic leadership per se. Questions should be raised about what predisposes individuals to enter into a charismatic relationship with a leader. What are the characteristics of the follower in a charismatic relationship? Might different individuals follow a leader who has been labeled charismatic for widely disparate reasons, only some of which pertain to a charismatic relationship? Under what social, political, economic, and ideological circumstances are charismatic relationships most likely to develop? If the nebulous concept of charisma is to be retained, social scientists should treat it as an intervening variable, and attempts should be made to identify precisely its antecedents and behavioral effects.

Notes

1. E. P. Hollander, *Leaders, Groups and Influence* (New York: Oxford University Press, 1964), p. 1.

2. N. T. Tillman, "Leadership," in J. Dunner, ed., *Dictionary of Political Science* (New York: Philosophical Library, 1964), p. 308.

3. M. Weber, *The Theory of Social and Economic Organization,* edited by T. Parsons (New York: Oxford University Press, 1947); M. Weber, *On Charisma and Institution Building,* edited by S. N. Eisenstadt (Chicago: University of Chicago Press, 1968).

4. Weber, *Theory of Social and Economic Organization,* p. 331.

5. Ibid., pp. 332-334.

6. Ibid., p. 333.

7. H. Gerth and C. Wright, eds., *From Max Weber: Essays in Sociology* (New York: Oxford University Press, 1946), p. 249.

8. Weber, *Theory of Social and Economic Organization*, pp. 331-332.

9. Ibid., p. 329.

10. Ibid., p. 330.

11. B. R. Wilson, *The Noble Savages* (Berkeley: University of California Press, 1975), p. 6.

12. E. Manheim, "Recent Types of Charismatic Leadership," in J. S. Roucek, ed., *Social Control* (New York: D. Van Nostrand, 1956), pp. 545-559.

13. Ibid., p. 552.

14. Ibid., p. 555.

15. Hollander, *Leaders, Groups and Influence*, p. 6.

16. For a history and analysis of the "great man" theory, see E. E. Jennings, *An Anatomy of Leadership: Princes, Heroes and Supermen* (New York: Harper, 1960).

17. E. S. Bogardus, *Leaders and Leadership* (New York: Appleton-Century, 1934); E. L. Munsen, *The Management of Men* (New York: Holt, 1921); R. Michels, *Political Parties* (New York: Macmillan, 1915), p. 6.

18. A. J. Murphy, "A Study of the Leadership Process," *American Sociological Review* 6 (1941):674-687.

19. For descriptions of these various positions, see, for example, F. E. Fiedler, *Leadership* (New York: General Learning Press, 1971); R. J. House, "A Path Goal Theory of Leader Effectiveness," *Administrative Science Quarterly* 16 (1971):321-338; and R. M. Stogdill, *Leadership: A Survey of the Literature: Selected Topics* (Greensboro, N.C.: Smith Richardson Foundation, 1968).

20. E. S. Bogardus, *Essentials of Social Psychology* (Los Angeles: University of Southern California Press, 1918).

21. Weber, *On Charisma and Institution Building*, pp. 46-80.

22. R. M. Stogdill, *Handbook of Leadership* (New York: Free Press, 1974).

23. E.g., H. Mintzberg, *The Nature of Managerial Work* (New York: Harper and Row, 1973).

24. Hollander, *Leaders, Groups and Influence*, p. 225.

25. Stogdill, *Handbook of Leadership*, p. 63.

26. Hollander, *Leaders, Groups and Influence*, p. 226.

27. For discussions of leadership functions, see S. M. Nealy and F. E. Fiedler, "Leadership Functions of Middle Managers," *Psychological Bulletin* 5 (1968):313-329; and Stogdill, *Handbook of Leadership*, pp. 28-31.

28. D. C. Pelz and F. M. Andrews, "Autonomy, Co-ordination and Stimulation in Relation to Scientific Achievement," *Behavioral Science* 11 (1966):89-97.

29. Hollander, *Leaders, Groups and Influence*, p. 331ff.

30. M. H. Lindemuth, "An Analysis of the Leader Behavior of Academic Deans" Ph.D. Dissertation, University of Michigan, 1969.

31. H. E. Roadman, "The Industrial Use of Peer Ratings," *Journal of Applied Psychology* 48 (1964):211-214.

32. Hollander, *Leaders, Groups and Influence,* p. 237.

33. J. V. Downton, *Rebel Leadership, Commitment and Charisma in the Revolutionary Process* (New York: Free Press, 1973), p. 209.

34. Ibid., p. 210.

Arthur S. Wilke

ART AND LITERATURE

An examination of the relationships between the arts and social control in community life requires a developed sociology of art, a field which in many ways is still in its infancy. The field remains much as James H. Barnett described it a generation ago, when he said it was characterized by "a point of view or attitude toward art, rather than a recognized area of study encompassing a specific subject matter, employing accepted methods of investigation, and secure in its possession of an established frame of reference."[1]

Contributing to the problems of the sociology of art is the difficulty of identifying and defining its subject matter. The vastness and indefiniteness of the arts, Thomas Munro notes, make even the most rudimentary task, that of classification, a difficult and controversial undertaking.[2] The arts, he notes, have been employed to designate many things: "literature, music and dance, theatre and film, the visual and decorative arts, and other equally diverse activities."[3] Form, medium, technique, and significance are among the many features used to classify the arts. Because so many of the classificatory schema reflect a social and historical relativism, their delineation for comparative study is no easy undertaking.

Compounding the problem of classification is the changing nature of the arts; over time, they change both in expression and significance. Painting and literary techniques, for example, change as do aesthetic principles. Furthermore, works once thought to be significant in one context change, and works not thought serious become viewed as works of art. *Gulliver's Travels* and *Robinson Crusoe*, for example, were once considered serious works but are now looked upon as children's literature, and Lincoln's Gettysburg Address, once shorn of its original context, has emerged a literary classic, although Lincoln's contemporaries viewed it as merely another speech.

Not only are the arts a varied set of expressions, but their appreciation is likewise varied. Unlike the sciences which tend to be judged by peers, art, especially art in the contemporary world, is subjected to judgments by diffuse audiences.

If the sociology of art is to assist in unraveling some of the issues dealing with social control, significant attention will have to be paid to matters of definition, classification, and significance.

The sociology of art is encompassed by a general field which Irvin Child identifies as aesthetics: "the study of man's behavior and experience in creating art, in perceiving and understanding art, and in being influenced by art."[4] Although work in the area has been fragmentary, psychologists (e.g., Arnheim, McCurdy, Barry, and Osgood) and anthropologists (e.g., Fischer)[5] have been prominent in some of these examinations. The renewed interest in the work of A. R. Luria[6] on comparative cognitive development may provide additional impetus in this area.

Within the general study of aesthetics, the sociology of art has examined proscribed concerns. With a tendency to accept the "beaux arts" or fine arts definition of art, with a smattering of interest in some popular forms, the principal foci for sociologists have been literature, music, and painting, with comparatively little attention paid to dance, architecture, pottery, weaving and so forth.[7] Most of the materials reviewed in this article focus on literature or painting. Music is dealt with separately in the following essay by Roucek.

Established Concerns

While the sociology of art is not well developed and little explicit investigation relating art to social control has been undertaken, a number of sociologists either have linked the arts to social control or have provided a foundation for such a consideration. Among the sociologists who have contributed to this concern are Pitirim Sorokin, Joseph S. Roucek, Talcott Parsons, and Don Martindale.

In his effort to construct a cyclical theory of history, Sorokin investigated art artifacts as one of the keys in verifying the existence of a predominant cultural type. The three types he considered were the sensate wherein bodily pleasures reign supreme; the ideational wherein faith predominates; and the idealistic in which reason is superordinate. His major effort in this regard is found in his multivolume study, *Social and Cultural Dynamics*.[8]

Joseph S. Roucek has done much to keep the concerns of art and social control alive in American sociology. Although he has not proposed a grand theory in the manner of Sorokin, he has, by and large, agreed with Sorokin's view that the arts and the predominant social forms of control are isomorphic. In his original symposium, *Social Control*, in which he identified art and literature as areas critical to the understanding of social control (a theme develoepd in that volume by Raymond F. Bellamy[9]), Roucek laid the foundation for this area of study. In recent years, Roucek has continued to outline the sociology of literature and art.[10] While he recognizes the manifold nature of social control and the arts, he has emphasized explicit control in an area made famous by Diderot during the French Revolution, the politicization of the arts. Although the arts have long dealt with political commentary, Diderot attempted to "identify artists with certain social and political causes."[11] Roucek has been particularly sensitive to this development in sociology, while other commentators have critically examined the connection between politics and the arts, especially literature.[12]

The noted functionalist Talcott Parsons has provided a theoretical key for examining the propagandistic role of artists. Artists, he maintains, have failed to fully professionalize themselves and have instead devoted their energies exclusively to cultivating the public's appreciation of art. The artist's major concern is making a living, a concern which, Parsons argues, undercuts professional development. Only through professional development, he says, can collectivities cope with the challenges and opportunities of increasingly bureaucratized societies.[13]

As people struggling to make a living, artists do not occupy a central position in community affairs; as a result, their symbolic expressions cannot serve as the unifying expressions of a community. Hence, they assume the intermediary role of propagandist. As propagandist, the artist employs expressive symbols and serves as an intermediary in the cultural processes of community life.[14]

One of the few American sociologists who has explicitly articulated a view on the integral role of art in sociocultural affairs is Don Martindale. A social behaviorist, Martindale conceives of much of art as arising from the unresolved problems of community life. Artistic works, along with other intellectual productions, provide imaginative ways of dealing with various problems of collective life, including social control, in which ready formulations and directives are not easily attained. As creative statements then, artistic works constitute sublimations wherein some of the unresolved problems of community life are raised to an idealized or imaginative status.[15] If this resolves the problems with institutionalized procedures for coping with collective problems, such art provides for a "higher" order of social control.

Long a student of social change in which individuals are seen as playing a decisive role, Martindale's conception of art provides a means for the social analyst to probe moments of decisive change. Unlike Sorokin who looked for representative and typical art expressions, Martindale remains sensitive to the changing and unfolding features of symbolic expression. To that end, in a recent work, *Sociological Theory and the Problem of Values*,[16] he has added a neo-Kantian aesthetic to his probe of art. Two general forms, abstract formalism and representational symbolism, are used to characterize the dominant modes of artistic execution and aesthetic discernment in community life. For Martindale it is both "a triumph and a tragedy" that vast opportunities for personal development and expression are provided at the same time as numerous other possibilities are thwarted.[17]

An area of expanding interest is the social historical study of art which was pioneered by Arnold Hauser's classic, *The Social History of Art*.[18] This work urged, among other things, the employment of the sociological perspective in this form of investigation. The tradition has since bloomed. Numerous efforts have been undertaken to account for the genesis of some of the contemporary aspects of the art scene. Vytautas Kavolis,[19] for example, has summarized a typology of artistic cultures in which varying degrees of internal and external controls on the creation and appreciation of art are witnessed. Among the artistic cultures he identifies as exhibiting principally internal controls are the genius culture, dominated by highly independent persons who boldly speak out for new values; the professional culture, wherein the personal aesthetic tastes of the artist set the direction for the products, even though the artist remains sensitive to the art market; the movement culture, exhibiting spontaneity, thereby breaking down rigid definitions separating artists and art from the regular routines of community life;[20] and avant garde culture in which the articulation of contemporary alienation predominates (e.g., plays by Bertolt Brecht and Edward Albee) and which may express the alienation with art itself (i.e., anti-art art).[21] These cultures, to the degree they are financed by the artists themselves, provide for a great amount of artistic diversity and creativity, some of which may, at times, border on anarchy, if not nihilism.[22]

Artistic cultures in which external controls predominate include the applied arts culture in which social engineering tends to predominate as a central technique (e.g., advertising, architecture, and design); the mass-arts culture in which a vast technostructure of personnel and appliances are positioned between the artist and diffuse audiences (e.g., by radio, television, and mass publications); the total demand culture in which all phases of art and artistic production are subjected to principles considered to be in harmony with a predominant political ideology and often exampled by the Soviet Union and Nazi Germany; the scientific-technological culture in which scientific research guides and directs vast capital, technical, and labor resources which glorify the achievements of the technical order;[23] and finally, amateur art-making in which the division between producer and consumer is blurred, but critical controls on the distribution of appliances and materials remain in the hands of others.

Another historic effort, *summarized by Francis Haskell,[24] traces the shifting organizational milieu of artists to account for some of the institutionalized practices associated with the contemporary art world. Some of the modern developments were spurred by events in sixteenth-century Rome where academies emerged in the wake of the decline of artist guilds. The academies helped launch the artists and thereby promoted some of their newly won gains in status. During the next several centuries, the art dealer came to play a more central role in the art world, breaking the direct relationship between the art consumer and the artist. This system encouraged specializations in subject matter which are witnessed even today. Simultaneous to the growth of art dealers were exhibitions in the form of the annual *salon*, providing artists a means of exhibiting their works. In response to the *salon* came the art critic. The first critics were advisors to patrons, but by the eighteenth century, pamphleteers emerged, creating a more pervasive form of art criticism. With the rise of the pamphleteer (today often a newspaper critic), the exclusivity of the artists' *salon* was broken and a much broader public was now exposed to the art world. At this time, the connoisseur became an important figure in the art world. A moderately affluent individual, the connoisseur could effect changes and developments in art that were not possible in the economic and political sectors of societies. With the growth in private collections, the art dealer, "the exhibition, the critic, and even the museum of modern art"[25] combined to lay the foundation for the contemporary art world. One additional element was added in the nineteenth century: the avant garde. The avant garde grew in significance during this period and could be ignored only at great risk to those trading as well as appreciating art. Like the products of the emerging industrial order, art became a matter of style, innovation, and obsolescence.[26]

During the 1960s, some new insights into the sociology of art grew out of the countercultural revolts and the emergence of the New Left. As new vehicles of expression surfaced and expanded, critical voices began to be heard—particularly those of Leo Lowenthal and Herbert Marcuse, formerly members of the Frankfurt Institute, the Frenchman Lucien Goldmann, and the Hungarian Georg Lukacs. The last three were vocal critics of capitalism and of the role of arts in that system.

Lowenthal's early study "Biographies in Popular Magazines"[27] was a content analysis of popular magazines, and noted that the heroes of biographical pieces had changed from heroes of production to consumption. While Lowenthal's work was significant for its effort to empirically verify changing features of cultural life, it did not appreciably add to the sociological understanding of art. Nonetheless, his work published over a decade later, *Literature and the Image of Man*,[28] probed issues that more closely identified him with the critical theory concerns of other former members of the Frankfurt Institute such as Marcuse.

Lowenthal did not gain as great recognition as Herbert Marcuse. As Marcuse observes, the fact that style is a central feature of the capitalist market system has had a significant effect on the role and meaning of art. Art in the capitalist market, instead of constititing a sublimation as Martindale notes, results in what Marcuse terms desublimation. In the changing avalanche of style, art is no longer capable of expressing the unresolved tensions found in community life, presumably a task it did fulfill for the bourgeoisie of an earlier period, and as a result, it loses its potential for subversion and change.[29] Only art in the service of new sensibilities could provide the necessary dynamic to mobilize resistance and challenge to an existing social order whose repressive features are seen to be expanding.[30] Nevertheless, as Marcuse readily acknowledges, such a new sensibility, expressed by the rebelling youth of the 1960s, did contain hazards, the chief of which was the possible renunciation of all historically identifiable art and culture.

Toward the end of the 1960s, attention began to center on writers such as Lucien Goldmann who had been heretofore inaccessible to English-speaking readers, especially those in the sociology of art. Goldmann maintains that the novel in capitalist society no longer serves to heighten group consciousness and as a result, does not assist in coordinating human affairs. In fact, Goldmann argues, such literature does not help compensate for the "frustrations created by a fragmented world."[31] (This view harmonizes with Marcuse's.) Further, Goldmann states that literary forms such as the novel are "increasingly realistic, individualistic and reified,"[32] and not capable of playing a profound role in human affairs. Contemporary novels highlight the changing centers of control and purpose in community affairs. Although neither Sorokin nor Martindale would contest this point, Martindale at least would undoubtedly view the significance of Goldmann's observations quite differently. For him the individualistic, even in a sublimated form, is a condition to be championed and not, as Goldmann does, condemned.

Within the past decade, George Lukacs has emerged as a major influence in the sociology of literature.[33] Like Goldmann, he is critical of bourgeois literature and maintains that literature should have purpose or a *telos* in community affairs. This view is expressed in the concept of totalization wherein art is seen as ideally providing a far more comprehensive engagement with the world than that found in, say, science which is seen to be the cultivation of partial perceptions. In the *Theory of the Novel*,[34] Lukacs advances the view that art must be faithful to the preconstituted reality of human beings, shorn of the reflective and interpretative apparatus so often used to understand human affairs. This concern provides a platform for Lukacs' criticism of both abstract idealism and romanticism. An engaged action is more than the pure action stressed in abstract idealism, and his concern clearly eschews the attention given in romanticism to expressing the feelings and emotions attached to what are taken to be contemplated actions.

Lukacs the dialectician comes to the forefront in his studies of literature. Unlike epochal theorists who see major contours in the changing cultural landscape, Lukacs is sensitive to the changing significance art may have for people within an epoch. This may provide an expanded vision for those who chart the changing significance of art in community affairs.

Evolving Concerns

Many of the works discussed above provide a foundation for considering the role the arts play vis-à-vis social control. First, however, there must be an understanding of how the arts become what they are. Mason Griff,[35] for example, suggests that it will be difficult to assess the role of the artist and his work in community affairs without understanding how artistic careers are selected and how artists become socialized. J. M. B. Edwards underscores the difficulty of assessing the influence of the arts in community affairs inasmuch as the audiences of the arts are so diffuse.[36]

There has long been an interest in the factors controlling and directing artistic creativity, which is one manifestation of social control. In *Canvases and Careers*[37] the Whites, for example, explore the relationship between the institutional changes and the painting world in nineteenth-century France. The subject of creativity, which has been of great concern to psychologists and philosophers, has been introduced in sociology by Vytautas Kavolis.[38] Though such concerns as creativity are still debated, the attention promises to provide new considerations for sociologically studying art and social control.

As attention is directed to increasingly rationalized aspects of contemporary life, the political and economic dimensions of the production, distribution, and consumption of art will take on greater significance.[39] Such concerns will shift attention away from the resulting control functions of art to how the arts are intricately linked to concentrated systems of control and domination in community affairs. This is highlighted in the growing concern over art forgeries.

The problem of art forgery is of growing significance because of the massive amounts of money invested in art. For holders of large amounts of accumulated wealth, investment in art is, among other things, a hedge against inflation. The art critic takes on a central role by aiding in the policing of possible forgeries. From the purchase of art masterpieces to their donation (with resulting tax benefits), the basis of the masterpieces' value is increasingly scrutinized by critics.

Besides elevating the art critic and the artist producing physical artifacts (painting and sculpture, for example, as opposed to performing arts) to more central roles in the cultural life of communities, the investment in art has another major implication for social control in community life. Inasmuch as investment in art or any precious item constitutes an orientation of preindustrial capitalism, the economic life in settings thought to be industrial capitalist may be viewed as a puzzle or a source of increasing contradiction. The implications for social control issuing from such conflicts and changes in the economic bases of community affairs may be immense.

Since the public has assumed a larger role in community affairs as regards the use and significance of the arts, the social control of the arts as well as social control through the arts have become important concerns. The changes in the cultural milieu[40] as well as the increase in literacy[41] have unleashed forces requiring changing modes of social coordination. Attention to the role of audiences has been developed by writers such as Escarpit[42] and Abercrombie.[43]

Further understanding of art within community life is to be anticipated with the renewed interest in ritual. The means of creating group solidarity, discussed by Turner[44] as ritual process, reintroduces subtle, nondiscursive items in considering art in community affairs. Turner, like Samuel Brandon,[45] focuses on ritual as it relates to religion. By contrast, the sociologist Hugh Dalziel Duncan is concerned with more commonplace ritual as it relates to art. Duncan suggests that art is integral to the rituals of everyday life, serving "as a dramatic rehearsal in the imagination of community roles...(to be) play(ed) to sustain social order."[46]

Attention to the role of the audience in the arts was generated by Sartre's sweeping essay *What Is Literature?*[47] Recognizing that art would have no meaning without an audience, Sartre argued for an engaged writer (and, by extension, artist), one not unlike the one urged by Lukacs. The awareness of the audience is not limited to political concerns, however, for as Escarpit observes, the trend has been to engage the audience by transforming them from passive, detached reviewers into active participants.[48] This is especially true of the performing arts. Even museum directors, under the guise of museology,[49] are promoting such a role for the audience. Hence, the scope of social control associated with the arts has been magnified. This growing awareness will direct scholarly attention into areas of community life that have previously gone unexamined.

For the past four centuries[50] the traditional arts and their interpretation have become increasingly less significant as a result of the expanding awareness of art production and experience. All indications point to accelerations of these trends in the future.[51] As artistic styles continue to shift dramatically and strategic efforts are expended in the production and appreciation of art, features once treated in perfunctory fashion, new problems regarding the role of art in producing social control and its relationship to vast networks of social control can be expected.

Summary

Although sociologists have outlined an area of concern in the study of the relationship of the arts and social control, the nature and significance of that relationship are fraught with controversy. Many debates center on the classification, definition, and significance of the arts. The growing awareness of the many facets of the arts and art experiences provide not only expanding means for extending social control but also unique challenges for establishing control in community affairs.

Notes

1. James H. Barnett, "The Sociology of Art," in Robert K. Merton, Leonard Broom, and Leonard S. Cottrell, Jr., eds., *Sociology Today: Problems and Prospects* (New York: Basic Books, 1959), pp. 197-214.

2. Thomas Munro, "Classification of the Arts," *The New Encyclopaedia Britannica*, Macropaedia, Vol. 2 (Chicago: Encyclopaedia Britannica, 1976), p. 81.

3. Ibid.

4. Irvin L. Child, "Aesthetics," in David L. Sills, ed., *The International Encyclopedia of the Social Sciences*, (New York: Macmillan and Free Press, 1968), Vol. 1, p. 116.

5. Ibid., pp. 116-120. Also see Charlotte M. Otten, *Anthropology and Art: Readings in Cross-Cultural Aesthetics* (Austin, Tex.: University of Texas Press, 1976); Anto Ehrenzwerg, *The Hidden Order of Art: A Study in the Psychology of Artistic Imagination* (Berkeley: University of California Press, 1976 [1967]); and Suen Hesselgran, *Man's Perception of Man-Made Environment: An Architectural Theory* (Stroudsberg, Pa.: Dowden, Hutchinson and Ross, 1976 [1975]).

6. A. R. Luria, *Cognitive Development: Its Cultural and Social Foundations*, translated by Martin Lopez-Morillas and Lynn Solotaroff and edited by Michael Cole (Cambridge, Mass. and London: Harvard University Press, 1976 [1974]).

7. The arts are given cursory treatment in *The International Encyclopedia of the Social Sciences*; see C. A. Doxiadis, "Architecture," Vol. I, pp. 392-397; Faubion Bowers, "Drama," Vol. 4, pp. 256-258; Daniel J. Crowley, "Crafts," Vol. 3, pp. 430-434; and Phillip H. Lewis, "Primitive Art," Vol. 12, pp. 477-480. Other works in these areas of interest to sociologists are: Constanios A. Doxiadis, *Architecture in Transition* (New York: Oxford University Press, 1953); Sigfried Giedion, *The Eternal Present: The Beginnings of Architecture* (New York: Pantheon Books, 1964); Lewis Mumford, *The City in History: Its Origins, Its Transformations and Its Prospects* (New York: Harcourt, Brace and World, 1961); Lewis Mumford, *Sticks and Stones: A Study of American Architecture and Civilization*, 2d ed. (New York: Dover, 1955 [1924]); Frank Lloyd Wright, *Frank Lloyd Wright on Architecture; Selected Writings, 1894-1940* (New York: Grosset and Dunlop, 1959 [1941]); Udo Kuttermann, *New Architecture in the World*, updated ed. (Boulder, Col.: Westview Press, 1976); and Franz Boas, *Primitive Art*, new ed. (New York: Dover, 1955 [1927]).

8. Pitirim A. Sorokin, *Social and Cultural Dynamics*, 4 vols. (New York: American Book Co., 1937), especially Vol. 1.

9. Raymond F. Bellamy, "Art and Literature," in Joseph S. Roucek, *Social Control* (New York: D. Van Nostrand, 1947), pp. 240-259. This wide-ranging discussion summarizes a number of historic works and remains a valuable resource.

10. Joseph S. Roucek, "The Sociology of Literature," *Indian Journal of Social Research* 2 (July 1961):22-30; and Joseph S. Roucek and Raj P. Mohan, "An Essay on the Developments in and the Implications of the Sociology of Art," *International Journal of Contemporary Sociology* 9(October 1972):214-230. As is characteristic of Roucek's work, both of these articles contain a wide-ranging selection of references.

11. Francis Haskell, "Fine Arts: I. Art and Society," *The International Encyclopedia of the Social Sciences*, Vol. 5, p. 445.

12. Among some writers addressing the political novel are: Joseph Blotner, *The Political Novel* (Garden City, N.Y.: Doubleday, 1955); Irving Howe, *Politics and the Novel* (New York: World, 1957); Paul von Blum, *The Art of Social Conscience* (New York: Universe Books, 1976); and Charles I. Glicksburg, *The Literature of Commitment* (Lewisburg, Pa.: Bucknell University Press, 1975). In a collection of autobiographical statements of authors who merged their political and artistic

concerns, see Richard H. S. Crossman, ed., *The God That Failed* (New York: Harper, 1959 [1949]).

13. Talcott Parsons, "Professions," *The International Encyclopia of the Social Sciences*, Vol. 12, p. 538.

14. Talcott Parsons, *The Social System* (Glencoe, Ill.: Free Press, 1951), pp. 411-412.

15. Don Martindale, *Social Life and Cultural Change* (Princeton, N.J.: D. Van Nostrand, 1962), pp. 51-54.

16. Don Martindale, *Sociological Theory and the Problem of Values* (Columbus, Ohio: Charles E. Merrill, 1974), p. 55.

17. Martindale, *Social Life and Cultural Change*, pp. 496-497.

18. Arnold Hauser, *The Social History of Art*, 2 vols. (New York: Alfred A. Knopf, 1951).

19. Vytautas Kavolis, "Social and Economic Aspects of the Arts," *The New Encyclopaedia Britannica*, Macropaedia, Vol. 2, pp. 97-108.

20. A popular portrait of the cultural revolt of the 1960s is Charles A. Reich, *The Greening of America* (New York: Bantam, 1971 [1970]), and R. Serge Denisoff and Richard A. Peterson, eds., *The Sounds of Social Change: Studies in Popular Culture* (Chicago: Rand McNally, 1972) for commentary and wide-ranging bibliography.

21. See Robert W. Corrigan, ed., *Theatre in the Twentieth Century* (New York: Grove, 1963).

22. For valuable reviews primarily of literature and stressing some of these themes; see the annual volumes *The Great Ideas Today* (Chicago: Encyclopaedia Britannica, various dates).

23. A foremost critic of these developments is Lewis Mumford. See *The Myth of the Machine: Technics and Human Development* (New York: Harcourt Brace Jovanovich, 1968), and *The Myth of the Machine: The Pentagon of Power* (New York: Harcourt Brace Jovanovich, 1970 [1964]).

24. Francis Haskell, "Fine Arts: I. Art and Society," *The International Encyclopedia of the Social Sciences*, Vol. 5, pp. 439-447.

25. Ibid., p. 445.

26. The social historical literature on literature and painting is rapidly increasing, and access to it should be quite easy.

27. Leo Lowenthal, "Biographies in Popular Magazines," in Paul F. Lazarsfeld and Frank Stanton, eds., *Radio Research 1942-43* (New York: Bureau of Applied Social Research, 1944).

28. Leo Lowenthal, *Literature and the Image of Man: Studies of European Drama and Novel, 1600-1900* (Boston: Beacon, 1957).

29. Herbert Marcuse, *One Dimensional Man: Studies in the Ideology of Advanced Industrial Society* (Boston: Beacon, 1964).

30. Herbert Marcuse, *An Essay on Liberation* (Boston: Beacon, 1969).

31. Lucien Goldmann, *Cultural Creation in Modern Society*, translated by Wm. Mayrl (St. Louis, Mo.: Telos Press, 1976).

32. Support for Goldmann can be found in Albert J. Geurard, "Discontinuities and Discoveries: Innovation in Recent American Fiction," *The Great Ideas Today, 1976* (Chicago: Encyclopaedia Britannica, 1976), pp. 108-151.

33. Robert Escarpit, "Literature: I. The Sociology of Literature," *The International Encyclopedia of the Social Sciences*, Vol. 9, p. 418.

34. Georg Lukacs, *The Theory of the Novel: A Historical-Philosophical Essay on the Forms of Great Epic Literature*, translated by Anna Bostock (Cambridge, Mass.: MIT Press, 1971). For a different philosophical treatment, see Joseph Chiari, *Art and Knowledge* (New York: Gordion Press, 1977).

35. Mason Griff, "Fine Arts: II. The Recruitment and Socialization of Artists," *The International Encyclopedia of the Social Sciences*, Vol. 5, p. 454.

36. J.M.B. Edwards, "Creativity: II. Social Aspects," *The International Encyclopedia of the Social Sciences*, Vol. 3, p. 444.

37. Harrison C. White and Cynthia A. White, *Canvases and Careers: Institutional Change in the French Painting World* (New York: John Wiley and Sons, 1965).

38. Vytautas M. Kavolis, "Community Dynamics and Artistic Creativity," *American Sociological Review* 31 (April 1966):208-217, and Vytautas Kavolis, *History on Art's Side: Social Dynamics in Artistic Efflorescences* (Ithaca, N.Y.: Cornell University Press, 1972).

39. See Richard A. Peterson, ed., *The Production of Culture* (Beverly Hills, Calif., Sage Publications, 1976), and Mark Blaug, ed., *The Economics of Art* (Boulder, Colo.: Westview Press, 1976).

40. Raymond Williams, *Culture and Society: 1780-1950* (New York: Harper Torchbooks, 1958); Raymond Williams, *The Long Revolution*. rev. ed. (New York: Harper Torchbooks, 1961); and R. D. Altick, *The English Common Reader: A Social History of the Mass Reading Public, 1800-1900* (Chicago: University of Chicago Press, 1957).

41. Richard Hoggart, *The Uses of Literacy: Aspects of Working-Class Life with Special Reference to Publications and Entertainments* (New York: Oxford University Press, 1957).

42. Robert C.E.G. Escarpit, *Sociology of Literature* (Painsville, Ohio: Lake Erie College Press, 1965 [1958]).

43. Nigel Abercrombie, *Artists and Their Public* (Paris: UNESCO Press, 1975).

44. Victor W. Turner, *The Ritual Process: Structure and Anti-Structure* (Chicago: Aldine, 1969).

45. Samuel George Frederick Brandon, *Man and God in Art and Ritual* (New York: Charles Scribner's Sons, 1974).

46. Hugh Dalziel Duncan, *Symbols in Society* (New York: Oxford University Press, 1968), p. 222.

47. Jean-Paul Sartre, *What Is Literature?*, translated by Bernard Frechtman and introduced by Wallace Fowlie (New York: Harper Colophon, 1965 [1949]).

48. Escarpit, "Literature: I. The Sociology of Literature," pp. 417-425.

49. Edmon Radar, "Art Centers and Participation," *Diogenes*, no. 94 (Summer 1976):94-109.

50. Escarpit, "Literature: I. The Sociology of Literature," p. 419.

51. J. Adler, "Innovative Art and Obsolescent Artists," *Social Research* 42 (Summer 1975):360-378.

Joseph S. Roucek

MUSIC

Music has been used effectively for social control throughout the history of mankind. Today, more than ever before, not only music but nearly all forms of art are viewed as initiators or mirrors of social change, and "much of modern criticism is based upon evaluation of such reform purposes."[1]

Music, is "by its nature. . . . suited more for the objectification and transmission of feelings, emotions, moods, or elusive mental states that defy verbal expression than of ideas or acts, and is therefore more often used for emotional than intellectual communication." The symbolic sound waves "induce a depressed state—sadness, despondency, or grief, with their corresponding overt reactions—while others elicit a sense of mirth, happiness, or joy, accompanied by the appropriate movements."[2] The exciting or depressing influence of music, Bohn claims, has been known since ancient days. "Besides funeral marches, accompanied by depressing moods and slow movements, there is also exciting music compelling people to move their bodies vigorously in marching or dancing, a thing which could not be even imagined without the music."[3]

The social control functions of art may be either unconscious or planned. Today music (as one of arts' tools) is increasingly used to deliberately influence men and events, although it should be noted that the actual effects are often quite different from those that are predicted. At any rate, a better understanding of music as a social force is important for a comprehension of contemporary life.

What people repeatedly see or hear daily in their surroundings become accepted as being normal and natural. Thus, when images depict the familiar, they are powerful supporters of things as they are, but when artists break away from the traditional, they help to bring about social changes. This especially happens when revolutionary leaders try to mobilize various mass media of communications (music, books, newspapers, plays, radio, television) in their efforts to reshape the mass mind, as shown, for instance, in John Greenway's *American Folksongs of Protest* (New York: A. S. Barnes, 1953).

In fact, many revolutionary thinkers consider the Gospel as presented in music to be one of the most effective means of propaganda. In a review of a collection of songs by Thomas Rousseau in the *Journal des hommes libres,* one of the leading revolutionary journals, it is asserted that music is probably older than language and certainly older than knowledge. The review argues that since music derived from nature itself, it had a powerful appeal to human beings, particularly the very young. "Few people read, everybody sings!" the journal observes. "Song is therefore one of the main avenues which must be opened up for public instruction."[4]

Mirroring the Time Periods

Unlike "classic" music, "popular" music is the product of the times. For instance, the progression of feeling during the American Depression in the 1930s can be traced in the songs of that era. First, the early songs were witty and hopeful; typical of these was "it will all come out all right if I keep painting the clouds with sunshine." Later, as the Depression deepened, the songs mirrored confused, uncertain conditions. Some of the songs attempted to make a joke of the Depression, as in "Brother can you spare a dime?" Others boldly asserted: "Just around the corner, there's a rainbow in the sky." The depth of hopelessness was probably reached in: "What to do about it, just put out the light and go to sleep."

These compositions exercised a great deal of control over the thinking and acting of the people, just as songs such as "Keep the Home Fires Burning" and "Smile, Smile, Smile!" had during World War I.[5]

Religious Music

Church music and songs cannot be separated from the other forms of religious social control, notably art, chants, rituals, and pageantry. We learn, for instance that

A distinguishing quality of Methodists even today is their singing, which at a great church convocation is an experience no hearer ever forgets. Methodism, it has been said, literally sung itself into the hearts of the people. The roots of the tradition go back to Charles Wesley, brother of founder John Wesley, who wrote the words to 6,500 hymns. . . . Until the Methodists, there was little hymn singing in church as we know it now. Music was limited largely to chants and Te Deums. Charles Wesley wrote hymns for every occasion: for rising and retiring, for washing dishes and laundry, for hewing wood and plowing. His genius as a hymn writer lay in the intensely personal quality of his works, which bristle with personal pronouncements: "Oh, for a thousand tongues to sing *my* great Redeemer's praise," "Jesus, love *my* soul.[6]

Or we learn that "recreational programs are not highly advanced in the Negro church, but choirs, instrumental ensembles, and other music attractions entertain those who attend."[7]

Modern anthropology claims that "the total accompaniment of religious rites, probably beginning with early man's magical incantations, hinge on the effect of instrumental and vocal tone in manipulating unseen powers. Early religious music was thus largely utilitarian, and this phase blended into the early historic religions with their more formalized music."[8]

According to Whitman, the "Song of Deborah" (Judges 5) in the Old Testament is the oldest recorded song in Judeo-Christian culture.[9] The oldest musical survivors are the Gregorian chants, many of which have become themes for today's hymnals. "As the scriptural heritage is shared, even the words of the best-loved hymns are echoed in Jewish and Christian hymns, in both Catholic and Protestant church, and in the spirituals."[10] In general, most religious music has been the language of faith and hope.

The basic system of church music in Western Europe can be traced to the sixth century and the administration of Pope Gregory the Great. (It probably originated in Byzantium.) This system is known variously as plain-chant, plain-song, or the Gregorian chant. The chant consisted of notes sung in unison. It lacked harmony and had little melody or fixed rhythm, but "its monotony produced an uplifting and almost hypnotic effect in church services."[11] Eventually, a number of varieties of plain-song developed, including the antiphonal, in which two choirs sang alternately, and the responsive, in which solo voice in the choir answered. It also included hymns, which were probably pagan in origin. During the eleventh century, a number of musicians devised the present system of notation with notes of the scale called by the first seven letters of the alphabet and with symbols on the staff to represent not only the note but also its duration. This system allowed the quick reading of music, instead of the former laborious training by memory, and promoted the rise of polyphonic music, which developed several themes at once by giving different parts to different voices. Aware of the value of the new system, churchmen attempted from time to time to introduce polyphonic music into the official ritual of the church; they were officially resisted inasmuch as the conservative church leaders preferred the traditional plain-song. Secular music, lacking the conventional restraints of church tradition, developed more freely and richly than ecclesiastical music. At the end of the Middle Ages, church music began to use the pipe organ to supplement choirs.

In general, the development of music responded to the same general social and cultural trends as those governing other art forms. Beginning in the fiftheenth century, the musician, like the artist and the writer, rose in status, until the composer and the virtuoso were no longer craftsmen or clerics but artists with independent positions in the aristocratic world. The medieval distinction between music as the science of harmonics (a branch of mathematics) and as a purely functional element in religious ritual and court ceremonials gradually disappeared, and music was recognized as an art form. The technical and social aspects of European music in the sixteenth and seventeenth centuries worked together to lay the groundwork for the accomplishments of musical giants such as Bach and Handel in the eighteenth century. Bach, known for his church music, counterpoint, and the fugue—all of which were marked by a strong intellectual appeal—also composed chamber music.

In America the first popular songs were religious—psalms and hymns. They were imported from the Old World and flourished in New England before the Revolution; they represented both a means of worship and a social pastime at home and town meetings. A continuous tradition was established with the landing of the Pilgrims at Plymouth Rock in 1620: they brought with them Henry Ainsworth's Book of Psalms. One of Ainsworth's compositions, "The Old Hundredth," is still sung today as the doxology to the words "Praise God from Whom all Blessings Flow."[12]

An important part of the musical heritage of several religious American denominations and sects was formed by the Moravian Brethren (Brothers), whose hymns and choir singing are known internationally. John Wesley, for example, composed his hymns based on the Moravian pattern.[13]

Eastern Orthodoxy maintains that its music has made definite contributions to all Christianity. Its divine liturgy is the most elaborate and colorful in Christendom, lasting from sixty minutes to three hours, it is always sung and is a dialogue between the priest and lay voices.[14] Lutheranism in America had its musical roots in Luther himself who emphasized the value of music, calling it "an inexpressible miracle of the Lord." Luther himself sang well and played the flute, and especially appreciated the inspirational value of choral music. To encourage hymn singing, he collaborated on the first Protestant hymnal, which included four of his own compositions. His towering hymn, "A Mighty Fortress Is Our God," is often called "The Battle Hymn of the Reformation." Luther also composed choir music based on the Gospel stories thus anticipating the eighteenth-century Lutheran genius, Johann Sebastian Bach, and his contemporary, George Frederick Handel.

The Baptists, with their church program suggesting "attack the problem, not the people," and with their large Negro membership, feature music very prominently in their services.[15] The choir is quite prominent in Episcopalian services[16] as well as in the Mormon church. (The Mormon Tabernacle Choir has a fine national reputation.)

The Government's Manipulation of Symbols of Music

While in recent times, fascism, nazism, and communism have manipulated music on a large and impressive scale, it has always been subject to government use, though less systematically and less consciously. Music has always been an important component of social, political, and religious ceremonials,[17] being utilized not only in work and play, but also in politics and warfare. It has nearly always been presented in conjunction with memorial days and periods, public ceremonies, parades, and public political gatherings.[18] As Merriam points out, "Music and song have contributed to the glorification of the power association in some of the most striking rhythms ever decided, rivaled again, however, by those of the church, and by the other types of music. What should we do without the 'Marseillaise,' 'Deutschland Über Alles,' the 'Internationale,' 'Giovanezza,' 'America,' 'God Save the King'?"[19]

The title of a study by Whitman, *Songs That Changed the World* (New York: Crown, 1969), is possibly somewhat of an exaggeration, but it is also partly true. Whether or not songs and music prove effective all the time, the fact remains that their long-term social action "has been a factor in history," as exemplified by "The World Turned Upside Down" played at the Yorktown surrender or "Go Down Moses" in Mississippi's history.

Martial Music

From time immemorial, men have marched to war to the strains of martial music; obviously, Plato's recommendation of martial music has been followed universally. For example, the "catchiest of marching tunes, 'The British Grenadiers,' ... must have led many a youth to take the king's shilling."[20] Interestingly, numerous songs which were written for one specific event became associated with other causes, and even different nations. "Yankee Doodle" began in England as a Roundhead song in Cromwell's revolution and stood for foreign, un-English influence among the royalists; brought to America, it inspired new verses and was played by the victors at Yorktown. When Claude-Rouget de Lisle wrote "La Marseillaise" in 1792, France was fighting invasion, and the composition began as a war song calling for enemy blood.[21] "John Brown's Body," written just before the American Civil War, "deserves its fame if only as inspiration for the 'Battle Hymn of the Republic.' "[22] The "Battle Hymn" was written by Julia Ward Howe and was set to the "brave music" of "John Brown's Body"; her song was sung in Westminster Abbey in World War II, was parodied during the anti-Vietnam war demonstrations as "Gory, gory, gory. What a Helleva Way to Die!" and was sung by dissenters at the 1968 Democratic Convention.[23] "Marching Through Georgia," a favorite Yankee tune of the Civil War, was played to welcome southern troops landing in Ireland during World War I.[24] "Tramp! Tramp! Tramp!" was successful with the Union Army and served as a marching song in later wars.[25] "Dixie," which started as a Civil War song, still "brings rebel yells and brought southern audiences to hysteria when Toscanini led it during the 'cold civil war' of our time."[26] "The

Bonnie Blue Flag" ran second only to "Dixie" in popularity, and "its enumeration of the seceding states was an honor roll cherished by diehards long after the war's end."[27] And "When Johnny Comes Marching Home" belongs to all the wars.[28]

"Quand Madelon" was one of the marching songs of World War I for both French troops and Americans who landed in France in 1917-1918.[29] "Around Her Neck She Wore a Yellow Ribbon," a folk song, was revived in World War I. "The original purple ribbon was changed to yellow for the cavalry, which retained its dash in that war although saber charges were over."[30]

Other military songs include "Anchors Aweigh," which has "a proper seafaring swing,"[31] and "The Marines' Hymn" ("Halls of Montezuma"), a well-loved and inspiring song for the American Marines.[32] "The Bell of Hell" originated with the British in World War I and was a Royal Flying Corps favorite.[33]

The Music of World War I and World War II

The outbreak of World War I exerted a profound effect on Tin Pan Alley, which had "developed into a well-oiled machine capable of manufacturing songs for every need. Not only was Tin Pan Alley cognizant of the way in which the war had changed the lives, thoughts, and emotions of the American people, but it was also in a position to give direct expression to such thoughts and emotions."[34]

The sentimentality of the Americans about their boys in the war in a foreign land, as well as the sentimentality of the soldiers about their homes and the girls they had left behind, were featured in such poignant songs as "Till We Meet Again" by Richard A. Whiting, possibly the most eloquent ballad of the war, and in Albert von Tilzeris' "I May Be Gone for a Long, Long Time" and "Au Revoir but Not Good-bye, Soldier Boy." In the same category belong Al Piantadosi's "Send Me Away with a Smile," written in collaboration with Louis Wesleyn; Pete Wendling's "Oh, How I Wish I Could Sleep until My Daddy Comes Home"; and Jean Schwartz's "Hello Central, Give Me No Man's Land."

The American's patriotic ardor and martial spirit were inspired by such songs as "Just Like Washington Crossed the Delaware, General Pershing Will Cross the Rhine" and Billy Baskere's "Good-bye Broadway, Hello France." Tunes such as "We're Going Over" and "The Navy Took Them Over and the Navy Will Bring Them Back" were hymns of praise of the various services. The hatred of the Kaiser was expressed in over a hundred songs such as "We're Going to Hang the Kaiser under the Linden Tree," while the affection for the ally, France, was sung in "Joan of Arc" and Fred Fisher's "Lorraine— My Beautiful Alsace Lorraine." The humorous aspects of army life during World War I were reflected in "K-K-Katy," Walter Donalson's "How Ya

Gonna Keep 'em Down on the Farm?" and Irving Berlin's "Oh! How I Hate to Get Up in the Morning."

The most famous World War I song was George M. Cohan's "Over There," which sold over two million copies of sheet music and a million records. President Woodrow Wilson wrote that it had been "a genuine inspiration to all American manhood." Many years later, the song brought Cohan a Congressional Medal of Honor, bestowed by President Franklin D. Roosevelt under a special act of Congress.[35]

In contrast to World War I, World War II produced few songs of lasting consequence. The two best ones were "The Beer Barrel Polka" and "Waltzing Matilda" (imported by the Australians). Apparently, it was not a singing war. One explanation is that neither soldiers nor civilians sang as much as they did during the previous decades. Although the military authorities tried to develop singing habits among the troops, all such attempts failed.[36] Possibly the war was too grim for singing. Refuting this theory is the fact that although the war was grimmer in China than anywhere else, the Chinese took up group singing for the first time. Another explantion proposed is the universality of radio music. The full explanation may eventually be found in a complex of causes.[37]

Music and Nationalism

"Near the end of the 18th century, music was generally regarded as an international or cosmopolitan art of which Italians and Germans (including Austrians) were especially gifted creators." The Italians were the special masters of vocal music, or "songs," and the Germans of instrumental music, such as the orchestral symphony.[38] A century later, English scholars began to study the English heritage both of folk music and Elizabethan popular music; composers like Ralph Vaughan Williams strove to use this heritage in order to create a distinctly English symphonic music. (Williams most admired the great Finnish national composer Jean Sibelius, rather than German composers.) In the United States, at the beginning of the present century the composer Arthur Farwell objected to the mode of seeing everything in music through German spectacles; he preferred the compositions of France and Russia and favored a distinctive "American" music. Before Farrell, much argument arose in American musical circles over the heavy use of Czech and Slavonic folk songs in Antonín Dvořák's compositions, especially "The New World Symphony." Dvořák was following in the tradition of Bedřich Smetana, the famed Czech composer of "The Bartered Bride."

During World War II, the Nazis prohibited the performance of Smetana's opera "Libuše" on the basis that it contained the prophecy that the Czech nation would never perish.

In the United States, the most popular and eloquent martial and nationalistic music was writted by John Philip Sousa (1854-1932). During his twelve-year leadership of the U.S. Marine Band, Sousa wrote "Semper Fidelis" (1888), "The Thunderer," and "The Washington Post" (1889). Even more popular were the marches he composed during his world tours with his own band: "The March King" and "The Liberty Bell" (1889). His most celebrated march is "The Stars and Stripes Forever." "It is American music to its very bone and marrow, as eloquent a patriotic utterance as has yet been written."[39]

In recent decades, much has been written about nationalism, but much less about its relationship to music. More than any other art, music expresses the basic kinship of nationalistically minded groups of people, the awareness of their common ideological needs and mutual ways of historical development, as expressed in folkways and mores. The collection and classification of folk music have reached great heights in our time, and adaptations of this national art has given us beautiful music by such composers as Ralph Vaughan Williams of England, Jean Sibelius of Finland, Leo Janáček, Bedřich Smetana and Antonín Dvořák of Czechoslovakia, Béla Bártok of Hungary, Aaron Copland, George Gershwin and Virgil Thompson of the United States, Manuel de Falla of Spain, Sergie Prokofiev and Aram Khachaturian of the Soviet Union, Heiter Villa-Lobos of Brazil, and Carlos Chávez of Mexico; Ernest Bloch, a Swiss-born composer but an American by adoption, sought in many of his compositions to express a Jewish national feeling.

"Musical nationalism," an offshoot of romanticism, began to flourish in the nineteenth century. (Romanticism applied to the movement in European literature and other arts, beginning at the end of the eighteenth century, that emphasized the imagination and emotions over reason and the intellect and revolted against the conventional strictness of neo-classicism.)[40]

Actually, folk music flourished centuries before the age of romanticism. For instance, "the past springs to life in Czech music, whose heritage of anthems, hymns and folksong goes back as far as the Hussite epoch and the counter-reformation and, with church support, was kept alive in the villages by schoolmasters who were also precentors."[41] In act, "the Slavs consider music as one of the greatest gifts of God. The Slav dances to his music, which is a kaleidoscopic blend of fiery songs showing his passionate soul and sanguine restlessness. His dance music abounds in originality of motifs and dynamic action. The treasure of the plain Slav music has been used in the compositions of Tchaikowsky, Hadyn, Strauss, Lehár, Czibulka, and others."[42] The Czechs and Slovaks especially have retained the music and dances of earlier epochs. These dances were based on the activities of daily life and were often accompanied on the bagpipe, the typical popular musical instrument, which joined forces with the violin and clarinet to make up the village band. "Some dances reflected social and political feelings in a very real way; there were Hussite dances" and a "dance of the corvée."[43]

All other Slavic nations, especially the Russians, Ukrainians, Yugoslavs and Poles, have made lasting contributions to the world of music. For instance, Frédéric Chopin found in folklore, popular legends, and Polish history the inspiration for his "Mazurkas," "Polonaise," and "Ballades." Balakirev, who published a collection of folksongs in 1866, was the leader of several Russian composers who constituted a truly original Russian music based on fold melodies.[44]

Afro-American Music

In recent decades, black music and dance have achieved great recognition. Music played a vital part in African life as well as in slave life in America. It is, of course, difficult to estimate how much of the African idiom remained in the New World's Negro song. The largest number of black folksongs collected thus far are spirituals. They were first presented to the world by the Fisk Jubilee Singers, who toured America and Europe from 1871 to 1878. Sharma points out that "the great spiritual events of *American history* were frequent subjects of spirituals. Slave songs throw light upon camp meetings, African colonization, the oral instruction of Negroes after 1831, work and leisuretime activities of Negroes, the Civil War with its soldiers, education, and evangelism, and the Reconstruction."[45] The Afro-American has also made continuous contributions through ragtime and jazz.[46]

Nationalistic Music

Dictatorships have historically been sensitive to the potential effects of nationalistic music and have often resorted to censorship of music. During World War I, for example, the Austro-Hungarian authorities prohibited the singing of Czech nationalistic songs by Karel Hašler. (Hašler was imprisoned by the Nazis during World War II.) Another example is Bedřich Smetana's famed folk opera "The Bartered Bride," which was periodically suspended by Austrian, Nazi, and Communist authorities.[47]

Small countries struggling for independence have produced some of the most enduring nationalistic songs; examples are the Czech hymn "Where Is My Home?", Scottish ballads, and the nostalgic songs of Irish exiles. Love of country has inspired moving songs ranging from "America the Beautiful" (a stirring national anthem, published in 1895), "Meadewand" (a favorite of the Red Army during the Revolution), "Killarney" (the best loved of all Irish songs, written in the nineteenth century by light opera composer M. W. Balfe), to "The Road of Eilat" (with words and music by Chaim Chager, celebrating Israel's reclaimed independence and the promise of the new-old land in our own times).

Another category of nationalistic music is that celebrating a nation's heritage—as exemplified by "My Country, 'tis of Thee," Karel Hašler's "The Czech Song...As long As It Will Live, Our Nation Will Also Live" and "Hatikvah" ("The Hope"), which is sung in Jewish homes around the world.

Music Under the Nazis

Under Hitler, German music was placed under severe government restrictions, as were all other aspects of the country's culture, but "music fared best, if only because it was the least political of the arts and because the Germans had such a store of it from Bach through Beethoven and Mozart to Brahms."[48] All Jewish compositions were, of course, prohibited; thus, the works of Mendelssohn and Paul Hindemith, for example, were proscribed. In addition, all Jews who were members of the great symphony orchestras and opera companies were quickly discharged. Interestingly, unlike nearly all writers, most of the great German musicians stayed in Germany and lent their names and abilities to the "New Order." For instance, Wilhelm Fürtwaengler, "one of the finest conductors of the century," according to Shirer, fell out of favor in 1934, but regained his position in 1935 and held it throughout the remainder of Hitler's rule; Richard Strauss became president of the Reich Music Chamber, and Alter Kieseking, a great pianist, toured foreign countries under the sponsorship of Goebbels' Propaganda Ministry, promoting German "culture" abroad.

Hitler once said: "Whoever wants to understand National Socialist Germany must know Wagner!" and indeed Wagner (who also hated the Jews) reigned supreme in Nazi Germany. Hitler loved Wagner's operas, which vividly recalled "the world of German antiquity with its heroic myths, its fighting pagan gods and heroes, its demons and dragons, its blood feuds and primitive tribal codes, its sense of destiny, of the splendor of love and life and the nobility of death, which inspired the myths of modern Germany."[49]

The German troops were inspired by "Horst Wessel Song" and "Der Wacht am Rheim" ("The Watch on the Rhine"), and the most popular song of all, "Deutschland Über Alles" ("Deutschland Above All"), the national anthem.[50]

Music In Soviet Russia

Any deviation in the Soviet Union from the official line—even in clothes and in music—has political implications. The Communist party determines what is musically acceptable and what is lacking in artistic taste. Because the party's primary interest is political, most Russian musicians find it quite difficult to give full scope to their creative genius. "The cynical atmosphere of slander, fabrication, and abject repentance, with promises to 'correct one's mistakes' and to be 'more careful,' the atmosphere in which humiliated musicians pretend to be happy and grateful to those who control them—this in reality is what constitutes the 'creative conditions' under which Soviet composers work."[51] All forms of musical experience—popular songs, operas, symphonic and ballet music, and chamber music—have been attacked by the party at one time or another. For example, during the early stages of the Bolskevik Revolution, Lenin himself considered opera to be a "remnant of the culture of gentility," and the organization known as "Proletkult" ("Proletarian Culture") even demanded the abolition of operatic art.[52]

During the New Economic Policy period, music was divided into two general schools: one sought to revive and develop prerevolutionary musical traditions, and the other to direct Soviet music toward proletarian goals. The first school was represented by the Association of Proletarian Musicians (ASMO) and the other by the Russian Association of Proletarian Musicians (RAPM). The members of the first group even openly praised Western Music. But the rise of Stalinism led to the virtual destruction of freedom; even Shostakovich was subjected to savage criticism by the party in 1935 for his opera "Lady Macbeth of Mtsenk Country."[53]

With Stalin's launching of the First Five-Year Plan, the criteria for all arts became purely propagandistic. Only works considered to be helpful in achieving the Plan were encouraged. In music, "Socialist realism has meant the composers are enjoined to send their audiences out into the streets whistling memorable tunes. Folk music and folk melodies woven into a somewhat more sophisticated musical setting enjoy official blessing."[54] At the same time, "the regime regards music as an important adjunct to the pomp and pageantry of state and involves its aid at all major diplomatic ceremonials";[55] foreign dignitaries are regaled with special performances at the opera and ballet and with concerts in the palaces where the finest artists perform. "As a result of their appearances at the Bolshoi and in the Kremlin the musicians see more of the present rulers of Russia than any other class of the population."[56]

The reasons are rather obvious. Such performances present fewer dangers to the current Communist ideology than the spoken or written word. Its appeal crosses all frontiers, and it supports the ideological claims that "no regime has done more to preserve and advance culture than the present one and that modern Soviet art is the legitimate heir to traditional Russian art and is in no way inferior to it."[57]

There is no such thing in Soviet Russia as "art for art's sake," and even a symphony or a quartet must tell a pro-Communist story. The Communist authorities are always pressing the composers to write operas, "since a spectacle is always likely to draw bigger audiences than a concert work."

Furthermore, "operas and ballet should not depict Tsars and enchantresses but events of contemporary life."[58] Unfortunately, "too often the finished product, after heavy and prolonged birth-pangs, plays before empty houses, and after the first opening nights the director sends an enthusiastic report to the Ministry of Culture and puts the score on the shelf. But when the day of reckoning comes he does not escape a rebuke for having failed to keep in step with demands of modern Soviet society."[59]

In 1936, the Communist party reversed its policy by promoting the staging of Ivan Dzerzhinski's "And Quiet Flows the Don," hailed as the first Soviet opera. Until the outbreak of World War II, it remained the official example of operatic art because it "ideally reflected all the elements of socialist realism."[60] Actually, the opera "merely completes the process of returning grand opera to the principles of vaudeville, of the 'drama of manners' in which songs and dances are interspersed in a literary drama."[61]

During World War II, the party exerted little control over music but reverted to its prewar policies after the war. Zhdanov, a full member of the Politburo after 1939, proclaimed that all composers must "support only a healthy and progressive trend in music, the trend of Soviet realism." This directive also stated that Prokofief, Khatchaturian, Shostakovich, Popop, Miaskovski, and Shevalin represented "most strikingly the formalistic perversions and anti-democratic tendencies in music which are alien to the Soviet people and their artistic taste."[62] This directive was also aimed at all musicians in the Communist orbit.

After Stalin's death, the party tried to create the impression that Stalin was responsible for the stagnation of art in Soviet Russia. More recently, Soviet composers have been allowed to participate in discussions with composers from other countries, and the public has heard orchestras and conductors from the United States, Britain, and other countries. Western music is gradually making its way into the U.S.S.R. For instance, Bach has been "rediscovered" and Bartók and Janáček have become quite popular thanks to the visits of Hungarian and Czechoslovak artists. The most popular Soviet composers are Shostakovich and Prokofief (also the two most popular Soviet composers in the West), but Soviet audiences are allowed to hear only a very limited selection of their works.[63]

For years Communist societies have been as troubled by the disaffection of their young as the rest of the world—and have found it just as difficult to solve the problem. In recent years, the authorities in the U.S.S.R. and all other East European countries have been very concerned with the impact of Western rock:

Teen-agers in worn work clothes twist and shake to the blaring Western-style rock of electric guitars in cities along the Volga River. . . . A gentle pop-style group has to compete with a loud rock band at the other end of a dance hall in Khabarovsk in far-

eastern Siberia. ... Boys with long hair and girls in treasured Western jeans
tape-record Western shortwave broadcasts and beg the latest discs from tourists
outside the big hotels in Moscow.[64]

The Communist authorities have tried to stamp out what they call "radio
hooligans," or unauthorized amateur radio operators. These "radio
hooligans" operate under such colorful names as "Demon," "Dynamite,"
"Dragon," "Ninochka," "King of the Either," or "Pharao." Forbidden foreign
music and songs still make the rounds, however. Hedrick Smith believes
that many young Russians "ache for a change of pace from the diet of
patriotic music, Red Army marches and semioperatic ballads fed them on
Soviet radio and television."[65]

Notes

1. Joseph S. Roucek, ed., *Social Control* (Princeton, N.J.: D. Van Nostrand, 1956;
Westport, Conn.: Greenwood Press, 1970), p. 255, bibliography, pp. 257-259. The
literature on sociological aspects of music is rather limited, but consult Don
Martindale, *American Society* (Princeton, N.J.: D. Van Nostrand, 1960), Chs. 20 and
21; Don Martindale, *Community, Character and Civilization: Studies in Social
Behaviorism* (Glencoe, Ill.: Free Press, 1963), Ch. 10; Max Weber's *Sociology of
Music* (with Johannes Riedel), pp. 365-393; E. Clements, *Introduction to the Study of
Indian Music* (London: Longmans, Green, 1913); Henry George Farmer, *A History of
Arabian Music* (London: Luzac, 1929); Carl Stumph, *Die Anfange der Musik*
(Leipzig: J. A. Barth, 1911); Curt Sachs, *The Rise of Music in the Ancient World: East
and West* (New York: W. W. Norton, 1943); Paul S. Carpenter, *Music: An Art and a
Business* (Norman: University of Oklahoma Press, 1950); D. D. Braun, *Toward a
Theory of Popular Culture: The Sociology and History of American Music and
Dance, 1920-1968* (Ann Arbor, Mich.: Ann Arbor Publishers, 1969); Charles Nanry,
ed., *American Music: From Storyville to Woodstock* (New Brunswick, N.J.:
Transaction Books, 1972); Christopher Headington, *History of Western Music* (New
York: Schirmer, 1977); Nick Tosches, *Country Music* (New York: Stein and Day,
1976); Alec Robertson, *Requiem: Music of Mourning and Consolation* (Westport,
Conn.: Greenwood Press, 1976); Jerome L. Rodnitzky, *Minstrels of the Dawn: The
Folk-Protest Singer as a Cultural Hero* (Chicago: Nelson-Hall, 1976); Theodor W.
Adorno, *Introduction to the Sociology of Music* (New York: Seabury Press, 1976); G.
Hindley, ed., *The Larousse Encyclopedia of Music* (New York: World, 1970); John
Greenway, *Ethnomusicology* (Minneapolis: Burgess, 1976); Henry Raynor, *Music
and Society Since 1815* (New York: Schocken Books, 1976); Henry Krehbiel, *Music
and Manners in the Classical Period* (Portland, Me.: Longwood, 1976); Ferenz Fedor,
The Birth of the Yankee Doodle (New York: Vantage, 1976); William P. Malm, *Music
Culture of the Pacific, the Near East, and Asia* (Englewood Cliffs, N.J.: Prentice-Hall,
1977); Pitirim A. Sorokin, *Society, Culture, and Personality* (New York: Harper,
1947); A. S. Tomars, *Introduction to the Sociology of Art* (privately printed,
1940); Hans Engel, "Music and Society." Pp. 566-575, in *The International
Encyclopedia of the Social Sciences*, Vol. 10 (New York: Macmillan, 1968); Warden

D. Allen, *Philosophies of Music History: A Study of General Histories of Music, 1600-1960* (New York: Dryden Press, 1958); P. R. Fansworth, *The Social Psychology of Music* (New York: Dryden Press, 1958); Larry Sandberg and Dick Weissman, *The Catalogue of North American Folk Music* (New York: Alfred A. Knopf, 1976); Harold Courlander, *A Treasury of Afro-American Folklore: The Oral Literature, Traditions, Recollections, Legends, Tales, Songs, Religious Beliefs, Customs, Sayings, and Humor of Peoples of African Descent in the Americas* (New York: Crown, 1976); Béla Bártok, *Turkish Folk Music from Asia Minor* (Princeton, N.J.: Princeton University Press, 1976); Carl Engel, *An Introduction to the Study of National Music: Comprising Researches into Popular Songs, Traditions, and Customs* (New York: AMS Press, 1976); Vera B. Lawrence, *Music for Patriots, Politicians and Presidents* (New York: Macmillan, 1975); John Stuart Blackie, *Scottish Song: Its Wealth, Wisdom and Social Significance* (New York: AMS Press, 1976); Hans-Hubert Schonzeler, ed., *Of German Music: A Symposium* (New York: Barnes and Noble, 1976); Leslie Orrey, ed., *The Encyclopedia of Opera* (New York: Charles Scribner's Sons, 1976); E. J. Dent, *The Rise of Romantic Opera* (New York: Cambridge University Press, 1976); John H. Mueller, *The American Symphony Orchestra: A Social History of Musical Taste* (Westport, Conn.: Greenwood Press, 1976); A. V. Olkovsky, *Music Under the Soviets: The Agony of an Art* (New York: Praeger Publishers, 1959); Geza Reversz, *Introduction to the Psychology of Music* (Norman: University of Oklahoma Press, 1946); Elie Siegmeister, ed., *Music and Society* (New York: Critics Group, 1938); Alphons Silbermann, *The Sociology of Music* (London: Routledge and Kegan Paul, 1957); Max Weber, *The Rational and Social Foundations of Music* (Carbondale: Southern Illinois University Press, [1921], 1958).

2. Pitirim A. Sorokin, *Society, Culture and Personality*, p. 54.

3. G. Bohn, *La Nouvelle Psychologie Animale*, pp. 166-168, cited by Sorokin, *Society, Culture and Personality*, p. 54.

4. Quoted by James A. Leither, *Media and Revolution* (Toronto: Canadian Broadcasting Corporation, 1968), p. 53. See also B. R. Cornwell, *The Spirit of Revolution in 1789: A Study of Public Opinion as Revealed in Political Songs and Other Popular Literature at the Beginning of the French Revolution* (New York: Greenwood Press, 1969); Wanda Willson Whitman, ed., *Songs That Changed the World* (New York: Crown, 1969), whose conclusions we have used extensively here.

5. Our study does not deal fully with opera, ragtime, the blues, jazz, the musical theater, comic opera, or country music, although all such musical forms are also important means of social control and social change. Only the limitations of space prevent a full discussion of these areas of music here. A good introduction to this music can be found in Whitman, *Songs That Changed the World*; David Ewen, *History of Popular Music* (New York: Barnes and Noble, 1961), bibliography, pp. 191-194; Carter Harman, *A Popular History of Music: From Gregorian Chant to Jazz* (New York: Dell, 1956); Sidney Finkelstein, *Composer and Nation* (New York: International Publishers, 1960).

6. Hartzell Spence, *The Story of America's Religions* (New York: Abingdon Press, 1960), p. 9.

7. David O. Moberg, *The Church as a Special Institution: The Sociology of American Religion* (Englewood Cliffs, N.J.: Prentice-Hall, 1962), p. 450.

8. Charles Winick, *Dictionary of Anthropology* (Ames, Iowa: Littlefield, Adams, 1953), p. 374.

9. Whitman, *Songs That Changed the World*, p. 99.

10. Ibid.

11. G. P. Judo, *A History of Civilization* (New York: Macmillan, 1966), p. 202.

12. Ewen, *History of Popular Music*, pp. 191-192; James E. Matthew, *The Literature of Music* (New York: Da Capo Press, 1969); H. Wiley Hitchcock, *Music in the United States, a Historical Introduction* (Englewood Cliffs, N.J.: Prentice-Hall, 1969). "Music History, Periods In," in Dagobert Runes and Harry G. Schrickel, eds., *Encyclopedia of the Arts* (New York: Philosophical Library, 1946), pp. 655-657, is an excellent, although quite brief, introduction to its topic; this encyclopedia also contains valuable studies of "Musicology," p. 657, "Origins of Music," p. 658, and "Psychology of Music," pp. 820-821.

13. Joseph S. Roucek, *The Czechs and Slovaks in America* (Minneapolis, Minn.: Lerner, 1967), pp. 21-23; G. L. Collin, *Moravians in Two Worlds* (New York: Columbia University Press, 1967); Joseph S. Roucek, "The Protestant Heritage in American Education," Ch. VI, in Richard E. Gross, ed., *Heritage of American Education* (Boston: Allyn and Bacon, 1962), pp. 206-211; Joseph S. Roucek, "The Moravian Brethren in America," *Social Studies* (February 2, 1952): 56-61; Joseph S. Roucek, ed., *Slavonic Encyclopedia* (Port Washington, N.Y.: Kennikat Press, 1949), pp. 824-825.

14. Spence, *The Story of America's Religions*, p. 123.

15. Ibid., p. 52.

16. William S. Pregnall, *Laity and Liturgy: A Handbook for Parish Worship* (New York: Seabury Press, 1975); William B. Gray, *The Episcopal Church Welcomes You: An Introduction to Its History, Worship, and Mission* (New York: Seabury Press, 1974); Carson I. A. Ritchie, *Frontier Parish: An Account of the Society for the Propagation of the Gospel and the Anglican Church in America* (New Brunswick, N.J.: Farleigh Dickinson University Press, 1975).

17. Charles E. Merriam, *Political Power* (New York: Collier, 1964), pp. 112ff.; H. L. Nieburg, *Culture Storm: Politics and the Ritual Order* (New York: St. Martin's Press, 1973); John J. Honingmann, *The World of Man* (New York: Harper, 1959), Ch. 31; A. K. Saran, "Art and Ritual as Methods of Social Control," *Ethics* 63 (1953): 171-179; Theodor Reik, *Ritual: Psycho-Analytic Studies* (New York: International Universities Press, 1958).

18. Merriam, *Political Power*, pp. 105-106.

19. Ibid., p. 112.

20. Spence, *Story of America's Religions*, p. 31.

21. The text and music in ibid., pp. 34-35.

22. Ibid., pp. 35-36.

23. Ibid., p. 37.

24. Ibid., pp. 37-38.

25. Ibid., pp. 38-39.

26. Ibid., p. 40.

27. Ibid., pp. 40-41.

28. Ibid., pp. 42-43.

29. Ibid., pp. 44-45.

30. Ibid., p. 45.

31. Ibid., pp. 46-47.

32. Text and music in ibid., p. 47.

33. Ibid., p. 49.

34. Ewen, *History of Popular Music*, p. 86.

35. For the music and the text, see Whitman, *Songs That Changed the World*, p. 44.

36. Roucek, *Social Control*, p. 255.

37. We accept here the theory of multiple causation, which recognizes the complex configuration of conditions under which specific instances of certain types of music may develop.

38. Joseph F. Zacek, "Nationalism in Czechoslovakia," in Peter F. Sugar and Ivo J. Lederer, eds., *Nationalism in Eastern Europe* (Seattle: University of Washington Press, 1969), p. 197. The relationship of nationalism to national hymns is discussed by Hans Kohn, *The Idea of Nationalism: A Study in Its Origins and Background* (New York: Macmillan, 1961), pp. 208ff., 512, 526, 647ff.

39. Ewen, *History of Popular Music*, p. 78. We must also note the impact of music on nationalism by such composers as Verdi, Wagner, Smetana, Tchaikovsky, Rimski-Korsakov, and Musorgski. For details, consult Finkelstein, *Composer and Nation*, Ch. 5; Vera Brodsky Lawrence, *Music for Patriots: Politicians and Presidents* (New York: Macmillan, 1975); Engel, *An Introduction to the Study of National Music.*

40. Alfred Einstein, *A Short History of Music* (New York: Vintage Books, 1954), p. 191; see also Ralph Vaughan Williams, *National Music* (New York: Oxford University Press, 1933).

41. Roger Portal, *The Slavs: A Cultural and Historical Survey of the Slavonic Peoples* New York: Harper and Row, 1969), pp. 359-360. See also "Music," pp. 842-859, and "Folk Music," pp. 330-335, in Roucek, ed., *Slavonic Encyclopaedia.*

42. Roucek, *Slavonic Encyclopaedia*, p. 842.

43. Portal, *The Slavs*, p. 241.

44. Ibid., p. 299.

45. Mohan Lal Sharma, "Afro-American Music and Dance." Pp. 139-172 in Joseph S. Roucek and Thomas Kiernan, eds., *The Negro Impact on Western Civilization* (New York: Philosophical Library, 1970), p. 144, and "Selected Bibliography," pp. 170-172; Albert Murray, *Stomping the Blues* (New York: McGraw-Hill, 1977); John F. Szwed, *Negro Music: Urban Renewal* (New York: Basic Books, 1968); Dorothy Scarborough, *On the Trail of Negro Folk-Songs* (Hatboro, Pa.: Folklore Associates, 1963).

46. E. L. Doctorow, *Ragtime* (New York: Random House, 1975); Hentoff, *The Jazz Life;* André Hodeir, *Toward Jazz* (New York: Da Capo Press, 1976); Whitney Balliett, *New York Notes: A Journal of Jazz, 1972-1975* (Boston: Houghton Mifflin, 1976); Robert Goffin, *Jazz, From the Congo to the Metropolitan* (New York: Da Capo Press, 1975); Nat Shapiro, ed., *The Jazz Makers* (Westport, Conn.: Greenwood Press, 1975); Bruce Cook, *Listen to the Blues* (New York: Charles Scribner's Sons, 1976); Nat Hentoff and Albert J. McCarthy, eds., *Jazz: New Perspectives in the History of Jazz* (New York: Da Capo Press, 1975); Rudi Blesh, *Shining Trumpets: A History of Jazz* (New York: Da Capo Press, 1976).

47. For details of Smetana's composition and influence, see Finkelstein, *Composer and Nation*, pp. 160-167.

48. William L. Shirer, *The Rise and Fall of the Third Reich* (Greenwich, Conn.: Fawcett Crest Book, 1968), p. 334.

49. Ibid., p. 148.

50. Whitman, *Songs That Changed the World*, pp. 21-22, 129. "Deutschland Über Alles" was adopted from Haydn's "Kaiser Quartet"; it also served as the Imperial hymn of Austria-Hungary.

51. Andrey Olkhovsky, *Music Under the Soviets* (New York: Praeger Publishers, 1955), p. 57.

52. Quoted in John Fizer, "The Arts and Sciences," in Joseph M. Bochenski and Gerhart Niemeyer, eds., *Handbook on Communism* (New York: Praeger Publishers, 1962), Ch. 3, p. 473. See also Gershon Swet, "Music." Pp. 371-374, in Michael T. Florinsky, ed., *McGraw-Hill Encyclopedia of Russia and the Soviet Union* (New York: McGraw-Hill, 1961); Robert M. Slusser, "Soviet Music Since the Death of Stalin." Pp. 116-125, in Alvin Toffler, ed., *The Annals of The American Academy of Political and Social Science* 303 (January 1956); Boris Scharz, *Music and Musical Life in Soviet Russia, 1917-1970* (New York: W. W. Norton, 1973); L. L. Sabaneev, *Modern Russian Composers* (New York: Da Capo Press, 1975); Max Eastman, *Artists in Uniform* (New York: Alfred A. Knopf, 1934); Juri Jelagin, *Taming of the Arts* (New York: E. P. Dutton, 1951); Alex Inkeles and Kent Geiger, eds., *Soviet Society: A Book of Readings* (Boston: Houghton Mifflin, 1961), pp. 484-490; Finkelstein, *Composer and Nation*, Ch. 11; Ivan Martunov, Dimitri *Shostakovich* (New York: Philosophical Library, 1949); Leonid Vladimirov, *The Russians* (New York: Praeger Publishers, 1968).

53. Fizer, "The Arts and Sciences," pp. 473-474.

54. W. W. Rostow et al., *The Dynamics of Soviet Society* (New York: New American Library, 1954), p. 115.

55. Cecil Parrot, "Music Expression in the U.S.S.R.," *Soviet Survey*, no. 27 (January-March 1959): 25-31.

56. Olkhovsky, *Music Under the Soviets*, p. 484.

57. Ibid., p. 485.

58. Ibid.

59. Ibid., p. 486.

60. Fizer, "The Arts and Sciences," p. 474.

61. Quoted in ibid.

62. Ibid., p. 475.

63. Finkelstein, *Composer and Nation*, Ch. 11; Martunov, *Shostakovich*.

64. David K. Willis, "Rock on Volga—Soviet Youths Are Twisting, Shaking," *The Christian Science Monitor*, September 28, 1976. See also G. A. Geyer, *The Young Russians* (Homewood, Ill: ETC Publications, 1975); Hedrick Smith, *The Russians* (New York: Ballantine, 1977), Ch. 7, "Youth: Rock Without Roll," pp. 228-263.

65. Smith, *The Russians*, p. 231.

John E. Owen

RECREATION AND LEISURE

That personality and behavior are conditioned by the society—its values and institutions—is a sociological truism. It is not as generally recognized, however, that one realm of values lies in leisure and that recreation today is becoming an institution. As a means of social control, their influence upon personality is very real and pervasive.

In the last two decades, sociologists have given more research priority to these aspects of society. The first part of this article describes trends in the growing concern with recreation and leisure in America, and the second reviews recent research and theories.

With the rise of automation and technology, several writers have noted changing patterns of human values in the transition to a postindustrial world. Emery and Twist see a new emphasis upon "self-actualization," "self-expression," "interdependence," and "capacity for joy."[1] There is also evidence of a rising humanistic approach to leisure as a means of attaining "the good life," and a concern with how its realization has been hindered by societal controls and restraints, and with how both work and leisure activities can give *meaning* to individuals.[2]

Recent Trends

During the 1950s and 1960s, there was a growing movement to organize a recreation service. Among the factors accounting for this trend were a national concern with physical fitness, programs for the disabled, outdoor recreation and park development, and increased government assistance and involvement in the arts. Other factors supporting a recreation movement since World War II have included an appreciable growth of leisure and affluence, higher levels of education, advances in technology, greater population mobility, a cultural explosion, and the expansion of social welfare.[3]

For the first time in their history, the American people may be entering an age of leisure. Leisure today is becoming an integral part of the life of the many and not just the few, and for the first time may become more significant than work in giving meaning to life. There is evidence that this trend is becoming permanent.

More Americans have more free time, more money to enjoy its varied use, and more diversified ways of spending both their time and money. They spend more on spare-time activities than on either national defense or new homes. In 1965, personal consumption for recreation was $26 billion; by 1976, the outlay had increased by $146 billion.[4] A rapid rise in personal income, a shorter work week, and earlier retirement are among the trends making for the growing significance of leisure in U.S. life.

Decline of the Work Ethic

An increase in leisure time is partly the result of automation and technology, though this is merely the most recent phase of an industrializing trend that has been discernible since the nation's founding.[5] The current pattern is one of increasing education and later entry into the job market, combined with a decline of the Puritan ethic that emerged from an economy of scarcity.

Work no longer has its traditionally significant place in U.S. values, particularly among younger workers. Among industrial employees, high absenteeism rates and a widespread tendency to look upon leisure as more meaningful and rewarding than work illustrate altered attitudes to work. Public opinion polls show that at least a fifth of all workers are discontented with their jobs. A new challenge to personnel managers and industrial executives arises in attempting to fill this new demand—that work be made "interesting," that it engage more facets of the worker's personality, and that it give him the opportunity to invest his talents and congenial drives. For many U.S. workers in the 1970s, the long-standing motivations of high wages, job security, and opportunities of getting ahead appear to have lost their appeal. Among blue collar factory workers, boredom and discontent have been seen by many industrial specialists as a potent threat to the nation's productivity, economic stability, and psychological health.

The idea that work is valuable in itself has been rejected by many; executives are tending to retire before the age of sixty, or are taking second careers that offer more fulfillment and less strain; and there is a tendency for industrial workers to refuse to work overtime.[6] A growing trend is toward the four-day week, which more than 3,000 firms have now instituted. By 1972, over 4,000 articles had been written on this subject.[7]

The new leisure applies to all groups—workers, the unemployed, children and youth, women, and the retired. Considerable attention has been paid to the recreational needs of the elderly, as part of the increasing emphasis on gerontology. With 10 percent of the U.S. population over sixty-five, the American Association of Retired Persons and other groups have been active in pointing out that old age, far from being a barrier to creative enjoyment of added leisure time, can in fact enhance it. False myths concerning the physical and mental capacities of the elderly no longer exert the same degree of harmful "social control" over them as in earlier decades. Retirement communities in Florida, Arizona, and California, for those who can afford them, are replete with many recreational facilities.

Sports

For youth, and in fact all segments of the population, the hunger for sports is insatiable. Literally millions of adults engage in skiing, surfing, and skin diving. At least one in five Americans bowls, and a lesser number play tennis or golf. Professional football attracts about 10 million spectators a year, major league baseball appeals to some 30 million, and the most popular spectator sport, horse-racing, draws some 70 million. The number who sit at home and watch these and other sports on TV greatly exceeds these figures. Sport is a popular culture, and the 1960s, like the 1920s, could be called a "golden age of sports."

The leading trend in sports since World War II has been a huge rise in participant sport. The number of participants has more than doubled since 1945, and with rising incomes more Americans find time for sports such as golf, once the privilege of the few. The rise of the suburbs, the "rush to the great outdoors," and the need to find physical relaxation after work have all had their part here. Swimming, camping, and winter sports have undergone a huge boom in popularity in the 1950 era.

Football and baseball are probably the most popular sports today. Significantly, the final match of the professional football season attracts a larger TV audience than did the astronauts who walked on the moon. Baseball's popularity was established during the drabness of the early industrial era. It afforded a relief from that dreariness, it created a different atmosphere— a freemasonry of social equality—and the large baseball field could be compared with the frontier. As a force controlling behavior, football provides the thrill of a sense of participation in excitement and danger on a mass scale, a heightened crowd unity that is contagious. Psychiatrists view this participation as a release of hostilities and aggressive urges, a catharsis for thousands. Football is comparable to U.S. society generally, in that it is a cluster of people living under heavy tension in a condition of continuing and perpetual change. Like all sports, it appeals to hidden depths of the spirit long celebrated by poets and writers—the need to "let go," to find a sense of togetherness, to escape reality, and to experience thrills collectively.

Women have been playing an increasing role in sports partly because of the women's liberation movement. As early as 1967, Sports Illustrated had included over 200 articles on women athletes. Complaints about lack of opportunity for girls to participate in high school and college sports have had an impact, and for women, as for blacks, traditional restraints are lessening. By 1968, almost a third of professional football players and about 60 percent of National Basketball Association players were black.[8]

Population Increase

On the community level, many public and voluntary agencies (the YMCA, YWCA, Boys' Clubs of America, Camp Fire Girls, and the Scouts) provide recreational facilities for youth. Partly as an escape from urban crowding and tensions, about a third of the U.S. population (over 70 million) spend part of the summer in the rural outdoors. About 3 million families have a second vacation home in the country, and with the extension of the four-day week, experts foresee a possible 6 million such homes by 1980.

Population pressure (a record 125 million Americans are now on the road for overnight trips every year) and pollution are affecting even the great outdoors. In order to help save the environment official proposals have been made to ration the visits to America's thirty-six national parks, visits that totaled over 200 million at the start of the 1970s. As in other areas of life, increasing population may lead to social controls over recreation. It has also been suggested that vacations, 99 percent of which are now taken in June, July, and August, should be spread evenly through the year. The demand for recreation is outstripping the supply, and it is anticipated that demand for outdoor recreational facilities in 1980 will be double what it was in 1960. The government is aware of this problem, as well as the attendant need for research on recreation. As early as 1968, the Bureau of Outdoor Recreation and the National Academy of Sciences sponsored a conference which resulted in a statement of research goals and priorities in outdoor recreation.[9]

More Federal Control?

The question arises whether this increasing federal interest might result in new federal controls over recreation. For example, government attempts at urban development and renewal involve urban planning for recreation and parks. Many government agencies, including the National Park Service, the Office of Education, and the Department of Commerce, are involved in projects affecting leisure. The new profession of town planning is now taking account of the recreational needs of communities, which was for the first time an important topic at the World Congress of the International Union of Architects in 1972. There is every indication that leisure will assume increasing significance in city and regional planning. City planners, thinking in terms of "neighborhood" and "community," now give attention to neighborhood play lots, parks, and playing-fields. In England, the planned "New Towns" have taken account of recreational needs, but there have been indications of popular discontent among residents uprooted from the familiar scenes and life-style of their former localities.

In America, over 230 state agencies are involved in park and recreational development for youth, the aged, the slum-dweller, and other groups. All fifty states have legislation that authorizes local govenment bodies to participate in recreational themes, through land acquisition, taxation functions, and the provision of special services. On the local level, government participation in recreation and park facilities has grown since 1950, a trend that had been operative since 1900.

The functions of the federal government in recreation include the direct management of outdoor recreation resources, conservation and resource reclamation, assistance to open-space programs, direct programs of recreation participation (e.g., in Veterans' Administration hospitals, other federal institutions, and the armed forces worldwide), advisory, consultative, and financial assistance programs, aid to professional education, and the promotion of recreation as an economic function. This last capacity includes the promotion of tourism, aid to rural folk in developing recreation enterprises, and assistance to Indian tribes in establishing facilities on their reservations.[10] The growth of government involvement is demonstrated by the fact that between 1961 and 1966 the number of federal agencies working in recreation grew from thirteen to seventy-two.

The National Park Service, the National Forest Service, the Bureau of Outdoor Recreation, the Children's Bureau, and other agencies under HEW, together with the federal antipoverty programs established in the early 1960s, are all functioning directly or indirectly in the recreational realm. Within the armed forces, the government provides facilities and extensive programs for "morale support"; these facilities employ many thousand full-time personnel and considerably more part-time workers. Counties and local government bodies are also functioning in this area to an appreciably greater extent than was the case prior to World War II, in such varied activities as municipal parks, summer programs, Little Theatres, arts and crafts, evening classes, sports facilities, services to the disabled, and a wide range of other activities.

Private and Commercial Recreation

The provision of recreational funds and facilities (and hence control over its variety and use) has never been left entirely to official bodies. America has always had the joint existence of private and official services, a duality that has shown its mark in the recreational realm as in others. The 1960s and 1970s have witnessed a marked growth in voluntary agencies, private agencies, and commercial recreation. The first two of these serve a large range of purposes, including youth, religious groups, community goals, and special-interest groups. They are voluntary in terms of their origin, membership and administrative control, and leadership. In contrast to government agencies, they are less subject to social control in that they are not so influenced by political considerations and thus are freer to set their own policies and aims. They enjoy more flexibility and can meet the specific needs of particular constituencies but, being dependent on their own efforts at fund-raising, may be less financially secure than government programs.[11]

One aspect of commercial recreation that has not received prime attention has been the provision by industrial and commercial firms of recreation for their employees. Many large corporations own and operate golf courses, parks, and camps for their employees, and in other ways they seek to maintain worker efficiency and morale. This is part of a long-term trend toward "human relations in industry" that treats workers as human beings rather than hired help. Criticisms from sources hostile to business frequently question the corporations' motives in these endeavors, claiming that they are essentially management-oriented in their purposes and provide a relatively inexpensive means of fostering productive efficiency. These endeavors are said to lessen worker discontent and to be a subtle means of social control and manipulation of employees. The degree of validity in these claims is problematical, but the fact remains that business firms *are* active in providing recreational programs. One estimate is that by 1965 the annual cost of these efforts to business reached $1.5 billion, and much higher by 1975. Organized labor has also increased its efforts in this area.

Education for Leisure

Another recent development has been a marked growth of the adult education movement, which now reaches an estimated 50 million people. Educators have also shown concern with the issue of education for the wise use of leisure. One writer claims that "the goals of recreation and education are not poles apart, since both are working toward enrichment of life for individuals. Learning is more rapid and lasting if it is pleasurable and satifying in itself, and the finest educational experiences take on a recreational nature."[12] The concern with education for leisure is not related solely to its cultural benefits, but also to the need to prepare persons for the changes likely to accrue with increasing leisure in an automating society.

In an urbanized mass society, a land in transition from the Puritan work ethic and small town values, it is perhaps symptomatic that more leisure time should bring the abuse of these extra hours for many, as shown in rising figures of alcoholism, drug addiction, and marital infidelity. With the lessening of traditional controls over behavior, what new controls will emerge in the coming leisure society? Concern with "the quality of life" is one of the new emphases among humanistic sociologists. But recent research and theory on leisure reflect other themes and approaches, some of which appear to bear relatively little connection with actual leisure trends, as the next section will indicate.

Theory and Research

In a report published in 1969, Rolf Meyersohn declared that "the study of leisure has not yet found a firm foothold among American sociologists."[13] Two years later, two other writers claimed that "there does not appear to be an overwhelming amount of solid leisure research in progress."[14] Yet (particularly if one includes work done in Europe), it would appear that the foothold of theory and research is becoming more solid.

Theories

The meaning of leisure in our civilization has been dealt with by many writers, most of whom are not sociologists. Within the social sciences and education, there is a growing literature, though little that relates specifically to social control. An exception is the work of Max Kaplan, who in 1960 outlined the elements of social control illustrated by activities in leisure. His thesis was that control is expressed in consensus and conformity ("everyone is doing it"), in tradition, representation (enhancing the self-image), hierarchy ("my idols and heroes are doing this"), knowledge (activity that will lead to self-improvement and wider horizons), exclusiveness (satisfaction from engaging in leisure activity not open to all), and imposition ("I have no choice, my wife got me into this"). In a later work, Kaplan notes the problem of relating these seven types of controls to types of conditions. For example, what conditions (age, time, income) are most likely to be affected by the theme of consensus? The dynamics of leisure selection affords a new field for research.[15]

Many definitions of leisure have been formulated, most of them viewing leisure (and recreation) as a form of activity or experience. Thus, games theory is one aspect of the psychological view of leisure and recreation.[16] Sociologists emphasize another approach, namely, the role of leisure and recreation in the total functioning of society rather than in relation to individual behavior. A leading British writer, Stanley Parker, points out that there are two main schools of thought on the relation of different segments of life in contemporary urban-industrial society. The first claims that people's lives are split into different realms of activity and interest, with each social segment lived out relatively independently of the others. Work is separated from leisure, education from religion, for example. The other school has a holist approach, viewing society as an integrated whole in which every part is affected by every other part.

Another point of theory revolves around nonwork variables. Does the type of education determine the occupation, which in turn determines work-leisure patterns, or does education exert an influence on work-leisure patterns quite independently of occupation? A parallel can be found between the two schools of thought mentioned above and types of work-leisure relationships.[17] Other writers have suggested the need to distinguish ideas from behavior in theories about leisure. Kenneth Roberts notes that relationships discovered between work and leisure (e.g., in giving meaning to life) might not necessarily be reflected in actual behavior. Talcott Parsons' functional theory has been applied to leisure and work by Edward Gross, who suggests that leisure performs functions that enable society to survive. It helps to keep the society intact, and it helps persons to learn how to play their roles in society and to reach collective goals.[18] Another attempt to classify the functions of leisure for the individual has been made by the French scholar Joffre Dumazedier, who perceives leisure as having three chief functions— relaxation, entertainment, and personal development.[19]

What Does Leisure Mean?

What leisure actually means in a society will be related to the meaning assigned to work in that society. A study in New Zealand concluded that the meaning of leisure (in the sense of defined satisfactions or reasons for engaging in a specific leisure activity) centered, in order of frequency, on the pleasure of doing it, a change from work, contact with friends, new experience, a way of passing the time, and the sense of being creative. The author of the study, Robert Havighurst, stated that the meanings of leisure are also the meanings of work, in that most of the same satisfactions are derived from each activity.[20]

More recently (1971), Kando and Summers have pointed to the desirability of integrating the study of *forms* of work and leisure and their underlying *meaning*. What does work (and leisure) actually mean to different types of participants? This stress on meaning, which can be traced back to Max Weber, is highly significant. As these authors have asked, what is the complex network of relationships within which work influences nonwork?[21] John Kelly, in studying the problem of meaning, points to the need for examining the work-leisure relation and the way in which social norms can affect the choice of leisure activity.[22] Stanley Parker, after summarizing these studies, notes that we have a long way to go before this complex relationship between work and leisure is understood. He concludes that "the subject is of wide concern, and relevant findings bear not only upon the way we attempt to influence and control social behavior and institutions but also upon the way in which we handle work and leisure problems and make choices in our own lives."[23]

Research

During the 1950s and 1960s, numerous research studies dealt with leisure from the standpoint of class and occupation, based on the idea that a person's class position tended to control his recreational and spare-time activity. During the 1960s, it was also recognized that many changes had occurred to render the concept of class very vague, if not outmoded.[24] A significant study of leisure surveyed fifteen counties in southern California through a careful sampling of the population, with regard to age, sex, and class status. It analyzed the ratio of time spent on various activities (eating, sleeping, work, leisure, travel, child care) in the course of a year and shorter periods.[25]

A new trend is seen in the popularity of cross-cultural research on leisure. Surveys have revealed, for example, that the leisure time of British management executives is not controlled by work-involved pursuits to the same extent as that of the U.S. executive, who is more "work-oriented" even in his leisure.[26]

An outstanding piece of international research appeared in 1972, the Multinational Comparative Time Budget Research Project organized by Dr. Alexander Szalai. A twelve-nation study, it was carried out in 1965 and 1966, using almost 30,000 interviews and 150,000 coded information cards. It sought to compare leisure among men and women, influences of urbanism and industrialism, differences in leisure between days of the week, and the use of mass media. Much of the research revolved around time-budgets in relation to other factors.[27]

The analysis of leisure emphasizes the fundamental value of free choice, and a sizable part of research has dealt with specific ways of exercising choice regarding budgeting *time*. The need for time-budgeting itself acts as a form of social control over behavior.

A new framework for research is that of the family life-cycle. Two erudite British scholars have suggested this perspective, since in all cultures persons change their activities and interests in the course of their life-cycle.[28] Another new field is the sociology of sport, in which some pioneering texts have appeared in the 1970s.

The foregoing is indicative of the nature of investigations recently in progress. They are marked by great methodological variety, including empirical inquiries, time-budgets, and a historical tradition, in a humanistic approach that is both germane to the field of leisure and recreation and well established in academic sociology. Significantly, the 1975-1976 *Directory of Members* of the American Sociological Association listed approximately 150 persons under the specialty "Leisure/Sports/Recreation"—another indication that augurs well for the growth of knowledge in this field.

Notes

1. F. Emery and E. Twist, *Towards a Social Ecology* (London: Plenum, 1973), p. 154.

2. See, for example, Max Kaplan and Philip Bosserman, eds., *Technology, Human Values and Leisure* (New York: Abingdon Press, 1971).

3. Richard Kraus, *Recreation and Leisure in Modern Society* (New York: Meredith Corp., 1971), pp. 6-13, 208-209.

4. Ibid., p. 316. See also "People Are Shelling Out More Than Ever for a Good Time," *US News and World Report*, February 21, 1977, p. 40.

5. John E. Owen, "Automation and the American Worker," *Rivista Internazionale di Scienze Economiche e Commerciali* 19 (October 1972):1006-1013.

6. John E. Owen, "An End to the Work Ethic in America?" *Rivista Internazionale di Scienze Economiche e Commerciali* 22 (January 1975):33-43.

7. Riva Poor, *4 Days, 40 Hours* (Cambridge, Mass.: Bursk and Poor, 1970), cited in Stanley Parker, *The Sociology of Leisure* (New York: International Publications Service, 1976), p. 70.

8. John E. Owen, "Millions Go For Sport in the USA," *Sport and Recreation* 16 (Summer 1975):8-13.

9. National Academy of Sciences, *A Program for Outdoor Recreation Research* (Washington, D.C.: Bureau of Outdoor Recreation, 1969).

10. Kraus, *Recreation and Leisure*, pp. 25-27.

11. Ibid., pp. 76-77.

12. Reynold Carlson, *Recreation in American Life* (Belmont, Calif.: Wadsworth, 1972), p. 13, cited in Parker, *Sociology of Leisure*, p. 92.

13. Rolf Meyersohn, "The Sociology of Leisure in the United States: Introduction and Bibliography, 1945-65," *Journal of Leisure Research* 1 (Winter 1969):53. In writing this article, Meyersohn lists 229 articles and books published during the period under review.

14. Theodore B. Johannis, Jr. and C. Neil Bull, *Sociology of Leisure* (Beverly Hills, Calif.: Sage Publications, 1971), pp. 5-6.

15. Max Kaplan, *Leisure in America, A Social Inquiry* (New York: John Wiley and Sons, 1960), Ch. 18, and *Leisure: Theory and Policy* (New York: John Wiley and Sons, 1975), pp. 103-105.

16. See, for example, Morton D. Davis, *Game Theory: A Non-technical Introduction* (New York: Basic Books, 1970).

17. Stanley Parker, *The Future of Work and Leisure* (New York: Praeger Publishers, 1971), pp. 99-110.

18. Ibid., p. 73.

19. Joffre Dumazedier, *Toward a Society of Leisure* (New York and London: Free Press—Collier-Macmillan, 1967), pp. 14-17.

20. M. N. Donald and Robert J. Havighurst, "The Meanings of Leisure," *Social Forces* 37 (May 1959):355-360.

21. Thomas M. Kando and Worth C. Summers, "The Impact of Work on Leisure: Toward a Paradigm and Research Strategy," *Pacific Sociological Review* 14 (July 1971):310-327.

22. John R. Kelly, "Work and Leisure: A Simplified Paradigm," *Journal of Leisure Research* 4 (Winter 1972):50-62.

23. Parker, *The Sociology of Leisure*, p. 74.

24. For a study of the impact of occupation on leisure, see Joel E. Gerstl, "Leisure, Taste and Occupational Milieu," in Edwin O. Smigel, ed., *Work and Leisure: A Contemporary Social Problem* (New Haven, Conn.: College and University Press, 1963), pp. 146-167.

25. *The Challenge of Leisure: A Southern California Case Study* (Claremont, Calif.: Southern California Research Council, 1967).

26. J. Child and B. Macmillan, "Managers and Their Leisure," in M. A. Smith et al., eds., *Leisure and Society in Britain* (London: Allen Lane, 1973).

27. Alexander Szalai, *The Use of Time, Daily Activities of Urban and Suburban Populations in Twelve Countries* (The Hague, Paris: Mouton, 1972). See also Kaplan, *Leisure: Theory and Policy*, pp. 269-271.

28. Rhona Rapoport and Robert N. Rapoport, *Leisure and the Family Life Cycle* (London and Boston: Routledge and Kegan Paul, 1975).

Jerome Krase

SECRET SOCIETIES AND GUERRILLAS

The Role of Secrecy in Social Control

Secrecy is a feature of almost every aspect of social life. Families, clubs, as well as businesses and governments, produce and maintain secrets. In American society, "confidentiality" in many matters is a constitutional right of citizens, which is protected by the Fourth and Fifth Amendments of the Constitution. Since 1974, Congress has defined and expanded these rights by the Privacy and Freedom of Information Acts.

A secret is a social relationship. Even a secret that no one else is privy to is "social" because it separates the person with the secret from others in society. The ways by which secrets act to control those who hold them are best described by Georg Simmel.[1] He argued that the power of secrecy to control behavior is derived from two sources: fascination and fear of betrayal. Fascination is associated with secrecy because secrecy creates a special sense of self-worth, an exceptional status and prestige that separates the individual from the uninformed. In order to maintain this social "adornment," the secret must be kept. Therefore, one is positively pressured to respect secrets. the drive for status and prestige is a major factor in all forms of social control.

Many secrets, if disclosed, would hurt the interests of those who maintain them. To protect themselves, holders of secrets establish explicit, or implicit, negative sanctions for betrayal. The person who betrays his fellows-in-secrecy injures himself as well and loses stature in the eyes of those both inside and outside the group. Benedict Arnold, for example, retains an unenviable place in American folklore even 200 years after his treason.

The means of reducing the possibility of betrayal range from murder to simply labeling violators "finks," "stool pigeons," or untrustworthy. The more violent punishments are meted out by criminal secret societies. Historically, the Camorra of Naples (1820) and the Tongs of American Chinatowns (1890), as well as other ethnically based secret criminal groups, have been noted for their fierce enforcement of in-group codes.[2] The greater the need for secrecy, the greater the sanctions for betrayal.

Both fascination and fear of betrayal are essentially intragroup social control mechanisms. Secret societies conceal those ideas or activities that threaten the greater social world. Secrecy therefore breeds further fascination and fear, as the group is always seen as a danger to society at large, even when it is quite innocuous.

Although secrecy is an age-old social form, as civilization becomes more advanced and complex, collective life becomes less clandestine and individual life more private. The desire for personal secrecy may be viewed as a response to the intrusion of larger social mechanisms into individual life. In modern society, collective secrets and secret groups, not individual ones, are seen as a threat to society and become the concern of social control agencies.

All secrets are not equally important to a group. Erving Goffman describes three types of group secrets: dark, strategic, and inside.[3] Dark secrets are critical to the existence of the group and are therefore the most concealed. A dark secret might be a discrepancy between the real aims of a group and their public ones. For example, criminal and revolutionary groups often pose as social or religious organizations. Strategic secrets concern the immediate aims and intentions of the group. The methods, times, and places for activities are strategic secrets. Inside secrets are the least important and generally involve such things as membership criteria and ritual.

Most social organizations have clandestine elements, but it is only the secret society that has as its *raison d'être* the maintenance of secrecy. Therefore, it has a specific organization of elements that differs from that of other social groups. According to Simmel, the following are typical social relations found in secret societies:[4] (1) Extreme confidence among members in each other and the ideas they share, often solemnized through pledges and oaths; (2) major efforts to conceal the operation of the groups, and sometimes its membership, from outsiders; (3) absolute silence about the group in the presence of nonmembers; (4) written or other formalized communications between members to concretize relations between them; (5) a group organization designed to promote secrecy—for example, a hierarchy of membership which accords members different degrees of confidence and prestige, earned via displays of commitment to group ideals; and (6) a special kind of freedom for members—by withdrawing from the outside world, the group gains a feeling that it is not governed by common social rules.

Because of these social relations, the secret society, to various degrees, separates itself from the outside world and becomes quite formal in its internal operation. Secret societies tend to have regular meetings and meeting ceremonies. The isolation of the group promotes an extreme consciousness of kind and a system of recognition signs, e.g., handclasps, passwords, or other codes, that differentiate them from nonmembers. Membership in the group is exclusive; all those not specifically included are excluded. This reinforces the sense of superiority, and a kind of ideological aristocracy ensues. Aristocratic notions are strengthened by degrees of initiation and membership that are often celebrated by elaborate ceremonies and awards.[5] The necessity for secrecy and the problems of coordinating the actions of members, particularly if widely dispersed, lead to the creation of a highly centralized control apparatus. Strict control is needed to keep the group from dissolving or from being destroyed by outside forces. Within the group there is a greater degree of equality among members than is present on the outside. The reason for this apparent internal equality is that the rewards within the group are the result of agreed-upon goals and values, whereas in the larger social world there is less agreement on social goals and greater differences in individual abilities to attain them.[6]

We can divide secret societies into three types, based on their scope of interests:[7]

1. Self-interest societies, which are concerned only with controlling their own members in the pursuit of interests limited to themselves.

2. Intermediate societies, which are concerned primarily with controlling their own members and indirectly with controlling outsiders or outside interests. Many self-interest groups develop into intermediate types when the pursuit of their own interests becomes dependent on influencing events in the outside world.

3. Societally active societies, which are concerned primarily with controlling people other than the already initiated and secondarily with controlling their own members in the pursuit of primary aims, i.e., where the control of members is designed to increase the probability of reaching primary goals. There are two types of societally active secret societies. One is the society whose members and interests represent the more dominant groups in the social structure, for example, the Ku Klux Klan. Dominant groups resort to secret organization when they believe that their own interests are threatened by rising, opposing interests, particularly in periods of social instability. The second type is the society whose members and interests represent the less dominant groups that want to improve their status, ultimately at the expense of the dominant ones. The Black Panthers, the old Knights of Labor, and revolutionary parties in general belong to this category. The most restrictive the social world, the more likely that less advantaged groups will employ secret organizational forms in the pursuit of their goals.

Secret Societies Throughout History

Anthropologists have recorded the existence of secret societies in most primitive tribes. Usually they are connected to pubertal or other rites of passage. As the primitive civilization advances and generates a more complicated division of labor, secret societies may emerge which are associated with more specialized social, economic, or political functions within the group.

The separation of religion from everyday social life leads to the creation of special religious secret societies. Secret cults, or sects, existed in advanced ancient civilizations—for example, the Cult of Isis in Ancient Egypt. The secret religious organization is common in the nondominant or oppressed religions found in modern societies.[8] Many of the current open or public rituals of Christian churches were dark or inside secrets during the days of the Roman Empire.

During the Middle Ages, politically and economically active (both self-interest and intermediate) secret societies came on the scene in significant numbers. Artisan and merchant guilds which at that time began to play greater roles in the operation of medieval society, were highly secretive. Much of the regalia, paraphernalia, and ritual of modern fraternal orders can be traced to this period in history. The symbols and rituals have continued through time; in the process they have become more mysterious and mythical, helping to control members through fascination.

One of the first societally active secret societies was the Assassins, the heretical Moslem sect that arose in Persia in about 1000 A.D. Their legendary exploits have been repeated by later political groups throughout the world seeking to influence national and international events through secret, coordinated terrorism. The Thugs of Colonial India are another example of early religio-political terrorist groups that have at least a theoretical connection to present-day groups such as the Palestine Liberation Orgranization and the Irish Republican Army.

In eighteenth- and nineteenth-century Europe, the breakdown of the great empires stimulated the growth of societally active and intermediate secret societies with ethinic or social class bases. They were in essence the prototypes of modern secret revolutionary movements and guerrilla organizations. It was during the nineteenth century that societally active secret societies became truly international in scope—the best example of which was the Communist International. It can also be argued that an international capitalist movement developed during this period.

Secret Societies in America

Secret societies of various types have been in America since colonization (for example, the Free Masons, anticolonial revolutionary parties, and the underground abolitionist movement). The heyday of American secret societies was the late nineteenth and early twentieth centuries.[9] During this era, U.S. population was swelling rapidly as a result of mass immigration, and social, economic, and political divisions were multiplying and increasing because of industrialization and urbanization. Dominant groups sought to maintain their advantages, and the less dominant to improve their position in the social structure. As rapid industrialization had earlier led to the birth of secret and semisecret labor organizations in Europe, the proletarianization of large segments of the American population created a great number of worker and radical political groups.

Societally active secret societies are more likely to be found in countries whose political systems offer little or no recourse to open resolution of conflicts of interest. Even though the American system has been one of the most open, there have been both dominant and oppressed groups that have had to resort to secrecy in order to attain their goals. The Grange Organization in the 1860s, the Ku Klux Klan during the Reconstruction, the Knights of Labor, the Molly Maguires of the Ancient Order of Hibernians (1860), and the Industrial Workers of the World are prominent examples of societally active secret societies in American history.[10]

In an open system, extreme or minority interests cannot be completely satisfied democratically. The American system is one of compromise and not of absolute victory for competitors. The lack of successful secret activity (especially revolutionary) in the United States since the Civil War is testimony to the compromising and mollifying forces of the American system. While similar class and ethnic conflicts existed in Europe during the nineteenth and twentieth centuries, the solution of conflicts there took much more drastic forms than in America.[11]

The Revolutionary Party and Underground Movements

The relationship between secret societies, irreconcilable differences, and the phenomena of revolutionary parties and underground movements deserves greater attention in the literature than has so far been exhibited.[12] Feliks Gross notes that the term *underground movement* first appeared in Russia and Poland during the period 1860-1870 to designate secret, political organizations opposed to the Russian Czarist regime. An underground movement has a wide network. In order to maintain its goals, it must extend itself both geographically and socially, and at some point it must appeal to the uninitiated masses. The masses are only peripherally involved in its struggle and are manipulated by the group in order to reach its goals. To the masses, the movement must appear to be more democratic than the existing social order, but for the movement to survive in the face of constant government attacks, its internal order must be secret, rigid, restricted, and elitist and its leadership unopposed.

Movements that are unsuccessful in gaining the support of a significant proportion of the population may become microparties—small groups that attempt to overthrow the existing government or to foster social change by creating chaos via terrorism or other operations designed to cause economic, political, and social dislocations. These actions are thought to decrease the support or confidence of the general population in the existing regime and to create a more favorable climate for revolution. Usually, further abuse and repression on the part of central authority results from these disturbances, which the microparty sees as a victory because repression tends to widen support for political change.[13]

In totalitarian countries, the overt support of the masses is not necessary for the successful overthrow of the government. Because it is so centralized, the government need only be "captured" by a relatively small group of people. The secret military conspiracy, the "Junta," is a common mode of political change in countries with existing military dictatorships; it has been a fact of political life for many South American and, more recently, African nations.[14]

Because underground movements create the sense that they are above normal moral constraints, members can almost routinely engage in "despicable" acts such as bombings and assassinations. The members' intense commitment to the aims of their group turn them into moral automatons. Initiation into the group may involve participation in acts that ordinarily would be repulsive to initiates. The act demonstrates the new member's allegiance to the group but, even more importantly, psychologically fuses the identity of the individual to the secret society.

Both "good" and "bad" secret movements operate essentially the same way, even though they may display different ideologies, symbols, and uniforms. The modern underground movement differs from the traditional secret society in that it is somewhat less ritualized. (i.e., it has less regalia and ceremony) and is more tactical, secular, pragmatic, and rational. In other words; modern secret societies reflect the modern social order and advanced technology.[15]

American Underground Movements in the 1960s and 1970s

During the middle of the twentieth century, major economic and social problems in America resulted in the birth of secret societies and movements of many types. Rising expectations of nonwhite minority groups in the face of continuing discrimination and frustration led to the creation of groups such as the Student Non-Violent Coordinating Committee, the Black Panthers, and the Black Muslims.[16] The interests of these groups were frequently parallel to those of left-wing underground political movements such as the Students for a Democratic Society, the Weathermen, and, more recently, the Symbionese Liberation Army.[17] The riots of the 1960s, although not a direct result of clandestine activity, indicated the existence of a widespread sense of despair and frustration within the Afro-American population. The assassinations of Martin Luther King, John F. Kennedy, and Malcolm X added to the chaotic atmosphere of the decade.[18]

The government itself responded to unrest in covert ways, and the abuse of political authority has been a subject of much debate in recent years. The Federal Bureau of Investigation and the Central Intelligence Agency—secret organizations by government mandate—have particularly been criticized for infiltrating suspected antigovernment groups and for committing illegal acts both here and abroad. The epitome of secret abuses of power was the Watergate debacle in which a small group of men, convinced that they were above the Constitution of the Republic, took it upon themselves to ensure what they thought was the best interests of the country by covertly interfering with the democratic election system.[19]

Secret organizations in the 1960s and 1970s were not limited to left-wing interests. Right-wing and reactionary groups also crystallized in the form of paramilitary groups that prepared for what they believed was the "inevitable" Communist takeover of the nation. Most notable among these organizations was the Minutemen society. Organizations such as the ultra-conservative John Birch Society and neo-Nazi microparties also became part of the broad collection of extremist political groups in America.[20]

Left-wing student and "community" group demonstrations were given impetus by foreign policy decisions which tended to give support to foreign dictatorships in the "national interest." In addition in the 1960s and 1970s, groups of exiles and refugees became active in attempts to influence foreign policy through demonstrations and occasional terrorist activities, such as the Cuban Exile Pragmatistas and others, who may be responsible for over 100 bombings and several assassinations in America. Groups concerned with the plight of Soviet Jewry or other "captive nations," such as the Jewish Defense League and the Armed Forces of National Liberation (which violently favors independence for Puerto Rico), are only a few of the underground or semi-underground organizations that have become a common feature of political life in America today.[21]

Guerrilla Organizations

One outgrowth of societally active secret societies and underground movements is the guerrilla group which tries to create social and political change through military activity. Guerrilla war is the "last resort" of societally active groups. Carl von Clausewitz argued that war is an extension of foreign policy;[22] we might say that guerrilla warfare is an extension of the national policy of an unrecognized government.

Guerrilla activity has been primarily considered a legacy of World War II, as the overseas empires of the Great Powers were voluntarily or involuntarily dissolved. It has also been connected with neocolonial empire-building by which "puppet" states have been set up to protect the interests of old or new colonial powers.[23] Guerrilla warfare, however, has a long history, going back at least to the resistance of primitive people to the extension of the Roman Empire.[24] "True" guerrilla warfare, that associated with the formation of modern political states, can only be found where the nation-state exists, however. Guerrilla warfare is not merely backward military technology.

The American Revolution and the Civil War are two examples of our own nation's early participation in guerrilla warfare. The term *guerrilla* is said to have begun in the "little wars" of Spanish resistance to Napoleon (1808-1814). The European rebellions during the nineteenth century, of urban and rural proletariates, can be considered guerrilla insurections, even though most of them were not extended engagements, because their aims and outcomes were political. Guerrilla (partisan) activity in the Balkans versus the German forces of occupation during World War II, the activities of T. E. Lawrence and his Arab irregulars against the Turks in World War I, and the guerrilla-terrorist acts of the Zionists in Palestine (1917-1945) are a small sample of the diversity of guerrilla activity in the first half of the twentieth century. Since World War II, there has been a drastic increase in the number and scope of guerrilla wars, particularly in the Third World. Increasingly, guerrilla wars are launched in developing nations with the support of foreign powers who attempt to extend or maintain their local influence.[25]

The basic hardcore commandments of guerrilla war were laid down 2,500 years ago by the Chinese author Sun Tzu and are still viable today. Some of his rules were: "Offer the enemy but to lure him . . . whenever he is strong avoid him . . . Pretend inferiority and encourage his arrogance. Keep him under strain and wear him down. When he is united divide him. Attack when he is unprepared."[26] Although there are many well-known contemporary guerrilla strategists such as Josip Broz Tito, Fidel Castro, and Kwame Nkrumah, Americans are most familiar with the actions and legend of Ernesto Che Guevara.[27] He argued that detailed knowledge of the terrain, the local population's ability to provide supplies, and complete mobility were necessary for successful guerrilla actions in the rough countryside in which he fought. Most modern guerrilla wars have taken place in rural areas. This fact seems to contradict Karl Marx's belief that the urban proletariate was to be the major force behind modern revolutions. However, it is obvious that the content of guerrilla warfare must conform to local realities and not to theoretical treatises, as argued and demonstrated decisively by Mao Tse-tung in China.[28]

As societies become more advanced, for guerrilla activity to be successful it must focus on the cities and the urban populations. The "Urban Guerrillas" such as the Uruguayan Tupamaros and the Irish Republican Army may be seen as a new form of guerrilla group. Martin Oppenheimer notes that modern society is more vulnerable than past societies to disruption by small bands of dedicated extremists.[29] The reason is that as any organism becomes more complicated, it also becomes more "delicate" and sensitive to problems in any part of its structure.

Recent Trends

Several recent trends in guerrilla and underground activity are certain to be carried over into the succeeding decades. In America, as noted by Robert Nisbet, radical youth movements have subsided as the age cohort has been absorbed into the mainstream of American life.[30] The grievances of the more established minority groups, such as the blacks, have been assuaged to some degree by increases in social and economic opportunity. The slack, however, is certain to be taken up by the "new" oppressed groups, in particular, the Hispanics.[31]

In Canada, regional and ethnic differences have already produced separatist groups like the Free Quebec party, but as in America the Canadian political system allows for the possibility of attaining all but the most radical political goals. Therefore, the need for secrecy and guerrilla activity is obviated.[32] Similarly, most Western European countries offer sufficient freedom to prevent the emergence of significant underground and guerrilla activity. In nations such as West Germany, radical student mass movements and support for groups such as the Baader-Meinhof organization are on the wane.[33] Exceptions to the Western European tranquillity will most certainly continue to be Northern Ireland and Spain, where ethnic and regional differences are marked, and the gap between the government and the aggrieved has not yet been bridged. A caveat in regard to trends in mass movements and terrorist activities must be stated. These trends can quickly be reversed in response to drastic changes in economic conditions and the responses of legitimate governments to expressions of economic and political grievances. For example, in 1977 there was a rash of kidnappings and other terrorist actions in Western Europe. Whether this indicates a new trend or not will be confirmed, not by foresight, but by hindsight.

The Soviet Union and other Eastern European nations tend to view even the slightest expression of dissent as a threat; therefore, all movements there take place in secrecy. The best example of this phenomenon is the Samizdat, the underground movement in Russia associated with art and literature.[34] Totalitarianism in an efficient, modern society, however, prohibits the possibility of a large-scale underground movements inasmuch as the government is able to penetrate almost every aspect of life.

In Latin America, increasing modernization is changing the character of guerrilla activity from traditional to urban forms.[35] Only on the frontier and in the most underdeveloped nations will the peasant-based guerrillas persist. A rise in youth and student movements can also be expected as the societies undergo further modernization. The totalitarian nature of most of the governments there should ensure that the "Junta" will continue to be a common political mode.

The familiar forms of guerrilla warfare are playing a more important role in the emerging nations of black Africa, such as Angola and Mozambique; the semifeudal North African nations entering the modern age, such as Morocco and Ethiopia; and the white minority-ruled areas such as Rhodesia. All the ingredients for large-scale guerrilla warfare are present there: rough terrain, poor transportation, wide ethnic and class divisions, isolated cities, and inefficient, undemocratic governments.[36]

The Middle East has been a hotbed of guerrilla activity for decades, and the situation there shows little improvement. The Israeli-Palestinian conflict and the Christian-Moslem battles in Lebanon, although prominent, are merely examples of the problems facing regions in which international interests fight each other through "proxies."[37] In South East Asia, many assumed that the end of American involvement in Vietnam would automatically decrease guerrilla activity in that area of the world. This has unfortunately not been the case. Ethnic and racial differences of people occupying the same territory, the strains of infant modernization, and the grievances of oppressed minorities in places like Laos, Cambodia, Malaysia, and the Philippines do not require outside intervention to be vented in open or clandestine struggles. These tensions are endemic to Asia and affect even the most developed countries there.[38]

As the world becomes a network of interconnected nations, guerrilla and underground activities are becoming international and not simply national problems.[39] The trend toward commonplace international terrorism has led to studies of methods for its control. J. J. Lador-Lederer has observed that part of the problem of control is that the legal status of international terrorists and their acts are ill-defined, or not defined at all.[40] Hence, worldwide cooperation to deal with the problem is almost impossible. For the United Nations, or any other supranational body, to adjudicate terrorist crimes, a set of laws must exist and mechanisms for cooperative effort to enforce them must be devised.

A final trend, though not the least important, is the growth of the women's movement in developed and underdeveloped countries, which has led to an increase in the participation of women in all aspects of social and political life as noted by Sheila Rowbotham.[41] For example, women have been playing important roles in the revolutionary organizations in Latin America, demonstrating the power of modernization as a major influence on the character and operation of covert, as well as overt, social and political activity.

Notes

1. Georg Simmel, *Sociology of George Simmel*, translated by Kurt Wolf (New York: Free Press, 1950), pp. 307-376. See also P. Bonacich, "Secrecy and Solidarity," *Sociometry* 39 (Summer 1976):200-208.

2. See P. Savigear, "Some Reflections on Corsican Secret Societies," *International Review of Social History* 19 (1974):100-114, and P. Unger, "Making and Breaking of Chinese Secret Societies," *Journal of Contemporary Asia* 5 (May 1973):483-487.

3. Erving Goffman, *The Presentation of Self in Everyday Life* (Garden City, N.Y.: Doubleday, 1959), pp. 141-144.

4. Simmel, *Sociology*, pp. 345-376.

5. Alvin Schmidt and Nathan Babchuk, "Unbrotherly Brotherhood: Discrimination in Fraternal Orders," *Phylon* 34 (Summer 1973):483-487.

6. See J. C. Van Es and D. J. Koenig, "Social Participation, Social Status and Extremist Political Attitudes," *Sociological Quarterly* 17 (Winter 1976):16-26.

7. Joseph S. Roucek and Charles Marden, "Secret Societies," Chapter XVIII, in Joseph S. Roucek (ed.) *Social Control* (New York: D. Van Nostrand, 1956).

8. Vittorio Lanternari, *The Religions of the Oppressed* (New York: Alfred A. Knopf, 1963).

9. E. J. Hobsbawm, *Primitive Rebels* (New York: Praeger Publishers, 1959), and Wendell King, *Social Movements in the United States* (New York: Random House, 1956), are excellent works on this American era.

10. See Eyre Damer, *When the Ku Klux Klan Rode* (Westport, Conn.: Negro Universities Press, 1970); Anthony Bimba, *The Molly Maguires* (New York: International, 1970); and Phillip Taft, *Organized Labor in the United States* (New York: Harper and Row, 1964).

11. Michael Bateman et al., eds., *The Fourth Dimension of Warfare: Volume 2. Revolt to Revolution: Studies in the 19th and 20th Century European Experience* (New York: Rowman and Littlefield, 1974).

12. For an excellent analysis of secret political groups, see Feliks Gross, *The Revolutionary Party* (Westport, Conn.: Greenwood Press, 1974).

13. See especially Feliks Gross, *The Seizure of Political Power* (New York: Philosophical Library, 1958), pp. 356-358.

14. See Norman Miller and Roderick Aya, eds., *National Liberation: Revolutions in the Third World* (New York: Free Press, 1971).

15. Arkin Daraul, *A History of Secret Societies* (New York: Pocket Books, 1969), is a good review of historical trends.

16. Robert Blauner, *Racial Oppression in America* (New York: Harper and Row, 1972) discusses these developments in detail.

17. See especially Gil Green, *The New Radicalism: Anarchist or Marxist* (New York: International, 1971).

18. See National Advisory Commission on Civil Disorders, *Report* (Washington, D.C.: U.S. Government Printing Office, 1968).

19. See Elie Flatto, *The Rise and Fall of the Presidency* (New York: Arica, 1974).

20. See Richard Hofstadter, *The Paranoid Style in American Politics and Other Essays* (New York: Alfred A. Knopf, 1964).

21. For an outline of these trends, see John R. Howard, *The Cutting Edge* (Philadelphia: J. B. Lippincott, 1974).

22. A good introduction to Clausewitz is Roger Leonard, ed., *A Short Guide to Clausewitz on War* (New York: Putnam, 1967).

23. See, for example, William Pomeroy, *American Imperialism* (New York: International, 1970).

24. Joseph S. Roucek, "Guerilla Warfare: Its Theories and Strategies," *International Behavioural Scientist* 6 (March 1974):57-80.

25. See Wayne Wilcox, ed., "Protagonists, Power and the Third World: Essays on the Changing International Systems," *Annals of the American Academy of Political and Social Change* 386 (November 1969).

26. Cited by Carleton Beals, *Great Guerrilla Warriors* (Englewood Cliffs, N.J.: Prentice-Hall, 1970), p. 8.

27. For views of Marxist guerrilla leaders, see William Pomeroy, ed., *Guerrilla Warfare and Marxism* (New York: International, 1968).

28. See J. Bowyer Bell, *The Myth of the Guerrilla: Revolutionary Theory and Malpractice* (New York: Alfred A. Knopf, 1971).

29. Martin Oppenheimer, *The Urban Guerrilla* (Chicago: Quadrangle, 1969).

30. Robert Nisbet, "Who Killed the Student Movement?," *Encounter* 34 (Fall 1970): 10-18, discusses these changes.

31. See especially John H. Burma, ed., *Mexican Americans in the United States* (Cambridge, Mass.: Schenkman, 1970).

32. Donald V. Smiley, "Federal Provincial Conflict in Canada," *Publicus* 4 (Summer 1974):7-24.

33. Neal Ascherson, "The Urban Guerrillas of West Germany," *New Society* 32 (April 10, 1975):66-68.

34. J. Telesin, "Inside Samizdat," *Encounter* 40 (Fall, 1973):25-33.

35. Chester A. Russell et al. "Urban Guerrillas in Latin America: A Select Bibliography," *Latin American Research* 9 (Spring 1974): 37-79, is a good survey of the works about this phenomenon.

36. See, for example, B. Rivers, "Angola, Massacre and Oppression," *Africa Today* 21 (Winter 1974):41-45, and J. Bowyer Bell, "Endemic Insurgency and International Order: The Eritrean Experience," *Orbis* 18 (Summer 1974):427-450.

37. N. Ashab, "Balance of World Forces and the Middle East Crisis," *World Marxist Review* 19 (March 1976):116-123.

38. Committee of Concerned Asian Scholars, *The Indo China Story* (New York: Bantam, 1970).

39. See Yonah Alexander, ed., *International Terrorism: National, Regional and Global Perspectives* (New York: Praeger Publishers, 1976).

40. J. J. Lador-Lederer, "A Legal Approach to International Terrorism," *Israel Law Review* 9 (April 1974):194-220.

41. Sheila Rowbotham, *Women, Resistance and Revolution: A History of Women and Revolution in the Modern World* (New York: Pantheon, 1973).

Joseph S. Roucek

CAPITAL PUNISHMENT

Capital punishment has periodically produced bitter philosophical, ideological, and legal arguments, especially in contemporary times.

The concept of capital punishment originally meant the loss of the head—hence the loss of life. Today it generally refers to the loss of life carried out usually on the basis of legal and judicial authorities, although the death penalty has also been used by terrorist, underground, and guerrilla organizations or their representatives. The latter is usually classified as illegal violence, terrorism, crime, homicide, assault, civil disobedience, assassination, and the like. Death is the ultimate weapon in the power struggle. With a paucity of alternatives to this weapon, expressions of violence and terror leading to death are used both by groups controlling the maximum means of social control and by those with the minimum control of power.

The line between political murder and execution by legal authorities is not always very sharply drawn, especially during revolutions and periods of "declared" and "undeclared wars." The Soviet purge trials of individuals who were later "rehabilitated" are an example. In Nazi Germany, between 1935 and 1945, after official verdicts of some 13,000 were "legally" executed. Many American Negroes sentenced to death and executed belong to the history of political orders rather than to the American constitutional cases of jurisprudence.

In our study, we shall limit ourselves to the survey of the problem of capital punishment as isolated from the general problems of political violence and terror.[1]

History of Capital Punishment

"Is it not absurd," wrote Cesare Beccaria in 1764, "that the laws which detest and punish homicide, in order to prevent murder, publicly commit murder themselves?"

More than a century after Beccaria, the abolition of the death penalty became a matter of serious dispute in most European countries, with many influential social thinkers and sociologists defending it. For example, Cesare

Lombrose, writing in the 1890s, believed that capital punishment should be retained for the "born criminal" incapable of reform.[2] Nevertheless, strong opposing voices were also heard. Enrico Ferri, Lombrose's friend, wrote in 1881 that the death penalty would have to be applied "resolutely in all cases" if "the only positive utility which it possessed, namely artificial selection," were to be drawn from it. He advocated the abolition of the death penalty on the grounds that no country would "have the courage" to apply it with unwavering determination to the great number of "born criminals, guilty of the most serious crimes of violence," which was the only way of making it effective as a deterrent.[3]

The number of executions began to drop during the nineteenth century—and even before. One after the other, the European countries heeded the ideological appeals for reason and humanitarianism. Belgium, Holland, Luxemburg, Portugal, Romania, and Italy dispensed with capital punishment by the end of the last century. Norway followed in 1905, Sweden in 1921, Denmark in 1930, Switzerland in 1942, Italy in 1944 (the Fascists having introduced it for certain crimes in 1931), Finland in 1949 (Hitler restored a uniformed headsman with ritualistic axes) in 1949, and Austria in 1950.

In the United States, as in England, the debate has long continued and remains unsolved. In early nineteenth-century England, capital punishment was known as the Blood Code. In its heyday, from 2,000 to 3,000 persons a year were executed for murder, burglary, picketing, and any of 220 other crimes.

The Death Penalty in American History

The U.S. Supreme Court decision reinstating the death penalty in 1976 is the latest chapter in a controversy that stretches back more than 300 years into colonial and American history. Ever since the 1650's, when colonists could be put to death for denying the true God or even for cursing their parents, advocates and opponents of capital punishment have clashed almost continuously in the forum of public opinion, in state legislatures, and, most recently, in the courts.

Generally, those seeking to curb or abolish the death penalty gained most ground in times of peace and internal security, while proponents of capital punishment advanced their cause in wartime and during periods of national concern over crime and subversion. Despite its continuous presence as an issue, capital punishment has gone through cycles, with alternating times of activity and success by abolitionists or adherents and long lulls of public indifference in between.[4]

The earliest laws of the American colonies, reflecting their British heritage, were very harsh by modern standards but more lenient than those in most of

Europe. In Virginia from 1612 through 1619, the death penalty could be imposed for stealing grapes, trading with Indians, or killing farm and household animals without permission. In New York in 1665, the eleven capital crimes included sodomy, kidnapping, traitorous denial of the king's rights, and striking a parent, as well as premeditated murder. An earlier Massachusetts code also included adultery, witchcraft, and being a rebellious son. The colonies of Pennsylvania and West Jersey, where the Quaker influence was strong, limited the death penalty to treason and willful murder; Rhode Island also had a relatively narrow code. Elsewhere, however, the prerevolutionary tendency was to increase steadily the number of crimes for which people could be put to death.

With the founding of the new nation in 1776, the British criminal justice system continued, more or less, for some years.

One of the first citizens to publicly advocate the abolition of capital punishment was apparently Dr. Benjamin Rush, a Philadelphia physician who in 1787 called the death penalty an "absurd and un-Christian practice." In 1794, Pennsylvania ended capital punishment except for first-degree murder, and a few states reduced the number of capital crimes over the next two decades.

In the early nineteenth century, some voices were heard for abolition, but the chief legislative result was the passage of statutes in the 1830s barring public hanging by Rhode Island, Pennsylvania, New York, Massachusetts, and New Jersey. The reason for passage was in the interest of taste and order rather than of conscience.

In 1837, Maine became the first state to declare a moratorium on capital punishment partly because of riots that had accompanied a public hanging in Augusta. The Maine law provided that those convicted of capital crimes would spend a year in solitary confinement and would be executed only on order of the governor. The result was no executions.

In the 1840s, abolition of capital punishment became a major public cause, with clergymen participating. Interestingly, the chief defenders of the death penalty were the more orthodox Protestant clergymen who relied on Genesis 9:6—"Whosoever sheddeth a man's blood, so shall his blood be shed." The abolition leaders attracted public attention but won passage of few laws. They played no part in Michigan's 1846 abolition of capital punishment— except for the virtually nonexistent crime of treason against the state. Michigan's lead was followed by Rhode Island in 1852 and by Wisconsin in 1853. For more than half a century following these actions, the abolitionist effort languished. In the decade between 1907 and 1917, ten states abolished the death penalty for murder, although by 1919 five of these had reintroduced it. During World War I, the rising hatred of foreigners and fear of radicalism, plus anticipation of a crime wave, induced four other states to reinstate capital punishment.[5]

The next significant abolitionist period did not arrive until after World War II, particularly in the 1960s and early 1970s. States executed fewer criminals after World War II than they had before that time. In 1950, the number was 82 and in 1955, only 76—down from 199 in 1935.

In this period, six states abolished the death penalty, with few or no qualifications: Oregon (1964); West Virginia, Vermont, Iowa, and New York (1965); and New Mexico (1969). During the 1960s, the last mandatory death penalties for first-degree murder were repealed—in the District of Columbia (1962) and New York (1963). These were replaced by optional death sentences at the discretion of a jury.

At the same time, new categories of crime were classed as capital offenses. At the federal level, air piracy was so designated (1961) and assassination of the president or vice president (1964). In 1970, the state of California provided the death penalty for anyone exploding a "destructive device" causing great harm or injury.

The report of the National Crime Commission (1967) promoted renewed efforts by opponents of capital punishment to secure the suspension of execution while a series of cases that had been appealed to the U.S. Supreme Court were under consideration. A major element in this campaign was the class action suit, initiated by an NAACP legal defense attorney; as a result, executions were blocked in Florida and, subsequently, in California. These actions, in turn, had the effect of halting other executions pending judicial determination of "due process" and "equal protection" issues. The following year, 1968, was the first in which no execution took place under American civil law.

In 1969, the U.S. Supreme Court for the first time heard arguments that the death penalty was unconstitutional under the Eighth Amendment, which prohibits "cruel and unusual punishments." After numerous legal delays and arguments, a divided U.S. Supreme Court handed down its 5-4 decision in 1972 in the case of *Furman* v. *Georgia*, overturning the death penalty in three capital punishment cases. Confusion resulting from the Supreme Court's ruling resulted in a variety of responses among the states to different—and frequently conflicting—interpretations of how the decision did affect their capital punishment laws. Some states vacated or abolished outright the death row and commuted to life imprisonment (or less) the sentences of those awaiting execution. In other states, a "wait and see" attitude prevailed, with condemned prisoners presumably no longer under threat of execution, but with their status not yet officially altered by state authorities and with the procedures and equipment of capital punishment in many cases left intact.

In June 1972, some 631 persons were under sentence of death, with most of them obtaining commutation to life or new trials resulting in their return to prison. But no person was executed, although twenty-eight states adopted a mandatory death sentence, with some 150 persons waiting death sentence.

Often working for days without sleep, criss-crossing the country with petitions to save defendents faced with certain execution, the lawyers working under the sponsorship of the NAACP Legal Defense and Education Fund, Inc., obtained considerable stature as they worked through case after case, gaining a definite victory or at least further delay. This was the period of Lyndon Johnson's "Great Society" and major civil rights efforts, especially in the South. Young lawyers saw themselves as participants in a new legal frontier; they believed the American people were unable to utilize the death penalty with overall consistency, thereby creating irrational and arbitrary sentences.

The initial strategy was to challenge the legal procedures that made the death sentence possible. First, it was noted that individuals who had scruples about the death penalty should be excluded from capital trials. Second, it was objected that jurors both determined guilt and fixed the sentence in capital cases, a procedure that was quite unlike that of other crimial trials where the juror determined guilt and the judge imposed the sentence. Third, there were no generalized legal standards or doctrines for making a decision with regard to using the death penalty. A fourth major stratagem was the race factor, generally perceived through the use of executions data appearing in the *National Prisoner Statistics* series then published by the Bureau of Prisons. Legal researchers conducted extensive research on the care of offenders and victims and provided some twenty-two variables. When analyzed by criminologist Marvin Wolfgang, these variables showed that "the disparity between the number of death sentences imposed on Negroes with white victims and all other racial combinations of convicted defendants and victims was such that it could have occurred less than twice in one hundred times by chance." This finding was in response to a comprehensive study carried out in Arkansas in connection with the 1966 federal district court hearings for the petitioner William L. Maxwell. Maxwell and many others laid the groundwork for continued appeals at the state level as well as in the District Court, the U.S. Circuit Court of Appeals, and finally the Supreme Court.

Capital Punishment Revived in 1976

After carefully reviewing the haphazard use of capital punishment, U.S. Supreme Court Justice Potter Stewart concluded in 1972 that the death penalty was cruel and unusual punishment "in the same way that being struck by lightning is cruel and unusual." A majority of five justices used words such as "arbitrary," "capricious," and "freakish" to describe the application of the penalty. They joined together to shut down the nation's death rows with a ruling which to many sounded like a constitutional ban on executions.

In a landmark ruling on July 2, 1976, however, the Supreme Court upheld the constitutionality of capital punishment and apparently sanctioned the execution of more than 600 prisoners on death rows. The Court, in three 7-to-2 decisions, declared that the death penalty did not violate the Eighth Amendment ban on "cruel and unusual punishment." "There is no question that death as a punishment is unique in its severity and irrevocability," wrote Potter Stewart for the majority. "But . . . it is an extreme sanction, suitable to the most extreme of crimes."[6]

The decision capped a week of major rulings. The ruling both permitted the resumption of executions in the United States (the last was in 1967) and made it easier for states that did not then have death penalties to enact them. Even as it upheld the constitutionality of the death penalty for murder, however, the Court in two separate 5-4 decisions struck down laws that made death mandatory for certain crimes. Mandatory sentences, wrote Stewart, are a kind of cruel and unusual punishment because they treat "all persons convicted of a designated offense not as uniquely individual human beings, but as members of a faceless, undifferentiated mass." However, in the fourteen states (including Florida) that allow judges and juries to consider mitigating or aggravating circumstances before imposing a death sentence, executions could presumably resume.

The 1976 ruling was the first decision on capital punishment since 1972, when it was held that the death penalty was so arbitrarily imposed that it was unconstitutional. In the aftermath of the 1972 decision, thirty-five states and the federal government wrote new statutes designed to make capital punishment less capricious. Many state legislators felt that they had accomplished this goal when they voted to make death mandatory for specific crimes (such as murder by an already convicted killer). The federal government made murder during the course of an air hijacking grounds for execution. In overturning the laws of North Carolina and Louisiana, however, the Supreme Court ruled that states should instead carefully review a defendant's background and take into consideration any special circumstances before sentencing him to death. Because of the "qualitative difference [between death and life imprisonment]", wrote Stewart, "there is a corresponding difference in the need for reliability in the determination that death is appropriate punishment."

In upholding capital punishment, the Supreme Court recognized that many states had enacted new death penalty laws since 1972. This trend, said the Court, was "a marked indication of society's endorsement of the death penalty for murder."

The Death Penalty as a Persistent Ideological Issue

In the wake of the death of murderer Gary Gilmore before a Utah firing squad in 1977, arguments over capital punishment again began to escalate. Supporters of the death penalty were encouraged that a ten-year period in which no executions occurred had come to an end. Opponents began to redouble their efforts to prevent executions from once again becoming a part of prison routine in the United States.

In 1977, 358 men and women were on death rows in twenty states. The action in Utah, on January 17, 1977, has raised several questions. Does it signal a rash of other executions? Will the circus-like atmosphere that surrounded Gilmore's death be endlessly repeated elsewhere? The consensus is that, while other condemned prisoners may die, a sudden flood of executions is unlikely.

The scenes in Utah were reminiscent of the sensationalism of the 1920s. Hordes of reporters, cameramen, gawkers, and profitseekers descended on the execution site, often camping on the prison grounds. Gilmore, unlike most of death row inmates, was demanding to die; twice he had tried suicide. In the process he had become a minor folk hero.

Supporters of the death penalty maintained that the sideshow trappings of Gilmore's death were an exception. Opponents, however, intended to capitalize on the gruesome aspects of the execution in their fight to abolish state-ordered death.

The campaign to block further executions called for appeals of every condemned prisoner's case, principally through the assistance of the ACLU and the NAACP Legal Defense and Educational Fund; pleas to governors for executive clemency for those on death row; intensive lobbying efforts by the ACLU and others to prevent enactment of more capital punishment laws—and to repeal existing laws; massive demonstrations to enlist the support of the public. Southern Coalition of Jails and Prisons scheduled the first big rally for Easter weekend in Atlanta; and legal assistance at trials for those accused of capital crimes, in hopes of preventing a death sentence in the event of a conviction. These efforts were focused mainly in the South, which houses more than half of the country's condemned prisoners.

It is against this background that the battle over the death penalty is again being waged. One of the leading opponents is Charles L. Black, Jr., professor of constitutional law at Yale and author of *Capital Punishment: The Inevitability of Caprice and Mistake* (New York: W. W. Norton, 1974). According to Black, the legal tools available are simply not good enough to distinguish those who should live from those who must die. He seeks to persuade the ordinary citizen—and any judges or legislators who may be listening—not only that mistakes are inevitable whenever fallible human beings attempt to apply fallible human rules, but also that "the official choices—by prosecutors, judges, juries and governors—that divide those who are to die from those who are to live are on the whole not made, and cannot be made, under standards that are consistently meaningful and clear." Instead, Black sets out to prove that there are no genuine standards at all. He demonstrates how prosecutors' discretion, in determining the charge a criminal must face and in accepting or rejecting a plea bargain to a lesser charge, circumvent the law's claim to objective justice. He shows how the traditional secrecy of the jury, which draws a veil of steel over the deliberative process, permits the jurors to indulge their prejudices and sympathies in the name of mercy—or in the name of death. Above all, he illuminates the ways in which the sentencing process, insulated by centuries of legal tradition from meaningful review, evades rational choice. Even clemency, arbitrarily denied to some and granted to others for reasons seldom articulated, contributes to the lawlessness of the law. For if the legal system is not adequate to choose between life and death, the suspicion arises that it is no more adequate to choose between five and twenty years in prisons, between probation and sixty days, between punishment and freedom at all. Black's repeated answer is that death is "supremely different," that in the continuum of criminal punishment it is a quantum leap so vast as to require a higher degree of clarity and precision than any other choice.

The answer may be correct as far as it goes—but it does not go far enough. Even one criminal conviction and one short jail sentence may profoundly alter a man's life. The American legal system is so arranged that few criminals ever stop paying for their crimes: jobs are lost, civil rights restricted, families stigmatized, and friends alienated. For the poor and uneducated—the great majority of those who actually go to prison—the traps proliferate. Probation and parole depend in part on family ties and prospects of employment. The ex-convict has to take what he can get—and quite often starts traveling on the road to recidivism. In a legal system so unforgiving, every mistake matters. Evidently, Black supports the status quo because, as a lobbyist against capital punishment, he may have no choice. The problem is ironic: capital punishment is not an easy issue to lobby for. The task of defending (and extending) the death penalty falls largely to the professionals of the criminal law, those police chiefs, district attorneys, prison wardens, and attorneys general who can be counted on to profess the necessity of legalizing killing to preserve our way of life. All of Black's arguments can be easily attacked by unsupported appeals to compassion, or a reckless acknowledgment that the entire system of criminal punishment is, in the words of Willard Gaylin, an "amazing disgrace."

Willard Gaylin (in his *Partial Justice, A Study of Bias in Sentencing*, New York: Alfred A. Knopf, 1975) documents, through perceptive interviews with more than forty judges, the enormous disparities in sentencing theory and practice that pervade the legal system. The sentence is never a judgment of the criminal's peer. In a system where the great majority of criminal cases are disposed of through bargained pleas of guilty, the sentence is all the judgment the ordinary criminal defendant ever gets. The deficiencies of this system are compounded by the differences among judges.

Black's and Gaylin's studies are only a few recent examples of the persistent arguments for and against capital punishment. Logic tells us that if killers are hanged or electrocuted, they will not be around to commit further crimes. Without the possibility of a death penalty, anyone threatened with a life term for hijacking a plan or kidnapping a child or shooting a man in the course of armed robbery would have no reason for refraining from murdering a third person (a policeman or an informer) in order to make a getaway.

The case for or against the death penalty as a deterrent rests on a preference for one of two risks. If capital punishment does not increase deterrence, we lose the life of an executed convict without saving anyone else. But if the death penalty does add deterrence, and we refrain from pronouncing it, we run the chance of losing the lives of future victims.

There can be miscarriages of justice, of course. Capital punishment is irrevocable, and if a man is hanged he will not be there to take advantage of new evidence proving his innocence. The logical case for the death penalty must rest on the presumption that, despite an occasional miscarriage of justice, more innocent lives will be saved than lost by invoking it.

We must also note that the murder rate in the United States is always many times that of Western Europe and Japan, and has risen terrifyingly in the last two decades. Obviously, life becomes cheaper as we become kinder to those who wantonly take it. Oddly, many of the people who reject capital punishment on humanitarian grounds have no prejudice against abortion or, in some cases, against euthanasia. The prospect of life imprisonment might be enough of a deterrent in itself. But murderers are frequently released for one reason or another, before they have completed their "mandatory" prison sentences. The modern convict, no matter what his crime, is entertained by TV and has access to social workers who may obtain sufficient freedom for him to commit additional crimes.

Ernest van den Haag's *Punishing Criminals: A Very Old and Painful Question* (New York: Basic Books, 1976) admits that crimes are, in many instances, "socially conditioned." Van den Haag's lively sense of paradox impels him to turn this argument against the followers of Rousseau. The idea of deterrence, if it becomes part of the expectations of a community, can be part of a "general determinism." If a criminal cannot help what he is doing, other members of society are equally "determined" in punishing culprits who menace their rights. According to van den Haag, "deterministic views of all kinds are entirely consistent with theories of deterrence, which actually require a causal (though not necessarily 'deterministic') view of human behavior."

The fact remains that a free society must rest on the presumption that all men are responsible for what they do, despite their genes or their "social conditioning." Morality has no relevance if all things are fated by environment on the one hand or by heredity on the other. Some poor people commit crimes and some do not; some rich people are responsible and some are not. Responsible people can only act on the theory that criminals must be incapacitated if society, in general, is to live in peace. Unfortunately, the Rousseauists among us today have made it more and more difficult to incapacitate thieves and cheaters and murderers. Knowing human nature, we can only reduce, not eliminate crime, and this includes the consideration of capital punishment. The task is not to dream up a social order that can do without punishment but, rather, to make the punishment it uses more just and effective.

Ongoing Debate

Evidently, both retentionists and abolitionists have developed nearly ritualistic arguments on this key issue.

Most of the controversy centers on the retentionists' premise that capital punishment is a unique deterrent to crime. This approach needs more investigation. Although it is a rather fundamental principle of learning theory that desired behavior should be awarded and undesirable behavior punished, the kind and degree of reward or punishment remain questionable. Then, too, most people are familiar with contradictory statistics as to the effect of capital punishment. In a few cases, the removal of capital punishment has been followed by a slight increase in homicide rates; in other cases, it has actually been followed by a decrease. The conclusion seems to be that the murder rate is influenced more by such factors as urbanization and geographical mobility than by capital punishment. One reason is that murder is usually a crime of desperation rather than of cool calculation.

Those who favor the death penalty also argue that it eliminates the criminal from society, thus ensuring that he will never commit another crime. In addition, they point out that it does away with expense to the state of supporting the incorrigibles in prison and that it is more humane to put a murderer to death than to imprison him for life. Retentionists maintain that only the death penalty can adequately protect society; the life sentence alternative does not offer adequate protection because criminals who are given life sentences are often paroled and are thus able to commit other crimes. Many who commit repeated capital cimes are adjudged legally insane and not executed, even in a capital punishment jurisdiction. Criminals under a life sentence have killed in attempts to escape, knowing their sentences cannot be increased if they fail in their attempts to escape.

Those who argue against the death penalty claim that it possibly deters only those disposed to deterrent influences. They also contend that it is useless to execute the mentally defective who are unable to make rational judgments. Moreover, the policy and court systems deal only with those who are caught and arrested, a large proportion of whom are freed through legal machinations. Those sentenced to life imprisonment often make the best prisoners, lending credence to rehabilitative possibilities. They stress that statistics support their arguments: where capital punishment has been abolished, the homicide rate is approximately the same as that in areas with the death penalty. Pointing out the paradoxical nature of capital punishment, opponents maintain that it is an inhumane, brutalizing process; that no one has the right to take human life; and that there have been cases where innocent persons have been executed. Murder cases frequently involve lengthy and sensational trials and endless appeals (as in the case of Caryl Chessman, a convicted criminal who was finally executed after twelve years of court battles). Another argument is that the penalty is applied with discrimination, since it is imposed more frequently on the poor, the ignorant, and minority group members; if capital punishment is not uniformly applied, they say, it should be abolished. In short, the abolitionists maintain that executions brutalize human nature and cheapen human life. Since society is to be blamed for the crminal's way of life, society ought to be more considerate of him.[7]

World Trends

There has been a gradual trend toward the abolition of capital punishment, which was widely employed throughout the world fifty or more years ago. Part of this trend can be attributed to the repeal of certain laws, but disuse of others is largely responsible for it.

Many countries still hold executions; these include West Germany and Britain. Others, such as Canada, are considering its abolition. Even many countries that still have the death penalty (there are 101 according to the United Nations) have either narrowed the range of capital offenses or have become more liberal in commuting sentences to prison terms ranging from thirteen to more than thirty years, or both. Some countries (like Belgium) retain capital punishment but refrain from utilizing it.[8]

The most vigorous use of capital punishment today appears to occur in Communist countries, where even embezzlement can bring death, and among the authoritarian Asian allies of the United States (most notably Taiwan and South Korea), where political dissent can be a capital crime.

Beginning near the end of World War II, the pace of the abolition movement quickened as a result of the general revulsion over that conflict's death toll and genocide.[10] In 1948, Italy abolished the death penalty for the second time, following its earlier reinstitution by Mussolini. Switzerland, which had shot seventeen men during the war, had its last execution. In 1949, West Germany abolished capital punishment. In October 1965, Britain's House of Commons, despite public opposition, voted to impose a five-year trial ban on execution, which was later made permanent. (Law enforcement authorities in England have said that the murder rate has not been appreciably higher than when hanging was the penalty.)

In contrast, in Kenya, a former British colony, there is no move afoot to end executions or public hangings, or to provide legal assistance for indigent defendants accused of capital crimes. France retains capital punishment (although only twenty-three persons—murderers of children, policemen, and the elderly—have actually gone to the guillotine). Spain has also kept the death penalty. Five convicted terrorists were executed there in the fall of 1976. An abolition movement has developed, and in November 1976, King Juan Carlos commuted eleven death sentences to life imprisonment. The Netherlands abolished capital punishment in 1870. Belgium has kept the death sentence but grants automatic clemency.

In Latin America, executions have been declining in use. Panama, Honduras, El Salvador, Costa Rica, and the Dominican Republic have no capital crimes. Some states in Mexico have kept the law, but there has been no legal execution in three decades.

With the exception of Australia, which has not executed anyone since 1967, Asia appears to remain a major stronghold for capital punishment. The Indian government, for instance, maintains professional executioners in every state, and some murderers are hanged every month. In South Korea, capital crimes include murder, sedition, and espionage on behalf of North Korea. In Thailand, which has one of the world's higher murder rates, there is no debate over the death penalty, and about eighty condemned men await their turn before the government's "official marksman" at Bang Kwang Prison. The Chinese Nationalist government of Taiwan executed nineteen convicted criminals by firing squads in 1976. In Japan, twenty to thirty people convicted of particularly brutal murders are executed every year. In Communist China executions are held every few months.

Andrew H. Malcom reported in the *New York Times* of July 3, 1976: "Sometimes in countries that have eliminated or cut back executions, movements develop to restore the penalty, especially after a rash of serious crimes. This has happened recently in Hong Kong, El Salvador and Britain."

All in all, in most of the states that still have capital punishment, the range of offenses have been drastically reduced and most states are becoming increasingly reluctant to apply, even when their laws permit it.

Notes

1. Among the numerous studies of violence and terror, see Paul Wilkinson, *Political Terrorism* (London: Macmillan and Co., 1974), bibliography, pp. 152-160; Joseph S. Roucek, "Sociological Elements of a Theory of Terror and Violence,"

American Journal of Economics and Sociology, 21, no. 2 (April 1962): 165-172; Gilbert Kais, "Violence and Organized Crime." Pp. 86-95 in *Patterns of Violence*, *Annals of The American Academy of Political and Social Science* 364 (March 1966); James F. Kirham, Sheldon G. Levy, and William J. Vrotty, *Assassination and Political Violence*, A Report to the National Commission on the Causes and Prevention of Violence (New York: Bantam Books, 1970), bibliography, pp. 733-752; Gerald Runkle, "Is Violence Always Wrong?" *Journal of Politics* 38(1976): 367-389; Robert A. Friedlander, "Sowing the Wind: Rebellion and Violence in Theory and Practice," *Denver Journal of International Law and Policy* 6, no. 1 (Spring 1976):83-93; M. Cherif Bassiouni, ed., *International Terrorism and Political Crimes* (Springfield, Ill.: C. C Thomas, 1974); V. Bowyer Bell, *Transnational Terror* (Washington, D.C.: American Enterprise Institute for Public Policy Research, 1975); Ernst Halperin, *Terrorism in Latin America* (Beverly Hills, Calif.: Sage Publications, 1976); Albert Parry, *Terrorism from Robespierre to Arafat* (New York: Vanguard, 1976).

2. This "social hygiene theory" was favored by Nazi Germany, where Lombrose was much misquoted. The theory was used to justify sterilization laws and was applied even to the congenitally blind and to alcoholics.

3. Stephen Schafer, *Theories in Criminology: Past and Present Philosophies of the Crime Problem* (New York: Random House, 1969), contains a valuable introduction to various theories on the death penalty. We have summarized here also: Joseph S. Roucek, "The Capital Punishment in Its Legal and Social Aspects," *International Journal of Legal Research* 6 (December 1971): 50-66, republished as Ch. 10 in James Van Patten, Joseph S. Roucek, Michael V. Belok, and Martin Schoppmeyer, eds., *Conflict, Permanency, Change and Education* (Moti Katra, Agra 3, India: Satish Book Enterprise, 1976).

4. Warren J. Weaver, "Death Penalty a 2-year Issue in America," *New York Times*, July 3, 1976; Frances A. Allen, "Capital Punishment," in *The International Encyclopedia of the Social Sciences* (New York: Macmillan, 1968), Vol. 2, pp. 290-294; Mary Peter Mack, "Beccaria," in ibid., pp. 237-238; Daniel Glaser, "Penology," in ibid., pp. 514-523; and respective bibliographies in each of the following three articles—Joseph S. Roucek, *Capital Punishment* (Charlotteville, N.Y.: SamHar Press, 1975), James A. McCafferty, ed., *Capital Punishment* (Chicago: Aldine-Atherton, 1972), bibliography, pp. 262-266, and The Law School, University of Chicago, *Capital Punishment* (The Center for Studies in Criminal Justice, 1966); H. A. Bodau, ed., *The Death Penalty in America: An Anthology* (Chicago: Aldine, 1968); Raymond T. Bye, *Capital Punishment in the United States* (Philadelphia: Committee on Philanthropy and Labor of Philadelphia Yearly Meeting of Friends, 1919), bibliography, pp. 102-110; David Felix, *Protest: Sacco-Vanzetti and the Intellectuals* (Bloomington: Indiana University Press, 1965); Julie Emily Johnson, ed., *Capital Punishment* (New York: H. W. Wilson, 1939), Reference Shelf, Vol. 13, bibliography, pp. 243-262; John Lawrence, *A History of Capital Punishment, With a Comment on Capital Punishment by Clarence Darrow* (New York: Citadel Press, 1960); C. H. S. Jayewardene, *The Penalty of Death: The Canadian Experiment* (Lexington, Mass.: Lexington Books, 1977).

5. Thomas F. Gossett, *Race: The History of an Idea in America* (New York: Schocken, 1963), especially Chs. 14 and 15; Thomas J. Curren, *Xenophobia and*

Immigration, 1820-1930 (New York: Twayne, 1975); Joseph S. Roucek, "Image of the Slavs in U. S. History and in Immigration Policy," *American Journal of Economics and Sociology*, 28 (January 1969): 29-48.

6. "Reviving the Death Penalty," *Newsweek*, July 12, 1976, pp. 14-15; Lesley Oelsner, "Justices Uphold Death Penalty: Require Guidance for Imposing It, Limit Laws Making It Mandatory," *New York Times*, July 3, 1972; "The Death Penalty Revived," *Time*, July 12, 1976, pp. 35-36; "The Death Penalty—Issue That Won't Go Away," *U. S. News and World Report*, January 31, 1977, p. 47.

7. Marshall B. Clinard, *Sociology of Deviant Behavior* (New York: Holt, Rinehart and Winston, 1968), pp. 211-212; Edwin M. Schur, *Law and Society: A Sociological View* (New York: Random House, 1968), pp. 7, 119, 131; Roucek, *Capital Punishment*, pp. 24-27; McCafferty, *Capital Punishment*, bibliography, pp. 262-266; Joseph S. Roucek, "Sociological Elements of a Theory of Terror and Violence," *American Journal of Economics and Sociology* 21, no. 2 (April 1962): 165-172; "Controversy over Capital Punishment," *Congressional Digest*, 52 (1973), 1-32.

8. Andrew H. Malcolm, "World Trend Is Toward Ending Executions for Crime," *New York Times*, July 3, 1976; James A. Joyce, *Capital Punishment: A World View* (New York: Grove Press, 1961), bibliography, pp. 275-279; George Rusche and Otto Kirchheimer, *Punishment and Social Structure* (New York: Columbia University Press, 1939); Clarence H. Patrick, "The Status of Capital Punishment: A World Perspective," *Journal of Criminal Law, Criminology, and Police Science* 56 (1965): 397-411.

Unquestionably, the urban societies that now appear to be reaching some sort of climax in our industrial-urban civilization were preceded by many human groups that spread out over the world for many thousands of years. In this long period, members of a given community were life-long associates from birth to death. They shared the same folkways and mores, and gossip and ridicule were sufficient means of control for most infractions of traditional ways. For extreme intransigence, death or, more frequently, outcasting resolved the problem once and for all. Even in the pre-civilization period of human development, however, the evidence points toward an increasing complication of community forms and a specialization of control devices.

The contemporary mass society is one product of processes which in the last thousand years have seen (1) the consolidation of power in the hands of ruling, including bureaucratic, elites; (2) the displacement of folkways and mores by law; (3) the shift of responsibility for the maintenance of order from the community at large to special institutions such as the police and the courts; and (4) the decline of informal communication processes and the rise of mass communication industries.

The most fundamental of all control mechanisms in the primitive society was routine communication or gossip. Since everyone knew everyone else from birth to death, this was a powerful weapon against deviance of any form or kind. The most basic control mechanisms in the modern mass society (whether it be of the democratic or communist type) are the mass media. The essays in the present section explore various ways in which the mass media are employed for control ends.

PART IV

Social Control in Mass Society

The problem to which Mohan devotes himself concerns the different ways in which mass media technology is employed for control purposes in the Communist (totalitarian) and democratic (mass society) national blocs. In both instances, control is concentrated at the top, with the Communist bloc nations' preferred method being censorship and intimidation and the democratic mass societies preferring advertising technologies and persuasion. Martin's essay on public opinion indicates that in theory it serves as a sounding board for authority in democracies whose leaders have the people's mandate to act in their behalf. Noland's chapter on brainwashing demonstrates that propaganda is not necessarily either good or bad, for it can be used for either end; it makes use of many devices to achieve the vested interests of some groups. One of the most extreme manifestations of conversionary propaganda is found in brainwashing which employs techniques of coercive persuasion. Reul's summary treatment of the most important communications media (radio, television, and motion pictures) shows them to be mirrors of society and to have a potent educational influence. These three mass media disseminate information, provide entertainment, and offer education, and therefore can greatly affect the values of a society. O'Keefe's coverage of journalism and advertising shows that the printed media and advertising have always enjoyed a very close relationship. Belok's analysis of the problem of minorities and ethnicity deals with the discrepancies between American ideals and American practices. The tensions resulting from these discrepancies are reflected in the social order as more and more individuals become conscious of the frustrations inherent in their positions. Ethnicity has become a vehicle for advancing the group demands of America's more aggressive minorities. Conrad and Schneider conclude that medicine's jurisdiction over deviant behavior and its social control functions have increased in the past few decades because of new technological "discoveries" and more subtle measurement of human variation (e.g., genetics). This expansion is expected to continue.

J.S.R.

Raj P. Mohan

SCIENCE AND TECHNOLOGY*

In discussing the effects of science and technology on the mechanisms of social control, it is necessary to clarify the terms *science*, *technology*, and *social control*.

Science is used here to refer to demonstrable knowledge about the facts of nature, including human beings.[1] Science has become an increasingly popular word. Those who wish to buttress their ideological, political, and personal beliefs increasingly appeal to science as an authority. The growing discussion and use of science and technology have resulted more from spectacular technological accomplishments than from much understanding of the procedures and attitudes of scientists.[2]

Technology is an impact channel of science. Through technology (technical inventions such as tools to make human life easier and safer), science manifests itself concretely. In the realm of the abstract, science is manifested through the number of abstract concepts that form a body of knowledge for explaining the nature of the universe.

While it is true that intellectual curiosity is one of the most effective forces in the creation of science, the fact remains that the scientist's behavior is determined to a large extent by factors unrelated to the pursuit of science per se. One of these factors is the reward that intellectual curiosity can bring in the form of popular recognition. The slowness of the development of science in ancient times can be traced in large part to social indifference. Then, as now, scientists frequently had to make exaggerated claims, to appeal to mystery, in order to attract public attention. The satisfaction of intellectual curiosity, however, is often contaminated with those ideas that come from acquiring a sense of power and domination, not only over nature but also over fellow scientists and others. Conflicts over priority[3] and professional competition[4] have always been common to all levels of scientific population (not barring such heroic figures as Newton and Pasteur).

*I appreciate the critical reading by my colleagues Fran French, Chester Hartwig, and Arthur Wilke; and the research assistance of Martha Baker.

Science, Technology, Values, and Change

To question the ultimate intellectual and moral value of science is a very ancient attitude.[5] Socrates' skepticism as expressed in Plato's dialogues has its counterpart in the discussion about the bankruptcy of science that was widespread in the literary and philosophical circles at the beginning of the present century. Until recently, however, the attitude of the skeptics was not one of hostility but rather one of impatience and disappointment at the fact that, despite oft-repeated promise, science had not solved for man the riddle of his nature and destiny. Along with an admiration for and awe at the power of science, there exists among the lay public a curious mistrust of the scientist himself, as if he were something scarcely normal and human. This modern attitude toward the scientist is not far removed from that of the primitives toward the shaman or medicine man—an individual regarded as essential to the group, but one who is feared and often hated.

Typical of this attitude is *The Tragic Sense of Life* (1913) by Miguel de Unamuno and Ortega y Gasset's *The Revolt of the Masses* (1930). Both stress what they regard as the bankruptcy of science. They recognize the contributions made by science and technology to human safety and comfort, but they are little impressed by the intellectual process involved in the technology that has produced these conveniences. Much scientific thinking corresponds to a mechanical performance of a rather low order. Both accept Francis Bacon's claim that the scientific method is so mechanical and foolproof as to be readily and effectively handled by small minds.

Technology is not just a listing of inventions based on scientific developments. Historians and social scientists are placing technology in an enlarged perspective within the history of ideas, linking technological developments with massive social and cultural changes That science and technology are major variables in contemporary social change needs no scholarly documentation. The power of science, scientists, and technology in today's world is visible in all realms.[6]

Smelser[7] advances a theory of a seven-phase sequence of social changes in technological revolution. Changes in one institution (industry) may outmode those in another institution (family). When this happens, the outmoded institution in turn changes to bring the institutional system back to equilibrium. One type of such institutional change, which occurs in changing social systems, is structural differentiation in which roles change from generalized (as in the domestic industry system) to specialized (as in factory capitalism). In Smelser's presentation, structural differentiation is the familiar process wherein, in the institutions noted, functions are shifted from inside to outside the family. Changes of this type, in any institution or subsystem, occur in a seven-phase sequence: (1) dissatisfaction with the prevailing conditions, (2) symptoms of disturbance such as emotional outbursts (e.g., the Luddites) or utopian thinking, (3) covert handling of the disturbances through a mobilization of motivational resources...to realize the implications of the existing value system, (4) encouragement of new and sometimes impractical ideas for resolving the disturbance, (5) efforts to select and channel the more practical of the new ideas, (6) responsible implementation of the ideas that have proved feasible, and (7) routinization of the implemented ideas.

In Rostow's influential volume[8] and other studies, Rostow posits that "in their economic dimension" all societies fit into "one of five categories." He labels these (1) traditional society, (2) the preconditions for take-off, (3) the take-off, (4) the drive to maturity, and (5) the age of high mass consumption.

According to Rostow, when the fourth stage of economic growth, the drive to maturity, is reached, modern technology spreads to practically all segments of society and the economy achieves technical maturity. The society is then confronted by three inescapable choices: (1) it can move into the state of high-mass consumption, (2) it can move into becoming a welfare state, or (3) it can divert a major portion of its resources to the construction of a military machine through which it can reach out beyond its borders to exert control on the world stage. According to Rostow, it is possible for a nation to choose parts of all three. It can be observed here that with increasing technical and scientific maturity, the capabilities of nuclear, chemical, and bacteriological warfare magnify unless such powers can agree on some effective means to control the spread of their technology. Short of such controls, Rostow argues, the world's only hope of passing through this critical phase is for the nonaggressive nations to maintain such massive means of retaliation that it would be suicidal for any aggressor to embark on technologically sophisticated warfare.

Assuming that the world will pass through this phase, a growing number of nations will reach technological and scientific maturity, and the stage of high mass consumption. What then? Is this the final goal of man's endeavor?

The rise of modern science and technology has made it possible for one society after another to shift from a predominantly agricultural base to an economy dominated by industry, communication, trade, and services. Before this happens in any society, certain preconditions must be met. The most important of these preconditions is that a significant number of people must discard their traditional outlook on life and accept the revolutionary idea that man can by means of science and technology control his environment—that science and technology can solve all his riddles. This leads to the development of technocracy.[9]

Technocracy...

Technocracy is nothing more than the *authority* side of science. It is based in the belief that technology has answers to all the problems and that technocrats can put us back on the right track. In fact, from the beginnings of the Industrial Revolution, a scientific technocratic legitimation has been proclaimed for the society.

Science and technology have brought us two evident processes: destruction of the traditional social orders and formation of new ones. Science and technology have destroyed traditional forms of control systems that existed in any society and have replaced them with other forms of social controls. These new forms of control mechanisms operate at the international level, between nations, within societies or social systems, and their subsystems. The traditional forms of controls and value systems that existed in preindustrial societies and communities have vanished or are gradually vanishing. This has created the need for nontraditional forms of control mechanisms. Technology and science comprise a great furnace, a great melting pot in which social life is molded and remolded.

...and Questions of Morality

Scientists achieved the first atomic chain reaction on December 2, 1942. This knowledge was put to devastating use in Hiroshima and Nagasaki almost three years later, which raised the questions of morality and responsibility that persist to the present day. The first computer data bank[10] was put into operation during the 1950s, making storage and retrieval of information possible. This development raised questions such as information about what and for whom and to be used in what way? We suddenly realized that it could invade our privacy and be used to control our life-style. More recently, we have found experiments dealing with the chemical molecule called DNA in the headlines. Explorations are going on with the basic thread of life which raises questions as to how someone might tinker with this thread. For what purposes, involving what moral issues? And what about tomorrow, and the years and decades to come? What new technological advances and scientific breakthroughs will raise disturbing new questions and control our way of life?

Technology,[11] science,[12] and scientists all are going through a "crisis of confidence." Their methods, values, and goals are being seriously questioned. The use of science and technology in everyday life raises serious and disturbing questions. Who should make the critical decisions concerning how, where, and why science and technology should be used and controlled by whom? Are social and scientific goals compatible? Hamilton, for example, provides valuable data on the worldwide consequences of technological progress.[13] What are the moral responsibilities of the scientists? Are the benefits of our technological age worth the potential danger to our environment, our well-being, and the future of this planet? Should we allow science, scientists, and technology to endanger and control the lives of people?

One of the basic contemporary problems is the relation of advancing science and technology to broader human values. If this advance continues to a point where science and technology may serve man with maximum efficiency, paradoxically, must they not destroy their own worth to him by coming to dominate his culture and enslave his spirit? Indeed, is it possible for an individual to recognize what science can tell him of his origin and of the manner in which his body and mind function, yet retain a sense of his significance as a human being, acting responsibly in ways that possess genuine value and importance? Or with our growing scientific enlightenment, must we credit such terms as *eternal values* and the *dignity of man* to the wishful thinking of past ages in which men did not know the plain facts about themselves?

Such questions have been debated frequently. The spokesmen in the field of human relations recognize the necessity of a clearer understanding of human values[14] and a truer perspective in which science and technology will be seen in their rightful roles as implements, not masters, of these values, if human welfare and civilizations are to be maintained.[15]

Our contemporary industrial civilization is characterized by a new scale of values: utility is the end to be pursued; violence has given way to toleration; the virtue of charity has gained a new emphasis; the eighteenth-century concept of civilization has taken shape. According to Nef, "The methods of science, technology and economics provide no key to divinity. Industrial man is not a god: we must find man again. That is the only way we can hope to lead him to God."[16]

Technological change has been much praised and often condemned.[17] A few claim that technological advance is a sufficient condition for the intellectual and spiritual development of the human race; and others claim that this is the necessary condition for such a development. Still others (Hutchins, Juenger, Gandhi) would hold that technological development is antagonistic to spiritual development.[18] Every year our contemporary civilization seems to be based more firmly upon a scientific foundation than the year before. From the mysteries of applied science (that oil furnace whose emotional behavior remains quite inexplicable) to the miracles of pure research that change our conceptions of the universe and threaten to demolish our own small corner of it, science baffles most nonscientists—the largest block of the human population.

Ross[19] once discussed enlightenment as a mechanism of social regulation. There are, of course, various types of enlightenments, but in our contemporary world we have come to accept science and technology as the harbingers of mental illumination. Many have come to accept science as an authority. The result has been that gradually our behavior has been shaped to align with scientific thought. For example, in the field of public health new knowledge and legislation have, to some degree, enforced a certain conformity on our part. Old customs and traditions concerning marriage and family have been drastically reduced or changed because of a developing scientific ideology concerning marriage and family. Even the customs concerning death have been taken over by trained professionals—the caretakers of the dead.

It cannot be denied that much of the modern world has been molded and remolded by science and technology. However, it is equally important to mention that modern science and technology have been shaped by society's placement of certain requirements and constraints on science. It would be fallacious to consider science as an external agent shaping and molding the type of civilization as is implied in the title of Bertrand Russell's *The Impact of Science on Society*.[20] Even Karl Mannheim in his famous essay on the sociology of knowledge, *Ideology and Utopia*,[21] fails to consider that science as an aspect of knowledge could be socially determined.

Culture and Technology—Their Reciprocal Relationship

At this point, it is necessary to illustrate how psychological and cultural factors affect science and technology. Interestingly, the Greeks and other ancients, especially the scientists and other inventors of Hellenistic Alexandria, possessed much mechanical genius, but they were more interested in probing material marvels and "miracles" than in adopting invention to production and transportation. This has often been attributed to the cheapness of slave labor. A more important factor was the Greek outlook on life, which gave little thought to using inventive powers to practical ends.[22]

Technology, in its ideological justification, became interrelated with the nineteenth-century doctrine of progress and perfectibility. It is true that science and technology have resulted in better material conditions for human living throughout the world, but the loosening of the bond of the primary group has been a serious disruption in social life. With the decline of the primary group, mechanisms of control once operating at the personal level have been taken over by bureaucratized, impersonal agencies of control. The social scientists of today have taken the position of earlier critics such as John Ruskin, William Morris, H. G. Wells, and George Bernard Shaw. Especially featured in modern sociological writings has been a characterization of "uselessness" as imposed on much of the work done in the factories, the result of a long historical process of industrialization and mechanization. "If it were desired to reduce a man to nothing," wrote Fyodor Dostoyevsky in the *House of the Dead*, ". . . it would be necessary only to give his work a character of uselessness."

Probably the oldest, most effective means of social control is physical violence, or the threat of physical violence. To keep a member of a society in line, to maintain social order, mechanisms of ultimate violence are there, though sometimes hidden from view.[23]

In most societies, the efficiency of this one-on-one meting out of violence has been far supassed by that of symbolic control systems which establish and maintain order. (The terms *society* and *order* are used here in their general connotative sense.) The order is the "world view," as it were, of "how things are done and are not done" and, consequently, of "how things should be done." It is, in effect, "how things are," or the accepted reality for that society.

Physical violence as a means of social control is almost passé. This can be seen in the nature of racial disturbances in the United States: so-called outbreaks of violence are actually in support of the system. People are not trying to get out; they want to get in more fully. It is only the form that these efforts take that is expected. "How things are," that all people should be able to participate in the benefits of this society, is still the generally accepted ideal.

The symbolic control system, then, encompasses and enforces the position that one finds himself in in society, at any given point in time. Religious beliefs, mores, folkways, laws, customs, habits, statutes, are all man-formed and man-forming. An in this control system are the elements for social change. Society as a dynamic process involves change. Supports are loosened; "how things are done" varies; other supports are adopted, keeping the system, or "how things are," moving.

As "how things are done" changes, man may stare and balk, but he usually comes along even if he is dragged, kicking and screaming all the way. He eventually incorporates these changes in "how things should be done" into his world view or *weltanschauung*.[24] Generally, one does not, not accept the marvels of modern science; one does not, not drive a car; one does not, not want a better vacuum cleaner. Shocking as perhaps the contradictions between myth, superstition, and science and technology once were to man and his *Weltanschauung*, science and the resultant technology have now lost much of their shock value.

Man, being a creature with an inquiring mind, always seeks some sort of explanation...in the world about him. Myth and science give him the answer. This same kind of mind, never content with leaving things as it finds them, leads man to tinker with the things he sees about him and to make other things of them. Thus, through the inventive process, tools and eventually technology develop. Finally, man is capable of transmitting both idea and tool to his posterity. We therefore live and move in...an environment of tested ideas on the one hand and of invented devices on the other.[25]

Science has come to mean authority. Verifiable cause and effect relationships are taken for granted in the scheme of things. It is no problem now for the scientific approach to hold sway over myth and the folly of superstition in our unscientific past. But whereas science and technology were once a means to an end in society, they are now both means and ends for society. It is "the way things are." This change is reflected in vocabulary. Progress and modernization, to name two concepts, have been hypostatized. One can "see" progress in a new plant coming to town; one can point to a modern building. And, as always, one can look through the world view and say "good" or "bad." Value judgments are routine, necessary, and uncomplicated. To be progressive is good; to be backward is bad. But in this modern instance, progress not only entails "the way things are done," but it also embodies the world view, "the way things are."

Herbert Marcuse in *One-Dimensional Man* elucidates quite clearly how the ideology surrounding the industrial means of production has become reality for modern man:

The rights and liberties which were such vital factors in the origins and earlier stages of industrial society yield to a higher stage in this society: they are losing their traditional rationale and content. Freedom of thought, speech, and conscience were—just as free enterprise, which they served to promote and protect—essentially *critical* ideas, designed to replace an obsolescent, material and intellectual culture by a more productive and rational one. Once institutionalized, these rights and liberties shared the fate of the society of which they had become an integral part. The achievement cancels the premises.[26]

Marcuse goes on to posit that independence of thought, autonomy, and the right to political opposition "are being deprived of their basic critical function in a society which seems increasingly capable of satisfying the needs of the individual through the way in which it is organized."[27] This organization has become a totalitarian reality. It has been effected through the operationalizing of reason—both method and behavior in the rational and efficient organization of the means of production to satisfy these individual needs. "For 'totalitarian' is not only a terroristic political coordination of society, but also a non-terroristic economic-technical coordination which operates through the manipulation of needs by vested interests."[28] Scientific progress has become the total administration of the populace to produce satisfaction of these needs. And progress, in the affluent society, has transformed social needs into individual needs.[29]

Thus, as individuals accept the laws of the society they come into, and whereas ideology has *become* reality, what emerges is a pattern of "one-dimensional thought and behavior." Any appeal to reason as it is now constructed (effectiveness of production and consumption) emasculates the critical power of reason. The "impact of progress turns reason into submission to the facts of life."[30] It is the same as saying that we are on the road to progress. How are we getting there? By progressing.

In modern industrial society, social control, taken in its broadest form as composite world view, is effecting itself. Participation in fulfillment of needs is both reasonable and rational. It seems that only the degree of participation is the proverbial sore spot. Whether the symbols of social control—the laws, customs, habits, statutes, and religious bent of the nations—have a democratic or communistic flavor, reflects only the eccentricities of this participation.

Notes

1. For a critical treatment of the concept of science, see, for example, Carlo L. Lastrucci, *The Scientific Approach. Basic Principles of Scientific Method* (Cambridge, Mass.: Schenkman Publishing Co., 1963 [1967]), especially Ch. 1; Abraham Kaplan, *The Conduct of Inquiry* (San Francisco: Chandler Publishing Co., 1964); Joseph S. Roucek, "Scientific Goals and Methods Versus Ideological Goals and Methods," *Wisconsin Sociologist* 2, no. 2, (Fall 1963): 1-6; Felix Marti-Ibanez, M.D., "The Concept of Science and the Sciences," *MD* 13, no. 2 (February 1969); B. Barber and W. Hirsch, eds., *The Sociology of Science* (New York: Free Press of Glencoe, 1962); Robert K, Merton, *The Sociology of Science: Theoretical and Empirical Investigations*, edited by Norman Storer (Chicago: University of Chicago Press, 1973).

2. For an excellent study dealing with the social structure of the scientific community and how that system operates to determine patterns of scientific behavior, see Jonathan R. Cole and Stephen Cole, *Social Stratification in Science* (Chicago: University of Chicago Press, 1973). See also J. D. Bernal, *The Social Functions of Science* (London: Routledge and Kegan Paul, 1939); D. J. de Solla Price, *Little Science, Big Science* (New York: Columbia University Press, 1963).

3. Cf. Robert K. Merton, "Priorities in Scientific Discovery: A Chapter in Sociology of Science," *American Sociological Review* 22, no. 6 (1957): 635-659. Reprinted in Merton, *Sociology of Science*. See also Robert K. Merton and R. Lewis, "The Competitive Pressure (1): The Race for Priority," *The Impact of Science on Sociology* 21, no. 2 (1971):151-161.

4. Jerry Gaston's work highlights an interesting dilemma in modern science. Gaston explores how scientists at the frontiers of knowledge often find themselves in direct competition with other scientists; the decision then arises whether to work cooperatively or to promote one's career by working in secret and maximizing the chance for recognition of an original discovery. See Jerry Gaston, *Originality and Competition in Science* (Chicago: University of Chicago Press, 1973).

5. C. Singer, *A Short History of Scientific Ideas to Nineteen Hundred* (Oxford: Oxford University Press, 1959); René Dubos, *The Drums of Reason: Science and Utopias* (New York: Columbia University Press, 1961).

6. John Diebold, *Man and the Computer: Technology as an Agent of Social Change* (New York: Praeger Publishers, 1969); Richard C. Dorf, *Technology, Society, and Man* (San Francisco: Boyd and Fraser Publishing Co., 1974); Emmanuel G. Mesthene, *Technological Change: Its Impact on Man and Society* (Cambridge, Mass.: Harvard

University Press, 1970); Lewis Mumford, *The Myth of the Machine: The Pentagon of Power* (New York: Harcourt Brace Jovanovich, 1970); Irene Taviss and William Gerber, *Technology and the Individual* (Cambridge, Mass.: Harvard University Program on Technology and Society, 1970).

7. Neil J. Smelser, *Social Change in the Industrial Revolution: An Application of Theory to the British Cotton Industry, 1770-1840* (Chicago: University of Chicago Press, 1959).

8. W. W. Rostow, *Stages of Economic Growth: A Non-Communist Manifesto* (New York: Cambridge University Press, 1960).

9. Among excellent surveys of technocracy, see W.H.G. Armytage, *The Rise of Technocrats: A Social History* (London: Routledge and Kegan Paul, 1965); Graham A. Laing, *Towards Technocracy* (Los Angeles, Calif.: Angelus Press, 1933); Harold Loeb, *Life in a Technocracy: What It Might Be Like* (New York: Viking Press, 1933); Theodore Geiger, *The Fortunes of the West; the Future of the Atlantic Nations* (Bloomington, Ind.: Indiana University Press, 1973).

10. For various implications of the computer technology and its impact on society, see H. Sackman, *Man-Computer Problem Solving* (Princeton, N.J.: Auerbach Publishers, 1970); H. Sackman and H. Borko, eds., *Computers and the Problems of Society* (Montvale, N.J.: AFIPS Press, 1972); John Platt, "What We Must Do," *Science* 166 (November 28, 1969):1115-1121.

11. For some critical literature on the role of technology and its social implications, see Charles A. Trall and Jerold M. Starr, eds., *Technology, Power and Social Change* (Carbondale, Ill.: Southern Illinois University Press, 1974); Victor C. Ferkiss, *The Future of Technological Civilization* (New York: G. Braziller, 1974); Alvis V. Adair, *Human Experimentation: An Ancient Notion in a Modern Technology* (Washington, D.C.: Institute for Urban Affairs and Research, Howard University, 1974); David Hamilton, *Technology, Man and the Environment* (New York: Charles Scribner's Sons, 1973) (this extensive review of the developments in major areas of technology provides valuable concepts and data on worldwide consequences of technological progress); Ernest von Khuon, *The Invisible Made Visible; The Expansion of Man's Vision of the Future Through Technology*, translated from the German by Paula Arne (Greenwich, Conn.: New York Graphic Society, 1973); E. J. Piel and J. G. Truxal, *Technology—Handle with Care*, (New York: McGraw-Hill, 1975); David M. Freeman, *Technology and Society: Issues in Assessment, Conflict and Choice* (Chicago: Rand McNally, 1974); Roberto Vacca, *The Coming Dark Age*, translated by J. S. Whale (Garden City, N.Y.: Anchor Books, 1974); Arnold Pacey, *The Maze of Ingenuity; Ideas and Idealism in the Development of Technology* (New York: Holme and Meier, 1975); Melvin Kranzberg and William H. Davenport, eds., *Technology and Culture: An Anthology* (New York: New American Library, 1975); Mihajlo Mesarovic and Edward Pestel, *Mankind at the Turning Point: The Second Report of the Club of Rome* (New York: E. P. Dutton, 1974); Thomas Hughes, ed., *Changing Attitudes Toward American Technology* (New York: Harper and Row, 1975); Harry G. Johnson, *Technology and Economic Interdependence* (New York: St. Martin's Press, 1976); Fred A. Olsen, ed., *Technology: A Regime of Benevolence and Destruction* (New York: MSS Information Corp., 1973); Edward R. Lawless,

Technology and Social Shock (New Brunswick, N.J.: Rutgers University Press, 1976); David Elliot and Ruth Elliot, *The Control of Technology* (London: Wykeham Publications, 1976); Oswald Spengler, *Man and Technics: A Contribution to Philosophy of Life* (Reprint ed.—Westport, Conn.: Greenwood Press, 1976; original ed.—New York: Alfred A. Knopf, 1932).

12. For a critical assessment of the impact of science and technology in the cultural and social realms, see Henry J. Steffens and H. N. Muller, eds., *Science, Technology and Culture* (New York: AMS Press, 1974); John T. Hardy, *Science, Technology and Environment* (Philadelphia: W. B. Saunders, 1975); For studies in the structure of thinking in technological sciences, see V. G. Afanasyev, *The Scientific and Technological Revolution—Its Impact on Management and Education* (Moscow: Progress Publishers, 1975); William R. Clark, *The Scientific Breakthrough: The Impact of Modern Invention* (New York: Putnam, 1974); Vannevar Bush, *Endless Horizons* (New York: Arno Press, 1975); Gabor Strasser and Eugene M. Simons, eds., *Science and Technology Policies, Yesterday, Today, and Tomorrow* (Cambridge, Mass.: Ballinger Publishing Co., 1974); George Lundberg, *Can Science Save Us?* (New York: Longmans, Green, 1961).

13. Hamilton, *Technology, Man and the Environment.*

14. For an excellent treatment of the problem, see Don Martindale, *Sociological Theory and the Problem of Values* (Columbus, Ohio: Charles E. Merrill, 1975).

15. R. N. Anshen, ed., *Science and Man: Twenty-Four Original Essays* (New York: Harcourt, Brace, 1942).

16. John V. Nef, *Cultural Foundations of Industrial Civilization* (New York: Cambridge University Press, 1958), p. 155.

17. See, for example, Alvin Toffler, *Future Shock* (New York: Random House, 1970).

18. Yale Brozen, "The Value of Technological Change," *Ethics* 62 (July 1952):249-265.

19. E. A. Ross, *Social Control: A Survey of the Foundations of Order* (New York: Macmillan Co., 1901).

20. London: Allen and Unwin, 1968.

21. London: Routledge and Kegan Paul, 1936.

22. G. D. H. Cole, "Industrialization," *Encyclopedia of the Social Sciences* (New York: Macmillan Co., 1930), Vol. 8, p. 19.

23. Peter Berger, *Invitation to Sociology* (Garden City, N.Y.: Doubleday and Co., 1963).

24. Raj P. Mohan and Glenn C. McCann, "A Note on the Individual and Social Situations: The Development of a Framework for Sociological Analysis," *Sociological Analysis and Theory* 6, no. 1 (February 1976).

25. Paul H. Landis, *Social Control* (New York: J. B. Lippincott Co., 1939), p. 309.

26. Herbert Marcuse, *One-Dimensional Man* (Boston: Beacon Press, 1964), p. 1.

27. Ibid., p. 2.

28. Ibid., pp. 3-7.

29. Ibid., p. 8.

30. Ibid., pp. 16-17.

L. John Martin

PUBLIC OPINION

To a person who feels powerless in the face of the awesome authority of government or the overwhelming potency of a major corporation, it cannot be very reassuring to be told that, ultimately, all power emanates from the people. There is no power other than human power, and the mandate to act derives from the society within which the action occurs. Claiming the right to rule by the "grace of God" is sheer bluff, as is the claim to a mandate from a "silent majority."

That many fall for such a bluff or struggle against it helplessly is not too surprising, however. An individual is as potent as the small particles in an iron bar. When a powerful magnet is passed over the bar, the particles align themselves in the same polar direction, turning the bar into a magnet. Then, and only then, does the bar acquire power. It is the aligning influence of the magnet that induces the power in the bar, although each particle in the bar holds neither more nor less magnetism after the passage than before. Similarly, it is the aligning influence of a leader, or of some instrument of leadership, that focuses public opinion so that it becomes a force in society.

As one may have gathered, governments have authority that stems from the underlying power of the people. This power, however, must be generated by the centripetal influence of a leader or some other instrumentality such as the mass media. It is this concentration of will—this consensus—that today is often referred to as public opinion and that forms the focus of the present article. It is both the instrument and the target of social control.

Concept of the Public

To understand public opinion, one must begin with a definition of "public." The concept of public is closely tied to public opinion. In fact, a public does not really exist conceptually without some common attitudes, beliefs, values, or opinions—these terms are closely interrelated—to cement individuals into a group. Political philosophers and sociologists have given their attention to the idea and the importance of publics since Plato, for whom the public was an undifferentiated mass of citizens in which there resided power. Plato was somewhat contradictory about the role and the power of the public. In Book VII of *The Republic* he said that there is an element of truth in the principle that the multitude should be supreme; but he also believed that rulers are qualified because of their superior knowledge and that it would therefore be superfluous for them to consult puplic opinion.

Aristotle disagreed about the relative wisdom of a ruler and his people. The collective wisdom of a people is superior even to that of the wisest lawgiver, he taught, since one person's knowledge supplements that of another. He interjected a new thought, however. While he retained the concept of an amorphous will, his analysis led him to conclude that there was more than one public, whose separate cohesions were the result of certain common objectives and, by implication, values. Today, we would call that opinion. In Book VI of his *Politics*, Aristotle speaks of "two classes out of which a state is composed—the poor and the rich." He sees a dichotomy between numerical and proportionate equality. True democratic justice, he says, requires that all should count equally, "for equality implies that the poor should have no more share in the govenment than the rich, and . . . that all should rule equally according to their numbers."[1]

Until the seventeenth century, little further progress was made in the analysis of publics. For the Roman and the medieval scholar and philosopher, the people manifested their common will through the law and through their leaders. Marsilio of Padua, in the thirteenth century, agreed with the prevailing sentiment that the community is absolutely omnipotent— *vox populi, vox dei*, as the Romans put it. Like Aristotle, however, he saw society as being composed of a number of classes or parts, such as soldiers, officials, and priests, and both their number and quality must be taken into account, he said.[2]

In the seventeenth century, John Locke added a new dimension to the study of publics. In "An Essay Concerning the True Original, Extent and End of Civil Government," he wrote that

when any number of men have, by the consent of every individual, made a community, they have thereby made that community one body, with a power to act as one body, which is only by the will and determination of the majority. For . . . it is necessary the body should move that way whither the greater force carries it, which is the consent of the majority.[3]

Three-quarters of a century later, Jean Jacques Rousseau was to distinguish in *The Social Contract* between "the will of all and the general will. The latter is concerned only with the common interest, the former with interests that are partial, being itself but the sum of individual wills."[4] By the "general will," Rousseau understood the arithmetic sum of wills—i.e., the sum of the positive and negative wishes of the people with sign taken into account. This net sum of wills or opinion amounts to the same thing as the majority opinion of Locke, except that Rousseau with his neat French logic saw individual wills of the minority canceling out a similar number of wills among the majority, leaving an unopposed set of wills that he called the general will.

Rousseau also wrestled with the problem of subgroups within the public. Unlike Aristotle, however, he did not let himself get caught in the dilemma of numerical versus proportionate equality. His arguments are not unlike those of the modern statistician discussing homogeneity within a sampling cluster. He says,

when intriguing groups and partial associations are formed to the disadvantage of the whole, then the will of each of such groups is general only in respect of its own members, but partial in respect of the State. *When such a situation arises, it may be said that there are no longer as many votes as men, but only as many votes as there are groups.*[5]

As the republican and democratic ideas of the late seventeenth and early eighteenth centuries began to come to fruition in the latter part of the eighteenth century, the question of quality versus quantity, first raised by Aristotle, began to acquire new significance. The controversy manifested itself in two forms. There were those, like Edmund Burke, who thought of the public as delegating its powers to its elected leaders, who, being better informed than their constituents, were guided solely by their intellect and conscience. This argument was rejected by others. Thomas Jefferson, for example, was more concerned about responsive government that served the majority will than about a stable central government. "The generalizing and concentrating all cares and powers into one body... has destroyed the liberty and the rights of men," he wrote.[6] Another form of the controversy was between those who believed that opinion within the public ought to be weighted according to its quality and those who believed in simple majority rule. Thus, John Adams wrote that "the people of all nations are naturally divided into two sorts, the gentlemen and the simple men." And, "Every democracy...has an aristocracy in it as distinct as that of Rome, France, England."[7] On the other hand, Thomas Paine championed the sovereign will of the common man as expressed through a simple majority.

The Industrial Revolution focused attention on a new phenomenon. The masses concentrated in urban centers, invested with at least philosophical sovereignty, became the objects of study by the new sociologists. Auguste Comte, the father of sociology, saw the individual as the product of his environment with values similar to the publics (or institutions) to which he belongs. These publics, according to the nineteenth-century sociologists and social psychologists influenced by Comte, had metaphysical qualities that made them different from the sum total of the individuals they comprised. French writer Gustave Le Bon singled out the crowd for special study, thus distinguishing between the metaphysical and the physical public.

By the turn of the twentieth century, thoughtful writers like James Bryce had decided that it was futile to try to describe, delimit, or categorize publics in terms of individuals. More important were the opinions they held in common. At least by implication, Lord Bryce suggested that a public is made up of all those who are giving their attention to public questions. And in this, he believed, there is little difference between the commercial or professional classes and the "humbler classes," the educated and the uneducated. Similarly, American political scientist A. Lawrence Lowell, writing in 1913, approached the problem of what constitutes a public not by counting heads but by focusing on the cement that bound them together into a single unit. Publics that neither have a common perception of a problem nor are willing to submit to a majority will might as well belong to different commonwealths, he wrote. Using a different approach, Harold D. Lasswell in 1935 showed that publics could be identified in terms of the symbols that united them. "We identify with others (a process which is not necessarily accompanied by acute self-awareness) by perceiving that they are from the same college, the same town, the same country; that they admire the same politicians."[8]

Thus, we finally arrive at a modern definition of public which, according to Herbert Blumer, refers to a group of people "(a) who are confronted by an issue, (b) who are divided in their ideas as to how to meet the issue, and (c) who engage in discussion over the issue."[9] W. Phillips Davison adds that while individuals in a public do not know one another, they "have formed beliefs concerning each other's attitudes on a particular subject and modify their behavior in accordance with these beliefs."[10] In the twentieth century, therefore, attention turned from the public to opinions. The question changed from "what opinions do publics spawn?" to "what publics swarm to or are united by particular opinons or symbols?"

Concept of Opinion

Having determined that opinion is what creates a public, one might well ask, "what, then, is an opinion?" Psychologists and sociologists have a hard time defining it. Some avoid the issue by terming it the "expression of an attitude in words."[11] But that makes it necessary to define an attitude.

The most often quoted definition of "attitude" is that of Gordon Allport, who termed it a "mental or neural state of readiness, organized through experience, exerting a directive or dynamic influence upon the individual's response to all objects and situations to which it is related."[12] Most definitions of attitude include some or all of the following attributes: (1) an attitude has a focus or object; (2) it includes an evaluative dimension; (3) it is learned rather than innate; (4) it is relatively enduring; and (5) it influences behavior in a consistent manner. Behavioral psychologists tend to look upon attitude more as a tendency to act in a consistent way toward particular objects or in given situations. In other words, it is a probability of action. Gestalt psychologists consider it to be a mental state or orientation toward objects and situations.

No one has seen an attitude. It is inferred from people's behavior, just as Isaac Newton, sitting under an apple tree, inferred the existence of gravity from the consistency with which apples dropped to the ground. The trouble is that occasionally, when we take two different behavioral measures of attitude, they turn out to be inconsistent. Thus, asking a person how he feels about tourists might elicit one response—known as an opinion, i.e., verbal behavior. From this, one can infer the person's "attitude" toward tourists. A second measure might be his actual behavior toward tourists. The two forms of behavior sometimes are inconsistent.

In an often quoted study of the early 1930s, Richard LaPiere found just such a discrepancy. Traveling all over the United States with a Chinese couple, he stopped at many restaurants and hotels. They were refused service only once. Later, he wrote to all these establishments and asked whether they would accept guests of the Chinese race. Some 93 percent of the restaurants and 92 percent of the hotels said they would not accommodate Chinese people.[13] Clearly, the verbal behavior and the actions of these caterers were at variance. Considering this and similar studies, Milton Rokeach offered an explanation for the discrepancy by proposing that expressed opinion or behavior change is the function of at least two attitudes: an attitude toward the object and an attitude toward the situation. Changes in behavior could result from changes in either of these two attitudes, he suggested, or even because of an interaction between the two.[14]

Martin Fishbein gives yet another explanation for the inconsistency with which attitudes and behavior are related. He states that "behavior toward a given object is a function of many variables, of which attitude toward the object is only one."[15]

If one considers an attitude as being an underlying force that impels one to act in a given way, then regardless of what one calls the "many variables" referred to by Fishbein, they all have attitudinal or directional force. Such attitudinal forces may be acquired through conditioning or cognitively— e.g., through being told what is right or wrong. When one is faced with a situation that requires action— whether verbal or nonverbal—a number of attitudinal forces come into play. These forces have both direction and intensity and may be thought of as vectors, which are mathematical concepts often represented by straight lines that are drawn in the proper direction and of the proper length. Vectors are additive, resulting in a single vector having both direction and length representing the combined force of the other vectors. Whenever one is faced with a situation that requires action, *all* relevant accumulated attitudes come into play. They exert a directional force that may favor one direction or the other, very strongly or weakly. But each of the relevant attitudes also has a relative importance, some being highly salient to the contemplated action while others are only of marginal, and therefore insignificant, intensity. The less important attitudes exert some, but proportionately less, force on the behavioral outcome.

Formation of Public Opinion

Having examined the complexity of the motivating factors behind an individual's opinions, one might well ask how one can even conceptualize public opinion, to say nothing of investigating its role as an instrument or a target of social control. This is where it is useful to consider once again what happens when an iron bar is stroked by a magnet. We have no idea what the various forces are that incline so many of the particles in the same direction. The outcome, however, is obvious and measurable. Similarly, we cannot really tell—or take into account—all the considerations that cause large numbers of people to adopt a common view of an issue. Nevertheless, public opinion is measurable and "can be mobilized on some particular issue and directed toward some kind of decision."[16]

For public opinion to exist on a particular issue one must have a public. As stated above, a public is a group of people who are confronted by and aware of an issue, and discuss and come to differing conclusions about it. If they did not come to differing conclusions, the issue would not be controversial. It would then not be an issue but a fact, and a fact is anything that is believed to be true by most people within a culture. Facts change. Until Copernicus, it was a fact that the heavenly bodies revolved around the earth.

If, however, people come to differing conclusions, public opinion cannot be unanimous. Public opinion is not a consensus but a concern. "Mobilizing public opinion" is merely a figure of speech which refers to the focusing of attention on an issue. The power of public opinion may be great or small, and it is always ideational rather than actual. It is nothing like an army that can be lined up with its guns. It may not even exist. President Richard Nixon conjured up a "silent majority" to support his actions.

Public opinion can be powerful if a large segment of the population is on one side of an issue because of the power such consensus lends to the authority or the government or organization it supports. Basically, however, it is an average opinion.[17] Thinking of public opinion as an average enables us to quantify it and to judge its power. It also makes possible comparisons of the power that supports various acts of government.

Measuring Public Opinion

Quantification of public opinion means measurement. "Straw votes" were conducted by newspapers in the United States as far back as 1824 to forecast the outcome of elections. These were not scientific polls but samples of opportunity to satisfy the curiosity of newspaper readers. Systematic methods of social data collection were developed in England, France, and Sweden in the midnineteenth century, and were used to study problems of the urban poor and of labor. But it was not until the 1930s that George Gallup applied scientific sampling to the study of public opinion. Since 1936, public opinion surveys have been done in the United States and, later, in other countries, on a continuing basis. The earliest opinion polls were taken to predict the outcome of national elections, but by the 1940s, surveys were being done to measure public opinion on all kinds of topics.

The rationale of an opinion survey is that opinions are distributed among the population in the same way that any other characteristics, such as sex or age, and that a randomly drawn sample should contain these characteristics or opinions in the same proportion as they exist in the population as a whole. An analogy would be the testing of a sack of grain for filth and other foreign bodies. A handful of grain would tell us pretty accurately what the proportion of foreign bodies is to good seed. One would not have to go through the entire sack. Of course, the grain would have to be well mixed, or else one would have to sample parts from all over the sack.

The latter is the procedure used in public opinion surveys. Samples are taken randomly from all over the population that is being studied, and the methods of sampling have been so highly refined that the distributions of population characteristics such as opinions can be measured to within less than one percent point of accuracy. While this kind of accuracy may require a sample as large as 10,000[18] Gallup and other national pollsters can, through scientific weighting, achieve fairly high accuracy with samples of 1,600.

Several questions have been raised regarding public opinion surveys, especially in connection with political election. One is the problem of the impact of the survey itself, and the publication of the findings, on the population. Is the press artificially creating public opinion by focusing public attention on an issue that would not otherwise have come to the attention of the public? As we said earlier, public opinion exists only when people are confronted by, aware of, and discussing an issue. What if the issue had not arisen before it was brought to the attention of a survey respondent? Unfortunately, people will give their "opinions" whether they have them or not on any issue that is brought to their attention.[19] Public opinion, as opposed to the individual opinions of the respondents questioned, does not in such cases emerge until after the results are published and people begin to think about and discuss the topic. The answer, therefore, is yes, the press is artificially creating public opinion. But this is no more artificial or unusual than the public opinion the press is creating all the time by focusing public attention on any topic it discusses.

Another question that has bothered many people is whether public opinion polls create a "bandwagon" effect by informing the public who the frontrunner is in an election. In other words, are people likely to change their vote in order to be on the winning side? Gallup and others have pointed out that it is just as likely that the polls create an "underdog" effect, that is, encourage people to switch to the "loser" out of pity or sympathy, or that it will make people who support the winner apathetic, since their candidate is winning. A study done during the 1968 presidential election to measure the influence on voters in California of election night television reports on the progress of the race on the East Coast supports Gallup. There was no measurable effect on either voter turnout or candidate choice.[20]

Public opinion surveys do, however, play an important role at least in the American political system. Without them, governments would receive much slower feedback from the public on their overt activities. Politicians have been known to take action or to refrain from taking action almost solely as a result of opinion poll showings. Geoge Romney (in 1968) and Hubert Humphrey (in 1976) decided against pursuing presidential aspirations because the polls indicated the race would be futile. Under pressure from public opinion as evidenced by poll results, President Ford changed his tactics in regard to Panama and detente, and Congressman Wayne Hayes was clearly driven to resignation from the chairmanship of his committee and later from Congress.

At the same time, there is no doubt that the mass media have been able to exploit public opinion surveys by publicizing them and thus focusing popular attention on issues and creating public opinion, if it did not already exist. On the other hand, there is no satisfactory evidence that the press can manipulate public opinion by influencing the direction it takes. The press can pick the issues but not the stand the public will take on them.

Influencing Public Opinion

At the beginning of this article, we implied that public opinion is powerful because power resides in the people if and when they are mobilized in a unified direction by some influence, such as an opinion leader or the mass media. We are now saying that the press cannot change attitudes—at least not in the short run. The press can only focus the attention of its readers on an issue. But in so doing, the press creates a public and, therefore, public opinion. The press does not determine how the public will react on the issue; the underlying or latent attitudes of each individual determine that.

At times, it may seem that the mass media not only bring up an issue but also dictate the direction of public opinion. This apparent influence can easily be explained. The editors and editorial writers, producers, and announcers who present the issue to the public are at the same time a part of that public and quite frequently, their views coincide with those of the majority of the public. Under such circumstances, they not only mobilize public opinion but agree with it—that is, their opinions coincide with the prevailing or majority opinion. Hence, the notion that they appear to influence public opinion. It is easy to be guilty of a *post hoc, propter hoc* fallacy, and one must be careful. "The so-called power of the editorialist is . . . a borrowed power. The reader may lend it during his perusal of one paragraph and withdraw it as he reads the next, or he may withhold it altogether," says *The New Yorker* in "The Talk of the Town."[21]

There is research evidence to support this idea. Numerous studies on the agenda-setting function of the press—the concept that the mass media tell the public what to think about—confirm that the press has little persuasive impact.[22] These studies also show, however, that in addition to alerting people to an event, the press suggests the relative importance of that event by the amount of coverage given to it.[23]

Now if we consider, once again, how an opinion (that is, verbal behavior) is formed, we can see that the mass media are not altogether innocent of influencing public opinion. Their influence, however, lies in rallying or creating public opinion rather than in determining its tenor or slant. We pointed out that behavior is determined by two things: numerous relevant attitudes that more or less favor the behavior, and the relative importance of each attitude in coming to a decision. As we have said, the press has little effect on the former, but it plays a crucial role in determining the latter. Obviously, the issues the press is playing up will incline the public in *both* directions; they would not otherwise be issues. The press may also play up "facts" that are nondebatable axioms within the culture. With the help of opinion polls and other methods of divination, the mass media can, if they seek to do so, focus on those issues and beliefs of the public that will maximize the chances of persuasion. But it must not be forgotten that the press can deal only with existing inclinations; it must work with what is there.

That public opinion is the power behind the authority of government is incontrovertible, but it is a power that needs much leading. The power is more evident in reaction than in action. It is more likely to tell the government what not to do than what to do. In a column analyzing President Carter's telephone chats with ordinary citizens, Joseph Kraft pointed out that "as a policy guide the session was useless." People have neither the ideas nor the know-how to run the country. "Just as the media can only be an element in opinion, so opinion can only be an element in policy."[24] The mass media can focus existing sentiment on an issue, and the resulting public opinion serves as a sounding board for those in authority who have the people's mandate to act in their behalf.

Notes

1. *Aristotle's Politics*, translated by Benjamin Jowett (New York: Modern Library, 1943), p. 262. Although Aristotle gives examples that suggest he believes in individual rather than group equality, he does express concern about the potential tyranny of the more numerous poor over the rich.

2. George H. Sabine, *A History of Political Theory* (New York: Henry Holt and Co., 1937), p. 297.

3. *Social Contract: Essays by Locke, Hume, and Rousseau* (New York: Oxford University Press, 1948), p. 57.

4. Ibid., p. 193.

5. Ibid., p. 194 (italics added).

6. Thomas Jefferson, *Writings*, edited by H. A. Washington (Washington, D.C., : U.S. Congress, 1853-1854).

7. John Adams, *Works: With a Life of the Author*, edited by C. F. Adams (Boston: Little, Brown, 1850-1856), Vol. 6, p. 516.

8. Harold D. Lasswell, "Nations and Classes: The Symbols of Identification," in Bernard Berelson and Morris Janowitz, eds., *Reader in Public Opinion and Communication*, 2d ed. (New York: Free Press, 1966), p. 31.

9. Herbert Blumer, "The Mass, the Public, and Public Opinion," in ibid., p. 46.

10. Quoted in H. Laurence Ross, *Perspectives on the Social Order* (New York: McGraw-Hill, 1968), p. 499.

11. Reed H. Blake and Edwin O. Haroldsen, *A Taxonomy of Concepts in Communication* (New York: Hastings House, 1975), p. 70.

12. Gordon W. Allport, "Attitudes," in C. Murchison, ed., *Handbook of Social Psychology* (New York: Russell and Russell, 1967), Vol. 2, p. 810.

13. Richard LaPiere, "Attitude vs. Action," *Social Forces* 13 (December 1934):230-237.

14. Milton Rokeach, "Attitude Change and Behavioral Change," *Public Opinion Quarterly* 30 (Winter 1966-1967), pp. 529-550.

15. Martin Fishbein, "Attitude and the Prediction of Behavior," in Martin Fishbein, ed., *Readings in Attitude Theory and Measurement* (New York: John Wiley and Sons, 1967), p. 491.

16. Joseph S. Roucek, *Social Control* (Westport, Conn.: Greenwood Press, 1970), p. 385.

17. If we gave a value of one to all individuals who support an issue and a zero to all those who oppose, the sum of the support divided by the total number in the population would give us an average or mean. This also happens to be the proportion of supporters. Let us say that 65 percent support an issue (which may also be written as 0.65), we can then say that the degree of support for an issue is 0.65. We can also say that each person in the public is, on the average, 0.65 in favor of the issue.

18. The size of the population is generally irrelevant unless it is less than, say, ten times the size of the sample.

19. See Philip E. Converse, "New Dimensions of Meaning for Cross-section Sample Surveys in Politics," *International Social Science Journal* 16 (1964):19-34.

20. Sam Tuchman and Thomas E. Coffin, "The Influence of Election Night Television Broadcasts in a Close Election," *Public Opinion Quarterly* 35 (Fall 1971):315-326.

21. Anon., "The Talk of the Town," *The New Yorker*, February 21, 1977, p. 27.

22. See L. John Martin, "Recent Theory on Mass Media Potential in Political Campaigns," *The Annals* 427 (September 1976):125-133.

23. Ibid., p. 131.

24. Joseph Kraft, "The Mythology of Public Opinion-Making," *The Washington Post*, March 8, 1977, p. A15.

John Moland, Jr.

PROPAGANDA AND BRAINWASHING

An important aspect of the study of present-day public opinion formation concerns the nature and role of propaganda as related to attitude change and social control.[1] Propaganda has to do with persuasion through the use of argument or other means of communication to influence people's attitudes and ultimately to affect their actions. It may be defined as any systematic and deliberate attempt by persons or groups to arouse and influence sentiments and attitudes by presenting social issues in a manner that may be wholly or partly true, confusing or false, so as to control the action and relationships of individuals and groups.[2]

The systematic and deliberate aspects of propaganda usage suggest the accompanying vested interest of certain persons or groups in presenting one side of a social issue in a manner designed to influence sentiments and opinions favorable toward that side while playing down the other side.[3] It is in this sense that propaganda is an organized, planned activity for influencing human action.

Although many dislike the word "propaganda" and some view it as something evil or sinister, propaganda is not necessarily either bad or good inasmuch as it can be used for either good or bad ends. It involves the use of selected techniques of communication by individuals or groups seeking to affect the attitudes and behavior of other individuals or groups. Its presentation may be open or concealed, obvious or subtle, crude or polished. Propaganda may have as its aim the broadest national good, or it may be directed toward extremely narrow and selfish concerns. From the standpoint of value judgment, a given propaganda effort may be viewed basically as an informative function of a socially beneficial and enlightening nature, or it may be viewed as a vested interest with exploitative aims.[4]

The History of Propaganda

The systematic design of propaganda and of counterpropaganda appears to have begun in Western civilization in about 500 B.C. with the codification of techniques of argument known as "rhetoric." Plato, Aristotle, and others in the Greek city-states compiled rules of rhetoric not only to make their own arguments more persuasive, but also to immunize "good" citizens against the use of logical fallacies and emotional terms by "bad" lawyers and demagogues.[5] A number of parallel developments appeared in other civilizations after 400 B.C. For example, Confucius in his *Analects* urged the use of truthful rhetoric and "proper" forms of speech and writing as means of persuading men to live the good life.[6]

The term *propaganda*, derived from the Latin word "propagate" (meaning to sow), was first used in the seventeenth century when Pope Gregory XV created the College of Propaganda, a committee of cardinals.[7] This organization was formed for the purpose of "propagating the faith" by training priests to become missionaries in a movement to convert people to Catholicism. The term retained its largely religious connotations until World War I when propaganda, involving obvious lies, was used as a means of influencing public opinion with respect to the war.[8]

Special usage and meanings were given to the word propaganda by Lenin in his collection of writings published in 1929 under the title *Agitation and Propaganda*.[9] Lenin made a distinction between propaganda as the reasoned use of arguments from history, philosoophy, and science in the spreading of doctrine, and agitation as incitement through the use of emotional slogans, "Aesopian" parables, and half-truths to influence acceptance of the doctrine. Lenin taught that the success of a social movement depends as much on use of the art and strategy of persuasion as on firmness of convictions.[10] Throughout history, propaganda and counterpropaganda, composed of mixtures of rhetoric, faith, and conviction, have been involved in every movement to spread social and political doctrines.

During World Wars I and II, propaganda (both domestic and foreign) was used extensively to arouse and intensify animosity against diplomatic and military rivals, and to attract and promote favorable support from allies and neutral nations. The postwar period and subsequent cold war were marked by prestige propaganda as nations vied for diplomatic dominance, aimed at inducing officials of the target nations to act as the propagandizing nation wished.

In recent decades, considerable attention has been given to the study of mass propaganda, with emphasis on examing the effects of the mass media on attitudes and behavior. Commercial propaganda and market research have focused on the study of detailed aspects of opinion, attitude, and behavior as related to and affected by "consumer motivation."

The Social-Psychological Nature of Propaganda

Propaganda is a method used to influence people to believe certain ideas or to follow certain courses of action. As such, to be effective it must have some appeal to the belief system—those deepest convictions which consist of fundamental attitudes and values that enter into a person's view of the world and one's relationship to it. The belief system has been defined by Kimball Young as an organized body of ideas, attitudes, and convictions centered around values or things regarded as important or precious to the group.[11] The content of belief systems includes myths, legends, stereotypes, clichés, and slogans. Also related to the belief system are valued symbols such as the flag, ceremonies, and words of strong sentimental value such as home, mother, love, security, justice, and peace. Propaganda is concerned with the deliberate creation and manipulation of myths, legends, and other character-istics of the belief system for the purpose of achieving attitude change and social control.

With suggestion as its mode of operation, propaganda is designed to affect our belief system by manipulating its content and thereby bring about a change in attitude and behavior.[12] It cannot, however, produce changes in opinion and attitudes without being supported by and supportive of the myths of the group and its members. Thus, propaganda can only alter attitudes and behavior in ways members of the group are already disposed to allow.

Propaganda Devices

The way propaganda is used may be better understood by classifying it according to the devices involved. Seven propaganda devices have been singled out and described in a study called *The Fine Art of Propaganda* by Alfred McClung Lee and Elizabeth Briant Lee.[13] They are listed and described as follows: (1) *Name Calling* involves labeling the opposition with words and symbols that produce an unfavorable response in the mind of the listener. "Nigger," "whitey," and "red" are examples. Another example is "socialized medicine," the label applied by the American Medical Association Campaign against President Truman's program for national medical insurance. This label was so effective that it remained attached to the program for more than a decade. (2) *Testimonial* consists in having some person of prestige and high status approve or disapprove of a given idea, program, person, or product. Sports stars and other well-known public figures often give their public support to a candidate or some public issue with the idea of gaining increased public support for the candidate or issue. (3) *Transfer* is the technique of association through identifying a negative or disapproved symbol with someone or something the propagandist would have us reject and disapprove; or it may transfer the authority or prestige of a high-status symbol to someone or something in order to make the latter more acceptable. "Guilt by association" and "acceptance by association" characterize the transfer technique. "Guilt by association" dominated McCarthyism. (4) *Plain Folks* is the device by which a speaker attempts to convince his listeners that he is an ordinary sort of person, not much different from them. His ideas and programs are good because they are of the people, his listeners. (5) *Card Stacking* involves the selected use of and selected emphasis upon facts or falsehoods, illustrations or distractions, and logical or illogical statements in order to give the best possible picture of one's own position and the worst possible picture of his opponent's position. (6) *Glittering Generality* is similar to transfer, except that a word or phrase of vague and general meaning is used. Examples include references to freedom, liberty, the Good Society, "the Great Society," "law and order," and the dignity of man. (7) *Band Wagon* emphasizes the theme "Everybody's doing it," and therefore you should follow the crowd and "jump on the band wagon."

The devices listed here overlap to some extent, and many are used simultaneously; however, they do not exhaust the devices used by the propagandist.

Aims and Conditions of Propaganda

Propaganda is a means of producing or impeding social change as related to the vested interest of some group, organization, or government. As such, its content, form, and effects can be understood only with reference to given conditions, including the target group and its members. The material and symbolic content, the particular procedure, and the psychological techniques employed are influenced by the aims and conditions under which propaganda take place. Thus, propaganda may be hidden or it may be open. It may be viewed as exploitative, conversionary, divisive, consolidating, or any combination of these in terms of aim and form.

Exploitative propaganda focuses on the sentiments and emotions of ill-informed and misinformed individuals and groups with the intent of using the group and its members for direct personal gain. As pointed out by Asch, the goal of the propagandist dictates the techniques used: deception, half-truths, and deliberate omissions.[14] The essential technique of divisive propaganda is that of "divide and conquer." Such propaganda is used extensively in wartime and during political campaigns.

Consolidation propaganda appeals to the habits, values, and deep-seated sentiments of the group or nation for the purpose of achieving and maintaining "togetherness" through promoting and maintaining morale. Under conditions of war and other crisis situations, this form of propaganda comes into play. Conversionary propaganda is more directly linked to social movements and advertisement campaigns. It relies heavily on persuasion and argument to get an individual to change his beliefs, attitudes, values, and ultimately his actions, so as to join the movement or buy a different product.

Type of Propaganda

War Propaganda

Modern warfare demands the use of all of a nation's resources at home as well as on the war front itself. Thus, one focus of war propaganda is to maintain morale not only among the armed forces, but also among the civilian population on the home front where the basic materials and supplies for the war effort are produced. In addition, propaganda activities are carried out to preserve the friendship of allies and neutral countries as well as to demoralize both the armed forces and the civilian populations of enemy nations.

The use of propaganda techniques during wartime has been designated "psychological warfare." Although considerable importance was given to psychological warfare operations during World War II as directed toward the German Army, studies of the German Army's morale and fighting effectiveness made during the last three years of the war cast doubt on the effectiveness of the propaganda used as well as the notion that human behavior can be extensively manipulated by mass communications.[15] These studies call attention to the role of the primary group in maintaining morale when faced with mass propaganda efforts. In addition, attention is called to the need to take into consideration different kinds of propaganda as related to different groups and variations in sets of conditions or situations of the group.

The so-called "cold war" involves the considerable use of propaganda exchange among nations during peace time. Postwar propaganda has centered largely around prestige campaigns and friendship propaganda. It is estimated that the propaganda efforts of the Soviet Union and the Communist block cost hundreds of millions of dollars annually.[16]

Commercial Propaganda

Much advertising is conversionary propaganda. The individual is persuaded to buy in terms of the superiority in quality, in terms of price structure (more for your money), in terms of availability on the market, and so on. Corporations may employ institutional advertising in the form of paid space in newspapers, magazines, and on billboards, or paid time on radio and television. Institutional advertising may be used to promote or oppose ideas by expounding on a general philosophy such as "free enterprise" and "private property" rather than advertising to promote a particular product. In this connection, prepared editorials and clipsheets may be disseminated as press releases. When such materials appear in the media, the impression is given of straightforward reporting or editorializing by the staff of the news media.[17]

Extensive advertising is conducted by organized pressure groups. For example, the American Medical Association has supported the preparation of pamphlets and articles opposing "socialized medicine." Employee and employer groups plead their respective positions during strikes through the use of newspaper advertisements and clipsheets. Every year vested interest groups spend billions of dollars in advertising campaigns for securing paid space or time from communication media.

In the area of market research, extensive in-depth studies have been made of opinion, attitude, belief, and behavior as related to consumer motivation through commercial propaganda and advertising. As a result, high power salesmanship techniques along with commercial advertising are used to sell everything from the smallest household item to land unseen.

Political Propaganda

Political propaganda is associated with political action and the attempt to achieve as well as exercise political power. Vested interest groups with their specialized promotional agents, including public relations personnel, are present in every level of government. These vested interest groups, as pressure groups, are well aware of the influence of public opinion. Accordingly, they cultivate public opinion through mass propaganda linked to public relations operations. Interest-group leaders may argue in terms of any widespread belief system and value system of the society such as freedom of speech, the free enterprise system, and individualism.

A frequently used political campaign tactic is scapegoating—the process of blaming one's opponent for unfortunate events that have occurred, while implying that they may occur again if the opponent or opposition party is reelected.[18] For example, voters are reminded of the depression or the war that occurred when the opposition party was in office and thereby the possibility of a repeat performance if the opposition party wins again is suggested.

Political campaigning involves extensive use of propaganda not only with respect to policy issues, but also in the presentation of the candidate as a personality attractive to the voters. Every candidate finds it necessary to construct a good public image and to sell it to the public, while at the same time trying to influence the creation of a negative image of his opponent. The candidate may emphasize any one or a combination of choices of images. The themes of these images include ideas that the candidate is "in good health," "a family man," "a religious man," or one who is fond of sports and outdoor life.

Candidates frequently make use of "propaganda-of-the-deed"—persuasion based on the use of personal examples. For instance, a congressman seeking public support can give his constituency the impression that he is a hard worker by reporting the number of bills he introduced and the number of hours he put in each day (sixteen or twenty hours) in their behalf. Propaganda-of-the-deed is further illustrated by President Roosevelt's decision during the campaign of 1944 to ride hatless in an open-top car through the rain in New York City, an action designed as an impressive display of his commitment to the people.[19]

Reformist Propaganda

Reformist propaganda is directed at broad or deep political, economic, and social changes by gradual modifications of an existing structure. This form of propaganda works for change in selected areas of the social order. It may be long range and general in purpose, or it may be limited in objective and temporary. Reformist propaganda is concerned with modifying conditions in the name of moral standards, as, for example, the efforts of prohibition movements against the drinking of alcohol or selling and recreating on "the Lord's Day."[20]

A method that has recently come into widespread use to influence public opinion and effect social change with respect to general societal problems is the mass demonstration. Reform has been sought through the use of mass demonstrations by civil rights groups such as the Southern Christian Leadership Conference, the National Association for the Advancement of Colored People, the Congress of Racial Equality, the Student Non-Violent Coordinating Committee, and others. In the 1960s, mass demonstrations were used as a means of focusing attention on the extent to which blacks have experienced discrimination and denial of opportunity in American society. These demonstrations, coupled with the nonviolent behavior (passive resistance) of the demonstrators and highlighted by mass arrest (which frequently involved "official brutality" by supporters of the power structure and the status quo), tended to arouse basic sentiments and values in support of the demonstrators and their movement for basic human rights. The leaders of the movement used slogans and symbols reflecting basic Christian doctrine and democratic values to solidify and maintain the morale of the members as well as convert new followers to the reform movement.

The "establishment" reacted with counterpropaganda of a divisive nature (divide and conquer) directed at the leadership of the civil rights movement. Thus, they publicized and magnified differences among leaders, attributed a selfish motive to them, labeled them and the movement Communist, and attempted to denigrate the leaders through devious means.

Racial and Ethnic Propaganda

An important class of propaganda is that related to race and ethnic group relations. Its purpose is to promote feelings of superiority among members of the in-group, while identifying and projecting members of the out-group as inferior. Positive in-group stereotypes involving deep-seated sentiments and strongly held values are contrasted with negative out-group stereotypes to provide the background and content for prejudice propaganda in intergroup conflict.

The propaganda of racism is clearly demonstrated by the verbal attack Senator Theodore Bilbo of Mississippi made on the issues and leaders of the desegregation efforts during the years of World War II.[21] In a speech before the Mississippi legislature, he verbally assaulted the Anti-Poll Tax Bill and A. Philip Randolph's proposed march on Washington. He also reiterated the traditional racist propaganda theme of amalgamation by repeating the question raised by Congressman McKenzie of Louisiana, "How can anyone be party to encouraging white girls into the arms of Negro soldiers at a canteen while singing 'Let Me Call You Sweetheart'?"[22] The traditional myths of preserving "the purity of white womanhood" and the "purity of white culture" provided the emotional symbols for arousing and maintaining opposition to the Anti-Poll Tax Bill and to efforts to desegregate the armed services and federal facilities.

In 1960, John F. Kennedy was the second Irish Catholic to be nominated by the Democratic party for the office of president of the United States. Anti-Catholic groups responded by having handbills printed and distributed to discourage Protestants from casting their vote for the Catholic candidate. Statements suggesting the takeover of the government by the Pope, the destruction of Protestant churches, and the loss of liberty provided the themes for the handbills.

The Jewish minority in the United States has also been the target of widely circulated propaganda. Anti-Semitic propaganda has had as its areas of emphasis the Jewish religion and the notion that Jews are engaged in a plot to gain a stranglehold on the economy.

Racial and ethnic propaganda is no less prevalent in the present decade than in the 1940s. The old familiar arguments are still expressed—the inherent inferiority of blacks, the dangers of miscegenation, and "Jewish money power."

Brainwashing

One of the most extreme manifestations of conversionary propaganda involves coercive persuasion which has been characterized by the term *brainwashing* as applied to the Communist attempt to propagandize American prisoners captured during the Korean conflict. Coercive persuasion emphasizes the complete control that the propagandist has over the subjects with respect to (1) social contacts and communication, and (2) the ability to manipulate rewards and punishments.[23] The goal is to bring about complete social change and social control in keeping with the ideological aims of the propagandist.

The objective of the Chinese Communists was to bring about true conversion by substituting within the person the values and belief systems of Communist ideology for that of Western democracy. To produce such a change, it was necessary to eliminate a person's self-identity by subjecting him to continual physical and psychological stress, with the manipulation of punitive treatment through increasing and reducing reward and punishment as the primary method of changing the individual. The approach was systematic, involving the elimination of leadership, group ties, and social interactions that sustained the old attitudes, beliefs, and values.

According to Schein, the Chinese approach to the treatment of prisoners seemed to emphasize "control over groups rather than individuals."[24] Mutual distrust was systematically fomented among group members by playing men off against one another. This was done by bestowing special privileges upon noncollaborating prisoners to make them appear to be collaborators, and by using false testimonials and signed statements from other prisoners to make them appear to be informers and collaborators when they were not. Incoming mail was manipulated so as to suggest that the prisoner had been abandoned by his loved ones. These tactics weakened the prisoner group's social structure, which resulted in increasing feelings of isolation among members.

Prisoners were compelled to attend lectures on the Communist doctrine followed by compulsory group discussion. Rewards were given for cooperation and collaboration, "while threats of death, non-repatriation, reprisal against family, torture, decreases in food and medicine, and imprisonment served to keep men from offering much resistance." Thus, through coercive persuasion an attempt was made to strip prisoners of their beliefs, values, and attitudes based upon democratic ideology and substitute beliefs, values, and attitudes based upon Communist ideology.

Research and Theory

The foregoing discussion of brainwashing and coercive persuasion emphasizes the importance of the social group in resisting or supporting propaganda efforts. In this context, the success or failure of propaganda becomes more meaningful when it is viewed as a special case of the theory of communication which has been treated as a subdivision of the general theory of social systems. Analysis in terms of the social system focuses on relations among persons, with emphasis upon group, status, role, and related social expectations.[25] A brief examination of the literature with respect to mass communication will shed some light on propaganda as a special case of communication theory.

In the decades prior to World War II, many viewed mass communication (including propaganda) as a means of providing messages for an atomistic mass of readers, listeners, and viewers, with these messages serving as direct and powerful stimuli that would elicit immediate response.[26] It has now become increasingly clear that the effects of communication depend upon (1) the location in the social structure of both the communicator and the person to whom communication is directed, and (2) their immediate relations to other persons and groups in the society.

The use of the panel technique by Lazarsfeld, Berelson, and Gaudet in the the study of voting behavior led to the "two-step flow of communication" hypothesis.[27] The two-step flow of communication suggests that ideas flow from the mass media to certain key persons and from these opinion leaders to less active individuals. In this process, the opinion leader serves not only as a relayer of the information but also as an influence agent. From further study of investigations of this hypothesis, Katz concluded that interpersonal relationships influence the effect of communication by serving as sources (1) of pressure to conform to the group's way of thinking and acting and (2) of social support for the individual.[28]

The importance of the primary group as a source of social support for attitudes in resisting propaganda efforts is emphasized by Shils and Janowitz.[29] According to findings from studies of the German Army's morale and fighting effectiveness, the most important factor accounting for the German troops' strong resistance to Allied propaganda was the German soldier's loyalty to his unit as a primary group, which provided the basis for maintaining a high level of morale.[30] The importance of interpersonal relationships in resisting propaganda efforts is further illustrated by the attempts of the Chinese Communists to brainwash American prisoners captured during the Korean conflict. Investigators conclude that the Chinese Communists were successful in destroying resistance and obtaining minor cooperation in part because primary groups were deliberately destroyed, as a result of which the average prisoner experienced feelings of isolation when facing his captors—even though he was physically in the presence of his fellow prisoners.[31] Thus, the nature and extent of interpersonal relations, including social pressures, expectation, and anticipation as properties of primary group and reference group relationships, set the stage for conditions under which different groups and individuals as members of these groups will respond to various types and devices of propaganda.

Trends

The foregoing discussion shows that propaganda efforts run the gamut from friendly verbal persuasion to coercive persuasion involving the direct use of physical, economic, or psychical means based upon the application and manipulation of punishment and reward.[32] The process by which people's attitudes and actions are changed by others, as well as the extent of such change, varies along the continuum between the poles of persuasion and coercive persuasion. Coercive persuasion in its ultimate form focuses upon removing from one's mind those political, social, and religious beliefs that are inconsistent with the goals of the propagandist and replacing them with ideas in keeping with his goals.[33]

Of considerable interest in the study of propaganda as a mechanism of influence and social control is the extent to which the propagandee's behavior and sense of self as aspects of his personality are affected by the devices of the propagandist.[34] Communication and symbolic interaction theory may serve as a framework for studying the effects of coercive persuasion upon one's personality and self-concept. Mind and selves, according to George H. Mead, are social products and must be accounted for in terms of communication and the social process.[35] The social self arises in social interaction and is dependent upon the social group to which it belongs.

If the achievement of selfhood is a gradual development in the life of the infant and child through the social process of role-taking, under what conditions and to what extent can this self-concept or selfhood be altered later in life? To what extent can the devices of the propagandist as involved in coercive persuasion affect one's sentiments, values, and behavior—and, ultimately one's self-concept and selfhood? In the light of recent developments involving coercive persuasion, better known as "brainwashing," these and related questions may be the focal point of attention for the next decade with respect to the study of propaganda and social control.

Notes

1. See, for example, Paul F. Secord and Carl W. Backman, *Social Psychology* (New York: McGraw-Hill, 1964), Ch. 6; Herbert C. Kelman, "Compliance, Identification, and Internalization: Three Processes Of Attitude Change," in Harold Proshansky and Bernard Seidenberg, eds., *Basic Studies in Social Psychology* (New York: Holt, Rinehart and Winston, 1966), p. 140-148; Eliju Katz, "The Two-Step Flow of Communication: An Up-to-Date Report on an Hypothesis," in Proshansky and Seidenberg, eds., *Basic Studies in Social Psychology*, pp. 196-209; Bernard Berelson and Morris Janowitz, eds., *Reader in Public Opinion and Communication* (New York: Free Press, 1966); P. F. Lazarsfeld, B. Berelson, and H. Gaudet, *The People's Choice* (New York: Columbia University Press, 1948).

2. Harold D. Lasswell, "Propaganda," in *Encyclopedia of the Social Sciences* (New York: Macmillan Co., 1959), Vol. 11, pp. 521-522; Bruce L. Smith, "Propaganda," in *The International Encyclopedia of the Social Sciences* (New York: Macmillan Co. and Free Press, 1968), Vol. 12, pp. 579-580; Leonard W. Doob, *Public Opinion and Propaganda* (New York: Henry Holt and Co., 1948); Kimball Young, *Social Psychology* (New York: Appleton-Century-Crofts, 1956), p. 460; Secord and

Backman, *Social Psychology*, p. 196; Solomon E. Asch, *Social Psychology* (New York: Prentice-Hall, 1955), p. 617; John M. Maclachlan, "Propaganda," in Joseph S. Roucek, ed., *Social Control* (Westport, Conn.: Greenwood Press, 1970), p. 408.

3. Jerry D. Rose, *Introduction to Sociology* (Chicago: Rand McNally College Publishing Co., 1976), p. 203; Young, *Social Psychology*, p. 357; Asch, *Social Psychology*, p. 620; Ralph K. White, "Propaganda: Morally Questionable and Morally Unquestionable Techniques," *Annals of the American Academy of Political and Social Sciences* 398 (November 1971):26-35.

4. Asch, *Social Psychology*, pp. 620-624; White, "Propaganda", pp. 26-27. Robert Waelder, "Demoralization and Re-Education," *World Politics* 14 (January 1962): 375-385.

5. Smith, "Propaganda," p. 580.

6. Ibid.

7. Young, *Social Psychology*, p. 457.

8. Read: James Morgan, *Atrocity Propaganda, 1914-1918* (New Haven, Conn.: Yale University Press, 1941), Chs. 2 and 4.

9. Smith, "Propaganda," p. 579; Frederick Barghoorn, "Soviet Doctrine and the Role of Propaganda," in Berelson and Janowitz, eds., *Reader in Public Opinion and Communication*, pp. 360-378.

10. Ibid.

11. Young, *Social Psychology*, p. 460. See also Chapter 9, "The Nature and Function of Belief Systems."

12. Young, *Social Psychology*, p. 461.

13. Alfred McClung Lee and Elizabeth B. Lee, *The Fine Art of Propaganda* (New York: Harcourt, Brace and Co., 1939), pp. 23-24.

14. Asch, *Social Psychology*, p. 619.

15. Edward A. Shils and Morris Janowitz, "Cohesion and Disintegration in the Wehrmacht in World War II," in Berelson and Janowtiz, eds., *Reader in Public Opinion and Communication*, pp. 402-417.

16. Barghoorn, "Soviet Doctrine," p. 373; Eugen Hadamovsky, *Propaganda and National Power* (New York: Arno Press, 1972).

17. William Ebenstein, C. Herman Pritchett, Henry A. Turner, and Dean Mann, *American Democracy in World Perspective* (New York: Harper and Row, 1973), p. 280.

18. Rose, *Introduction to Sociology*, p. 203.

19. Robert K. Merton, *Mass Persuasion* (New York: Harper, 1946), p. 92.

20. Lasswell, "Propaganda," p. 523.

21. From an address by Senator Theodore G. Bilbo before the Mississippi legislature reprinted in *The Poisoned Tongue*, Stanley Feldstein, ed. (New York: William Morrow and Co., 1972), pp. 288-295.

22. Ibid., p. 289.

23. Secord and Backman, *Social Psychology*, p. 221; Waelder, "Demoralization and Re-education," pp. 375-385; Anthony Storr, "Torture Without Violence," *New Statesman* 59 (March 12, 1960):358; George L. Williams, "Political Indoctrination of Secondary School Sudents in Fascist Italy," *School and Society* 100 (Summer 1972):312-317; Robert J. Lifton, "Brainwashing in Perspective," *New Republic*, May 13, 1957, pp. 21-25; Jacques Ellul, *Propaganda* (New York: Alfred A. Knopf, 1966),

pp. 311-313; James Roland Pennock and John W. Chapman, eds., *Coercion* (New York: Aldine-Atherton, 1972); Albert D. Biderman, "The Image of 'Brainwashing,' " *Public Opinion Quarterly* 26 (Winter 1962):547-563; Edgar H. Schein, Inge Schneier, and Curtis H. Barker, *Coercive Persuasion* (New York: W. W. Norton, 1961).

24. Edgar H. Schein, "Reaction Patterns to Severe, Chronic Stress in American Army Prisoners of War of the Chinese," in Proshansky and Seidenberg, eds., *Basic Studies in Social Psychology*, pp. 638-645; Jay A. Lifton, *Thought Reform and the Psychology of Totalism* (New York: W. W. Norton, 1961), pp. 152-184.

25. Talcott Parsons, *The Social System* (Glencoe, Ill.: Free Press, 1951).

26. Lazarsfeld, Berelson, and Gaudet, *The People's Choice*; Elihu Katz, "Two-Step Flow of Communication," p. 197.

27. Ibid.

28. Katz, "Two-Step Flow of Communication," p. 208; John P. Robinson, "Interpersonal Influence in Election Campaigns: Two-Step-Flow Hypotheses," *Public Opinion Quarterly* 40 (Fall 1976):304-319.

29. Shils and Janowitz, "Cohesion and Disintegration," pp. 416-417.

30. Ibid.

31. Schein, "Reaction Patterns," p. 641; Storr, "Torture Without Violence," p. 358.

32. Lifton, *Thought Reform*, p. 181; Michael A. Weinstein, "Coercion, Space, and the Modes of Human Domination," in Pennock and Chapman, eds., *Coercion*, pp. 63-80.

33. In this connection, see the numerous news articles involving current issues dealing with propaganda and attempts to change political and religious beliefs. For example, "Was She Brainwashed?," *Time*, October 6, 1975, p. 33; "The Hearst Case: Which Patty to Believe?," *Time*, October 6, 1975, pp. 30-32; "What Is Brainwashing?," *Newsweek*, March 1, 1976, p. 31; "Battle Over Patty's Mind," *Time*, March 8, 1976, pp. 25-31; "Brainwashing—Echoes of Korean War," *U.S. News and World Report*, February 23, 1976, p. 26; "Rescue from a Fanatic Cult," *Reader's Digest*, April 1977, pp. 129-133; "Deprogramming the Brainwashed: Even a Moonie Has Civil Rights," *The Nation*, February 26, 1977, pp. 238-242; "A Psychiatrist's Notes," *Newsweek*, February 16, 1976, p. 24.

34. Anne E. Freedman and P. E. Freedman, *The Psychology of Political Control* (New York: St. Martin's Press, 1975), pp. 217-250; Richard I. Evans, Richard M. Rozella, Thomas M. Lasater, Theodore M. Dembroski and Bem P. Allen, "Fear Arousal, Persuasion, and Actual Versus Implied Behavioral Change," *Journal of Personality and Social Psychology* 16 (1970):220-227; I. L. Janis, "Effects of Fear Arousal on Attitude; Recent Developments in Theory and Experimental Research," *Advances in Experimental Social Psychology* 4 (1967):166-224; H. Leventhal, R. P. Singer, and S. Jones, "Effects of Fear and Specificity of Recommendation upon Attitudes and Behavior," *Journal of Personality and Social Psychology* 2 (1965): 20-29.

35. George H. Mead, *Mind, Self and Society* (Chicago: University of Chicago Press, 1967); Charles Horton Cooley, *Human Nature and the Social Order* (New York: Schocken Books, 1964), pp. 36-37; J. D. Cardwell, *Social Psychology: A Symbolic Interaction Perspective* (Philadelphia: F. A. Davis Co., 1971), pp. 77-83; Joseph Luft, *Group Process* (New York: National Press Books, 1970), pp. 59-60.

Myrtle R. Reul

MOTION PICTURES, RADIO, AND TELEVISION

There is no quarrel with the need for social control, for without some kind of constraint we would have no social order, no culture, no social norm. The question is not whether there should be social control, but rather, as A. F. Nadel and others have pointed out, the question is "where should control reside?"[1] An even more important question is, Should social control stereotype one segment of the general population more than others? To attempt to answer such questions we must consider what society uses as a measure of social control.

The mass media have been one of the major influences—both positive and negative—in shaping values and reinforcing attitudes in this country. This is especially true of motion pictures, radio, and television, which have affected the self-concept of countless individuals, the behavior of groups, and the world image of the nation as a whole. One explanation of their impact is offered by Chaffee and Petrick who point out that entire populations are frequently exposed to the same stimuli, presented in the same way, and usually within the same time frame.[2] Such exposure can not but result in considerable uniformity of attitudes and behaviors.

In many instances, this influence has had detrimental consequences. For example, all three media have been guilty of presenting biases and negative stereotypes that have adversely affected large segments of the population. The stereotyping of women and women's roles has probably been the most common of such biases. Let us now take a brief look at the social control which motion pictures, radio, and television exert in general and their role in stereotyping women in particular.

Motion Pictures

Historical Background of Films

From the earliest days, the functions of motion pictures were said to be recreation, education, and propaganda.[3] Clearly, recreation won out in the long run. While internationally motion pictures appealed to lower income groups, by the end of World War I they were becoming the leading form of entertainment in this country. By 1930, between 85 and 100 million people of all incomes flocked to local movie theaters each week. Hollywood gave them what they wanted—entertainment and escape from the grim realities of the Depression and later a war into a world of fantasy and make-believe.

Phrases like "sex appeal" and "sex symbol" appeared in the scripts of the 1920s, but Hollywood did an abrupt about-face in 1934 when fear of censorship or boycott made producers switch from explicit (for their day) sex movies to juvenile classics and "gangbusters" films in which actresses like Jean Harlowe were assigned the new role of "tough-girl comedy."

In the mid-1930s, theaters tried to combat a temporary decline in attendance with double features, giveaways, cash prize drawings, and bingo games. The industry declined gradually through the 1940s and 1950s, beset by war, increased production costs, and the development of its arch competitor, television.

For the motion picture industry there seemed to be two solutions. The first was to turn the studios to the production of television films; the second was to reach new audiences. the drive-in theater was one such attempt. Other attempts included pictures with more stark realism. Nudity scenes increased and visual and verbal boldness became the order of the day. But in the 1970s, the Hollywood epic was reborn with films like *The Towering Inferno*, *Jaws*, and *Airport*, which attracted crowds unprecedented since the advent of television.

By the mid-1970s there was noticeable interest in the early days of motion pictures which were re-created in films such as *That's Entertainment*, Parts I and II, and *Nickelodeon*. The mid-1970s also saw increasing interest in the production of educational films on a wide variety of topics for business, industry, government, and educational institutions.

Influence of Motion Pictures on Public Opinion

Motion pictures have had strong appeal to all ages and tastes, and have also had strong psychological impact, for several reasons. Linden points out that a film script is deliberately written in the present tense and has the "appearance of an objective dream."[4] Members of the audience therefore remain individuals directly related to the events on the screen, instead of being welded into a group, as they are, for example, in spectator sports. Merleau-Ponty adds that, because the film *shows* the audience what is happening, viewers do not really need to be *told* in words what is happening. Thus, the spoken words become reinforcement of the action and lead to a greater degree of belief in what is seen.[5]

In one of the few psychoanalytic assessments of the cinema, psychiatrist Harvey R. Greenberg contends that movies bestow both omniscience and omnipotence on the viewer because he has knowledge of things supposedly unknown to the characters on the screen. The size of the screen and the darkness of the theater increase the viewer's involvement and suggestibility.[6]

Film's Effect on the Image of Women

According to Kanin, the majority of adolescent girls and young women harbored the same dream: of becoming a rich, famous, adored star and, above all, of being beautiful in the Ziegfeld tradition.[7] Movie producers used this theme for new film scripts. The advertising industry fanned the flames of adulation by using stars to endorce products and to set fashions and clothing styles (e.g., the Sweater Girl of 1937-1938).[8]

Although women were often presented as sex symbols, Greenberg sees this as a disguise for more damaging images in a number of movies ranging from *Casablanca* to *The Exorcist*.[9] Using the psychoanalytic frame of reference, he points out that women in films are seen repeatedly as adversaries or monsters, as untrustworthy people, or as victims of situations created by their own ignorance.

Radio

Historical Background of Radio

Radio was an instant success in 1920 when the Westinghouse Electric Company set up Station KDKA in East Pittsburgh and broadcast the Harding-Cox election results. By 1929, one family out of every three owned one.[10] While radio undeniably enlightened people about national and world events and brought top-flight talent into the most remote living rooms, the fact is that neither news nor cultural programs were the most popular. That honor must go to the serials—daytime, afternoon, and evening programs that were broadcast daily or weekly, sometimes for decades.

The so-called soap operas (most of them advertised soap) were directed at homemakers from late morning to early afternoon. They were succeeded by the after-school adventures of children's heroes like Captain Midnight, which went on until the suppertime news. Evenings were for family listening: "The Thin Man," "The Hit Parade," and, of course, comedians like Jack Benny.

By the 1960s—with television taking over day and nighttime serials, news, and much of the entertainment radio previously provided—stations filled their schedules with talk shows, record request programs, or pop music programs with glib disc jockeys introducing and playing the latest favorites. Radios literally became smaller as portability and personal listening became their forte.

In the late 1970s, the citizen's band low-frequency two-way radio began to appear in private cars, boats, campers, and homes. The long-range effect of so many voices crowding the air waves remains to be seen. Meanwhile, police and fire departments have mobilized this new radio network to help in emergencies.[11]

Influence of Radio on Public Opinion

Sociologists were quick to point out that radio produced a quickened general interest in current events, as well as other beneficial social effects. It standardized speech and, like the automobile, broke down regional, ethnic, and national culture barriers. The 1928 presidential campaign made extensive use of radio, as did many campaigns thereafter. President Roosevelt owed much of his popularity to his fireside chats. Before and during the Depression, radio is credited with promoting a greater feeling of social solidarity.

Although early hopes for a so-called university of the air failed to live up to expectations, the radio did inform vast portions of the population by airing tips, on health, homemaking, scientific farming, and other useful subjects. Radio has long been used as an educational tool in the public school systems, but the advent of two-way radio communication opened up the additional possibility of using shortwave radio to permit students to contact countries throughout the world.[12]

Dynes and his associates, among others, have defined the social responsibility of the media as follows: they must provide sufficient information so that free citizens in a democracy can determine the truth for themselves.[13] According to this definition, society depends on mass communication media to use three strategies: (1) to provide agreement on certain basic values by presenting those values to citizens; (2) to encourage citizens to evaluate these basic values; and (3) to encourage the expression of opposing viewpoints.

Whether or not radio has demonstrated such social responsibility is debatable at best. Both radio and television have had difficulties living up to this concept because they are dependent upon advertisers for all their revenue. We will discuss this problem further in the section on television.

Radio's Effect on the Image of Women

Since fewer women were employed during the heyday of radio, and much of the nine-to-three programming and advertising was aimed at them, how did radio influence women and the image of women?

Perhaps the popularity of the "soaps" ("Ma Perkins" and "The Romance of Helen Trent" ran uninterrupted for over thirty years) lay in their ability to assuage loneliness; to bring vicarious romance and tragedy into otherwise uneventful lives; and to put personal problems and dissatisfactions in a different, less disturbing perspective.

The women featured in the soap operas were deluged by crisis and unhappiness. Most of them were victims of romantic triangles, near-fatal accidents, deaths of loved ones, and jealousies which were usually based on unfounded fears. The key word here is *victims*. Women in the soap operas were either victimized by people or by circumstances they brought upon themselves through their inability to cope.

Nor was the role of women portrayed in a more flattering light during the evening series of comedies, mysteries, and adventure stories. In comedies, the woman usually played the clown—the foolish inept one whom everyone laughs at—while the casts of action and adventure stories were almost 100 percent male.

In its heyday, radio, perhaps more than any of the other media, portrayed women in a stereotyped sexist way. It reinforced what was even then an old-fashioned life-style, and it failed to provide realistic role models for children.

Television

Historical Background of Television

The big spurt in television's phenomenal growth began when the first commercial broadcasting license was granted in 1941. In its short history, television has made its mark as the nation's most popular medium of communication. By the early 1970s, 96 percent of all American households had one or more television sets, which for many were their only source of news.

Educational television has the greatest potential for growth at present. Closed circuit television is already an accepted method of instruction in elementary schools, high schools, professional schools, colleges, and even many preschool programs. Agler and Pohrte describe one experiment in using open circuit public television to offer college credit courses—a method of instruction they predict will become increasingly common.[14]

Griffin and Turner extol the virtues of television for course enrichment,[15] while Kalba foresees greater use of low-cost portable television recording equipment, with tape exchanges taking place between schools, libraries, museums, and community agencies. He believes the time is coming when "increasingly important portions of our community life will occur on television, through television, or as a result of television."[16]

The list goes on. Via communications satellites, we can send and receive news instantaneously to and from any part of the globe. Closed circuit television has been used in a school for the deaf,[17] for observing various manufacturing and safety systems in industry, and for monitoring surgery in hospitals. Television has been used so successfully to teach reading to preschoolers[18] that Coleman and Morton believe it also has potential for raising children's general intelligence.[19]

Television's Influence on Public Opinion

Television's impact on society is unprecedented. "Television is now the most influential of all the media," according to Hancock,[20] while Kalba sees it as a powerful purveyor of social roles, attitudes, and information.[21] Much of this impact can be attributed to its versatility. "It can act as newspaper, theater, variety entertainer, political platform, school, and advertiser."[22]

Because people are more impressed by what they see or hear than by what they read, and *most* impressed by what they see, television is more influential than radio or the printed word. Unlike the motion picture, television can also give live coverage of events as they happen, instantaneously in living rooms all over America.

More specifically, television may have bolstered John F. Kennedy's and Jimmy Carter's election victories. The influence of such authoritative newscasters as Walter Cronkite, Mike Wallace, David Brinkley, and John Chancellor on other national events cannot be underestimated. Recently, the impact of the televised version of Alex Haley's *Roots* was likened to that of Harriet Beecher Stowe's *Uncle Tom's Cabin*, which is often credited with changing the social consciousness of the entire nation.[23]

But what *kind* of impact are we talking about? The social control exercised by television programs, newscasts, and commercials is not always salutary. On the contrary, television's sense of social responsibility—or lack of it—continues to be the subject of scorching criticism.

Both Hall and Cirino have pointed out that newscasters do, in fact, express personal opinions by "the choice to film *this* aspect of an event rather than *that*."[24] Cirino agrees that this is a way to control public opinion because there is no way of knowing how many news items are not reported, or even why certain ones are selected.[25]

There seem to be two criticisms of television which underly more specific attacks: that television creates an artificial world unrelated to the real lives of real people, and that it is controlled by sponsors rather than by viewers.

According to Agee and associates, among others,[26] since the 1960s not only television, but also films and radio, have been charged with overemphasizing behavior and situations that occur only rarely in real life and are far beyond the experience of most people. Novak adds that "the writers, producers, actors and journalists of television are separated from most of the American population not only by economic standing and education, but also by the culture in which their actual lives are lived out."[27]

In addition, Telser points out that radio and television are the only media solely supported by advertising,[28] which results in their being "saturated with the attitudes of the advertisers, in editorial content as well as in the direct appeal of commercial advertisements."[29] Pitofsky concedes the need for some advertising but cites "a widespread sense of dissatisfaction with the present performance of the advertising industry," reflected in proposed legislation designed to modify or curtail advertising by the Federal Trade Commission among others.[30] Perhaps more insidious than the industry's more obvious lapses in honesty or good taste is its *indirect* appeal to the consumer. The industry draws on stock images to construct, as Millum puts it, "a 'social world' around the product" which goes beyond a specific message about that specific product.[31]

Television's Effect on the Image of Women

In a 1972 study, Dominick and Rouch concluded that commercials showing the so-called modern woman are virtually nonexistent.[32] Komisar agrees that the Madison Avenue woman is a "combination sex object and wife and mother who achieves fulfillment by looking beautiful and alluring for boy friends and lovers, and cooking, cleaning, working and polishing for her husband and family."[33] Too little of advertising recognizes that women have "many things to do, many interests in life besides washing dishes or clothes," Martineau finds.[34]

According to Silverstein and Silverstein, social scientists have been able to establish that the improper depiction of women in television commercials does lead to misconceptions and stereotyping.[35] Suelze points out, for example, that commercials repeatedly show a woman standing helpless before a pile of soiled laundry until the male overvoice of authority tells her to use Brand X detergent.[36]

In a study of female characters in family-oriented shows, Long and Simon found that they are presented in dependent, traditional, and often silly roles.[37] It was not until 1970 in the "Mary Tyler Moore Show" that a woman—and a *single* woman at that—was shown holding a job other than a clerical one.

Women like Lesley Stahl, Marilyn Berger, and Catherine Mackin are doing a knowledgeable, professional job of reporting national news on evening newscasts. Yet only three years ago, news directors questioned for a study through viewers would prefer a man as the evening newscaster, mainly because viewers would find news more believable if it were reported by a man.[38]

Some argue that this kind of stereotyping is not social control, that it is merely a reflection of existing social values. In fact, several studies maintain that television only *reinforces* existing ways of thinking, since people tend to ignore, avoid, or forget anything that disagrees with the ideas they already hold.[39]

Trends

Never in the history of the world has anything had the impact for social change as has television. During its short history, this medium has become purveyor of social roles, attitudes, and information as well as entertainment. It took motion pictures nearly forty years to reach their peak of popularity, radio became a household necessity in twenty years, but television was seemingly indispensable in less than ten years.

Television's spectacular climb as a social influence is directly related to the many areas into which television was introduced in addition to its multicommunication role as a medium carrying entertainment, marketing messages, newscasts, educational programs, and talk shows. These widely differing uses of television range from satellite stations that broadcast events around the world, to computer monitors that reflect corporate decision-making or graphic art, to electric directors that control air traffic in and out of airports, and to surveillance cameras that protect areas of security.

The total possibility of television in the educational sense has not been tapped. Television permits visual demonstration and illustration which radio cannot provide, and it has the advantage of instant playback which motion pictures do not. Closed circuit television is used to monitor student teaching, to observe surgery, and to address staff meetings in widely scattered areas, to mention only a few uses.

On-the-spot coverage of events—Queen Elizabeth's Silver Jubilee, kidnappings in Holland and Italy, political conventions in the United States, world events, storms and disasters—has brought the effect of a "global village" to the world. Few things can be contained within one country, or event in one section of that country due to television coverage. International television holds out the unique promise of spreading ideas and information across national boundaries. This widespread use of television raises questions of social control in the interests of national well-being.

Competition with television brought extreme changes to radio, as seen in its programming, uses, and the size and portability of its sets. Radio as a means of popularizing and promoting phonograph records and electronic and spatial sound effects is one example of the extreme change in program directions. The trend to smaller sets can be seen in the popularity of the tiny transistor. The widespread new uses for radio can be illustrated by the popularity of two-way radios, especially citizens' band radios, and by radio telescopes to monitor the stars of the galaxy and to record cosmic radio waves. Radio as a means of social control has less influence now that television has taken over that major role.

The position of motion pictures as a primary means of social control has also changed as television has taken the lead. Trends in motion pictures seem to be toward more documentaries and educational films which can be used for television programming.

Presently, television viewers are voicing louder demands for control. Special-interest groups continue to demand more input into the type of programs presented. For example, NOW, the National Organization for Women, has formally asked that the language of the television code be revised in order to strengthen the image of women in programming and advertising.

In this country, both radio and television broadcasting companies are dependent upon advertisers for all their revenues; hence, broadcasters are saturated with the attitudes of advertisers. In turn, the attitudes of sponsors produce a form of control as to both content and style of program. The control comes mostly through business and industry's advertising dollars which support the programs they think will appeal to potential buyers of their products. Money patrons pay at the box office to see a film helps determine what the motion picture industry will produce.

Because public opinion can be deeply affected by the mass media, equality of rights and opportunities must be protected through encouraging the input of all groups and not merely those representing the program sponsors. The trend for this kind of input is being shaped as a result of consumer surveys.

The most data have been gathered in the area of children's television, where over 2,000 studies and reports seem to agree that it has a decidedly negative effect on children. According to Gerbner, "Television has profoundly affected the way in which members of the human race learn to become human beings."[40] Perhaps the only conclusive information on social control we have so far is that the media do reinforce attitudinal concepts, especially biased concepts or those that tend to stereotype. Much of the social behavior of the public is being controlled by the constant repetition of points of view which reinforce existing opinions and values.

Notes

1. S. F. Nadel, "Social Control and Self-Regulation," in Walter Buckley, *Modern Systems Research for the Behavior Scientist* (Chicago: Aldine Publishing Co., 1968), pp. 401-408.

2. Steven H. Chaffee and Michael J. Petrick, *Using the Mass Media: Communication Problems in American Society* (New York: McGraw-Hill, 1975), pp. 47-52.

3. For individuals interested in the early history of motion pictures and the attempts in England to evaluate the influence of the cinematograph on young people (with the

possibility of its development as a medium of education), see *The Cinema, Its Present Position and Future Possibilities* (New York: Arno Press and the *New York Times*, 1970). This book is a reprint of a 1917 report.

4. George W. Linden, *Reflections on the Screen* (Belmont, Calif.: Wadsworth Publishing Co., 1970), p. 3.

5. Maurice Merleau-Ponty, *Sense and Non-Sense* (Evanston, Ill.: Northwestern University Press, 1964), pp. 56, 58.

6. Harvey R. Greenberg, *The Movies on Your Mind* (New York: E. P. Dutton, 1975), p. 7.

7. Garson Kanin, *Hollywood: Stars and Starlets, Tycoons and Flesh-Peddlers, Moviemakers and Moneymakers, Frauds and Geniuses, Hopefuls and Has-Beens, Great Lovers and Sex Symbols* (New York: Viking Press, 1974), p. 56; Una Stannard, "The Mask of Beauty," in Vivian Gornick and Barbara K. Moran, eds., *Woman in Sexist Society* (New York: Basic Books, 1971), p. 118; Florenz Ziegfeld identified the determining factors for the selection of females in his productions. They were beauty of face and body, followed by grace in movement, and lastly personality and individuality.

8. Kanin, *Hollywood: Stars and Starlets*, p. 57. The powerful influence of the movie stars of this period on the nation's economy was illustrated when Clark Gable in *It Happened One Night* took off his shirt in one scene and revealed he did not wear an undershirt. Sales of undershirts dropped immediately throughout the country.

9. Greenberg, *The Movies on Your Mind*, pp. 9, 13-32, 79-104, 169-194, 244-248.

10. Lawrence H. Lichty and Malachi C. Topping, eds., *American Broadcasting: A Sourcebook on the History of Radio and Television* (New York: Hastings House, 1975).

11. See J. C. Zurcher and R. M. Blackwell, "Public Safety's Additional Eyes and Ears: Palo Alto Police Department Community Radio Watch," in *Police Chief* 43, no. 6 (1976);68.

12. Louis Hockstra, Jr., "Kids on the 'Ham' Band," *Instructor* 88, no. 2 (October 1976):74-75.

13. Russell R. Dynes, Alfred C. Clarke, Simon Dinitz, and Twao Ishino, *Social Problems: Dissension and Deviation in an Industrial Society* (New York: Oxford University Press, 1974), pp. 266-267; Wilbur Schramm, *Responsibility in Mass Communication* (New York: Harper, 1957), pp. 343-352.

14. Linda S. Agler and Theodore W. Pohrte, "College-Credit Courses by Open-Circuit Television," *Educational Technology* 16, no. 10 (October 1976):39-41.

15. Robert J. Griffin, "Any Teacher Can: An Approach to Producing 'Camera Culture Capsules,' " *Hispania* 56, no. 3 (September 1973):627-630; Thomas Turner, "A Model Television Cultural Lectures Series for Beginning Spanish Programs," *Hispania* 59, no. 3 (September 1976):473-480.

16. Kas Kalba, "The Electronic Community: A New Environment for Television Viewers and Critics," in Douglass Cater and Richard Adler, eds., *Television as a Social Force: New Approaches to TV Criticism* (New York: Praeger Publishers, 1975), pp. 141-163.

17. Herbert Shuey, "Video Tapes in the Classroom," *American Annals of the Deaf* 121, no. 4 (August 1976):370-372.

18. J. P. Seyforth, "Use of Television to Teach Reading to Young Children," *AEL Evaluation Report* (Charleston, W. Va.: Appalachia Educational Laboratory, 1969); "Preschool Reading by Television," *Reading Newsreport* 4 (1970):12-20, 21-27.

19. Edmund B. Coleman and Charles E. Morton, "Modest Plan to Raise the National Intelligence," *Educational Technology* 16, no. 9 (September 1976):7-17.

20. Alan Hancock, *Mass Communication* (London: Longmans, Green and Co., 1968), p. 32.

21. Kalba, "The Electronic Community," p. 154.

22. Hancock, *Mass Communication*, p. 33.

23. Meg Greenfield, "Uncle Tom's Roots," *Newsweek* (February 14, 1977), p. 100.

24. Stewart Hall, "Media: Power: The Double Bind," *Journal of Communication* 26, no. 4 (Autumn 1976):23.

25. Robert Cirino, *Don't Blame the People* (Los Angeles, Calif.: Diversity Press, 1971), pp. 137-146.

26. Warren K. Agee, Phillip H. Ault, and Edwin Emery, *Introduction to Mass Communications* (New York: Harper and Row, 1976), pp. 149-152.

27. Michael Novak, "Television Shapes the Soul," In Cater and Adler, eds., *Television as a Social Force*, pp. 18-19.

28. Lester G. Telser, "Advertising and the Consumer," in Yale Brozen, *Advertising and Society* (New York: New York University Press, 1974), p. 35.

29. Hancock, *Mass Communication*, p. 71.

30. Robert Pitofsky, "Changing Focus in the Regulation of Advertising," in Brozen, ed., *Advertising and Society*, p. 125.

31. Trevor Millum, *Images of Women* (Totowa, N.J.: Rowman and Littlefield, 1975), Introduction, p. ix.

32. Joseph R. Dominick and Gale Rouch, "The Image of Women in Network TV Commercials," *Journal of Broadcasting* 16, no. 3 (Summer 1972):259-265.

33. Lucy Komisar, "The Image of Women in Advertising," in Vivian Gornick and Barbara K. Moran, eds., *Woman in Sexist Society*, p. 208.

34. Pierre Martineau, *Motivation in Advertising: Motives That Make People Buy* (New York: McGraw-Hill, 1971), p. 89.

35. Arthur Jay Silverstein and Rebecca Silverstein, "The Portrayal of Women in Television Advertising," *Federal Communication Bar Journal* 27, no. 1 (1974):71-98.

36. Marijean Suelze, "Women in Labor," *Trans-Action* (November-December 1970):50-58.

37. M. Long and R. Simon, "The Roles and Statuses of Women on Children and Family TV Programs," *Journalism Quarterly* 51 (Spring 1974): 107-110.

38. Vernon A. Stone, "Attitudes Toward Television Newswomen," *Journal of Broadcasting* 18 (Winter 1973-1974):49-62.

39. D. Graber, "The Press as Opinion Resource During the 1968 Presidential Campaign," *Public Opinion Quarterly* 35 (Summer 1971):168-182; Joseph Klapper, *The Effects of Mass Communication* (Glencoe, Ill.: Free Press, 1972); Charles Steinburg, *The Communicative Arts* (New York: Hastings House, 1970).

40. George Gerbner, dean of University of Pennsylvania's Annenburg School of Communications, quoted in "What TV Does to Kids," *Newsweek*, February 21, 1977, p. 63.

M. Timothy O'Keefe

JOURNALISM AND ADVERTISING

For the purposes of this discussion, the term *journalism* will refer only to the printed media, although it is recognized that the word is often used for all the media engaged in the dissemination of news. The term *press* refers only to the newspaper industry, although it too can be interpreted as more encompassing.

The printed media and advertising have always enjoyed a very close relationship. Without the development of advertising as an important economic force in the 1800s, newspapers and magazines would probably be very different from what they are today.

The first American newspapers were primarily propaganda vehicles for their respective political or religious organizations. The 'news' content in the papers had to reflect the prevailing philosophy of the sponsoring organization. Otherwise, the editor would be replaced or the subsidy terminated.

Between 1833 and 1837, American newspapers began to move away from partisan control. Newspapers during this period began to be edited differently in an attempt to attract a wide audience of ordinary people. This was done first through sensational news stories, but as the papers attracted a wide following, they gradually matured and their news treatment became more objective.

In addition to changing the content of this new mass-oriented press, editors reduced the price of newspapers from six cents to a penny, thereby giving the era the name the "penny press." Through its combination of editorial content and low price, the penny press, best typified by the *New York Sun*, which was begun in 1833 by Benjamin Day, soon attracted a large following. In turn, newspapers became very desirable vehicles to advertisers.[1]

As more and more advertisers began giving financial support to these independent newspapers, the press gradually disentangled itself from the partisan support on which it had relied. Advertising essentially freed the American press from its previous religious and political dominance.

The rise of the telegraph was another important contributor to the greater freedom and objectivity of the American press system. The telegraph made it possible to instantly alert people throughout the country to the latest

happenings. Cooperative news gathering began in 1848 with the establishment of the Associated Press (AP), the oldest news-gathering service in the
United States.

Since the AP was serving newspapers throughout the country, it could not
afford to take sides in its news coverage for fear of alienating editors and
readers. Therefore, reporting tended to become even more objective so that
no one would be displeased with the wire service coverage. Many local
newspapers apparently imitated the more objective AP style, which helped
make American newspapers even less biased.[2]

While the introduction of one technological development, the telegraph,
further helped free the press from bias, another development firmly placed
the system within the confines of one socioeconomic class. This was the
introduction of the high speed rotary press in the 1880s. From this time
onward, no person of average means would be able to begin his own
newspaper. The initial investment costs for production machinery ensured
that only those with significant financial backing could begin their own
publication. In 1835, a newspaper could be started for as little as $500; by
1900, it took an investment of at least $1 million; and today the cost is
estimated at $6 million.[3]

The rising cost of production became so great that many newspapers found
they could not survive on their own and had to merge with former
competitors. This consolidation, which began in the early 1900s, has become
so extensive that today it is unusual for competing newspapers (those owned
by different companies) to exist in other than the largest cities. Many cities
have both morning and afternoon papers, but normally such newspapers
have the same ownership.

Thus, in the majority of American communities, newspapers have become
a monopolistic enterprise and will likely remain so. Economic realities make
it difficult for a second newspaper to begin operation in a monopolistic or
one-newspaper town. Advertisers want to invest only in the publication with
the largest circulation, which will automatically be the older, established
newspaper. Ironically then, advertising, which in earlier times helped free the
press from religious and political control, has ultimately helped maintain
class control and reduce the free exchange of news and opinion. Newspapers
today depend on advertising for 75 to 80 percent of their income.

Rising costs have not only forced many papers to merge but have also
encouraged the rise of newspaper chains. In some chains, as many as fifty
newspapers are owned by one parent company. Such companies sometimes
require that all chain members publish certain editorial opinion and columns
supplied to them. Other chains keep only nominal control over the editorial
content of their members and allow the editors to act fairly independently.

Broadcasting chain ownership is limited to fourteen stations by government regulation.

The rise of television lured away many advertisers and had a lasting effect on newspapers. Today newspapers are becoming more news oriented since television has taken much of the entertainment function away from them. In the future, newspapers will probably have to increase in-depth reporting and news and analysis in order to compete with television news. Television news, because of time constraints, can devote only a small amount of time to each story. Recent surveys show that most Americans receive their national and international news primarily from television, and local and state news from newspapers.

Because of its traditional emphasis on local reporting, no national newspaper has yet emerged in the American press system. While several newspapers have national stature, such as the *New York Times*, their reading audience is not widespread enough for the publication to be considered truly a national one. In contrast, most of the other Western nations do have national newspapers, newspapers that are read by numerous people at all levels of society throughout a country.[4] As a result, the influence of American newspapers is primarily at the local level.

The American journalism tradition has always placed the reporting of political news and disaster stories above other categories. The one possible exception is human interest material, which at any rate should not strictly be categorized under "news" but rather under features.

Consequently, the main influence of the American press is in the political sphere. Yet, the power of the press in forming political decisions apparently is not as strong as might be thought. Studies have shown that the majority of American newspapers lean toward the Republican party. In several national elections where the majority of newspapers have endorsed Republican presidential candidates, Democrats have still easily won. This fact suggests that the power of the press in determining national elections may be somewhat limited. However, its power may be more substantial when it endorses local candidates.

Two aspects of newspapers have recently disturbed some citizens: the lack of accountability by the press to the public, and the fact that the average person has no access to it. In the latter respect, if an individual desires to express a certain view in the newspaper to counter something previously published, the only recourse he has is to write a letter to the editor. There is no requirement that this letter be published. Under the guarantees of the First Amendment to the Constitution, no outside influence can dictate or affect the content of a publication without its consent.[5]

Because broadcasting is regulated by the federal government, radio and television are responsible to the public for their content. A broadcast station license is granted only in the "public interest, convenience and necessity."

Licenses are renewed every three years following government review. In contrast, anyone with the financial means to do so can start a newspaper or magazine.

Broadcasters are also required by law to give equal time to all opposing views. Once a statement has been aired on one side of a controversy, equal opportunity by a spokesman for the opposition must be granted, or a station will be in danger of running afoul of its federal regulatory agency, the Federal Communications Commission.

Several recent developments have illustrated public discontent with the newspaper's relative immunity from any control. First was the widespread favorable reaction to then Vice-President Spiro Agnew's speech in 1969 in which he denounced the media for their liberal bias and their failure to concern themselves with the important issues of the day. Even though this speech was politically motivated, its philosophy apparently was shared by many Americans who felt they were not being responsibly served by the mass media, including the newspaper.

Coincidentally, a few years later (1973) the National News Council was formed to investigate charges of irresponsible conduct on the part of the media. This press council, an adaptation of a similar council that has operated in Great Britain since the early 1950s, for the first time allowed individuals to complain about press performance and asked that a quasi-independent body examine these charges. Conversely, the press was also given the opportunity to voice to the News Council criticism against those whose actions were impairing the free flow of news.

The National News Council originally limited its scope primarily to the broadcast networks and only the larger newspapers. Despite these investigatory boundaries (many felt they impaired the effectiveness of the Council since the smaller rather than the larger media are often charged with acting irresponsibly), no great crush of complaints came from the public.

At the same time, small local press councils began or continued operating in various communities. However, the existence of such a council at the local level is an exception. Still, for the first time many newspaper readers were given the opportunity to voice their concerns about press conduct.[6]

The tenacity with which newspapers will fight for their editorial independence was illustrated in 1974 when a number of publishers fought to overturn a 1913 Florida statute making it mandatory that political candidates editorially attacked by newspapers be given the right of reply. In deciding the case of *Miami Herald* v. *Tornillo*, the U.S. Supreme Court found the law unconstitutional, even though the Florida Supreme Court had interpreted the Law as one which enhanced the freedom of expression and would add to the free flow of ideas and information. The U.S. Supreme Court considered the law a violation of the First Amendment.[7]

Thus, the immunity from public influence remains in effect for the newspaper. As various groups bring pressure to make newspapers more

responsive to the public, however, it appears there will be more developments in this area of access to the press.

Despite increasing production costs and continued competition from
television, the newspaper industry today is quite healthy. In 1975, there were
an estimated 1,750 daily newspapers printing approximately 63 million
copies a day. Half of the dailies were small papers with less than 10,000
circulation. Of the total number of daily newspapers, 1,440 were afternoon
newspapers. In addition, there were an estimated 9,600 weekly newspapers
serving various small communities and suburbs.

A recent development in the newspaper field has been the growth of the
suburban or community press. These suburban papers, as opposed to the
large metropolitan dailies, attempt to cover the news gaps left by the larger
papers. Because of their content, suburban papers are normally not generally
considered in competition with the metropolitan papers. Small advertisers in
suburban areas have been very responsive to these new publications.

In terms of newspaper readership, publishers in the 1970s are becoming
increasingly concerned that persons in the eighteen to thirty-five age
group—the group most advertisers are interested in—are not regular
newspaper readers. Various studies are currently being conducted to
determine what type of content would appeal to this audience. These studies
are concurrent with the special programs which many newspapers have
developed to interest elementary school children in reading newspapers. One
such program involves the training of local teachers in the daily use of the
newspaper as a classroom teaching tool in all subject areas. By attempting to
instill the habit of newspaper usage at an early age, publishers are attempting
to ensure a large reading audience in the future.

In the middle of the 1970s, the average American spent about 30 minutes a
day with a newspaper, compared to 6 to 7 hours with the broadcast media.

Magazines

Like newspapers, magazines have had to make changes because of
economic and competitive factors. The dominance of television as the
country's primary medium of entertainment dealt severe blows to many
magazines in terms of advertising revenue. Advertising is as critical to the
growth and success of most magazines as it is to newspapers.

In 1956, the beginning of the end to many flourishing years of magazine
publishing began in the United States as the impact of television was felt. The
large-circulation mass magazines were most noticeably affected. *Collier's,
Look, The Saturday Evening Post*, and, finally the giant of them all, *Life* (in
1972), disappeared from regular publishing schedules.

Essentially, what had happened was that these large general-interest
magazines found themselves competing for the same audience as many
popular television programs. Realizing this fact, advertisers spent their

money in the medium that would give them the largest audience for the least money: television. At the time of its demise, it cost about $64,000 for a full page of color advertising in *Life* magazine, not including the cost of producing the ad. *Life* would deliver a circulation of about 8 million for this fee. A prime-time television program cost about the same amount for one commercial minute but could deliver an audience many times larger. Furthermore, television allowed a product to be demonstrated and to be seen in use—something the static print medium could not do. Thus, even with large circulations some magazines found they could not survive.[8]

While many of the magazine giants fell in the late 1960s and early 1970s, magazines in general have never been healthier. Content emphasis, however, has changed significantly. With television in 96 percent of all homes, people are no longer interested in general interest content in magazines; they can see this type of material on television.

Special interest magazines, catering to one particular segment of the public instead of everyone, have continued to flourish, while many new ones have begun operation in recent years.

Americans have shown a willingness to pay a dollar or more for a publication whose specialized content is of particular interest to them. Advertisers too are pleased with the health of these magazines, since the publications deliver an audience that would not be available as inexpensively. Virtually every reader of a special interest publication, such as boating, is a prospective consumer for the advertiser whose products are related to the magazine content.[9]

There are many recent examples of success stories in the magazine publishing field. On a regional level, *Southern Living*, a magazine intended and designed only for one region of the country, has built up a circulation of over 1 million.

A small state publication which caters even more to a limited audience, *Florida Sportsman* magazine of Miami, has managed to build a circulation of 70,000 within a few short years, giving it a circulation larger than that of most daily newspapers in the country.

People magazine, a Time Inc. publication specializing in human interest items about famous people, has been immensely successful on a national level. It is sold only on newstands and the reader, not the advertiser, provides most of the revenue. Not surprisingly the magazine with the largest total monthly circulation, *TV Guide*, is highly specialized.

Reader's Digest is perhaps the only large general interest magazine still surviving. Circulation for its single monthly issue (*TV Guide* comes out weekly) is in excess of 28 million, 11 million of which are sold outside the United States. Yet, some would argue that even the *Reader's Digest* is aimed at a particular type of audience because of the nature of its content. The *Digest* audience is generally an aging, conservative, Protestant-ethic one.

Even magazines on a downward trend in the 1960s and 1970s found that if they would limit themselves only to a certain audience segment and not try to appeal to everyone they could be very successful. The magazine *Cosmopolitan* is a case in point. Doing very poorly in the early 1960s, it changed its format from a general interest women's magazine to one aimed at the single working girl. No other magazine was then catering to this group. Readers wanted it, and advertisers wanted space in the publication since no other medium could deliver this type of audience. It has been extremely successful, spawning many imitators.

The same type of success was met earlier by *Playboy*, pioneer in the men's magazine field. As time went on, more and more imitators of such successful publications found that acceptance was not as easy to attain: reader and advertising interest had already been well satisfied.

In addition to helping kill off the general interest magazine, television seems effectively to have eliminated the magazine audience for fiction. The reason again is that television can present this kind of content better, often with more audience involvement. Today the ratio of nonfiction to fiction in magazines is three to one. Several decades ago it was reversed.

Garnering perhaps as large an audience overall as magazines intended for generally distributed magazines are the trade or business publications. Most of these are not seen by persons outside a particular industry or profession. These magazines generally are also doing well because of their specialized nature. Moreover, some receive a subsidy from a particular organization which wishes to communicate with their employees and clients. News magazines such as *Time* and *Newsweek* have shown a continued increase in circulation in recent years, despite their steeply rising subscription rates.

The greatest problem facing magazines in the 1970s is not a lack of readers but continually rising production and mailing costs. Production costs forced some magazines like *McCalls* to adopt a smaller page size. Magazines that had previously been printed entirely on a slick paper went to cheaper paper grades, such as newsprint, to reduce costs. Changing to newsprint eliminated the use of color photographs by these publications because of the poor reproduction quality of the lesser grade of paper.

Striking a kind of compromise, a number of publications went to newsprint for the majority of their pages but retained several slick pages with color photographs at the beginning and end of each issue. Such hybrids did not appear to alienate substantial numbers of readers.

Increases in the postage rates by Congress were forcing some publishers to consider new methods of distribution. Magazines (as well as newspapers) enjoy a government subsidy in the second-class mailing privilege, designed to promote the efficient flow of information at a cost significantly less than that of first-class mail. Steady increases in the second-class rate were forcing some publishers to attempt to cut down on the number of subscribers and to have readers purchase their publication at the newsstand.

One device several publishers employed was to raise the subscription rate to their magazines to such a level that there was no longer any significant savings in a subscription to the magazine. The reader would do just as well to purchase his copy from a newsstand where previously, by subscribing, he could get as much as 30 to 50 percent off the regular retail price.

Advertising

It would not be too extreme to say that advertising is the life blood of American mass media. In essence, advertising totally supports the broadcast industry. It is the most important income source for the print media as well, although the print media does gain added income from circulation sales. Without advertising support, the mass media would be structured and controlled far differently from the present system.

More than $27 billion is spent annually on advertising in the United States—a figure larger than the total national budgets of some countries. The newspaper, the oldest of all the mass media, is also the largest in terms of advertising dollar volume.

Advertising is differentiated from the closely allied field of public relations in that all advertising messages are paid for, whereas publicity is often provided without charge. Furthermore, the advertising message is controlled in a way a public relations message can rarely be: each advertisement is carefully controlled as to content and as to when and where it will appear. The public relations specialist often is content if his material is used at all; he usually expects to have little control over whether the content is altered and in which media it will appear.[10]

All advertising money is spent with one goal in mind: to persuade prospective consumers to purchase the advertised product. Once this goal has been accomplished, advertising helps persuade the consumer that he is satisfied with his choice so that he will repurchase the item. The word "persuasion" is the key term which reflects the common element of almost all advertising messages.[11]

The advertiser may employ various techniques in order to motivate people to try his product. Given a choice, most advertisers appeal to the emotions of consumers, since individuals are normally easier to motivate through emotional rather than rational appeals. This technique is sometimes criticized for fear the consumer is being unfairly taken advantage of, that he is being manipulated to buy items which, if presented more objectively, he would not purchase.

Advertisers respond that, as long as they are being truthful and not misleading, the consumer has nothing to fear. The advertiser also argues that under our competitive economic system, an appeal to the emotions is as legitimate a sales strategy as any other.

Most large advertisers employ advertising agencies to create their advertising campaigns, to produce the ads, and to arrange in which media they will appear. These agencies normally conduct research to determine consumer attitudes toward a client's product, the best types of appeals that might be used to promote it, and whether any intrinsic changes in product features are needed.

In general, only one dominant appeal appears in an advertisement, for to include more than one would create the potential of detracting from the ad's impact. The consumer might be given so many ideas at one time that none would make a lasting impression.

Each manufacturer has his own special reason for advertising. Depending on his particular needs and problems, it may be one or several of the following:[12]

To show many possible uses of a product
To extend the length of the buying season for a specific item
To dispel wrong impressions about a product
To make known the organization behind the advertisement (institutional advertising)
To help render a public service
To meet substitution by competitors' products
To attract a new generation of consumers

Advertising pervades the American society. To accomplish its goal to sell, whether it be ideas or products, it continually bombards the consumer to such an extent that it is sometimes felt advertising is too much with us. According to some estimates, the average person is deluged with between 2,500 and 5,000 different messages each day, depending on the type of media he uses and the amount of time he spends with them.

The advertising industry has reached the point where it has been termed an instrument of social control comparable to the school and the church in the extent of its influence upon society.[13] Of particular concern to many critics are the values expressed in the content of ads—values many people apparently imitate in the belief that proper conformity to them is necessary for success.

Does advertising create or reflect the values shown in its messages? Many advertisers tend to argue that they simply reflect society as it is. Opponents counter that the opposite is true, that advertising actually tends to create values in the society inasmuch as the consumer is bombarded with a concept so continually that he comes to adopt it without consciously realizing he is doing so.

As an example of this debate, the advertiser argues that he is not responsible for debasing the language and degrading the culture, as is often charged. He insists that, in order to most effectively persuade consumers, he must talk to them in their own language. Therefore, if the language of advertising is often at a low level, it is a reflection of the educational level of the population as a whole, that it is the society that sets the tone of the messages, not the advertiser. To talk above or below the intellectual level of the consumer would be detrimental to the success of any message, according to the advertiser. Some critics charge that even if this be the case, it is the job of advertising, because of its pervasiveness, to help raise the level of language and not keep it at its present low status.

Other social consequences of advertising that are of concern to critics include the following:

Does advertising play on previous insecurities already existing in people, or does it help bring them into existence?

Does advertising foster the philosophy that what you own is more important than what you are as a person, that things instead of people provide happiness?

Does advertising create psychological consumer deficit in substantial numbers of people and thereby threaten the good of the society as a whole? Psychological consumer deficit occurs when people are continually shown goods and services they themselves will never be able to afford, which causes unrest and dissatisfaction.

Whether advertising creates or reflects values is a moot question that can probably never be answered very simply. One thing that is obvious, however, is that advertising is extremely sensitive to values and tastes and is quick to highlight social changes in its messages.

The problem of fraudulent or misleading advertising has haunted advertisers from the beginning. The consumer's recognition that much advertising is often less than honest has given advertising somewhat of a tarnished image. Not helping the situation is the fact that advertising is but one of business's many sales tools and that commerce itself does not enjoy the highest of reputations. The old adage "let the buyer beware" was not based on the businessman's advertising messages but on his other practices.

People in general have come to expect a certain amount of exaggeration in advertising. Most consumers are skeptical of the claims that various brands are "the best." Such claims, known as puffery, are permitted by the federal govenment as long as they do not develop misleading impressions.[14] The Federal Trade Commission, the agency which regulates advertising, has adopted the attitude that puffery is so widespread that consumers are accustomed to it and are perceptive enough to recognize if for what it is. However, when an advertiser does something blatantly misleading, such as placing marbles in a soup bowl to make it appear the soup contains more vegetables than it actually does, he will be ordered to end such a deceptive practice, and he faces financial penalties for failure to comply.[15]

In order to correct misleading impressions made by previous ads, the practice of using counter and corrective advertising is becoming more common. A counter advertisement is one normally produced by someone other than the advertiser to refute or contradict the claims made by him, or to point out potential hazards from the use of a particular product that the advertiser does not make apparent. The large antismoking campaign is perhaps the largest counteroffensive ever launched in the field of advertising.

Corrective advertisements are those produced by the advertiser himself, often at the direction of the FTC, to clarify what previous commercials had stated in an unclear or misleading manner. For instance, one advertiser recently was made to explain what the term *food energy* meant as used in its advertisements. Many persons interpreted the term to refer to vitamins when it actually related to calories.

Advertising is subject to many forms of regulation. In addition to review by various federal agencies, there are the advertising codes of the various media, media censors, professional advertising organizations, better business bureaus, and consumer affairs bureaus, all of which attempt to prevent or examine complaints about misleading and deceptive messages.

An area of great concern is the increased practice of merchandising political candidates by means of regular advertising techniques, with the result that a candidate is packaged and sold to the consumer in the same manner as a bar of soap.

Since 1960 and the debates between Richard Nixon and John F. Kennedy, American political advertising has relied heavily on the concept of selling a candidate's image rather than making known a candidate's stance on various issues. This image politics has serious consequences since it manipulates the voters' emotional rather than intellectual reaction in helping determine candidate selection. It is argued that the offices for which candidates are competing are much too important for the candidates to be presented for public inspection in such a superficial manner.

While many complaints have been voiced about the practice, little is being done to curb it. Politicians and their campaign managers realize that advertising, especially TV commercials, is the most effective way to become known. Advertising is the cheapest, most efficient means of reaching the average voter, who is sometimes very apathetic about the entire electoral process.

According to many recent studies, many voters appear to make their decision on the basis of whether they "like" a candidate (primarily an emotional response to the candidate's appearance and mannerisms), and not on the basis of the candidate's intellectual abilities and stated policies.[16]

Despite the problems related to the way advertising sometimes operates, it is a central force in the economy of the country. No other means is available which as effectively turns potential consumers into actual customers. As such, it provides for mass production which allows the manufacture of goods and services at lower costs, and further stimulates sales in general.

Even societies that formerly disapproved of advertising as wasteful and unnecessary, such as the Soviet Union, are finding that when consumer production equals or exceeds consumer demand advertising is a necessary force if the economy's progress is to be sustained.[17]

Notes

1. Edwin Emery, Phillip H. Ault, and Warren K. Agee, *Introduction to Mass Communications* (New York: Dodd, Mead and Co., 1970), pp. 52-53.

2. Donald L. Shaw, "Surveillance vs. Constraint: Press Coverage of a Social Issue," *Journalism Quarterly* 46 (1969):707-712.

3. Frederick C. Whitney, *Mass Media and Mass Communications in Society* (Dubuque, Iowa: William C. Brown Co., 1975), pp. 161-168.

4. John C. Merrill, Carter R. Bryan, and Marvin Alisky, *The Foreign Press* (Baton Rouge: Louisiana State University Press, 1970), p. 41.

5. Donald M. Gillmor and Jerome A. Barron, *Mass Communication Law, Cases and Comment* (St. Paul, Minn.: West Publishing Co., 1974), pp. 553-572.

6. Robert J. Glessing and William P. White, *Mass Media, The Invisible Environment Revisited* (Palo Alto, Calif.: Science Research Associates, 1976), pp. 245-251.

7. Thomas W. Hoffer and Gerald A. Butterfield, "The Right to Reply: A Florida First Admendment Aberration," *Journalism Quarterly* 53 (1976):111-117.

8. Whitney, *Mass Media and Mass Communications*, p. 183.

9. Glessing and White, *Mass Media*, pp. 56-62.

10. Phillip Ward Burton and J. Robert Miller, *Advertising Fundamentals* (Scranton, Pa.: International Textbook Co., 1970), pp. 3-12.

11. S. Watson Dunn, *Advertising, Its Role in Modern Marketing* (New York: Holt Rinehart and Winston, 1969), pp. 3-16.

12. Otto Kleppner, *Advertising Procedure* (Englewood Cliffs, N.J.: Prentice-Hall, 1966), pp. 47-60.

13. David M. Potter, cited by Roe M. Christenson and Robert O. McWilliams, eds., *Voice of the People* (New York: McGraw-Hill, 1962), p. 456.

14. Kenneth G. Sheinkopf and M. Timothy O'Keefe, *Advertising Principles and Practices, Selected Readings* (Washington, D.C.: College and University Press, 1975), pp. 148-152.

15. Ibid., pp. 153-155.

16. M. Timothy O'Keefe and Kenneth G. Sheinkopf, "The Voter Decides: Candidate Image or Campaign Issue?," *Journal of Broadcasting* 18, no. 4 (1974):403-412.

17. M. Timothy O'Keefe and Kenneth G. Sheinkopf, "Advertising in the Soviet Union: Growth of a New Media Industry," *Journalism Quarterly* 53 (1976):80-87.

Michael V. Belok

MINORITIES AND ETHNICITY

The American image of minorities has been an ambivalent one from the very beginnings of the nation. The colonists (Englishmen for the most part) had mixed attitudes toward the native Americans. On one hand, they wished to convert them to Christianity, but implicit in their view of the natives was the notion that they were uncivilized. The natives were "raw material," and somehow they had to be processed and transformed into Christians and civilized people. It appears to be a peculiarity of the Anglo-Saxons to consider themselves the majority even when this is counter to the facts.

The early colonists came to the New World for many reasons, not the least of which was to educate the heathens and teach them the rudiments of the Christian faith. Thus, the early settlers in New England, led by the "Apostle to the Indians" John Eliot, soon began the process of acculturation of the natives. The charter of the Massachusetts Bay Company set forth the main objective of the colony: "to win and incite the natives of the country, to the knowledge and obedience of the only true God and saviour of mankind" (as Samuel Eliot Morison tells us in his *Builders of the Bay Colony*). The seal of the colony contained the cry "Come over and help us," placed in the mouth of an Indian. Samuel Eliot Morison good humoredly relates a dialogue between two Indians and members of the General Court. The Indians supposedly indicated a desire to reverence the God of the English "because we see he doth better to the English than other gods do to others."[1] In 1654, John Eliot produced an Indian primer to teach the Indians how to read. Eliot also prepared various religious tracts and translated the Bible into the English language of his locale. He was tireless in his efforts.[2]

The Massachusetts Bay Colony was not alone in its efforts. The Virginia Colony also had entertained high hopes of converting and educating the Indians. The original charter of the Virginia Company contained a reference to the need for "propagating of Christian religion to such people, as yet live in darkness and miserable ignorance of the true knowledge and worship of God, and may in time bring the infidels and savages . . . to human civility and quiet government." One of the plans was to form Henrico College for this purpose, but the plans were aborted by an Indian uprising and massacre.[3] The great educational theorist of the early seventeenth century, John Brinsley, wrote a plan of education for this very purpose entitled *A Consolation for Our Grammar Schools* (1622). Brinsley also included the Irish and other "Papists" as needing civilizing. In Pennsylvania, Anthony Benezet labored long and mightily to educate and civilize Negroes and Indians. Benjamin Franklin introduced another idea which was to become part and parcel of the American scene, the fear of the foreigner. He was much concerned that the German settlers would become an alien force in Pennsylvania and advocated education in the English language for them. Nowhere were there any suggestions that the minorities might enrich American life and that they should be allowed to continue their own culture and language.

When the American school system came into being, its purpose was to Americanize the immigrants. Cultural pluralism was not yet in evidence. American schools would make everyone Americans. Some resisted, and the tendency of bypassing the Protestant-dominated school began to emerge. Roman Catholics early began to set up their own schools.[4] Even earlier, there had been religiously oriented schools, but these were the exception rather than the rule. It was with the development of the American Common School that the movement toward parochial schools emerged.

The coming of the Irish in the antebellum period exacerbated the problem. Not only were they Catholics but they were perceived as an unruly lot. Poverty-stricken, alien in their religion, and just plain different, they were regarded with great suspicion. Almost anything negative one could say about a people was attributed to the Irish. Marcus Lee Hansen put it best: "They were regarded as stupid and dirty, superstitious and untrustworthy, diseased and in despair. They were viewed as beggars and thieves, the overflow of the Irish poorhouses and outcasts from overpopulated estates."[5] They were also not content to be kept in their place and so they moved to improve their lot and to maintain their traditions; the result was that they became a problem for many.

Their presence in New York City was felt by the New York Public School Society, a private, nonsectarian organization devoted to educating the poor. Poor the Irish were, and the New York School Society began the process of improving them. Their children were rounded up, cleaned up, and shaped up. As they were regarded as being dirty, superstitious, criminally inclined, and running free in the streets, they were seen as threats to the public order. Where better to change them and control them than in the schools.

The Roman Catholic clergy saw the situation differently. They believed that the Irish children were being subverted from the faith by the Protestant-dominated Public School Society. During the 1830s, a battle between the Catholics and the Public School Society took place, and the Roman Catholics pushed for their own schools and public funds to support them. They charged the Public School Society with using schoolbooks hostile to the Roman Catholic religion. The Roman Catholics wanted their own schools and their own schoolbooks and Bible. The school authorities offered to delete offensive passages in schoolbooks, but Bishop Hughes did not consider this condescension to be enough. "Where are the Catholic heroes?" he asked. The cultural objections the Catholics made then were very similar to those expressed by minority groups today. The Roman Catholics believed (with good cause) that the schoolbooks were biased against Catholics, presenting negative images and attitudes. Hughes pointed out that the schoolbooks did not contain positive images for Catholic children and neglected Catholic writers, inventors, explorers, and poets.

In 1840, the Roman Catholics approached the legislature for funds, and Governor Seward supported them. The Public School Society worked against them. Meanwhile, the New York Common Council decided against the Roman Catholics. The Public School Society's victory was short-lived, however. The Catholic recourse was to politics, and they managed to make their presence felt. In 1842, a bill passed the New York legislature in which the Public School Society was placed under the authority of elected public officials. Gradually, the Public School Society's position was weakened, and in 1853 it turned over its schools to the Board of Education.[6]

The controversy between the Catholics and the Public School Society was a significant one. Although the Catholics could not secure what they wanted most, public funds, they did manage to undo the Public School Society and to show that the Catholics were a political force to be reckoned with. Much of the classic techniques used by minorities were evident in this controversy: the use of political means to secure results, the charges of discrimination, and the development of a sense of cohesion and solidarity. If the Public School Society was an instrument of social control, it could be countered.

The Roman Catholics went their own way and eventually established a system of parochial schools. They have not yet given up the fight for public funds, but for a period the controversy was muted. Probably not too soon because the 1840 riots between Catholics and Protestants were related to the school issue and were a result of both groups escalating a conflict beyond manageable proportions.

With the advent of immigrants from Central-Eastern-Balkan-Russian Europe in the 1880s, the problem of acculturation became acute. Joseph S. Roucek gives a vivid description of this group:

... the strongest group coming to America was represented by the rather illiterate peasants from Central-Eastern-Balkan-Russian Europe, whose culture represented a folk society integrally associated with plantings, feasts and fasts, with the father having the role of a benevolent despot. The family was characterized by family cohesion and mutual responsibility, with individual roles ritualized in terms of culturally patterned systems of privileges and obligations; but this form did not fit the American scene, where the father could no longer command the obedience of children who allegiance to school and factory now competed with that of the family. Then, to all the social class disadvantages which the immigrant shared with the native working population (of low class standing) were added the ethnic and religious differences that set the immigrant and his family apart from the mainstream of the culture around him. The second (that is American born) generation soon made the painful discovery that the two worlds were incompatible, that it was a handicap to stick to the Family's "old-fashioned" and "non-American" folkways and mores, and that social rewards went to those who could most completely slough off the sign of their origins.[7]

The story of the attempts to Americanize these immigrants is well told in numerous books. The story is not without significance, as we have seen with the case of the Irish and the New York school controversy. Much of the minorities' problems, tactics, and future are adumbrated in the earlier story of these immigrants.

Some Theoretical Considerations

First, let us make clear that minority problems are not peculiar to the United States; *every* part of the world faces these problems. Whether it be North America, South America, Europe, Africa, or Asia, the problem of ethnic groups exists. The shift to the term *ethnic groups* should alert the reader to the close association of minorities and ethnicity in problem situations. Although the two terms are not synonymous, they are very closely related in many practical situations. Even the term *problem* is closely related. Minorities, ethnicity, and problems seem very often to go together, as does conflict. If a society is homogeneous, then minorities, ethnicity, and conflict of the sort associated with our discussion are nonexistent. But this is seldom the case. We can start with the basic premise that both minority and ethnic groups are associated with potential conflict and that both are conceived as potentially disintegrative elements in most societies. In a society, such as that of the United States, where the very sense of identity and nationhood was a problematic one, the threat of minorities or ethnic groups perceived as alien to the society is exacerbated even more. When the United States came into being, it did not represent a nation in its fullest sense; a sense of national identity and national character had to be created. The population was by no means homogeneous—a fact we tend to forget.[8] Thus Americans, composed of many peoples, have always been concerned with defining themselves.

For any society to exist, it must maintain self-sufficiency and order. This requires a broad commitment to the values of the society—the common values; they are the cement of societal self-sufficiency. While all members of the societal unit need not agree on all values, they must share at least a small core of values. For most societies, order is of primary importance and the maintenance of the society depends upon it. Without this minimal agreement, there would be chaos and a breakdown of the system. Values are an integrating factor.

As far as the dominant group is concerned, the values of minority groups are frequently dysfunctional. They see the immigrant or, as in the case of the

United States, the native population and the imported group (the blacks) as a threat. Blacks and immigrants cannot be done without, but they are still a threat to the social cohesiveness of the society. Witness the frequent riots characterizing American society, whether it be early black slave riots, Catholics rioting against Protestants, Irish rioting against free blacks in New York City during the Civil War, or the more recent black riots of the 1960s.[9]

In times of accelerated social change, people tend to perceive their world as threatening and dangerous. This attitude is especially significant to the institutions of the society entrusted with the task of socialization and enculturation. According to Seymour Martin Lipset, the dominant values of American society have been equality and achievement, and their "dynamic interaction . . . has been a constant element in data determining American institutions and behavior."[10] These institutions attempt to maintain the status quo in order to preserve some semblance of order and stability.

As the process of industrialization and modernization developed, the values of achievement and equality were especially useful. American society moved toward a rationally organized, bureaucratic structure. Following Parsons, we may speak of the structural components of norms, values, collectivities, and roles. The aspects of the developmental process are inclusion, value generalization, differentiation, and adaptive upgrading. Probably the most important socializing agency is the school. Adults, with some exceptions, are socialized elsewhere. It is the school that prepares the individual for adult roles, and that gives him the technical knowledge and skills necessary to adequately perform these roles. Individuals must be socialized so that they adequately perform the roles required by the society and be committed to their performance. In other words, they must internalize the behavior expected of them in these social roles as they also learn the necessary roles to keep society functioning. Here it might be useful to mention some pattern alternatives available such as universalism versus particularism, achievement versus ascription, and specificity versus diffuseness.[11]

Minority groups do not often share the commitment to the values mentioned above. Basically members of traditional societies, they are usually oriented more toward particularism and ascription than toward universalism and achievement. Since American society is based upon equality and achievement, however, minorities have always been required to adapt and learn new things in order to become part of the society in the fullest sense. Very often they chose not to. Not having been socialized to American society and its values, the immigrants were strangers. Following Gerald Rosenblum, the term *basic socialization* may be introduced. It means that the individual has incorporated the "generalized norms and values characterizing a society" so he can perform the social roles adequately both in the area of skills and attitudes. Intermediate socialization is specialized socialization. The individual learns the special behavior patterns expected in "differentiated subsystems," such as work settings.[12] The individual is an "expedient member" of the society, not a "genuine member" who has been basically socialized. With the immigrants this pattern applied to most adults; the second generation became more "genuine" members of American society. Probably, a similar process is now being experienced by other minorities as they are moving more and more from something resembling "expedient membership" toward "genuine membership" in the larger society.

Alternative Responses to Minorities

Although the minority "problem" has been around since the very beginnings, the response of the dominant American group has not been uniform or consistent. In the beginning, the Indians were to be civilized and made into Christians; very soon thereafter, the response changed and the Indians were considered by many as a "nuisance" and a group to be exterminated. Others deplored this approach and continued their efforts to convert the tribes to Christianity. Some felt that exclusion or isolation was the best policy (the reservation policy), and others that assimilation was a possibility. The various tribes had other ideas: some fought the whites until exhausted; others, such as the Cherokee, tried to conform to the white man's way; and still others tried isolation.

The immigrant's situation was different, for he came of his own accord. In some cases, he did not intend to stay; as soon as he made his "fortune," he would return to his native land. In the meantime, he worked hard as long as work was available. He fit the pattern we have identified as an "expedient member" of the society, trying all the time to stay clear of flagrantly flouting local mores and laws. Gradually his position changed, and he found himself either unable to return to his homeland or committed to staying in the new land.

At first, America welcomed the immigrants. After all, was not America the "asylum" of the world opening its doors to all?[13] Moreover, work was usually plentiful—at least menial tasks that the older groups no longer cared to do. There was also plenty of land, and the immigrants were often a source of profit to the old American. From time to time, the antagonisms between the "new" groups and the "old" flared up in riots and in certain political parties which viewed the foreigners with suspicion. For the most part, however, the various groups were able to accommodate themselves to each other.

Thus, there arose the three basic responses to the minorities (excluding the Indians and the blacks). The first response was the *policy of assimilation or acculturation*. Under this approach, the minorities would be made into Anglo-Saxons, and they and their children would become Americans. If not "true" Anglo-Saxons, at least they would learn the dominant ideas of the

American culture. They would be taught the virtues of cleanliness, hard work (as if they needed it), thrift, order, and respect for the American Constitution and system of laws. Except for some extremists, most Americans were willing to accept the new minorities on these terms. All the vehicles of socialization and acculturation would be used—the schools, the press, and the factory. Not only the children but also the adults went to school to learn the American language and to be indoctrinated in the American beliefs and values. The factory would socialize the adult into the pattern of behaviors appropriate in the work settings. The irrational patterns of the peasant past would have to be forgotten. Mills and mines did not defer to feast days and religious holidays. If the immigrants could not read English, there was the immigrant press that could be manipulated to acculturate the immigrant and help him adapt to the American scene. If it did not succeed in this respect, at least it provided him with a release: a place to air his woes, a vehicle for catharsis. American advertisers could be used to subsidize the press and to keep editors in line. The American immigrant press was also a vehicle to help the immigrant find out who he was. Many were peasants and had no real sense of identity. They were men of a particular locale, and only in America did many discover a wider sense of identity. Their ethnic identifications were often born in America, and they became Italians, Russians, Slovaks, and the like.[14]

The second response was the *Melting Pot* thesis put forth by many Americans. The immigrants would be fused with other Americans to form a new race. They would, in the words of Israel Zwangwill, become a "super race." The "Melting Pot" idea was not new. Hector St. John de Crevecoeur had written of a new man in the early period of the republic. Even Benjamin Rush had written of the "melting of the youth of all states into one mass of citizens."[15] The melting pot became a popular idea but one that many writers agree failed. Some did not want to be "melted"; these were not racists but simply believers in their own ethnic values and culture. They did not want to be homogenized into a uniform American type.

Those who wished to retain their ethnic identity and, as often was the case, even forge it brought forth the third response—*cultural pluralism*. Basic to this position was the belief that various ethnic groups could retain much of their culture while still remaining an integral part of American society. Ethnic groups had always maintained a certain degree of identity from the earliest times in colonial America. What actually occurred was a form of segregated pluralism with various immigrant groups concentrated in certain geographical areas: the Germans in Pennsylvania, the Dutch in New York, the English in New England and Virginia. This pattern continued late into the nineteenth century, with regional settlements the rule rather than the exception. With the coming of the "new" immigrants during 1880-1920, significant changes occurred and immigrants began settling in groups all over the country. The result was a new pattern that could be characterized as integrated pluralism. Various ethnic groups were in close and continual contact with one another.

Conflicts were inevitable. The dominant group in American society found conflict threatening. Although some did not view this development with alarm, many did. All the familiar charges were brought forth. The new immigrants threatened the racial integrity of the Anglo-Saxons; they were inferior, unclean, criminally inclined, and subversive, both politically and in the area of religion. Demands for immigrant restrictions were made. Literacy tests were advocated, exclusion by state laws was tried, laws for Asiatic exclusion were successfully passed, and, finally, the National Origins Quota Act of 1924 was passed.[16]

Some Minority Groups

Many have assumed that the "white ethnics" have been more or less assimilated into the dominant culture and have achieved success commensurate with their individual abilities. The evidence is mixed to say the least. The white ethnics refuse to go away; they are still labeled by others as "Polacks," "Wops," "Hunkies," and the like. They also often seem to perceive themselves in terms of their ethnic identities. The Melting Pot has been declared a failure countless times, but some continue to adhere to the notion. Although assimilation or "Anglo-conformity" still has its adherents, increasingly, there has been a recognition of the persistence of ethnic identification well into the third and fourth generations.[17]

Whatever the reasons for the recent revival of white ethnicity—nostalgia, search for roots, opportunism, or a reaction to the efforts of the blacks, Indians, and Hispanic Americans—there is no doubt that the movement has made considerable headway in recent years. The white ethnics, however, do not appear to be a genuine danger to the societal integration and order. Their tactics are mostly those used within the system and considered appropriate. Even though Michael Novak and other ethnic leaders have suggested that white ethnic gains have been less than impressive, there is no evidence that the white ethnics are likely to unite in any efforts to upset the status quo. Michael Novak can present figures showing that Poles, Italians, Slavs, and Greeks are not very well represented on the boards of large corporations, but whether such representation will make a difference in the composition of these boards is another question. The fact remains that the white ethnics are borrowing many of the tactics used so successfully by the blacks, Chicanos, and Indians. It is also true, however, that many of the ethnic groups used these tactics much earlier. The Irish, for example, were not averse to the use of force, and they were especially adept at the use of political power.[18]

The case of black, Indian, and Hispanic American minorities, in which most sociologists have been interested during the past two decades, is a different one. First, unlike the white ethnics, they are a highly visible group. The white ethnic, if he wishes, can opt out of his group by changing his name and adapting the dominant group's behavior patterns; the visible ethnics cannot. Second, the blacks, Chicanos, and Indians are descendants of either conquered or enslaved people, although this is not really true for all these peoples. Many blacks were free, and the Chicanos that make up the vast majority of the present American population are immigrants or descendants of immigrants, the bulk of them entering the United States during the same period as the so called new immigrants.

Characteristics of the Disadvantaged Minorities

Since 1960, one of the impressive features of American life has been the great concern for the disadvantaged segments of our society. The disadvantaged have too often been the blacks, Indians, and Hispanic Americans. For them, the tension between the values of equality and achievement identified by S. M. Lipset as the dominant values of American life has been acute. They are most often the groups who were more or less bypassed in the quest for equality and achievement.

Before moving to the population characteristics of these minorities, the point must be made that they are not homogeneous groups—neither the individual groups nor the larger group. It is an easy error to consider them homogeneous. There are differences within each group, and there are social and cultural differences among the different groups. It is well to keep in mind that what will be discussed here are averages and that averages are not all the same.

As one reads the literature about the minority groups, the constant reference to poverty is striking. It is a recurrent theme. Roessel, a leading figure in Indian education, stresses the poverty aspect.[19] Roucek quotes Hubert Humphrey: "Poverty is the everyday life of the American Indian. No other group is so victimized."[20] Bass and Burger give figures to back up their contention that the American Indian is the most disadvantaged rural group. According to them, the American Indians, when compared to the general population, suffer grievously. The Indian's income is only two-tenths as much, the unemployment rate about ten times greater, the life expectancy seven years less, and the infant mortality rate 50 percent higher.[21]

The situation of the Mexican-American is also deplorable. Mexican-Americans face discriminatory practices in most areas of the Southwest. Simmons, in his study of a south Texas town labeled "Border City," details the conditions and problems. In the city, Mexican-Americans account for about 56 percent of the population, but they are in the bottom level of the occupational hierarchy, serving as domestics, farm laborers, shed and cannery workers.[22] Glick, writing in 1966, comments, "Two ethnic, or racial, groups in the United States are currently distinguished by their inferior economic status as compared with the nation as a whole. These are the Negroes and the Spanish-speaking."[23]

A 1969 study by Galarza, Gallegos, and Samora states: "poverty and minority are synonymous for a large segment of the Mexican-American population. According to the 1960 census there were 243,000 families in the Southwest who were living in poverty commonly described as stark."[24] Greeley, in *Ethnicity* (1974), presents data showing that the position for Spanish-speaking groups has not changed significantly: they are still at the bottom.[25]

The same situation prevails in regard to the Puerto Ricans. They too suffer heavily because of discrimination. Their employment rate is lower than that of the general population, and poverty for them is a way of life. The influx of Puerto Ricans into the mainland has been a continuing one since 1940. From approximatley 100,000 in 1940, the Puerto Rican population of New York City has moved over the 900,000 mark. For a time, the influx seemed to be reversing itself, but recent figures show that the Puerto Rican migration is setting a new record. The new migrants will now be competing with their fellows in an economy that is suffering a very high unemployment rate.

The plight of the blacks is also very well known, and the literature is fast approaching unmanageable limits. Even a cursory review of the literature indicates that the blacks are now identified with the big cities. The blacks have been moving into the cities in ever-increasing numbers since World War II, and the whites have been in a rapid flight to the suburbs. Whites are estimated to be moving out of New York City at the rate of 50,000 annually. The figure for Chicago is 15,000, and for Cleveland it is estimated at 3,000. As the whites retreat, the blacks move in; the estimate is that one-half of all blacks will soon live outside the South.[26]

The familiar problems are all evident—poverty, low standards of conduct, language differences and verbal problems, different values, cultural conflicts and low social status, all resulting in prejudice, poor motivation, and inadequate self-images. Unemployment is much higher for blacks than for whites, reaching dangerously high levels for young black males. Frequently, the mother is the dominant figure and the chief support for the family. Living conditions in the ghetto are abominable for many. Noise and violence are continuing problems.

In a classic study entitled *The Mark of Oppression*, Abram Kardiner and Lionel Oversay present a picture of the life cycle of the blacks. In the lower classes, the situation of the family is often an unsettled one. The father is usually absent, and the mother is the head of the family. Broken families are very common, with the father deserting the family before the children are sixteen and often before the child is born or within two to three years after birth.

The black family of ghetto areas produces more than its share of delinquency, illiteracy, illegitimacy, and other ills. Most black families parallel
the national pattern of good behavior and self-improvement, but the
pathological end of the black family spectrum is in desperate need of help.
There are a variety of conditions responsible, but too often it is the absence of
a father in the home and the circumstance of a deserted wife living with
several children in a ghetto flat. More often than not, economic conditions
play a fundamental part. The father is often unemployed, he may absent
himself from the home to allow the family to receive relief. (As soon as a man
appears in the home, welfare payments come to an end.) However one may
feel about the problem, there is no denying it is a severe one. Conflict,
delinquency, and social disintegration are all part of the situation.[27]

If achievement and equality are American ideals, the school and education
are often considered the keys to realize them. What is the situation with
regard to education and the minorities? The most comprehensive recent
study is that referred to as the Coleman Report. This study (entitled *Equality
of Educational Opportunity*) dealt with six racial and ethnic groups: blacks,
American Indians, Oriental Americans, Puerto Ricans, Mexican-Americans,
and whites other than Mexican-Americans and Puerto Ricans. The Coleman
Report found that most American children attend segregated schools and
that black children are the most segregated of the minorities. Their schools
are often inferior in respect to some facilities related to possible academic
success. Their homes are less likely to have books and encyclopedias. The
report summarizes as follows:

Clear differences are found on these items. The average Negro family has fewer
children whose mothers graduated from high school: his classmates more frequently
are members of large rather than small families; they are less often enrolled in college
preparatory curricula: they have taken a smaller number of courses in English,
mathematics, foreign languages, and sciences.[28]

The situation varies according to regions, but this is the basic picture. The
black achievement in school is below that of white children based on average
scores from the first grade throughout high school.

The Mexican-American children also fare poorly when compared to the
white group. In the first grade, the Mexican-Americans are already behind
the Indians and the white groups and far behind the blacks in verbal
achievement. By the fourth grade, the children's median grade on reading
tests was 1.5 grade points below the norm. Ortego presents figures on the
Mexican-American's educational status that can only be called shocking. He
points out that in Texas 39 percent of the Mexican-Americans have less than a
fifth grade education, and that Mexican-Americans twenty-five years or
older have as little as 4.8 years of schooling. His conclusion is that almost half
of the Mexican-Americans in Texas are functional illiterates.[29]

Concluding Remarks

The discrepancies between the American ideal and practice result in tension in the social order as more and more individuals become conscious of the frustrations inherent in their positions. Ethnicity has become a vehicle for pushing group demands. The blacks, the Chicanos, and Indians have turned to violence, politics, and the courts to achieve their goals.[30] The black strategy is instructive. First, they used the courts to push their demands for civil rights, then they moved to violence to achieve civil rights and substantive social and economic rights, at the same time using the ideology of cultural pluralism to push their demands for cultural separatism. Black became beautiful, white seemed to become ugly. Blacks denigrated much of their white culture. Conflicts were escalated to dangerous levels and then gradually muted. In the meantime, blacks demanded special consideration for years of maltreatment. The values of universalism and achievement were repudiated in favor of particularism and ascription. Blacks were entitled to special treatment—in university admissions, in hiring for jobs usually based on merit, and in other areas.[31] The question becomes: Can cultural pluralism conceived as a form of cultural relativism and ethical relativism be defended in a society holding other values? Does not this position actually jeopardize the stability of the society, or is it possible to realize stability while allowing for considerable change in the society's norms and values?[32] Only time will tell.

Notes

1. Samuel Eliot Morison, *Builders of the Bay Colony* (Boston: Houghton Mifflin Co., 1930), pp. 288-289.

2. Ibid., pp. 288-313.

3. Edgar W. Knight and Clifton L. Hall, *Readings in American Educational History* (New York: Appleton-Century-Crofts, 1951), pp. 1-2.

4. Joseph S. Roucek, "Educational Problems Arising from the Minorities in the U.S.," *V.O.C. Journal of Education* (December 1964):33-34.

5. Marcus Lee Hansen, *The Immigrant in American History* (New York: Harper Torchbook, 1964), p. 161.

6. Carl F. Kaestle, *The Evolution of the Urban School System: New York City, 1750-1850* (Cambridge, Mass.: Harvard University Press, 1973). See also Vincent Lannie, *Public Money and Parochial Education* (Cleveland: Case Western Reserve Press, 1969).

7. Roucek, "Educational Problems," pp. 34-35.

8. Michael V. Belok, *Forming the American Minds: Early Schoolbooks and Their Compilers, 1783-1837* (Agra, India: Satish Book Enterprise, 1973).

9. Joseph S. Roucek, "The American Way of Violence: The Rise of Black Power," in James Van Patten et al., eds., *Conflict, Permanency, Change and Education* (Moti Katra; Agra 3, India: Satish Book Enterprise, 1976), pp. 230-251.

10. Seymour Martin Lipset, *The First New Nation* (Garden City, N.Y.: Doubleday, 1967), p. 115.

11. Talcott Parsons, *The Social System* (Glencoe, Ill.: Free Press, 1951), p. 67. See also Parsons, *The System of Modern Societies* (Englewood Cliffs, N.J.: Prentice-Hall, 1971).

12. Gerald Rosenblum, *Immigrant Workers* (New York: Basic Books, 1973), p. 29.

13. The term *asylum* is suggestive of hidden meaning and social control. See Erving Goffman, *Asylums* (Garden City, N.Y.: Doubleday, 1961).

14. Robert E. Park, *The Immigrant Press and Its Control* (New York: Harper, 1922).

15. Andrew M. Greeley, *Ethnicity in the United States: A Preliminary Reconnaissance* (New York: John Wiley and Sons, 1974), p. 299.

16. Peter I. Rose, *They and We* (New York: Random House, 1974), pp. 37-60.

17. Michael Novak, *The Rise of the Unmeltable Ethnics* (New York: Macmillan, 1971).

18. Andrew M. Greeley, *That Most Distressful Nation: The American Irish* (New York: Quadrangle Books, 1972).

19. Robert A. Roessel, *Handbook for Indian Education* (Los Angeles, Calif.: ERA Publishers, 1964), p. 21.

20. Joseph S. Roucek, "The Most Oppressed Race in the United States, The Indians," *Educational Forum* (May 1965):477.

21. Willard Bass and Henry G. Burger, *American Indians and Educational Laboratories* (Albuquerque, N.M.: Southwestern Cooperative Educational Laboratory, 1967).

22. Ozzie G. Simmons, "Ethnic Groups in American Life," *Daedalus* (Spring 1961):286-289.

23. Julian Samora, ed. *La Raya* (Notre Dame, Ind.: University of Notre Dame Press, 1966), p. 95.

24. Ernesto Galarza, Herman Gallegos, and Julian Samora, *Mexican-Americans in the Southwest* (Santa Barbara, Calif.: McNally and Loftin, 1969), pp. 30-31.

25. Andrew M. Greeley, *Ethnicity*, pp. 63-73. The *Arizona Republic*, December 10, 1976, reports similar data for 1975.

26. Although the data are not quite clear, this appears to be the case. See ibid., pp. 47-51.

27. Abram Kardiner and Lionel Oversay, *The Mark of Oppression* (New York: World Publishing Co., 1951), p. 396.

28. James S. Coleman et al., *Equality of Educational Opportunity* (Washington, D.C.: U.S. Government Printing Office, 1966), p. 9.

29. Philip D. Ortego, "Montezuma's Children," The Center Magazine (November 1972):23-24.

30. *Arizona Republic*, December 19, 1976. Also see *Arizona Republic*, January 2, 1977.

31. Kevin Phillips, "U.S. Seems to Be Going Minority-Crazy," *Arizona Republic*, December 6, 1976. See also Nathan Glazer and Daniel P. Moynihan, *Ethnicity Theory and Practice* (Cambridge, Mass.: Harvard University Press, 1975).

32. I have relied heavily on Richard Pratte's unpublished paper, "Cultural Pluralism and Its Relativistic Component," for the ideas expressed in the last paragraph.

Peter Conrad
and Joseph W. Schneider

MEDICINE

To consider medicine as an institution of social control requires a perspective on medical work and workers that is foreign both to popular as well as to much of sociological writing. We are not accustomed to thinking of medicine and physicians as "controllers," but rather as "healers" or "helpers" of people who are sick and in need. These common views must be suspended in order to focus on the ways in which medicine defines, orders, constrains, intervenes in, and treats the social world and the individuals who comprise it. To analyze medicine as an institution of social control is to emphasize the ways in which it serves to secure conformity or adherence to a particular set of values and norms in human societies.

On the most abstract level, medical social control may be identified as the "medicalization of life,"[1] meaning the definition and/or treatment of any phenomena of human existence in terms of their medical significance.[2] Since medicine addresses itself most generally to the protection and enhancement of "health" and the prevention and control of disease and sickness, medicalization raises the question of the boundaries of medical authority.

Medicine also controls social phenomena through its position as the dominant authority with respect to the designation and treatment of illness in modern societies. In the processes of diagnosis and treatment, medicine controls the deviation from health and "normality" that illness represents. Parsons[3] defines the "sick role" as the major cultural mechanism mitigating the potentially disruptive consequences of illness for society. Freidson[4] argues that aside from its potential impact on role performance, illness is deviance because it carries a virtually universally found evaluative quality: it is what might be called a "disvalued state." Medical institutions function to control such deviance in complex industrial societies.

Finally, in perhaps the most specific sense, medical social control may be seen as the medicalization of deviance.[5] The emphasis shifts from illness-as-deviance to deviance increasingly defined as illness. The process of defining phenomena in terms of their medical significance is applied in this case to a wide range of formerly sinful or criminal behaviors, resulting in their being redefined as illnesses, e.g., mental illness, alcoholism, drug addiction, homosexuality, hyperactivity, obesity, and violence. The boundaries of medical authority and jurisdiction become elastic and increasingly expansive.[6] It is in this more specific sense of the medicalization of deviance that medical social control becomes more direct and allows perhaps the greatest insight into the location of medicine in modern technological societies. Hence, the following discussion of sources and types of medical social control will focus primarily on medical control of deviant behavior.

Sources of Medical Social Control

The sources of medical social control, particularly of the medicalization of deviance, may be identified as a set of conditions that increase the likelihood of any phenomena being defined as a problem legitimate to medical intervention.[7] Primary among these are conditions that encourage people with problems to consult others they believe to be problem-solvers. Second, these problem-solvers must agree to accept the problem presented as a condition in fact relevant to medical diagnosis and treatment.

Healers, whether in the person of the shaman or the professional physician, have always been seen as people to whom one takes problems of unusual suffering, discomfort, or impairment. These specialists then have the responsibility to help and/or comfort the troubled person. The preeminently practical, problem-solving, and individual-focused nature of much medical work predisposes the physician to action against the presented problem, occasionally even in the face of only sketchy general knowledge.[8] In taking such action, the practitioner-physician is inclined to rely heavily on his direct, first-hand experience of past diagnosis and treatment as essentially "wise" and "successful," somewhat independently of their ultimate consequences. In seeking and subsequently submitting to this medical opinion and advice, the patient assumes a subordinate role in what has become in modern societies a system of virtually unchallenged medical authority. Although in principle subject to state approval and surveillance, the authority of physicians and medical institutions over matters of the definition and treatment of illness and maintenance of health and the conditions to which these labels apply is dominant.[9]

Medical treatment as a form of social control was first discussed systematically by Parsons[10] in his well-known description of the "sick role." He identified four components of this role: (1) its occupant is exempt from routine role performances and social responsibilities, contingent upon medical legitimation by a physician; (2) the individual is absolved of responsibility for the condition that has allowed this exemption; (3) the sick person must want to "get well" and leave the undesirable state of illness; and (4) as evidence of such proper motivation, the patient must seek technically competent help from the physician toward this end. In such legitimation and management of sickness, the physician controls the deviance that illness represents, and he redirects it, through the process of treatment, toward socially and personally stabilizing ends.

The fact that application of both the labels "ill" and "deviant" involves a moral evaluation, the designation of some state as undesirable and a violation of social norms, highlights the similar logical and social processes in identifying sick people and criminals.[11] Both are normative violations that have associated social control structures which serve to process and further define the cases brought forth: medicine and medical institutions on the one hand, and what is now called the criminal justice system on the other. The historical articulation of these cultural and structural forms is discussed in works on the rise and development of modern psychiatry[12] and the concept of mental illness[13] as rather clear attempts to control disagreeable public behavior. This social control function in the name of health is seen also in the practice of public health medicine[14] and its attempt to regulate behavior according to certain social and medical norms.

Such qualities of medicine emphasize the expansiveness of its social control function in modern societies. This suggests that a sufficient condition for the medicalization of anything, but most specifically here, of behavior defined as deviant, is that it first must be identified as a cause, consequence, or component of an illness. Failing that, it must in some way be perceived as a threat to health as defined by the medical profession. The widely inclusive definition of health provided by the prestigious World Health Organization is illustrative here: "Health is a state of complete physical, mental, and social well-being and not merely the absence of disease or infirmity." Zola[15] has perhaps captured this expansive dimension of medicine's authority most clearly: "My contention is that if anything can be shown in some way to effect the inner workings of the body and to a lesser extent the mind, then it can be labelled an 'illness' or jurisdictionally a 'medical problem' "[16]

A second set of conditions propitious for the development of medical social control involves the availability of specific knowledge and techniques that may be applied toward this end.[17] Without question, the success of modern medicine and medical practice in achieving its dominant position in Western industrial societies is in large part the result of the greatly increased effectiveness of medical intervention that began at the turn of the century in Europe and America.[18] Before the latter part of the nineteenth century, physicians were relatively unorganized, inconsistently trained, poorly paid, and limited in their therapeutic techniques and abilities. The apparently remarkable impact of medicine in the control of communicable diseases[19] and improvements in clinical medicine and surgery contributed substantially to the reputation of medicine and physicians as effective specialists in healing and treatment. As science became the dominant and trusted system for understanding and controlling the natural world, traditional religious and mystical explanations of sickness and discomfort declined. Notwithstanding these advances in medical knowledge, it is medical technology that has gained for modern medicine the dubious reputation as capable of virtually unlimited achievement; indeed, the inevitability of death itself has been challenged in the face of these "medical miracles." The rise and development of modern psychiatry in the United States, although generally regarded as considerably less effective than other medical interventions, has contributed significantly to this image of medicine as capable of handling virtually any problem of human experience.

The effectiveness of physicians and modern medicine in solving problems individuals present them is quite significant, then, in understanding the authority they enjoy and its implication for social control. Freidson[20] cautions, however, that their reputation should not be seen solely as a result of actual achievements, but also as the product of negotiation, persuasion, and impression management by the powerful interests involved in the health care system. This distinction between the reputation and reality of modern medicine points to a third set of conditions important as a source of medical social control: the congruence between medical and popular conceptions of health, sickness, and treatment.

To the extent that popular and professional definitions of what constitutes health and illness and appropriate forms of treatment coincide, the control of illness by medical institutions becomes significantly easier as a result of the "moral weight" of what comes to be defined as "normal," everyday, or commonplace. Such congruence may be seen as equally the product of lay and professional expectations and behavior,[21] or as primarily the consequence of popular socialization into a dominant ideological point of view.[22]

To analyze the reputation and apparent increasing voluntary solicitation of medical institutions[23] as in part a product of a dominant ideology is to portray the components of medical institutions as having vested interests in the medical status quo and its protection. This status quo is seen to serve particularly the needs of those having the most power and control as against those with few such resources. Critics of the American medical system have little difficulty identifying such interested participants, particularly represented in the form of the American Medical Association, state and county medical societies, the American Hospital Association, Blue Cross and Blue Shield and other health insurance carriers, and perhaps most undeniably, the medical equipment and drug industries.[24] An analysis of the political economy of the American health care system in particular leads to the conclusion that all of these parties have an investment in what might be called "sick care," its maintenance and even growth.

The question of growth attributable to economic and power interests relates directly to the expansive boundaries of medical care noted above. Such enlarged jurisdiction seems to be illustrated rather clearly by deviant behaviors that are increasingly defined as illness, such as obesity, hyperactivity in children, and violence. If many of the "miracles" of modern medicine are the direct result of technological knowledge and its implementation through material commodities, and, given the interest the suppliers of these commodities have in such events, then, as Ellul[25] and others have suggested, medical technology must be studied as a potentially independent source of such medicalization. Indeed, these "new" areas of illness and disease, constructed by redefining deviant behavior as sickness, may be seen as "frontiers" not only of medical research, discovery, and treatment, but also in terms of new "markets" for the economic interests involved in modern medical care, particularly in the United States. That such medicalization is a form of medical hegemony[26] or medical imperialism has been suggested by some critics. These analyses are, of course, not psychological, but focus on the economic and social characteristics of the society and interested groups involved, including scientists and physicians as well as business persons.[27] Although speculative, it is suggested that this medical establishment in the United States is characterized by a kind of scientific, economic, technological, and bureaucratic "dynamic inertia" that serves both to maintain the system and to stimulate it toward increased dominance and control.

The development of medical social control discussed thus far, particularly the medicalization of deviance, has been in terms of the "pull" by medical institutions of an increasingly broad range of deviant behaviors under medical jurisdiction. Such an analysis directs attention to historical changes that might simultaneously "push" such behavior toward medical social control. These exclusionary processes of other institutional arrangements in society represent a fourth set of conditions for increased medical social control.

Changes in the criminal justice system in the United States, which have occurred almost parallel to those discussed above, have encouraged and reinforced the expansion of medical control, particularly psychiatric control. Affected by the same scientific world view that provided the basis for modern medical practice, criminal law has undergone a process of "divestment"[28] of a broad range of offenses for which individuals are considered incapable of willful or criminal intent, the keystone of assessing responsibility in the criminal law. In place of traditional forms of punishment, such individuals have been directed toward treatment, therapy, and rehabilitation conducted typically under either direct medical auspices or indirect medical supervision in community-based treatment programs. Kittrie[29] and Szasz[30] have identified this process as the rise of the "therapeutic state." Rieff[31] discusses this same development in terms of the diffusion of Freudian ideas, and he suggests that it represents a "triumph of the therapeutic" in which the hospital has increasingly come to replace the church and parliament as the symbolic center of Western society. Szasz sees this development as leading not only to the corruption of psychiatry, but, more importantly, to a growing absence of individual responsibility for a wide range of rule-breaking behaviors.

As Kittrie points out, this development has its roots in the positivist criminology of the nineteenth century. Contrary to classical notions that individuals behaved, for better or worse, as a result of their own free-will choices based on a hedonistic calculus, the "new" criminology saw individual wrong-doing in terms of either social or biological-genetic determinism. The causes of this rule-breaking behavior could be studied and treated scientifically. Such an argument was historically congenial in that it satisfied the growing desire for humanitarian treatment, addressed the ineffectiveness and distastefulness of traditional criminal punishments, and still allowed the state to meet its responsibility to protect society from repeated offenses. Certain categories of deviant actors, particularly those who appeared to act on the basis of diminished self-control, were increasingly seen as subject to forces either internal or external to them over which they had only limited, if any, control. Treatment of the mentally ill, juveniles, psychopaths, drug addicts, and alcoholics was to be pursued, as in medical treatment, in terms of the needs of individual cases.

Through the conjunction of scientific criminology and the medical model, the state comes to act in a *parens patriae*[32] role toward categories of "sick" deviants, acting on their behalf while simultaneously serving the interests of the state acting for the community. In such cooperation, the physician must divide his or her loyalties between the interests of the patient, considered a sacred commitment, and those of the state. This cooperation serves to increase rather dramatically medicine's social control while, paradoxically, simultaneously limiting its autonomy to make decisions in such cases. A prime contemporary example is the highly politicized practice of psychiatry in the Soviet Union. What is perceived typically as a supportive relationship between medicine and the state[33] comes in such situations to assume coercive qualities as physicians and medical personnel are implicated explicitly in political control in the name of health.[34]

Types of Medical Social Control

On the most abstract level, medical social control is the acceptance of a medical perspective as the dominant definition of certain phenomena. When medical perspectives of problems and their solutions become dominant, they diminish competing definitions. This is particularly true of problems related to bodily functioning and in areas where medical technology can demonstrate effectiveness (e.g., immunization, contraception, antibacterial drugs), and is increasingly the case for behavioral and social problems.[35] This underlies the construction of medical norms (e.g., what is healthy) and the "enforcement" of both medical and social norms. Medical social control also includes medical advice, counsel, and information that is part of the general stock of knowledge: eat a well-balanced diet, cigarette smoking causes cancer, being overweight increases health risks, exercising regularly is healthy, teeth should be brushed twice daily, etc. Such aphorisms, even when unheeded, serve as roadsigns for desirable behavior. At a more concrete level, medical social control is professional medical intervention qua medical treatment (although it may include some types of self-treatment). This intervention aims at returning sick individuals to a state of health and to their conventional social roles, adjusting them to new (e.g., impaired) roles, or, short of these, making individuals more comfortable with their condition. Medical social control of deviant behavior is usually a variant of medical intervention that seeks to eliminate, modify, isolate, or regulate behavior, socially defined as deviant, with medical means and in the name of health.

Traditionally, psychiatry and public health have served as modes of medical control. Psychiatry's social control functions with mental illness, especially in terms of institutionalization, have been widely analyzed.[36] Recently, it has been argued that psychotherapy itself is an agent of social control and a supporter of the status quo.[37] The mandate of public health medicine—the control and elimination of conditions and diseases deemed a threat to the health of a community—is more diffuse. It operates as a control agent by setting and enforcing certain "health" standards in the home, workplace, and community (food, water, sanitation) and by identifying, preventing, treating, and, if necessary, isolating persons with communicable diseases.[38] The clearest example of the last-named is the detection of venereal disease. Indeed, public health has exerted considerable coercive power in attempting to prevent the spread of infectious disease.

There are a number of types of medical control of deviance. The most common forms include medicalizing deviant behavior—i.e., defining the behavior as an illness or a symptom of an illness or underlying disease—and subsequent direct medical intervention. This medical social control takes three general forms: medical technology, medical collaboration, and medical ideology.

The growth of specialized and technological medicine and the concomitant development of *medical technology* has produced an armamentarium of medical controls. Psychotechnologies, which include various forms of medical and behavioral technologies,[39] are the most common types of medical control of deviance. Since the emergence of phenothiazine medications in the early 1950s for the treatment and control of mental disorder, there has been a virtual explosion in the development and use of psychoactive medications that control behavioral deviance: tranquilizers like Librium and Valium for anxiety, nervousness, and general malaise; stimulant medications for hyperactive children; amphetamines for over-eating and obesity; antabuse for alcoholism; methadone for heroin; and many others. These pharmaceutical discoveries. aggressively promoted by a highly profitable and powerful drug industry,[40] often become the treatment of choice for deviant behavior. They are easily administered, under professional medical control; quite potent in their effects (i.e., controlling, modifying, and even eliminating behavior; and generally less expensive than other treatments and controls (e.g., hospitalization, altering environments, long-term psychotherapy).

Psychosurgery, surgical procedures meant to correct certain "brain dysfunctions" alleged to cause deviant behavior, was first developed in the early 1930s as prefrontal lobotomy as a treatment for mental illness. Early forms of psychosurgery fell into disrepute in the early 1950s because the side effects (general passivity, difficulty with abstract thinking) were deemed too undesirable and many patients remained institutionalized (and besides, new psychoactive medications were becoming available to control the mentally ill). Nonetheless, during this period, approximately 40,000 to 50,000 such operations were performed in the United States. In the late 1960s, a new and technologically more sophisticated variant of psychosurgery (including laser technology and brain implants) emerged and was heralded by some as a treatment of uncontrollable violent outbursts. While psychosurgery for violence has been criticized from both within and without the medical profession and relatively few operations have been actually performed, in 1976 a blue ribbon national commission reporting to the Department of Health, Education and Welfare endorsed the use of psychosurgery as having "potential merit" and judged its risks "not excessive." This endorsement may encourage increased use of this form of medical control.

Behavior modification, a psychotechnology based on the theories of B. F. Skinner and other behaviorist learning advocates, has been adopted by some medical professionals as a treatment modality. A variety of types and variations of behavior modification exists (token economies, positive reinforcement schedules, aversive conditioning, operant conditioning). While they are not medical technologies per se, physicians have used them to treat mental illness, mental retardation, homosexuality, violence, hyperactive children, autism, phobias, alcoholism, drug addiction, and other disorders. An irony of the medical use of behavior modification is that behaviorism explicitly denies the medical model (that behavior is a symptom of illness) and adopts an environmental, albeit still individual, solution to the problem. This has not, however, hindered its adoption by medical professionals.

Human genetics is one of the most exciting and rapidly expanding areas of medical knowledge. Genetic screening and genetic counseling are becoming more commonplace. Genetic causes are proposed for such a variety of human problems as alcoholism, hyperactivity, learning disabilities, schizophrenia, manic-depressive psychosis, homosexuality, and mental retardation. At this point in time, apart from specific genetic disorders such as phenylketonuria (PKU) and certain forms of retardation, genetic explanations tend to be general theories, with only minimal (if any) empirical support, and are not the level at which medical intervention occurs. The most well-publicized genetic theory of deviant behavior is that an xyy chromosome arrangement is a determinant factor in "criminal tendencies." While this xyy research has been severely questioned,[41] the controversy surrounding it may be a harbinger of things to come. Genetic anomalies may be discovered to have a correlation with deviant behavior and may become a causal explanation for this behavior. Medical control, in the form of genetic counseling, may discourage parents from having offspring with a high risk (e.g., 25 percent) of genetic impairment. Clearly, the potentials for medical control go far beyond present use. One could imagine the possibility of licensing selected parents (with proper genes) to have children and of further manipulating gene arrangements to produce or eliminate certain traits.

Medicine acts not only as an independent agent of social control (as above), but frequently *medical collaboration* with other authorities serves social control functions. Such collaboration includes roles as information provider, gatekeeper, institutional agent, and technician. These interdependent medical control functions highlight the interwoven position of medicine in the fabric of society. Historically, medical personnel have reported information on gunshot wounds and venereal disease to state authorities. More recently, these have been extended to reporting child abuse to child welfare or law enforcement agencies.

The medical profession's status as official designator of the "sick role," which imbues the physician with authority to define particular kinds of deviance as illness and exempt the patient from certain role obligations, is a general gatekeeping and social control task. In some instances, the physician functions as a specific gatekeeper for special exemptions from conventional norms; here the exemptions are authorized due to illness, disease, or disability. The classic example is the so-called insanity defense in capital crime cases. Other more commonplace examples include medical deferment from the draft or a medical discharge from the military; requiring doctors' notes to legitimize missing an examination or excessive absences in school; and, before abortion was legalized, obtaining two psychiatrists' letters testifying to the therapeutic necessity of the abortion. Halleck[42] has termed this "the power of medical excuse." In a slightly different vein, but still forms of gatekeeping and medical excuse, are medical examinations for disability, or workman's compensation benefits. Medical reports required for insurance coverage and employment, or medical certification of an epileptic as seizure free to obtain a driver's license, are also gatekeeping activities.

Physicians in total institutions have one of two roles. In some institutions, such as schools for the retarded or mental hospitals, they are usually the administrative authority; in others, such as the military or prisons, they are employees of the administration. In total institutions, medicine's role as an agent of social control (for the institution) is more apparent. In both the military and prisons, physicians have the power to confer the sick role and to offer medical excuse for deviance.[43] For example, medical discharges and sick call are available designations for deviant behavior. As physicians are in the hire of and paid by the institution, it is difficult for them to be fully an agent of the patient, engendering built-in role strains. An extreme example is in wartime conflict when the physician's mandate is to return the soldier to combat duty as soon as possible. Under some circumstances, physicians act as direct agents of control by prescribing medications to control unruly or disorderly inmates or to help a "neurotic" adjust to the conditions of the total institution. In such cases, "captive professionals"[44] are more likely to become the agent of the institution than of the individual patient.

Under rather rare circumstances, physicians may become "mere technicians," applying the sanctions of another authority who hires their medical skills. An extreme, although more complex, example would be the behavior of the experimental and death physicians in Nazi Germany. A more mundane example is physicians who perform court-ordered sterilizations.[45] Perhaps one could imagine sometime in the future, if the death penalty becomes commonplace again, physicians administering drugs as the "humanitarian" and painless executioner.

Medical ideology is a type of social control that involves defining a behavior or condition as an illness primarily because of the social and ideological benefits accrued by conceptualizing it in medical terms. These latent functions of medical ideology may benefit the individual or the dominant interests in society, or both, but is quite separate from any organic basis for illness or any available treatment. Waitzkin and Waterman[46] call one latent function of medicalization "secondary gain," arguing that assumption of the sick role can fulfill personality and individual needs (e.g., gaining nurturance or attention) or legitimize personal failure.[47] One of the most important functions of the disease model of alcoholism, and to a lesser extent drug addiction, is the secondary gain of removing blame from, and constructing a shield against condemnation of, individuals for their deviant behavior. Alcoholics Anonymous, a nonmedical, quasi-religious self-help organization, adopted a variant of the medical model of alcoholism quite independently of the medical profession. One suspects the secondary gain serves their purposes well.

Disease designations can support dominant social interests and institutions. A poignant example is prominent New Orleans physician S. W. Cartwright's antebellum conceptualization of the disease drapetomania, a condition that only affected slaves. Its major symptom was running away from their masters.[48] Medical conceptions and controls often support dominant social values and morality: the nineteenth-century Victorian conceptualization of the illness of and addiction to masturbation, and the medical treatments developed to control this "disease" make chilling reading in the 1970s.[49] The recent Soviet labeling of political dissidents as mentally ill is a further example of the manipulation of illness designations to support dominant political and social institutions. These examples highlight the sociopolitical nature of illness designations in general.[50]

It is clear that medicine's jurisdiction over deviant behavior and its social control functions have increased in the past few decades. With new technological "discoveries" and more subtle measurement of human variation (e.g., genetics), this expansion is expected to continue.

Notes

1. Ivan Illich, *Medical Nemesis* (New York: Pantheon Books, 1976).

2. One of the earliest and clearest discussions of medicalization is found in Irving K. Zola, "Medicine as an Institution of Social Control," *Sociological Review* 20 (1972):487-504.

3. Talcott Parsons, *The Social System* (New York: Free Press, 1951), pp. 428-479.

4. A widely cited and clear discussion of illness as deviance is found in Eliot Freidson, *The Profession of Medicine* (New York: Dodd, Mead and Co., 1970), pp. 205-223.

5. The concept medicalization of deviance is discussed in Thomas Szasz, *The Manufacture of Madness* (New York: Dell, 1970); Nicholas Kittrie, *The Right to Be Different* (Baltimore: Johns Hopkins University Press, 1971); and Peter Conrad, *Identifying Hyperactive Children: The Medicalization of Deviant Behavior* (Lexington, Mass.: D. C. Heath, 1976).

6. Barbara Ehrenreich and John Ehrenreich, "Medicine and Social Control," in B. Mandell, ed., *Welfare in America* (Englewood Cliffs, N.J.: Prentice-Hall, 1975), pp. 138-167, discuss this expansive characteristic of medical control.

7. See Conrad, *Identifying Hyperactive Children*, pp. 93-99.

8. Freidson, *Profession of Medicine*, p. 163.

9. Ibid.

10. Parsons, *The Social System*, pp. 436-437.

11. Ibid., pp. 312-314, 475-479.

12. Michael Foucault, *Madness and Civilization* (New York: Pantheon Books, 1965).

13. Szasz, *The Manufacture of Madness*.

14. See George Rosen, "The Evolution of Social Medicine," in H. E. Freeman, S. Levine, and L. Reader, eds., *Handbook of Medical Sociology* (Englewood Cliffs, N.J.: Prentice-Hall, 1972), pp. 30-60, for an historical discussion of public health and its development.

15. Zola, "Medicine as an Institution of Social Control."

16. Ibid., p. 495.

17. Conrad, *Identifying Hyperactive Children*.

18. Freidson, *Profession of Medicine*, pp. 16-22.

19. René Dubos, *The Mirage of Health* (New York: Harper and Row, 1959) discusses the medical control of communicable diseases in human history.

20. Freidson, *Profession of Medicine*, p. 83.

21. Zola, "Medicine as an Institution of Social Control," and in "In the Name of Health and Illness," *Social Science and Medicine* 9 (1975):83-87, argues that this medicalization is the result of both lay demand and medical interests.

22. For representative discussions of the concept of medical ideology, its sources and functions, see Freidson, *Profession of Medicine*; H. K. Waitzkin and B. Waterman, *The Exploitation of Illness in Capitalist Society* (Indianapolis: Bobbs-Merrill, 1974); Ehrenreich and Ehrenreich, "Medicine and Social Control"; and Michael Radelet, "Medical Hegemony as Social Control: The Use of Tranquilizers," Society for the Study of Social Problems Annual Meetings (1977).

23. See Zola "Medicine as an Institution of Social Control," and David Mechanic, "Health and Illness in Technological Societies," *The Hastings Center Studies* 1 (1973):7-18, for discussions of such increasing utilization of medical institutions, particularly in advanced technological societies.

24. James Goddard, "The Medical Business," *Scientific American* 229 (September 1973):161-68, provides an insightful overview of the drug industry and other medical industries.

25. Jacques Ellul, *Technological Society* (New York: Vintage, 1964).

26. Radelet (1977) elaborates on the concept of medical hegemony in his discussion of drug companies and the use of tranquilizers.

27. Mechanic, "Health and Illness."

28. Kittrie, *The Right to Be Different*, pp. 4-8, 46-47, 32-36.

29. Ibid.

30. Szasz, *The Manufacture of Madness*.

31. Philip Rieff, *The Triumph of the Therapeutic* (New York: Harper and Row, 1966).

32. Kittrie uses this term to identify the role of the state as "parent" in such cases.

33. Freidson, *Profession of Medicine*, pp. 72-73.

34. Zola, "In the Name of Health and Illness."

35. Mechanic, "Health and Illness."

36. Szasz, *The Manufacture of Madness*.

37. Seymour Halleck, *The Politics of Therapy* (New York: Science House, 1970), and Nathan Hurvitz, "Psychotherapy as a Means of Social Control," *Journal of Consulting and Clinical Psychology* 40 (1973):232-239, present cogent analyses of psychotherapy's social control functions.

38. Rosen, "The Evolution of Social Medicine."

39. Stephen Chorover, "Big Brother and Psychotechnology," *Psychology Today* (October 1973):43-54, enumerates types and consequences of such technologies.

40. Goddard, "The Medical Business."

41. See Richard G. Fox, "The XYY Offender: A Modern Myth?," *Journal of Criminal Law, Criminology and Police Science* 62 (1971):1-15, for a careful critique of the alleged connection between XYY and crime.

42. Halleck, *The Politics of Therapy*.

43. See, for example, Arlene K. Daniels, "The Captive Professional: Bureaucratic Limitation in the Practice of Military Psychiatry," *Journal of Health and Social Behavior* 10 (December 1969):255-265; Waitzkin and Waterman, *Exploitation of Illness*.

44. Daniels, "The Captive Professional."

45. See Kittrie, *The Right to Be Different*, pp. 325-333.

46. Waitzkin and Waterman, *Exploitation of Illness*.

47. For example, see Judith T. Shuval and Aaron Antonovsky, "Illness: A Mechanism for Coping with Failure," *Social Science and Medicine* 7 (1973):259-265.

48. S. A. Cartwright, "Report on the Diseases and Physical Peculiarities of the Negro Race," *New Orleans Medical and Surgical Journal* 7 (May 1851):691-715.

49. H. T. Englehardt, Jr., "The Disease of Masturbation," *Bulletin of the History of Medicine* 48 (Summer 1974):234-48, gives a clear and carefully documented analysis of the "disease" of masturbation.

50. Zola, "In the Name of Health and Illness."

SELECTED BIBLIOGRAPHY

Books

Abrahamsson, Bengt. *Bureaucracy or Participation.* Beverly Hills, Calif.: Sage Publications, 1977.

Abramson, Paul R. *The Political Socialization of Black Americans.* New York: Free Press, 1977.

Adelam, Iram. *Theories of Economic Growth and Development.* Stanford: Stanford University Press, 1961.

Agus, Jacob B. *Jewish Identity in an Age of Ideologies.* New York: F. Ungar Publishing, 1977.

Alex, Nicholas. *New York Cops Talk Back.* New York: John Wiley and Sons, 1976.

Andreas, Carol. *Sex and Caste in America.* Englewood Cliffs, N. J.: Prentice-Hall, 1962.

Ball, Donald W., and John W. Loy. *Sport and Social Order.* Reading, Mass.: Addison-Wesley, 1975.

Bane, Mary Jo. *Here to Stay: American Families in the Twentieth Century.* New York: Basic Books, 1976.

Barner, Bernard, John J. Lally, Julia Loughlin Makarushko, and Daniel F. Sullivan. *Research on Human Subjects. Problems of Social Control in Medical Experimentation.* Beverly Hills, Calif.: Sage Publications, 1973.

Barnett, James H. "The Sociology of Art." In *Sociology Today. Problems and Prospects,* ed. by Leonard Broom and Leonard S. Cottrell. New York: Basic Books, 1959.

Barth, Hans. *Truth and Ideology.* Berkeley: University of California Press, 1976.

Bayley, David H., ed. *Police and Society.* Beverly Hills, Calif.: Sage Publications, 1977.

Bean, P. *The Social Control of Drugs.* New York: Halstead Press, 1974.

Bedau, Hugo Adam. *The Courts, the Constitution, and Capital Punishment.* Lexington, Mass.: Lexington Books, 1977.

Bedow, Hugo Adams, and Chester M. Pierce. *Capital Punishment in the United States.* New York: AMS Press, 1976.

Becker, Howard Paul. *Man in Reciprocity: Introductory Lectures on Culture, Society and Personality.* Westport, Conn.: Greenwood Press, 1973.

Bell, Daniel. *The Coming of Post-Industrial Society.* New York: Basic Books, 1973.

Bendix, Reinhard. *Nation-Building and Citizenship: Studies of Our Changing Social Order.* Berkeley: University of California Press, 1977.

Berger, Monroe. *Real and Imagined Worlds: The Novel and Social Science.* Cambridge, Mass.: Harvard University Press, 1977.

Berger, Peter L., and Brigitte Berger. *The Homeless Mind: Modernization and Consciousness*. New York: Vintage Books, 1974.

Birnbaum, Arnold, and Edward Sagarin. *Norms and Human Behavior*. New York: Praeger Publishers, 1976.

Boas, Georg. *Vox Populi: Essays in the History of Ideas*. Baltimore, Md.: Johns Hopkins University Press, 1969.

Boaz, John K., and Dennis C. Martin. *Persuasive Communication*. Dubuque, Iowa: Kendall/Hunt Publishing, 1975.

Boulding, Kenneth E. *Economics As a Science*. New York: McGraw-Hill, 1970.

Bowen, Peter. *Social Control in Industrial Organizations*. Boston: Routledge and Kegan Paul, 1976.

Burns, Tom R., and Walter Buckley, eds. *Power and Control: Social Structures and Their Transformation*. Beverly Hills, Calif.: Sage Publications, 1976.

Cahn, Edgar S. *Our Brother's Keeper: The Indian in White America*. Cleveland: World Publishing, 1969.

Calder, Nigel. *Technopolis: Social Control of the Uses of Science*. New York: Simon and Schuster, 1975.

Camp, John. *Magic, Myth and Medicine*. New York: Taplinger Publishing, 1974.

Carpenter, Paul S. *Music: An Art and a Business*. Norman: University of Oklahoma Press, 1950.

Casler, Lawrence. *Is Marriage Necessary?* New York: Human Science Press, 1974.

Cassell, Eric J. *The Healer's Art: A New Approach to the Doctor-Patient Relationship*. Philadelphia: J. B. Lippincott, 1976.

Cater, Douglass, and Richard Adler, eds. *Television As a Social Force: New Approaches to Television Criticism*. New York: Praeger Publishers, 1975.

Chaffee, Stern H., and Michael J. Petrick. *Using the Mass Media: Communication Problems in American Society*. New York: McGraw-Hill, 1975.

Chapman, Jane Roberts, and Margaret Gates, eds. *Women into Wives: The Legal and Economic Impact of Marriage*. Beverly Hills, Calif.: Sage Publications, 1977.

Chapman, William E. *Roots of Character Education: An Exploration of the American Heritage from the Decade of the 1920s*. Schenectady, N.Y.: Character Research Press, 1976.

Clayre, Alasdair. *Work and Play: Ideas and Experiences of Work and Leisure*. New York: Harper and Row, 1974.

Coaley, Jay J. *Sport in Society: Issues and Controversies*. St. Louis: C. V. Mosby, 1978.

Cockerham, William C. *Medical Sociology*. Englewood Cliffs, N. J.: Prentice-Hall, 1978.

Cole, Barry, and Mal Oettinger. *Reluctant Regulators: The FCC and the Broadcast Audience*. Reading, Mass.: Addison-Wesley, 1978.

Cole, George Douglas Howard. *Studies in Class Structure*. Westport, Conn.: Greenwood Press, 1976.

Coles, Robert. *Eskimos, Chicano, Indians*. Boston: Little, Brown, 1977.

Condon, John C. *Interpersonal Communication*. New York: Macmillan, 1977.

Csikszent, Mihalayi. *Beyond Boredom and Anxiety: The Experience of Play in Work and Games*. San Francisco: Jossey-Bass, 1975.

Curtis, Charlotte. *The Rich and Other Atrocities*. New York: Harper and Row, 1976.

Danielson, Michael N. *The Politics of Exclusion*. New York: Columbia University Press, 1976.

Davies, James C. *Human Nature in Politics: The Dynamics of Political Behavior*. Westport, Conn.: Greenwood Press, 1978.

de Crespigny, H., and K. Minogue, eds. *Contemporary Political Philosophers*. London: Methuen, 1976.

De Gré, Gerald. *Society and Ideology: An Inquiry into the Sociology of Knowledge*. New York: Columbia University (Bookstore), 1943.

Delucchi, V.L., ed. *Studies in Biological Control*. New York: Cambridge University Press, 1976.

Demaris, Ovid. *Brothers in Blood*. New York: Charles Scribner's Sons, 1977.

Denby, David, ed. *Awake in the Dark: An Anthology of American Film Criticism 1915 to the Present*. New York: Vintage Press, 1977.

Denisoff, R. Serge, and Richard A. Peterson, eds. *The Sounds of Social Change: Studies in Popular Culture*. Chicago: Rand McNally, 1972.

Dischman, Robert. *Urban Utopias in the Twentieth Century*. New York: Basic Books, 1978.

Domhoff, G. William. *The Bohemian Grove and Other Retreats: A Study in Ruling-Class Cohesiveness*. New York: Harper and Row, 1975.

Donajgrodzki, A. P., ed. *Social Control in Nineteenth Century Britain*. Totowa, N. J.: Rowman and Littlefield, 1977.

Dorf, Richard C. *Technology, Society and Man*. San Francisco: Boyd and Fraser Publishing, 1974.

Downs, Robert B. *Books That Changed America*. New York: Macmillan, 1970.

Downton, J. V. *Rebel Leadership: Commitment and Charisma in the Revolutionary Process*. New York: Free Press, 1973.

Duberman, Lucile. *Social Inequality: Class and Caste in America*. Philadelphia: J. B. Lippincott, 1976.

Edelman, Murray. *Political Language: Words That Succeed and Policies That Fail*. New York: Academic Press, 1978.

Ederi, Ronald S. *Social Change*. Dubuque, Iowa: Wm. C. Brown, 1976.

Engel, Haris. "Music and Society." In *The International Encyclopedia of the Social Sciences*, Vol. X, pp. 566-575. New York: Macmillan and Free Press, 1968.

Erikson, E. *Childhood and Society*. New York: W. W. Norton, 1963.

Fansworth, P. R. *The Social Psychology of Music*. New York: Dryden Press, 1958.

Farber, Bernard, ed. *Kinship and Family Organization*. New York: John Wiley and Sons, 1966.

Flacks, Richard. *Conformity, Resistance, and Self-Determination: The Individual and Authority*. Boston: Little, Brown, 1973.

Fogelson, Robert N. *Big-City Police*. Cambridge: Harvard University Press, 1977.

Form, William H., and Delbert C. Miller. *Industry, Labor and Community*. New York: Harper and Row, 1960.

Foucault, Michel. *Discipline and Punishment: The Birth of the Prison*. New York: Pantheon, 1978.

Francis, E. K. *Interethnic Relations: An Essay in Sociological Theory*. New York: Elsevier, 1976.

Freedman, Anne E., and P. E. Freedman. *The Psychology of Political Control.* New York: St. Martin's Press, 1976.

Freeman, David M. *Technology and Society: Issues in Assessment, Conflict, and Choice.* Chicago: Rand McNally, 1974.

Freeman, Howard E., Sol Levine, and Leo G. Reeder, eds. *Handbook of Medical Sociology.* Englewood Cliffs, N. J.: Prentice-Hall, 1962.

Freeman, Richard B. *The Over-Educated American.* New York: Academic Press, 1976.

Friedlander, Saul. *History and Psychoanalysis.* New York: Holmes & Meier, 1978.

Freidson, Eliot. *Doctoring Together: A Study of Professional Social Control.* New York: Elsevier, 1976.

Freud, Sigmund. *Totem and Taboo.* New York: W. W. Norton, 1920.

Galbraith, John Kenneth. *The Affluent Society.* Boston: Houghton Mifflin, 1958.

————. *The Age of Uncertainty.* Boston: Houghton Mifflin, 1977.

Gibbs, Jack P. *Crime, Punishment, and Deterrence.* New York: Elsevier, 1975.

Gibson, George H. *Public Broadcasting: The Role of the Federal Government, 1912-1976.* New York: Praeger Publishers, 1977.

Giddens, Anthony. *The Class Structure of the Advanced Societies.* New York: Harper and Row, 1975.

Glazer, Nathan, and Daniel P. Moynihan. *Beyond the Melting Pot.* Cambridge, Mass.: The MIT Press, 1963.

Gassett, Thomas F. *Race: The History of an Idea in America.* New York: Schocken Books, 1963.

Gordon, Milton Myron. *Human Nature, Class, and Ethnicity.* New York: Oxford University Press, 1978.

————. *Social Class in American Sociology.* Durham, N. C.: Duke University Press, 1958.

Gornick, Vivian, and Barbara K. Moran, eds. *Woman in Sexist Society.* New York: Basic Books, 1971.

Gouldner, Alvin W. *The Dialectic of Ideology and Technology: The Origins, Grammar, and Future of Ideology.* New York: Seabury Press, 1976.

Grambs, Jean Dresden. *Schools, Scholars, and Society.* Englewood Cliffs, N. J.: Prentice-Hall, 1978.

Greeley, Andrew M. *Why Can't They Be More Like Us: America's White Ethnic Groups.* New York: E. P. Dutton, 1971.

Greenfield, Jeff. *Television: The First Fifty Years.* New York: Harry N. Abrams, 1977.

Greenway, John. *Ethnomusicology.* Minneapolis, Minn.: Burgess Publishing, 1976.

Griffin, Emory A. *The Mind Changers: The Art of Christian Persuasion.* Wheaton, Ill.: Tyndale House, 1976.

Grolling, Francis X., and Harold B. Haley, eds. *Medical Anthropology.* The Hague: Mouton, 1976.

Gross, Richard, ed. *Heritage of American Education.* Boston: Allyn and Bacon, 1962.

Gulliver, Philip H. *Social Control in an African Society.* New York: New York University Press, 1963.

Hacker, Frederick F. *Crusaders, Criminals, Crazies: Terror and Terrorism in Our Time.* New York: W. W. Norton, 1976.

Hamilton, David. *Technology, Man and the Environment.* New York: Charles Scribner's Sons, 1973.

Hardy, John T. *Science, Technology, and the Environment.* Philadelphia: W. B. Saunders, 1975.

Häring, Bernard. *Ethics of Manipulation: Issues in Medicine, Behavior Control and Genetics.* New York: Seabury Press, 1975.

Hauser, Arnold. *The Social History of Art.* New York: Alfred A. Knopf, 1951.

Hayek, Frederick A. *The Road to Serfdom.* Chicago: University of Chicago Press, 1944.

Hazleton, Lesley. *Israeli Women: The Reality Behind the Myths.* New York: Simon and Schuster, 1977.

Heertie, Arnold. *Economics and Technical Change.* New York: John Wiley and Sons, 1977.

Heisler, Martin O. *Ethnic Conflict in the World Today,* Vol. 433. Philadelphia: American Academy of Political and Social Science, 1977.

Henley, Nancy. *Body Politics: Power, Sex, and Nonverbal Communication.* Englewood Cliffs, N. J.: Prentice-Hall, 1977.

Hodges, Robert W. *Trends in Social Stratification.* Chicago: Markham, 1973.

Horowitz, I. L. *Ideology and Utopia in the United States 1956-1976.* New York: Oxford University Press, 1977.

Hutschnecker, Arnold A. *The Drive for Power.* New York: Bantam, 1976.

Hutten, Ernest Hirschlaff. *The Origins of Science: An Inquiry into the Foundations of Western Thought.* Westport, Conn.: Greenwood Press, 1978.

Illich, Ivan. *Medical Nemesis.* New York: Bantam, 1977.

Islver, Isidor, ed. *The Crime Control Establishment.* Englewood Cliffs, N. J.: Prentice-Hall, 1974.

Isenberg, Irwin, ed. *The Death Penalty.* New York: H. W. Wilson, 1977.

Jacobson, Howard B., and Joseph S. Roucek, eds. *Automation and Society.* New York: Philosophical Library, 1959.

James, Anthony. *Capital Punishment.* New York: Tower Publications, 1977.

Janowitz, Morris. *Social Control of the Welfare State.* New York: Elsevier, 1976.

Jayewardene, C. H. S. *The Penalty of Death: The Canadian Experiment.* Lexington, Mass.: Lexington Books, 1977.

Jennings, R. Kent, and Richard G. Niemi. *The Political Characteristics of Adolescence: The Influence of Families and Schools.* Princeton, N. J.: Princeton University Press, 1974.

Jones, R. Kenneth, and P. A. Jones. *Sociology in Medicine.* New York: John Wiley and Sons, 1965.

Josephson, Eric, and Eleanor E. Carroll, eds. *Drug Use: Epidemiological and Sociological Approaches.* New York: Halsted Press, 1974.

Kando, Thomas. *Leisure and Popular Culture in Transition.* St. Louis, Mo.: C. V. Mosby, 1975.

Kastelein, T. J., ed. *Twenty-five Years of Economic Theory: Retrospect and Prospect.* Leiden: Martinus Nijhoff, 1977.

Kavolis, Vytautas. *Artistic Expression: A Sociological Analysis.* Ithaca, N. Y.: Cornell University Press, 1968.

Kelso, William Alton. *American Democratic Theory: Pluralism and Its Critics.* Westport, Conn.: Greenwood Press, 1978.

Kerckhoff, Alan C. *Socialization and Social Class.* Englewood Cliffs, N. J.: Prentice-Hall, 1972.

Kilson, Martin, ed. *New States in the Modern World.* Cambridge, Mass.: Harvard University Press, 1976.

Kohn, Hans. *The Idea of Nationalism: A Study in Its Origins and Background.* New York: Macmillan, 1961.

Kohn, Melvin L. *Class and Conformity: A Study in Values.* Homewood, Ill.: Dorsey Press, 1969.

Krauss, Irving. *Stratification, Class and Conflict.* New York: Free Press, 1976.

Krickus, Richard. *Pursuing the American Dream: White Ethnics and the New Populism.* New York: Anchor Press, 1976.

Kroes, William H. *Society's Victim, The Policeman: An Analysis of Job Stress in Policing.* Springfield, Ill.: C. C. Thomas, 1976.

Landy, David., ed. *Culture, Disease, and Healing.* New York: Macmillan, 1977.

Langer, Suzanne K. *Problems of Art.* New York: Charles Scribner's Sons, 1957.

LaPiere, Richard T. *A Theory of Social Control.* New York: McGraw-Hill, 1954.

Lasky, Melvin J. *Utopia and Revolution. On the Origins of a Metaphor, or Some Illustrations of the Problem of Political Temperament and Intellectual Clomaye and How Ideas, Ideals and Ideologies Have Been Historically Related.* Chicago: University of Chicago Press, 1977.

Laqueur, Walter. *Terrorism.* Boston: Little, Brown, 1977.

Laumann, Edward G. *Social Stratification: Research and Theory for the 1970s.* Indianapolis, Ind.: Bobbs, Merrill, 1970.

Lerman, Paul. *Community Treatment and Social Control. A Critical Analysis of Juvenile Correctional Policy.* Chicago: University of Chicago Press, 1975.

Leslie, Gerald R., and Elizabeth McLaughlin Leslie. *Marriage in a Changing World.* New York: John Wiley and Sons, 1977.

Lipset, S. M., and Earl Raab. *The Political Unreason: Right-Wing Extremism in America 1790-1970.* New York: Harper and Row, 1970.

Lockwood, William O. *Toward a Theory of Ethnicity.* Monticello, Ill.: Council of Planning Librarians, 1977.

Lomax, Alan. *Folk Song Style and Culture.* Washington, D.C.: American Association for the Advancement of Science, 1968.

MacNamara, Donal E. J. *Sex, Crime, and the Law.* New York: Free Press, 1978.

Mankiewicz, Frank, and Joe Swerdlow. *Remote Control: Television and the Manipulation of American Life.* New York: Times Books, 1978.

Marcuse, Herbert. *One Dimensional Man: Studies in the Ideology of Advanced Industrial Society.* Boston: Beacon Press, 1964.

Martindale, Don. *American Society.* Huntington, N.Y.: Robert E. Krieger Publishing, 1972.

––––––. *Institutions, Organization and Mass Society.* Boston: Houghton Mifflin, 1966.

––––––. *The Romance of a Profession. A Case History in the Sociology of Sociology.* St. Paul, Minn.: Windflower Publishing, 1976.

Martineau, Pierre. *Motivation in Advertising: Motives That Make People Buy.* New York: McGraw-Hill, 1971.

Mason, Philip. *Patterns of Dominance.* New York: Oxford University Press, 1970.

Matthews, Brander. *Americanisms and Briticisms, With Other Essays on Other Isms.* Folcroft, Pa.: Folcroft Library Editions, 1976.

McDougall, William. *An Introduction to Social Psychology.* London: Methuen, 1908.

McKeown, Thomas, and C. R. Lowe. *An Introduction to Social Medicine.* Philadelphia: J. B. Lippincott, 1974.

McKnight, G. *The Terrorist Mind: Why They Hijack, Kidnap, Bomb and Kill.* Indianapolis, Ind.: Bobbs-Merrill, 1975.

McLuhan, Marshall, and Quentin Fiore. *The Medium Is the Massage.* New York: Bantam, 1967.

Mechanic, David. *Politics, Medicine, and Social Science.* New York: John Wiley and Sons, 1974.

Meltsner, Michael. *Cruel and Unusual: The Supreme Court and Capital Punishment.* New York: Random House, 1973.

Merriam, Charles E. *Political Power.* New York: Collier, 1964.

Merton, Robert K. *Social Theory and Social Structure.* New York: Free Press, 1957.

Mesthene, Emmanuel G. *Technological Change: Its Impact on Man and Society.* Cambridge, Mass.: Harvard University Press, 1970.

Miller, Gerald R. *New Techniques of Persuasion.* New York: Harper and Row, 1973.

Miller, Wayne Charles. *A Handbook of American Minorities.* New York: New York University Press, 1976.

Mises, Ludwig von. *The Anti-Capitalist Mentality.* Princeton, N.J.: D. Van Nostrand, 1956.

Moberg, David G. *The Church As a Special Institution. The Sociology of American Religion.* Englewood Cliffs, N. J.: Prentice-Hall, 1962.

Monaco, James. *How to Read a Film: The Art, Technology, Language, History, and Theory of Film and Media.* New York: Oxford University Press, 1977.

Mosse, George, ed. *Police Forces in History.* Beverly Hills, Calif.: Sage Publications, 1975.

Mueller, John H. *The American Symphony Orchestra: A Social History of Musical Taste.* Westport, Conn.: Greenwood Press, 1976.

Muir, William Ker, Jr. *Police: Streetcorner Politicians.* Chicago: University of Chicago Press, 1977.

Mumford, Lewis. *The Myth of the Machine: Technics and Human Development.* New York: Harcourt Brace Jovanovich, 1968.

Murphy, Patrick V., and Thomas Plate. *Commissioner: A View from the Top of American Law Enforcement.* New York: Simon and Schuster, 1978.

Negley, Glenn Robert. *Utopian Literature: A Bibliography with a Supplementary Listing of Works Influential in Utopian Thought.* Lawrence, Kansas: Regent Press of Kansas, 1977.

Orr, John. *Tragic Realism and Modern Society: Studies in the Sociology of the Modern Novel.* Pittsburgh: University of Pittsburgh Press, 1977.

Orum, Anthony M. *Introduction to Political Sociology: The Social Anatomy of the Body Politic.* Englewood Cliffs, N. J.: Prentice-Hall, 1976.

Pace, Denny F. *Handbook of Vice Control*. Englewood Cliffs, N. J.: Prentice-Hall, 1971.

Pareto, Vilfredo. *The Mind and Society*. New York: Harcourt, Brace, 1935.

Parsons, Talcott. *Social Structure and Personality*. New York: Free Press, 1964.

Patterson, Orlando. *Ethnic Chauvinism: The Reactionary Impulse*. New York: Stein and Day, 1977.

Patterson, Horace Orlando. *The Tribal Tradition: A Critical Study of Ethnicity*. New York: Stein and Day, 1977.

Pepinsky, Harold E. *Crime and Conflict: A Study of Law and Society*. New York: Academic Press, 1976.

Persell, Caroline Hodges. *Education and Inequality*. New York: Free Press, 1977.

Phares, E. Jerry. *Locus of Control in Personality*. Morristown, N.J.: General Learning Press, 1976.

Pines, Maya. *The Brain Changers: Scientist and the New Mind Control*. New York: New American Library, 1975.

Polhemus, Ted., ed. *The Body Reader: Social Aspects of the Human Body*. New York: Pantheon Books, 1977.

Pool, Ithiel de Sola. *The Social Impact of the Telephone*. Cambridge, Mass.: MIT Press, 1977.

Potholm, Christian P., and Richard E. Morgan. *Focus on Police: Police in American Society*. New York: Halsted Press, 1976.

Pound, Roscoe. *Social Control Through Law*. New Haven: Yale University Press, 1944.

Pratte, Richard. *Ideology and Education*. New York: David McKay, 1977.

Presthus, Robert. *Elites in the Policy Process*. New York: Cambridge University Press, 1974.

Queen, Stuart A., and Robert W. Habenstein. *The Family in Various Cultures*. Philadelphia: J. B. Lippincott, 1967.

Robertson, Leon S., and Margaret C. Heagart. *Medical Sociology: A General Systems Approach*. Chicago: Nelson-Hall Publishers, 1975.

Rada, Richard T. *Clinical Aspects of the Rapist*. New York: Grune and Stratton, 1978.

Radine, Lawrence B. *The Taming of the Troops: Social Control in the United States Army*. Westport, Conn.: Greenwood Press, 1977.

Reichert, John. *Making Sense of Literature*. Chicago: University of Chicago Press, 1978.

Reik, Theodor. *Ritual: Psycho-Analytic Studies*. New York: International Universities Press, 1958.

Ringer, Robert J. *Winning Through Intimidation*. New York: Funk and Wagnalls, 1975.

Robertson, Alec. *Requiem: Music of Mourning and Consolation*. Westport, Conn.: Greenwood Press, 1976.

Rodnitzky, Jerome L. *Minstrels of the Dawn: The Folk Protest Singer As a Cultural Hero*. Chicago: Nelson-Hall, 1976.

Rosenberg, Nathan. *Perspectives on Technology*. New York: Cambridge University Press, 1976.

Rossides, Daniel M. *The American Class System. An Introduction to Social Stratification.* Boston: Houghton Mifflin, 1976.

Roszak, Theodore. *Where the Wasteland Ends: Politics and Transcendence in Post-industrial Society.* New York: Doubleday, 1972.

Roucek, Joseph S., ed. *The Challenge of Science Education.* New York: Philosophical Library, 1959.

————, ed. *Juvenile Delinquency.* Freeport, N. Y.: Books for Libraries Press, 1970.

————, ed. *Sociological Foundations of Education.* New York: Thomas Y. Crowell, 1942.

————, ed. *Social Control.* Westport, Conn.: Greenwood Press, 1970.

————, ed. *Sociology of Crime.* Westport, Conn.: Greenwood Press, 1969.

Rubel, Robert J. *The Unruly School: Disorders, Disruptions, and Crimes.* Lexington, Mass.: D. C. Heath, 1977.

Rule, James B. *The Private Lives and Public Surveillance: Social Control in the Computer Age.* New York: Schocken Books, 1974.

Sammons, Jeffrey L. *Literary Sociology and Practical Criticism: An Inquiry.* Bloomington: Indiana University Press, 1977.

Sanders, William B. *Detective Work: A Study of Criminal Investigation.* New York: Free Press, 1978.

Sarason, Seymour B. *Work, Aging, and Social Change.* New York: Free Press, 1977.

Sartre, Jean-Paul. *Existentialism and Human Emotions.* New York: Philosophical Library, 1957.

Scanlan, Tom. *Family, Drama, and American Dreams.* Westport, Conn.: Greenwood Press, 1978.

Scase, Richard, ed. *Industrial Society: Class, Cleavage and Control.* New York: St. Martin's Press, 1977.

Schafer, Stephen. *Theories in Criminology: Past and Present Philosophies of the Crime Problem.* New York: Random House, 1969.

Schneider, Carl D. *Shame, Exposure and Privacy.* New York: Harper and Row, 1977.

Schneider, Louis. *Classical Theories of Social Change.* Morristown, N.J.: General Learning Press, 1976.

Schiller, Herbert I. *Communication and Cultural Domination.* White Plains, N.Y.: International Arts and Sciences Press, 1976.

Schramm, Wilbur, and Donald F. Roberts, eds. *The Processes and Effects of Mass Communication.* Urbana, Ill.: University of Illinois Press, 1971.

Schur, Edward M. *Law and Society: A Sociological View.* New York: Random House, 1968.

Scientific American. *Scientific Technology and Social Change.* San Francisco: W. H. Freeman, 1974.

Sedlacek, William E., and Glenwood C. Brooks, Jr. *Racism in American Education. A Model for Change.* Chicago: Nelson-Hall, 1976.

Seliger, Martin. *The Marxist Conception of Ideology: A Critical Essay.* New York: Cambridge University Press, 1977.

Seligson, Marcia. *The Eternal Bliss Machine: America's Way of Wedding.* New York: William Morrow, 1973.

Sharp, Rachel, and Anthony Green. *Education and Social Control: A Study in Progressive Primary Education.* Boston: Routledge and Kegan Paul, 1975.

Simmel, Georg. *Conflict.* New York: Free Press, 1955.

Simoes, Anton, ed. *The Bilingual Child: Research and Analysis of Existing Educational Themes.* New York: Academic Press, 1976.

Sites, Paul. *Control: The Basis of Social Order.* New York: Dunnellen, 1974.

Skinner, B. F. *Beyond Freedom and Dignity: Science and Human Behavior.* New York: Alfred A. Knopf, 1972.

Skolnick, Arlene S., and Jerome H. Skolnick, eds. *Family in Transition.* Boston: Little, Brown, 1977.

Slaby, Andrew Edmund, and Lawrence Tancredi. *Collusion for Conformity.* New York: J. Aronson, 1975.

Sobel, Robert. *The Manipulators: America in the Media Age.* Garden City, N.Y.: Anchor Press/Doubleday, 1976.

Sorokin, Pitirim A. *Social and Cultural Dynamics.* New York: American Book Co., 1937-1941.

————. *Social Mobility.* New York: Harper and Row, 1927.

Spiller, Robert E., ed. *Social Control in a Free Society,* by Loren C. Eiseley. Westport, Conn.: Greenwood Press, 1975.

Steinberg, Charles. *The Communicative Arts: An Introduction to Mass Media.* New York: Hastings House, 1970.

Stone, Christopher D. *Where the Law Ends: The Social Control of Corporate Behavior.* New York: Harper and Row, 1975.

Stroman, Duane F. *The Medical Establishment and Social Responsibility.* Port Washington, N.Y.: Kennikat Press, 1976.

Susser, M. W., and W. Watson. *Sociology in Medicine.* New York: Oxford University Press, 1971.

Tedeschi, James E., ed. *Perspectives on Social Power.* Chicago: Aldine Publishing, 1974.

Thomas, W. I., and Florian Znaniecki. *The Polish Peasant in Europe and America.* New York: Alfred A. Knopf, 1927.

Thomson, David. *America in the Dark: Hollywood and the Gift of Unreality.* New York: William Morrow, 1977.

Thrall, Charles A., and Jerold M. Starr, eds. *Technology, Power and Social Change.* Carbondale, Ill.: Southern Illinois University Press, 1974.

Toch, Hans. *Living in Prison: The Ecology of Survival.* New York: Free Press, 1978.

Tönnies, Ferdinand. *Community and Society.* East Lansing, Mich.: Michigan State University Press, 1957.

Treiman, Donald J. *Occupational Prestige in Comparative Perspective.* New York: Academic Press, 1977.

Turner, Victor M. *The Ritual Process: Structure and Anti-Structure.* Chicago: Aldine, 1969.

Van Patten, James, ed. *Conflict, Permanency, Change and Education.* Agra (India): Satish Book Enterprise, 1976.

Veblen, Thorstein. *The Theory of the Leisure Class.* New York: Mentor, 1953.

Walker, Samuel. *A Critical History of Police Reform: The Emergence of Professionalism.* Lexington, Mass.: D. C. Heath, 1977.

Walzer, Michael. *Just and Unjust Wars: A Moral Argument with Historical Illustrations.* New York: Basic Books, 1978.

Walkins, Cecil Kenneth. *Social Control*. New York: Longmans, 1975.

Weber, Max. *Max Weber on Law in Economy and Society*. Trans. by Max Rheistein and Edward Shills. Cambridge, Mass.: Harvard University Press, 1954.

———. *The Theory of Social and Economic Organization*. Trans. by A. M. Henderson and Talcott Parsons. New York: Oxford University Press, 1947.

Weil, Mildred W. *Marriage, the Family, and Society: Toward a Sociology of Marriage and the Family*. Danville, Ill.: Interstate Printers, 1977.

Weinberg, S. Kirson. *Deviant Behavior and Social Control*. Dubuque, Iowa: Wm. C. Brown, 1974.

Welch, Claude E., Jr., ed. *Civilian Control of the Military: Theory and Cases from Developing Countries*. Albany, N.Y.: State University of New York Press, 1976.

Wells, Alan, ed. *Mass Communication: A World View*. Palo Alto, Calif.: National Press Book, 1974.

White, G. Edward. *The American Judicial Tradition*. New York: Oxford University Press, 1978.

Willis, Roy, ed. *The Interpretation of Symbolism*. New York: John Wiley and Sons, 1975.

Willner, Ann Ruth. *Charismatic Political Leadership: A Theory*. Princeton, N. J.: Center of International Studies, 1968.

Wilson, Amy Auerbacher, ed. *Deviance and Social Control in Chinese Society*. New York: Praeger Publishers, 1977.

Wilson, B. R. *The Noble Savages: The Primitive Origins of Charisma and Its Contemporary Survival*. Berkeley: University of California Press, 1975.

Wood, Arthur L. *Deviant Behavior and Control Strategies: Essays in Sociology*. Lexington, Mass.: Lexington Books, 1974.

Zeitlin, Irving M. *Ideology and the Development of Sociological Theory*. Englewood Cliffs, N. J.: Prentice-Hall, 1968.

Ziegenhagen, Eduard A. *Victims, Crime, and Social Control*. New York: Praeger Publishers, 1977.

Articles

Akers, R. L. "Problems in the Sociology of Deviance: Social Definitions and Behavior," *Social Forces* 46 (June 1968): 455-465.

Chein, I. "There Ought to Be a Law. But Why?" *Journal of Social Issues* 31 (1975): 221-244.

"The Computer Society." *Time* 111, February, 1978, pp. 44-59.

Closer, L. A. "Unanticipated Conservative Consequences of Liberal Theorizing." *Social Problems* 16 (Winter, 1969): 263-272.

Coleman, J. S. "The Competition for Adolescent Energies." *Phi Delta Kappan* 42 (March 1961): 231-236.

Dentler, R. A., and Kai T. Erikson. "The Function of Deviance in Groups." *Social Problems* 7 (1959): 98-107.

Goldberg, S. "What Is Normal? Logical Aspects of the Question of Homosexual Behavior." *Psychiatry* 38 (August 1975): 227-243.

Gottlieb, David. "The Neighborhood Tavern and the Cocktail Lounge: A Study of Class Differences." *American Journal of Sociology* 62 (May 1957): 559-562.

Green, E. C. "Social Control in Tribal Afro-America." *Anthropological Quarterly* 50 (July 1977): 107-116.

Hagan, J., and J. Leon. "Rediscovering Delinquency. Social History, Political Ideology and the Sociology of Law." *American Sociological Review* 42 (August 1977): 587-598.

Hawkes, R. K. "Norms, Deviance, and Social Control: A Mathematical Elaboration of Concepts." *American Journal of Sociology* 80 (January 1975): 886-908.

Himes, Joseph S. "The Function of Racial Conflict." *Social Forces* 45 (September 1966): 1-10.

Hollingshead, A. B. "The Concept of Social Control." *American Sociological Review* 6 (1941): 217-233.

Janowitz, Morris. "Sociological Theory and Social Control." *American Journal of Sociology* 81 (July 1975): 82-108.

Keniston, Kenneth. "The Sources of Student Dissent." *Journal of Social Issues* 23 (1967): 109-115.

Merton, R. K. "Social Structure and Anomie." *American Sociological Review* 3 (October 1938): 672-683.

Muraskin, W. A. "Social Control Theory in American History: A Critique." *Journal of Social History* 9 (Summer, 1976): 559-569.

Norbeck, E. "African Rituals of Conflict." *American Anthropologist* 65 (December 1963): 1254-1279.

Saran, A. K. "Art and Ritual As Methods of Social Control." *Ethics* 63 (1953): 171-179.

Schubert, G. "Political Culture and Judicial Ideology: Some Cross- and Subcultural Comparisons." *Comparative Political Studies* 9 (January 1977): 363-408.

Schnessler, K. F., and D. R. Cressey. "Personality Characteristics of Criminals." *American Journal of Sociology* 55 (March 1950): 476-484.

Schur, E. M. "Reactions to Deviance: A Critical Assessment." *American Journal of Sociology* 75 (November 1969): 309-322.

Scott, J. W., and Mohammed El-Assal. "Multiversity, University Size, University Quality and Student Protest: An Empirical Study." *American Sociological Review* 34 (October 1969): 702-709.

Slater, M. K. "My Son the Doctor: Aspects of Mobility Among American Jews." *American Sociological Review* 34 (June 1969): 359-363.

Solomon, W. E., and Alan T. Walters. "The Relationship Between Productivity and Prestige of Graduate Sociology Departments: Fact or Artifact." *American Sociologist* 10 (November 1975): 229-236.

Spitzer, S. "Toward a Marxian Theory of Deviance." *Social Problems* 22 (June 1975): 638-45.

Stollery, P. L. "Searching for the Magic Answer to Juvenile Delinquency." *Federal Probation* 41 (December 1977): 28-33.

Taft, D. R. "Nationality and Crime." *American Sociological Review* 1 (October 1936): 724-736.

Trondsen, N. "Social Control in the Art Museum." *Urban Life* 5 (April 1976): 105-119.

Turk, A. T. "Conflict and Criminality." *American Sociological Review* 31 (June 1966): 338-352.

————. "Law As a Weapon in Social Conflict." *Social Problems* 22 (1976): 276-291.

Vanneman, R., and F. C. Pampel. "American Perception of Class and Status." *American Sociological Review* 42 (June 1977): 422-437.

Warner, L. G., and Rutledge M. Dennis. "Prejudice Versus Discrimination: An Empirical Example and Theoretical Extension." *Social Forces* 48 (June, 1970): 473-484.

Waters, H. F., Martin Kasindorf, and Betsy Carter. "Sex and TV." *Newsweek* 91, February 20, 1978, pp. 54-61.

Wrong, D. H. "The Over-Socialized Conception of Man in Modern Sociology." *American Sociological Review* 26 (1961): 183-193.

Yinger, J. M. "Presidential Address: Countercultures and Social Change." *American Sociological Review* 42 (December 1977): 833-853.

INDEX

NOTES ON CONTRIBUTORS

MICHAEL V. BELOK, professor of education, Arizona State University, received his Ph.D. from the University of Southern California. He has published some sixty articles in scholarly journals, and has authored or coauthored nine books. He served as guest editor of three issues of the *Indian Journal of Social Research* devoted to Parsons and Sociology. His latest book is *Conflict, Permanency, Change and Education* with Joseph S. Roucek, James Van Patten, and Martin Schoppmeyer.

WILLIAM R. BROWN, assistant professor of sociology, Florida Technological University, received his Ph.D. from Purdue University. He has authored or coauthored over twenty articles and reports. He has served on several community committees and boards, including the Orange County Human Services Planning Council, Youth Programs Incorporated, and PACE School for Learning Disabled Children.

PETER CONRAD, assistant professor of sociology at Drake University, Des Moines, Iowa, received his Ph.D. from Boston University. His major research interests include the medicalization of deviance and hyperactivity in children. He is presently engaged in a study of epilepsy (with Joseph W. Schneider). He has written a number of articles in these areas and one book, *Identifying Hyperactive Children: The Medicalization of Deviant Behavior* (1976).

ROBERT A. FRIEDLANDER received his Ph.D. from Northwestern University in the fields of European and American history, and he obtained his J.D. from the De Paul University College of Law. He has written twenty-five articles and review essays dealing with law and politics, both domestic and international; he has written extensively in the fields of terrorism, human rights, and American foreign policy. He is currently associate professor of law at Northern University College of Law, Ada, Ohio, and a visiting faculty member of the De Paul University School for New Learning.

RAJ S. GANDHI studied as a Fulbright scholar at the University of Minnesota and received his Ph.D. in sociology from that institution. At present he is associate professor of sociology at the university of Calgary, Alberta, Canada. He is the author of the monograph *Locals and Cosmopolitans of Little India*, and has contributed numerous chapters to sociological anthologies, as well as articles to scientific journals in India, the United States, Canada, France, and Germany.

KAREL HULICKA, professor of history at the State University of New York at Buffalo, received his Ph.D. from the University of California at Berkeley. He has coauthored *Soviet Institutions, the Individual and Society* with Dr. Irene M. Hulicka and *European Politics and Government* (1962). He has also published numerous articles in journals such as *Soviet Studies, Land Economics, The American Slavic and East European Review, The Midwest Quarterly*, and *The South African Journal of Economics*.

MORRIS JANOWITZ, a distinguished service professor in the Department of Sociology, University of Chicago, has published extensively in the area of political and urban sociology. He is the editor of the multivolume series on the heritage of sociology and is presently engaged in preparing a comprehensive theoretical study on macrosociology and social control. He has served as vice-president of the American Sociological Association and is a fellow of the American Academy of Arts and Science.

JEROME KRASE, assistant professor and deputy chairman in the Sociology Department of Brooklyn College of the City University of New York, received his Ph.D. from New York University. With Ronald D. Corwin as co-author, he has published two monographs on demographic changes in New York City and Greenwich Village; he has also published a monograph on modern social problems. He is currently writing a book on the social-psychological aspects of inner-city living.

KENNETH V. LOTTICH has taught at Elon College, S.U.N.Y., Willamette University, Portland State University, the University of Hawaii, Boise State University, the University of Montana, and the University of California. He has published over 300 articles and reviews in leading social science, education, and history journals in the United States and abroad. Among his monographs are *Foundations of Modern Education* (1961 and 1970); *Behind the Iron Curtain* (with Joseph S. Roucek, 1963); *New England Transplanted* (1963 and 1971); and *The Great Educators* (1972).

L. JOHN MARTIN received his Ph.D. in political science from the University of Minnesota, and is professor of journalism and director of research for the Division of Arts and Humanities at the University of Maryland. He has worked for newspapers both in the United States and abroad, and has served as a consultant on terrorism to the U.S. government. He is author of *International Propaganda* (1958, 1969), has edited two issues of *The Annals* on propaganda and on the American press and politics, and has contributed to a number of journals, encyclopedias, and anthologies.

DON MARTINDALE is professor of sociology at the University of Minnesota. He is co-editor and co-translator of four books by Max Weber: *Ancient Judaism, The Religions of India, The Rational and Social Foundations of Music*, and *The City*. Among his major monographs are *Small Town and the Nation* (with R. Galen Hanson), *Social Dimensions of Mental Illness, Alcoholism and Drug Dependence* (with Edith Martindale), *Psychiatry and the Law* (with Edith Martindale), *Psychiatry and the Law* (with Edith Martindale), and *The Romance of a Profession: A Case*

History in the Sociology of Sociology. He is series editor of Greenwood's Contributions in Sociology.

RAJ P. MOHAN, assistant professor and coordinator of graduate studies in sociology at Auburn University, earned his Ph.D. in sociology from North Carolina State University. He has published over forty papers in journals all over the world, and since 1963 he has been editor of the *International Journal of Contemporary Sociology*. With Don Martindale, he wrote *Handbook of Contemporary Developments in World Sociology* (Greenwood Press, 1975).

JOHN MOLAND, JR., professor of sociology and director of the Center for Social Research at Southern University, holds the Ph.D. in sociology from the University of Chicago. His major academic and research interests include social psychology, juvenile delinquency, and community studies. The author of numerous articles and book reviews, he is currently preparing reports from research projects on rural community development.

M. TIMOTHY O'KEEFE, is associate professor of communication at Florida Techno-logical University in Orlando, where he founded the journalism program when the school opened in 1968. He has written numerous articles in scholarly journals and has presented papers at national and international meetings. With Kenneth G. Sheinkopf he is coauthor of *Advertising Principles and Practices: Selected Readings*. He received his Ph.D. from the University of North Carolina at Chapel Hill.

JOHN E. OWEN, professor of sociology at Arizona State University, received his Ph.D. from the University of Southern California. He is the author of *L. T. Hobhouse, Sociologist* (1974) and of over 200 articles for journals in sixteen countries.

MYRTLE R. REUL, the Equal Employment Opportunity Affirmation Action Officer at the University of Georgia, earned the Ed.D. degree at Michigan State University. She was formerly on the faculty at Michigan State University and associate dean in the School of Social Work at Albion College. She is a frequent contributor to professional journals, and her most recent book is *Territorial Boundaries of Rural Poverty: Profiles of Exploitation.*

JOSEPH S. ROUCEK, professor of social sciences, City University of New York (retired), has taught in numerous American, Canadian, and European universities and colleges, including New York University, the University of Southern California, the University of Washington, Hofstra College, and Pennsylvania State University. He has written, coauthored, edited, or coedited more than forty books, including *The Slavonic Encyclopedia, One America* (revised as *Our Racial and National Minorities*), *Politics of the Balkans,* and *The Czechs and Slovaks in America.* The Royal Government of Romania awarded him the Knighthood of the Star of Romania, and the Royal Government of Yugoslavia, the Knighthood of the Crown of Yugoslavia—both in the rank of Commander. He is the American editor or a member of the editorial board of numerous foreign journals.

JOSEPH W. SCHNEIDER, associate professor of sociology at Drake University, Des Moines, Iowa, received his Ph.D. from the University of Iowa in Iowa City. His research interests include the sociology of deviance and social control and the sociology of knowledge.

MARTIN W. SCHOPPMEYER earned his Ed.D. from the University of Florida, and is presently a member of the faculty of the University of Arkansas. He has written a number of articles in journals. He currently serves as executive secretary of the Arkansas School Study Council.

CHARLES M. UNKOVIC, professor and chairman of the Sociology Department at Florida Technological University, received his Ph.D. at the University of Pittsburgh. He has written four books and over forty articles for journals. He has served on several state and national advisory groups, such as the 1970 White House Conference on Children and Youth.

JAMES VAN PATTEN received his Ph.D. from the University of Texas (Austin) and has taught at Central Missouri State University and the University of Arkansas (Fayetteville). He has written over 100 articles and book reviews for professional journals, and he is the editor and publisher of *The Journal of Thought*, an interdisciplinary quarterly journal.

ARTHUR S. WILKE, assistant professor of sociology at Auburn University, received his Ph.D. from the University of Minnesota. His articles and book reviews have appeared in a variety of journals, including *The Journal of Political and Military Sociology*, *The Sociological Quarterly*, *Teaching Sociology*, *American Sociological Review*, and *Rural Sociology*. His most recent article was published in a special issue of the *International Journal of Contemporary Sociology* devoted to the life and work of Carle Zimmerman. His most recent volume, *The Hidden Professoriate*, will be published by Greenwood Press in 1978.

CHARLOTTE WOLF, associate professor of sociology and chairperson of the Department of Sociology/Anthropology at Ohio Wesleyan University, received the Ph.D. degree in 1968. Her main research interests are in the areas of community and identity theory, military sociology, and the sociology of women, as reflected in such studies as *Garrison Community, A Study of an Overseas American Military Colony* (Greenwood, 1969) and articles published in *Women's Studies*, *Sociological Quarterly*, and other journals. Active in the women's movement, she has chaired the American Sociological Association's Committee on the Status of Women.

OLEG ZINAM, professor of economics at the University of Cincinnati, received his doctorate in economics from the University of Cincinnati in 1963. He has published numerous articles in economics and sociology in professional journals in the United States, Canada, Germany, Italy, Spain, and India. He is presently teaching economics at the University of Cincinnati and the Russian language at Xavier University.